Reconciliation

The Children of Abraham

Reconciliation

The Children of Abraham

by
Duane Andry

Preface

There came a man Jesus. He was conceived by the overshadowing of the Holy Ghost and born of a virgin named Mary, who, along with Joseph her husband, is of the seed of David the king.

This same man Jesus was sanctified by God with the filling of the Holy Ghost, which remained upon him. At this time he was announced to those with him and thus to the world as the beloved Son of God. And we were directed by the voice of God to "hear ye him". This is the one called the Son of man and the Son of God.

This same man Jesus after the anointing of the Holy Ghost continued his ministry on the earth with mighty signs and wonders. Because of these signs he engendered the displeasure of the religious/political powers of his day. They thinking to rid the world of this *nuisance* crucified and killed this body on the cross. And by doing so brought into effect God's will for the salvation of mankind and for the return of all His children to Him. Jesus Christ, the Lamb of God, is the last sacrifice sanctioned by God to carry away the sins of the world through his blood. "It is finished."

This same man Jesus is spoken of throughout the pages of the Bible, the Holy Word of God. And this Bible was transcribed by holy men moved by the Spirit of God. And this Bible is sealed until the time of the end of this current earthly reality. It is in the light of this Bible that I present this message; for the remission of sin and the salvation of mankind.

Contents

viii

Introduction

The promise and presence of the God of the Universe to a man named Abram began with a very simple directive and an equally simple response. This first contact with the human origin of some of the largest religious groups of today is recorded in the following verses from Scripture.

> *Now the LORD had said unto Abram, Get thee out of thy country, and from thy kindred, and from thy father's house, unto a land that I will show thee: And I will make of thee a great nation, and I will bless thee, and make thy name great; and thou shalt be a blessing: And I will bless them that bless thee, and curse him that curseth thee: and in thee shall all families of the earth be blessed.*

> *So Abram departed, as the LORD had spoken unto him; and Lot went with him: and Abram was seventy and five years old when he departed out of Haran.*
>   (Genesis 12:1-4)

There is a most powerful declaration in these words, "*and in thee shall all families of the earth be blessed*". It doesn't mention that this man would have an impact on some sections of the world, but on all families. Please note, also, that the LORD did not put a timeframe on that declaration. It is just as active now as it was when it was first made.

Today we know even more about the impact of this man, and his offspring, on the entire earth. To fully understand this impact, let us take a closer look at the components of the covenant that was established by God with the man Abram.

The first part of the covenant is the establishment of Abram, now renamed Abraham, as the source of many nations with a large population base.

> *And when Abram was ninety years old and nine, the LORD appeared to Abram, and said unto him, I am the Almighty God; walk before me, and be thou perfect. And I will make my covenant between me and thee, and will multiply thee exceedingly.*

And Abram fell on his face: and God talked with him, saying, As for me, behold, my covenant is with thee, and thou shalt be a father of many nations. Neither shall thy name any more be called Abram, but thy name shall be Abraham; for a father of many nations have I made thee. And I will make thee exceeding fruitful, and I will make nations of thee, and kings shall come out of thee.
(Genesis 17:1-6)

God continues His declaration of the covenant by establishing a relationship between the seed of Abraham, throughout their generations, and Almighty God. There is no limit on this relationship between the seed of Abraham and God. Throughout all history there will always be this relationship between the seed of Abraham and God.

And I will establish my covenant between me and thee and thy seed after thee in their generations for an everlasting covenant, to be a God unto thee, and to thy seed after thee.
(Genesis 17:7)

This relationship is later extended not just to the seed of Abraham but also to anyone who became a part of the nations of Abraham, even those who served and those who entered by displaying the character of Abraham. This is that character which is the foundation of the relationship between Abraham and God. The character trait which Abram displayed is known as *faith in God*.

But who is the God that set up a covenant with Abraham? The Scriptures give us a view of God as having the following attributes and characteristics and powers (this is the extremely short list).

One who possesses heaven and earth
And Melchizedek king of Salem brought forth bread and wine: and he was the priest of the most high God. And he blessed him, and said, Blessed be Abram of the most high God, possessor of heaven and earth:
(Genesis 14:18-19)

One who commands perfection
And when Abram was ninety years old and nine, the LORD appeared to Abram, and said unto him, I am the Almighty God; walk before me, and be thou perfect.
(Genesis 17:1)

One who is Master over nature and the elements

Then the LORD rained upon Sodom and upon Gomorrah brimstone and fire from the LORD out of heaven; And he overthrew those cities, and all the plain, and all the inhabitants of the cities, and that which grew upon the ground.

And it came to pass, when God destroyed the cities of the plain, that God remembered Abraham, and sent Lot out of the midst of the overthrow, when he overthrew the cities in the which Lot dwelt.
(Genesis 19:24-25, 29)

One who does not tolerate sin

And God said unto him in a dream, Yea, I know that thou didst this in the integrity of thy heart; for I also withheld thee from sinning against me: therefore suffered I thee not to touch her.
(Genesis 20:6)

One who controls human birth

So Abraham prayed unto God: and God healed Abimelech, and his wife, and his maidservants; and they bare children. For the LORD had fast closed up all the wombs of the house of Abimelech, because of Sarah Abraham's wife.
(Genesis 20:17-18)

Abraham had the most marvelous human attribute of being reverent to God. He so respected the word of God that he was willing to give God both of his talent and of his substance; and he was even willing to give God his family and self. Abraham's reverence for God was total. When God asked for an action of Abraham he was instant in performing it. It is this Abraham and his many nations that we will explore in the discussion that follows.

But why do so?

There is a great need in the day that I am living for some form of reconciliation between the many nations that have been spawned from the man Abraham. There are many of them who have formed alliances, some weak and some strong. Others of them, however, have developed an intense hatred for others of the nations of Abraham. This is not consistent with the covenant given to the nations of Abraham.

Many people only relate to the land covenant given by God, which we haven't even mentioned up to this point. The first part of the covenant is the establishment of many nations. However, the second part of the covenant from God is for Him "to be a God unto thee, and to thy seed after thee". This part has been lost in the dealings of nation to nation among the nations of Abraham. We will attempt, through the Spirit of God, to show the way back to true honor and reverence for God for all the nations of Abraham.

Reconciliation: this is our objective.

Reconciliation: this can only be accomplished by the nations yielding to the Spirit of God.

Reconciliation: this has to start with all the nations of Abraham respecting all the other nations of Abraham.

Reconciliation; let us begin to evaluate how this must be done. Let all nations of Abraham return to the covenant of God and let God be God. We will first, focus on the covenant with Abraham and the peace that it offers to all the nations of Abraham. Sprinkled throughout this discussion are some thoughts on the later covenants; none of which invalidated the relationship of God with Abraham. The relationship between God and Abraham is "an everlasting covenant".

Furthermore, we will explore some of the benefits that have been introduced to humanity as a result of the relationship of God with Abraham. These are the benefits that are available to all the children of Abraham. Though the benefits have come through a particular set of descendants of Abraham, they carry the mark of God and are thus available to all. Please keep this in mind as you read of the various facets of the design of God for all mankind that started with Abraham.

Please consider your place in the design of God revealed through Abraham, and as children of Abraham know that your responsibility is to God to use all that He has provided. You cannot afford to restrict yourself to just the subset that has historically marked your existence. All is available and all must be used in righteousness before God.

The nations of Abraham,
You know who you are;
For in God's crown
You each are a star:

A part of the covenant
Between God and a man
Who lived on this earth
In an ancient land.

Revering his God
He found great favor,
Which we in this day
Should rightly savor;

Working toward the things
That guided his life:
The elimination of
Needless strife,

The quest to serve God
In all that we do,
And to our families
To forever be true.

Abraham stood before God
As the start of many nations,
Whose name they share
As their common relations;

With God Most High
The power binding them all,
So that none of them
Into sin need ever fall;

Never caught in Satan's trap
To establish a place supreme,
By the destruction of any other
To fulfill one nations dream.

Nations before God,
Brother to brother;
Commanded by God
To respect one another.

For, for a brother or cousin,
Or even just a friend,
We must never plot
To cause their end.

The Word from the Bible

Deuteronomy 6:1-8

Now these are the commandments, the statutes, and the judgments, which the LORD your God commanded to teach you, that ye might do them in the land whither ye go to possess it: That thou mightest fear the LORD thy God, to keep all his statutes and his commandments, which I command thee, thou, and thy son, and thy son's son, all the days of thy life; and that thy days may be prolonged. Hear therefore, O Israel, and observe to do it; that it may be well with thee, and that ye may increase mightily, as the LORD God of thy fathers hath promised thee, in the land that floweth with milk and honey.

Hear, O Israel: The LORD our God is one LORD: And thou shalt love the LORD thy God with all thine heart, and with all thy soul, and with all thy might. And these words, which I command thee this day, shall be in thine heart: And thou shalt teach them diligently unto thy children, and shalt talk of them when thou sittest in thine house, and when thou walkest by the way, and when thou liest down, and when thou risest up. And thou shalt bind them for a sign upon thine hand, and they shall be as frontlets between thine eyes.

Isaiah 44:21-28

Remember these, O Jacob and Israel; for thou art my servant: I have formed thee; thou art my servant: O Israel, thou shalt not be forgotten of me. I have blotted out, as a thick cloud, thy transgressions, and, as a cloud, thy sins: return unto me; for I have redeemed thee.

Sing, O ye heavens; for the LORD hath done it: shout, ye lower parts of the earth: break forth into singing, ye mountains, O forest, and every tree therein: for the LORD hath redeemed Jacob, and glorified himself in Israel. Thus saith the LORD, thy redeemer, and he that formed thee from the womb, I am the LORD that maketh all things; that stretcheth forth the heavens alone; that spreadeth abroad the earth by myself; That frustrateth the tokens of the liars, and maketh diviners mad; that turneth wise men backward, and maketh their knowledge foolish; That confirmeth the word of his servant, and performeth the counsel of his messengers; that saith to Jerusalem, Thou shalt be inhabited; and to the cities of Judah, Ye shall be built, and I will raise up the decayed places thereof: That saith to the deep, Be dry, and I will dry up thy rivers: That saith of Cyrus, He is my shepherd, and shall perform all my pleasure: even saying to Jerusalem, Thou shalt be built; and to the temple, Thy foundation shall be laid.

Isaiah 45:1-6

Thus saith the LORD to his anointed, to Cyrus, whose right hand I have holden, to subdue nations before him; and I will loose the loins of kings, to open before him the two leaved gates; and the gates shall not be shut; I will go before thee, and make the crooked places straight: I will break in pieces the gates of brass, and cut in sunder the bars of iron: And I will give thee the treasures of darkness, and hidden riches of secret places, that thou mayest know that I, the LORD, which call thee by thy name, am the God of Israel. For Jacob my servant's sake, and Israel mine elect, I have even called thee by thy name: I have surnamed thee, though thou hast not known me. I am the LORD, and there is none else, there is no God beside me: I girded thee, though thou hast not known me: That they may know from the rising of the sun, and from the west, that there is none beside me. I am the LORD, and there is none else.

Malachi 1:8-10

But ye are departed out of the way; ye have caused many to stumble at the law; ye have corrupted the covenant of Levi, saith the LORD of hosts. Therefore have I also made you contemptible and base before all the people, according as ye have not kept my ways, but have been partial in the law. Have we not all one father? hath not one God created us? why do we deal treacherously every man against his brother, by profaning the covenant of our fathers?

Chapter One

God Is One

The revelation of God to man starts with the words in Genesis 1:26-27 where we read the following:

> *And God said, Let us make man in our image, after our likeness: and let them have dominion over the fish of the sea, and over the fowl of the air, and over the cattle, and over all the earth, and over every creeping thing that creepeth upon the earth. So God created man in his own image, in the image of God created he him; male and female created he them."*

That God said *let us* has been misinterpreted by some to indicate that there were multiple, at least two, power sources in the creation scenario. This may not be such a bad interpretation if it were not followed by an addition to the text. This additional thought is that because God said *let us* there must have been someone or something else there of equal power with God. To those who hold this view it is as if God had to consult with someone or something else to accomplish the creation.

However, if we look closely at the text we note that it is God who calls forth the creation of man and who is thus the author thereof. This does not, however, eliminate the presence of others with power, existing in the midst of God at the creation. Nor does it eliminate the possibility that God called others into action to effect the creation. It does say that God is directly responsible for the creation. How he did it is not mentioned in this text. In any case, the servant does not earn credit for the work of the master by being called into service to do the work.

Consider the text in Genesis 2:7 which reads

> *And the LORD God formed man of the dust of the ground, and breathed into his nostrils the breath of life; and man became a living soul.*

This text does not say how God performed the creation. Did God bend down and scoop up some dirt and sculpt it into a man? Could it be that God told the dirt to form itself into a certain shape? Did God call forth a wind to blow the dirt into a particular shape? The text above doesn't give us an answer of the how God did it; only of what God did.

Let's evaluate some of the ways that God has accomplished His work as recorded in the Bible. To begin this discovery we will have to introduce one additional set of characters in the Kingdom of God that are caused by God to do His bidding. These characters are the angels. The Scriptures are full of both encounters by man with angels as well as listing many accounts of the service of the angels to God and on behalf of God. We will look at two forms in which the angels appear to man.

Angels can come to man shaped like humans. This seems to be the case of the meeting with Hagar, who was the handmaid of Sarai who was the wife of Abram who we know as Abraham. This appearance seems to be in human form.

> *And the angel of the LORD found her by a fountain of water in the wilderness, by the fountain in the way to Shur. And he said, Hagar, Sarai's maid, whence camest thou? and whither wilt thou go? And she said, I flee from the face of my mistress Sarai.*
> (Genesis 16:7-8)

Another Scripture which indicates that angels can come in human form is recorded in the following:

> *And there came two angels to Sodom at even; and Lot sat in the gate of Sodom: and Lot seeing them rose up to meet them; and he bowed himself with his face toward the ground;*
>
> *But before they lay down, the men of the city, even the men of Sodom, compassed the house round, both old and young, all the people from every quarter: And they called unto Lot, and said unto him, Where are the men which came in to thee this night? bring them out unto us, that we may know them.*
> (Genesis 19:1, 4-5)

The human form is not the only form of angel that is presented in Scripture. Angels can also come in non-human form. Below are some references that describe such angels.

> *Now Moses kept the flock of Jethro his father in law, the priest of Midian: and he led the flock to the backside of the desert, and came to the mountain of God, even to Horeb. And the angel of the LORD appeared unto him in a flame of fire out of the midst of a bush: and he looked, and, behold, the bush burned with fire, and the bush was not consumed.*
> (Exodus 3:1-2)

> *And the angel of God, which went before the camp of Israel, removed and went behind them; and the pillar of the cloud went from before their face, and stood behind them: And it came between the camp of the Egyptians and the camp of Israel; and it was a cloud and darkness to them, but it gave light by night to these: so that the one came not near the other all the night.*
> (Exodus 14:19-20)

The presence of angels shows us that God has established a system whereby He can delegate authority to act on His behalf to others: ethereal, elemental and other types of beings. We read in the preceding Scriptures of God delegating certain tasks to His angels. Sometimes in these encounters between the angel and man, the angel is viewed as being God. This is only the view from the standpoint of the person receiving the visitation; and it indicates that the power that is represented is of a magnitude that is easily recognized as being from God.

Hagar thinks that the angel that appeared to her is actually God. However, we know that the angel is only performing the mission assigned to it. It does not by doing so become eligible to be considered equal with God. It is only, so to speak, doing its job.

> *And she called the name of the LORD that spake unto her, Thou God seest me: for she said, Have I also here looked after him that seeth me?*
> (Genesis 16:13).

There are others to whom God delegates His authority to act. Let's look at a few more. God delegates to men. One of the most powerful example of this recorded in the Old Testament in the Bible is done directly by God.

> *And the LORD said unto Moses, See, I have made thee a god to Pharaoh: and Aaron thy brother shall be thy prophet. Thou shalt speak all that I command thee: and Aaron thy brother shall speak unto Pharaoh, that he send the children of Israel out of his land.*
> (Exodus 7:1-2)

God also delegates to animals. God, as we know, has the power to directly and immediately remove sin. There are many reasons why He might have chosen not to do so in the Old Testament times. One of the terms that come to mind is one that has come into popular use; it is the term "personal responsibility". By using a visible representative to denote the removal of sin, God is able to keep man's mind on the fact that there is a price that has to be paid by someone or something for every sin that we commit. This lot fell to the scapegoat.

> *Thus shall Aaron come into the holy place: with a young bullock for a sin offering, and a ram for a burnt offering. He shall put on the holy linen coat, and he shall have the linen breeches upon his flesh, and shall be girded with a linen girdle, and with the linen mitre shall he be attired: these are holy garments; therefore shall he wash his flesh in water, and so put them on. And he shall take of the congregation of the children of Israel two kids of the goats for a sin offering, and one ram for a burnt offering.*

> *And Aaron shall offer his bullock of the sin offering, which is for himself, and make an atonement for himself, and for his house.*

> *And he shall take the two goats, and present them before the LORD at the door of the tabernacle of the congregation. And Aaron shall cast lots upon the two goats; one lot for the LORD, and the other lot for the scapegoat. And Aaron shall bring the goat upon which the LORD'S lot fell, and offer him for a sin offering.*

*But the goat, on which the lot fell to be the scapegoat,
shall be presented alive before the LORD, to make an
atonement with him, and to let him go for a scapegoat
into the wilderness.*
(Genesis 16:3-10)

Furthermore, sometimes God selects out an animal to speak on his
behalf. This is the case in the following passage of Scripture.

*And Balaam rose up in the morning, and saddled his ass,
and went with the princes of Moab. And God's anger was
kindled because he went: and the angel of the LORD
stood in the way for an adversary against him.*

*Now he was riding upon his ass, and his two servants
were with him. And the ass saw the angel of the LORD
standing in the way, and his sword drawn in his hand:
and the ass turned aside out of the way, and went into the
field: and Balaam smote the ass, to turn her into the way.*

*But the angel of the LORD stood in a path of the
vineyards, a wall being on this side, and a wall on that
side. And when the ass saw the angel of the LORD,
she thrust herself unto the wall, and crushed Balaam's
foot against the wall: and he smote her again.*

*And the angel of the LORD went further, and stood in
a narrow place, where was no way to turn either to the
right hand or to the left. And when the ass saw the angel
of the LORD, she fell down under Balaam: and Balaam's
anger was kindled, and he smote the ass with a staff.*

And the LORD opened the mouth of the ass, *and
she said unto Balaam, What have I done unto thee, that
thou hast smitten me these three times?*

*And Balaam said unto the ass, Because thou hast
mocked me: I would there were a sword in mine hand,
for now would I kill thee.*

*And the ass said unto Balaam, Am not I thine ass, upon
which thou hast ridden ever since I was thine unto this
day? was I ever wont to do so unto thee?*

And he said, Nay. Then the LORD opened the eyes of Balaam, and he saw the angel of the LORD standing in the way, and his sword drawn in his hand: and he bowed down his head, and fell flat on his face.

And the angel of the LORD said unto him, Wherefore hast thou smitten thine ass these three times? behold, I went out to withstand thee, because thy way is perverse before me: And the ass saw me, and turned from me these three times: unless she had turned from me, surely now also I had slain thee, and saved her alive.
(Numbers 16:21-33)

There is one other delegate that we should store in our minds; that is the delegate known as a nation. God selects nations to send forth His word and to perform his works in the world. One such nation is the nation of Israel. In the delegation described below, the nation was chosen to show forth the beneficence and longsuffering of God to the world.

And Moses went up unto God, and the LORD called unto him out of the mountain, saying, Thus shalt thou say to the house of Jacob, and tell the children of Israel; Ye have seen what I did unto the Egyptians, and how I bare you on eagles' wings, and brought you unto myself. Now therefore, if ye will obey my voice indeed, and keep my covenant, then ye shall be a peculiar treasure unto me above all people: for all the earth is mine: And ye shall be unto me a kingdom of priests, and an holy nation. These are the words which thou shalt speak unto the children of Israel.
(Exodus 19:3-6)

There have been other nations that were selected to show forth the standards that God requires of all mankind. This is most often seen in a nation that has fallen under the judgment of God, but it can also be seen in a nation that has been selected to produce fruit for God. Such a nation was the nation of Persia under King Cyrus.

Now in the first year of Cyrus king of Persia, that the word of the LORD by the mouth of Jeremiah might be fulfilled, the LORD stirred up the spirit of Cyrus king of

Persia, that he made a proclamation throughout all his kingdom, and put it also in writing, saying, Thus saith Cyrus king of Persia, The LORD God of heaven hath given me all the kingdoms of the earth; and he hath charged me to build him an house at Jerusalem, which is in Judah.

Who is there among you of all his people? his God be with him, and let him go up to Jerusalem, which is in Judah, and build the house of the LORD God of Israel, (he is the God,) which is in Jerusalem. And whosoever remaineth in any place where he sojourneth, let the men of his place help him with silver, and with gold, and with goods, and with beasts, beside the freewill offering for the house of God that is in Jerusalem.

Then rose up the chief of the fathers of Judah and Benjamin, and the priests, and the Levites, with all them whose spirit God had raised, to go up to build the house of the LORD which is in Jerusalem. And all they that were about them strengthened their hands with vessels of silver, with gold, with goods, and with beasts, and with precious things, beside all that was willingly offered. Also Cyrus the king brought forth the vessels of the house of the LORD, which Nebuchadnezzar had brought forth out of Jerusalem, and had put them in the house of his gods;

(Ezra 1:1-7)

With all this delegation it might be assumed that some of the power of God might leave Him or at least some might remain on those to whom He delegates. If such could happen there might be one who would gain equal status with God; but not so. God is the Most High.

And Melchizedek king of Salem brought forth bread and wine: and he was the priest of the most high God. And he blessed him, and said, Blessed be Abram of the most high God, possessor of heaven and earth: And blessed be the most high God, which hath delivered thine enemies into thy hand. And he gave him tithes of all.

(Genesis 14:18-20)

God, being the Most High, has none who is as high as He is, and there is none who is higher than He. There is none with power that equals or exceeds that of God. In fact, there is none who has power that does not derive from God. God is the Most High and has full control of all power. Any power held by anyone in Heaven or on the earth, or anywhere else for that matter, is a gift and a responsibility given to them from God. Their ability to hold onto the power is by the allowance of God.

The fact of His supremacy was made most clear by God, when He stated that He swears by Himself. This He had to do because there is no other name higher than God by whom God can make an oath or seal a covenant.

> *And the angel of the LORD called unto Abraham out of heaven the second time, And said, By myself have I sworn, saith the LORD, for because thou hast done this thing, and hast not withheld thy son, thine only son: That in blessing I will bless thee, and in multiplying I will multiply thy seed as the stars of the heaven, and as the sand which is upon the sea shore; and thy seed shall possess the gate of his enemies; And in thy seed shall all the nations of the earth be blessed; because thou hast obeyed my voice.*
> (Genesis 22:15-18)

> *And we desire that every one of you do show the same diligence to the full assurance of hope unto the end: That ye be not slothful, but followers of them who through faith and patience inherit the promises. For when God made promise to Abraham, because he could swear by no greater, he sware by himself, Saying, Surely blessing I will bless thee, and multiplying I will multiply thee. And so, after he had patiently endured, he obtained the promise.*

> *For men verily swear by the greater: and an oath for confirmation is to them an end of all strife. Wherein God, willing more abundantly to show unto the heirs of promise the immutability of his counsel, confirmed it by an oath: That by two immutable things, in which it was impossible for God to lie, we might have a strong consolation, who have fled for refuge to lay hold upon the hope set before us:*
> (Hebrews 6:11-18)

Let's finish by taking a look at the word *Godhead*. We want to take a good look at this word, for man sometimes equates this word with God. The word *Godhead* is in the Bible in the following places.

> *God that made the world and all things therein, seeing that he is Lord of heaven and earth, dwelleth not in temples made with hands; Neither is worshipped with men's hands, as though he needed any thing, seeing he giveth to all life, and breath, and all things; And hath made of one blood all nations of men for to dwell on all the face of the earth, and hath determined the times before appointed, and the bounds of their habitation; That they should seek the Lord, if haply they might feel after him, and find him, though he be not far from every one of us: For in him we live, and move, and have our being; as certain also of your own poets have said, For we are also his offspring. Forasmuch then as we are the offspring of God, we ought not to think that the Godhead is like unto gold, or silver, or stone, graven by art and man's device.*
> (Acts 17:24-29)

> *For the wrath of God is revealed from heaven against all ungodliness and unrighteousness of men, who hold the truth in unrighteousness; Because that which may be known of God is manifest in them; for God hath showed it unto them.*

> *For the invisible things of him from the creation of the world are clearly seen, being understood by the things that are made, even his eternal power and Godhead; so that they are without excuse: Because that, when they knew God, they glorified him not as God, neither were thankful; but became vain in their imaginations, and their foolish heart was darkened. Professing themselves to be wise, they became fools, And changed the glory of the uncorruptible God into an image made like to corruptible man, and to birds, and fourfooted beasts, and creeping things.*
> (Romans 1:20-23)

For I would that ye knew what great conflict I have for you, and for them at Laodicea, and for as many as have not seen my face in the flesh; That their hearts might be comforted, being knit together in love, and unto all riches of the full assurance of understanding, to the acknowledgment of the mystery of God, and of the Father, and of Christ; In whom are hid all the treasures of wisdom and knowledge. And this I say, lest any man should beguile you with enticing words. For though I be absent in the flesh, yet am I with you in the spirit, joying and beholding your order, and the stedfastness of your faith in Christ.

As ye have therefore received Christ Jesus the Lord, so walk ye in him: Rooted and built up in him, and stablished in the faith, as ye have been taught, abounding therein with thanksgiving.

Beware lest any man spoil you through philosophy and vain deceit, after the tradition of men, after the rudiments of the world, and not after Christ. For in him dwelleth all the fulness of the Godhead bodily.
(Colossians 2:1-9)

Though it is not directly mentioned in the Bible, the Godhead is believed to be the Father, the Son (Christ), and the Holy Ghost. Though it may seem that Colossians 2:2 is pointing in that direction, it is in fact not. It only mentions that there was a mystery about the workings *of God, and of the Father, and of Christ*.

There is another passage of Scripture that is used to develop the notion of a trinitarian Godhead.

Whosoever believeth that Jesus is the Christ is born of God: and every one that loveth him that begat loveth him also that is begotten of him. By this we know that we love the children of God, when we love God, and keep his commandments. For this is the love of God, that we keep his commandments: and his commandments are not grievous. For whatsoever is born of God overcometh the world: and this is the victory that overcometh the world, even our faith.

> *Who is he that overcometh the world, but he that*
> *believeth that Jesus is the Son of God? This is he that*
> *came by water and blood, even Jesus Christ; not by water*
> *only, but by water and blood. And it is the Spirit that*
> *beareth witness, because the Spirit is truth. For there are*
> *three that bear record in heaven, the Father, the Word,*
> *and the Holy Ghost: and these three are one. And there*
> *are three that bear witness in earth, the Spirit, and the*
> *water, and the blood: and these three agree in one.*
> (1 John 5:1-8)

The singularity of the three is hypothesized from the phrase "*and these three are one*". Those who hold this position consider the word *one* to refer to a being. We state, however, that it refers in this instance to a process. They are one in the process that they "*bear record in heaven*". Thus, they are one in mission and in purpose; but there is no way of jumping from this to a position that makes them one in *person*. Nor can we imply from this that the manifestations exhibit the same power and responsibilities. Yes, they are three of one type. They are three divine, eternal outreaches of the Spirit of God.

To say the word Godhead is not to create equivalence with God: Godhead does not equal God. The Godhead is also not more than God, even if the Father is a member thereof. The Godhead is neither a nickname for God nor a membership club in which there are three elite members. The Godhead seems rather to be the manifestation of the loving concern of God for mankind.

The Godhead must be viewed only as the method God chose to represent His working in the kingdom of man. These three are the ways of outreach that God has established for man's understanding. These three are the Creation, Authority and Consciousness of God: they are not the *person* of God. ALL in divinity (Heaven) bow to God, as it will be on earth when He chooses to finalize matters of existence.

God is not diminished by having established the Godhead. The power of the *members*, I say this from a human perspective, are derived from the delineation by God of their roles to them. Jesus told us that he had received power from God.

> *And Jesus came and spake unto them, saying, All power*
> *is given unto me in heaven and in earth.*
> (Matthew 28:18)

The word *given* indicates that he did not have it at some time before and that it was bestowed on him by someone: that someone being God.

The Holy Ghost is sent unto man by the Father. The Bible also gives us an understanding of the mission and origin of the Spirit known as the Comforter, the Holy Ghost.

> *And I will pray the Father, and he shall give you another Comforter, that he may abide with you for ever; Even the Spirit of truth; whom the world cannot receive, because it seeth him not, neither knoweth him: but ye know him; for he dwelleth with you, and shall be in you.*
> (John 14:16-17)

> *But the Comforter, which is the Holy Ghost, whom the Father will send in my name, he shall teach you all things, and bring all things to your remembrance, whatsoever I have said unto you.*
> (John 14:26)

The most direct statement of the differentiation of the Father is also made by the Messiah, Jesus Christ.

> *Peace I leave with you, my peace I give unto you: not as the world giveth, give I unto you. Let not your heart be troubled, neither let it be afraid. Ye have heard how I said unto you, I go away, and come again unto you. If ye loved me, ye would rejoice, because I said, I go unto the Father: for my Father is greater than I.*
> (John 14:27-28)

> *My sheep hear my voice, and I know them, and they follow me: And I give unto them eternal life; and they shall never perish, neither shall any man pluck them out of my hand. My Father, which gave them me, is greater than all; and no man is able to pluck them out of my Father's hand.*
> (John 10:27)

This statement is only for human understanding and does not reflect any act of domination of divinity by divinity. The Father has a different position which from a human perspective can be seen to be more powerful. Furthermore, the Father does have greater responsibility than does the Son. This does not indicate that there is an overbearing, dominating hierarchy between the Father and the Son, only a difference of function and level of responsibility. Each function performed on God's behalf is of equal importance. There is no respect of persons, even in the heavenly realm. There is especially no need for it in Heaven; because there everyone not only knows, but also joys in their assignment for the Kingdom of God. The Father and the Son relate to one another in love, as we should also do with the Father, the Son and each other.

For completion sake, let me continue with the quotation that follows John 10:27. This is also one of the expressions of Jesus that causes some to denote that he and God are the same. However, right after making the statement and seeing the confusion of the religious folk, Jesus explained what he meant by the expression. He also gave them the milder form that would fit with their ability to understand the unity of mission of the Son and the Father. This he did when he said, "*because I said, I am the Son of God*".

> *I and my Father are one.*
>
> *Then the Jews took up stones again to stone him.*
>
> *Jesus answered them, Many good works have I shewed you from my Father; for which of those works do ye stone me?*
>
> *The Jews answered him, saying, For a good work we stone thee not; but for blasphemy; and because that thou, being a man, makest thyself God.*
>
> *Jesus answered them, Is it not written in your law, I said, Ye are gods? If he called them gods, unto whom the word of God came, and the scripture cannot be broken; Say ye of him, whom the Father hath sanctified, and sent into the world, Thou blasphemest; because I said, I am the Son of God? If I do not the works of my Father, believe me not. But if I do, though ye believe not me, believe the works: that ye may know, and believe, that the Father is in me, and I in him.*
> (John 10:30-38)

God is now, always has been and always will be, the Most High. All will bow to him as such, and all will recognize His representations in the Godhead. At God's bidding all will bow to their place in the Kingdom of God.

Shunning the message to Adam,
To listen for God's voice;
Man decided that he
Had to have a choice

Among the things in nature,
To give each one a name;
To establish for time to come
Something that he can blame

For the things that in life,
Of dark and light hue,
Are beyond his ability
To totally subdue:

Yes, man knew that it was not he
Who brought the sunshine and rain,
Or made the heat so intense
In the desert plain.

Something had to be doing
The wonder that came to be;
In the sky above, in the earth,
And in the expansive sea.

Men saw many signs,
But never heard a voice;
So, in their mind they
Weaved their own course.

Now, as in the time of the beginning,
Man thinks it is up to him
To establish names for the force
That move him by their whim.

Many names were created,
But all were titled, as god;
For man thought that each one
Ruled with an iron rod:

The god of the sun and the sky,
The god of the sea and the plain,
The god that brought sunshine,
The god that sent rain.

Then, the God of the universe
Told to us He is one,
And our journey in His presence
Had now once again begun.

New Testament References to One God

Mark 12:28-34

And one of the scribes came, and having heard them reasoning together, and perceiving that he had answered them well, asked him, Which is the first commandment of all?

And Jesus answered him, The first of all the commandments is, Hear, O Israel; The Lord our God is one Lord: And thou shalt love the Lord thy God with all thy heart, and with all thy soul, and with all thy mind, and with all thy strength: this is the first commandment. And the second is like, namely this, Thou shalt love thy neighbour as thyself. There is none other commandment greater than these.

And the scribe said unto him, Well, Master, thou hast said the truth: for there is one God; and there is none other but he: And to love him with all the heart, and with all the understanding, and with all the soul, and with all the strength, and to love his neighbour as himself, is more than all whole burnt offerings and sacrifices.

And when Jesus saw that he answered discreetly, he said unto him, Thou art not far from the kingdom of God. And no man after that durst ask him any question.

Luke 18:18-19

And a certain ruler asked him, saying, Good Master, what shall I do to inherit eternal life?

And Jesus said unto him, Why callest thou me good? none is good, save one, that is, God.

Romans 3:28-31

Therefore we conclude that a man is justified by faith without the deeds of the law.

Is he the God of the Jews only? is he not also of the Gentiles? Yes, of the Gentiles also: Seeing it is one God, which shall justify the circumcision by faith, and uncircumcision through faith.

Do we then make void the law through faith? God forbid: yea, we establish the law.

1 Corinthians 8:3-6

But if any man love God, the same is known of him.

As concerning therefore the eating of those things that are offered in sacrifice unto idols, we know that an idol is nothing in the world, and that there is none other God but one. For though there be that are called gods, whether in heaven or in earth, (as there be gods many, and lords many,) But to us there is but one God, the Father, of whom are all things, and we in him; and one Lord Jesus Christ, by whom are all things, and we by him.

Galatians 3:16-26

Now to Abraham and his seed were the promises made. He saith not, And to seeds, as of many; but as of one, And to thy seed, which is Christ. And this I say, that the covenant, that was confirmed before of God in Christ, the law, which was four hundred and thirty years after, cannot disannul, that it should make the promise of none effect. For if the inheritance be of the law, it is no more of promise: but God gave it to Abraham by promise.

Wherefore then serveth the law? It was added because of transgressions, till the seed should come to whom the promise was made; and it was ordained by angels in the hand of a mediator. Now a mediator is not a mediator of one, but God is one.

Is the law then against the promises of God? God forbid: for if there had been a law given which could have given life, verily righteousness should have been by the law. But the scripture hath concluded all under sin, that the promise by faith of Jesus Christ might be given to them that believe. But before faith came, we were kept under the law, shut up unto the faith which should afterwards be revealed.

Wherefore the law was our schoolmaster to bring us unto Christ, that we might be justified by faith. But after that faith is come, we are no longer under a schoolmaster. For ye are all the children of God by faith in Christ Jesus.

Ephesians 4:1-6

I therefore, the prisoner of the Lord, beseech you that ye walk worthy of the vocation wherewith ye are called, With all lowliness and meekness, with longsuffering, forbearing one another in love; Endeavouring to keep the unity of the Spirit in the bond of peace.

There is one body, and one Spirit, even as ye are called in one hope of your calling; One Lord, one faith, one baptism, One God and Father of all, who is above all, and through all, and in you all.

1 Timothy 2:1-7

I exhort therefore, that, first of all, supplications, prayers, intercessions, and giving of thanks, be made for all men; For kings, and for all that are in authority; that we may lead a quiet and peaceable life in all godliness and honesty. For this is good and acceptable in the sight of God our Saviour; Who will have all men to be saved, and to come unto the knowledge of the truth.

For there is one God, and one mediator between God and men, the man Christ Jesus; Who gave himself a ransom for all, to be testified in due time. Whereunto I am ordained a preacher, and an apostle, (I speak the truth in Christ, and lie not;) a teacher of the Gentiles in faith and verity.

James 2:18-22

Yea, a man may say, Thou hast faith, and I have works: show me thy faith without thy works, and I will show thee my faith by my works. Thou believest that there is one God; thou doest well: the devils also believe, and tremble. But wilt thou know, O vain man, that faith without works is dead? Was not Abraham our father justified by works, when he had offered Isaac his son upon the altar? Seest thou how faith wrought with his works, and by works was faith made perfect?

Chapter 1a

Israel – Muscle
(Movement)

I like to think of the broader structure of the things of God. In doing this I look at the kingdom of God on the earth as an example of the creation of God known as man. When I read "*And God said, Let us make man in our image, after our likeness*" in Genesis 1:26, I don't just see the physical structure known as man. I look beyond that to see the structure of mankind on a spiritual level.

I think you'd agree that the spiritual world is not limited to physical forms that match our own. However, the structure that God revealed when He said "*our image*" may also be a representation of the spiritual kingdom of God. The spiritual world has many different forms, including thrones, powers, and hierarchies. This also has been given to the kingdom of man.

As I think about the kingdom of man it makes me wonder why humans were created. I will touch briefly on that thought. Let me share with you the words of the Psalmist as he thought about the same matter.

> *When I consider thy heavens, the work of thy fingers, the moon and the stars, which thou hast ordained; What is man, that thou art mindful of him? and the son of man, that thou visitest him? For thou hast made him a little lower than the angels, and hast crowned him with glory and honour. Thou madest him to have dominion over the works of thy hands; thou hast put all things under his feet: All sheep and oxen, yea, and the beasts of the field; The fowl of the air, and the fish of the sea, and whatsoever passeth through the paths of the seas. O LORD our Lord, how excellent is thy name in all the earth!*
> (Psalm 8:3-9)

Now, on the matter of image, please think about this: what if God created not just man in the form of a body, but what if the body of man is an illustration of the kingdom of God with man? This would mean that all mankind is made in the image of God and after His likeness, not just each individual person in the kingdom of man. The Scriptures give me some justification for thinking on these lines: consider the following.

> *For the wrath of God is revealed from heaven against all ungodliness and unrighteousness of men, who hold the truth in unrighteousness; Because that which may be known of God is manifest in them; for God hath showed it unto them. For the invisible things of him from the creation of the world are clearly seen, being understood by the things that are made, even his eternal power and Godhead; so that they are without excuse: Because that, when they knew God, they glorified him not as God, neither were thankful; but became vain in their imaginations, and their foolish heart was darkened.*
> (Romans 1:18-21)

This thought caused me to begin to form a map of the place held by each of the nations in the kingdom of man. I looked at the world as a body built of nations. I started this evaluation with the nation of Israel. How might this nation fit into the kingdom of God with man, if it is viewed as a body?

Being a Christian (yes, I freely admit this, but don't throw the book away yet), and thus an adopted child in the line of David, who is of the sons of Abraham, I am thus linked with all the other children of Abraham. The concept of faith in God gained its greatest exposure in the writings about Abraham, so men of faith are indebted to Abraham for starting us down this road. As a Christian, I am reminded of the statement of the apostle of Jesus Christ named Paul, where he describes the church that is being built on the truth of Christ as a body.

> *For as the body is one, and hath many members, and all the members of that one body, being many, are one body: so also is Christ. For by one Spirit are we all baptized into one body, whether we be Jews or Gentiles, whether we be bond or free; and have been all made to drink into one Spirit.*

For the body is not one member, but many. If the foot shall say, Because I am not the hand, I am not of the body; is it therefore not of the body? And if the ear shall say, Because I am not the eye, I am not of the body; is it therefore not of the body? If the whole body were an eye, where were the hearing? If the whole were hearing, where were the smelling?

But now hath God set the members every one of them in the body, as it hath pleased him. And if they were all one member, where were the body? But now are they many members, yet but one body. And the eye cannot say unto the hand, I have no need of thee: nor again the head to the feet, I have no need of you. Nay, much more those members of the body, which seem to be more feeble, are necessary: And those members of the body, which we think to be less honourable, upon these we bestow more abundant honour; and our uncomely parts have more abundant comeliness. For our comely parts have no need: but God hath tempered the body together, having given more abundant honour to that part which lacked: That there should be no schism in the body; but that the members should have the same care one for another. And whether one member suffer, all the members suffer with it; or one member be honoured, all the members rejoice with it.

Now ye are the body of Christ, and members in particular. And God hath set some in the church, first apostles, secondarily prophets, thirdly teachers, after that miracles, then gifts of healings, helps, governments, diversities of tongues. Are all apostles? are all prophets? are all teachers? are all workers of miracles? Have all the gifts of healing? do all speak with tongues? do all interpret? But covet earnestly the best gifts: and yet show I unto you a more excellent way.
(1 Corinthians 12:12-31)

For such a powerful body as is the body of the kingdom of God with man, it does not seem proper to construct it of men or even of organization. It seems more in keeping with the awesome power of God that it be composed of nations, principalities, powers and divinely selected entities. Therefore, in reverence to the Scriptures we begin with the nation of Israel.

> *Remember the days of old, consider the years of many generations: ask thy father, and he will show thee; thy elders, and they will tell thee. When the Most High divided to the nations their inheritance, when he separated the sons of Adam, he set the bounds of the people according to the number of the children of Israel. For the LORD'S portion is his people; Jacob is the lot of his inheritance.*
> (Deuteronomy 32:7-9)

Studying the history of the nation of Israel and knowing the systems of the body, it seems that the one that fits the nation of Israel best is the muscular system. This is the system that is assigned the function of creating movement for and demonstrating the power of the body. These are functions that the nation of Israel has done throughout its history.

The most widely known demonstration of the power of the kingdom of God with man was illustrated to Pharaoh when he was *persuaded* to let the children of Israel go. It started with the call of Moses to action by God.

> *Now Moses kept the flock of Jethro his father in law, the priest of Midian: and he led the flock to the backside of the desert, and came to the mountain of God, even to Horeb. And the angel of the LORD appeared unto him in a flame of fire out of the midst of a bush: and he looked, and, behold, the bush burned with fire, and the bush was not consumed. And Moses said, I will now turn aside, and see this great sight, why the bush is not burnt.*
>
> *And when the LORD saw that he turned aside to see, God called unto him out of the midst of the bush, and said, Moses, Moses. And he said, Here am I. And he said, Draw not nigh hither: put off thy shoes from off thy feet, for the place whereon thou standest is holy ground. Moreover he said, I am the God of thy father, the God of Abraham, the God of Isaac, and the God of Jacob. And*

Moses hid his face; for he was afraid to look upon God. And the LORD said, I have surely seen the affliction of my people which are in Egypt, and have heard their cry by reason of their taskmasters; for I know their sorrows; And I am come down to deliver them out of the hand of the Egyptians, and to bring them up out of that land unto a good land and a large, unto a land flowing with milk and honey; unto the place of the Canaanites, and the Hittites, and the Amorites, and the Perizzites, and the Hivites, and the Jebusites. Now therefore, behold, the cry of the children of Israel is come unto me: and I have also seen the oppression wherewith the Egyptians oppress them. Come now therefore, and I will send thee unto Pharaoh, that thou mayest bring forth my people the children of Israel out of Egypt.
(Exodus 3:1-10)

The illustration was finished with the demonstration of God's power over life and death.

And Moses said, Thus saith the LORD, About midnight will I go out into the midst of Egypt: And all the firstborn in the land of Egypt shall die, from the first born of Pharaoh that sitteth upon his throne, even unto the firstborn of the maidservant that is behind the mill; and all the firstborn of beasts. And there shall be a great cry throughout all the land of Egypt, such as there was none like it, nor shall be like it any more. But against any of the children of Israel shall not a dog move his tongue, against man or beast: that ye may know how that the LORD doth put a difference between the Egyptians and Israel. And all these thy servants shall come down unto me, and bow down themselves unto me, saying, Get thee out, and all the people that follow thee: and after that I will go out. And he went out from Pharaoh in a great anger.
(Exodus 11:4-8)

This message was not limited to the kingdom of Egypt but resounded throughout the region. Those who saw the children of Israel were also convinced of the power of God in their midst.

And Balak the son of Zippor saw all that Israel had done to the Amorites. And Moab was sore afraid of the people, because they were many: and Moab was distressed because of the children of Israel. And Moab said unto the elders of Midian, Now shall this company lick up all that are round about us, as the ox licketh up the grass of the field. And Balak the son of Zippor was king of the Moabites at that time. He sent messengers therefore unto Balaam the son of Beor to Pethor, which is by the river of the land of the children of his people, to call him, saying, Behold, there is a people come out from Egypt: behold, they cover the face of the earth, and they abide over against me: Come now therefore, I pray thee, curse me this people; for they are too mighty for me: peradventure I shall prevail, that we may smite them, and that I may drive them out of the land: for I wot that he whom thou blessest is blessed, and he whom thou cursest is cursed.

And the elders of Moab and the elders of Midian departed with the rewards of divination in their hand; and they came unto Balaam, and spake unto him the words of Balak.

And he said unto them, Lodge here this night, and I will bring you word again, as the LORD shall speak unto me: and the princes of Moab abode with Balaam.

And God came unto Balaam, and said, What men are these with thee?

And Balaam said unto God, Balak the son of Zippor, king of Moab, hath sent unto me, saying, Behold, there is a people come out of Egypt, which covereth the face of the earth: come now, curse me them; peradventure I shall be able to overcome them, and drive them out.

And God said unto Balaam, Thou shalt not go with them; thou shalt not curse the people: for they are blessed.

And Balaam rose up in the morning, and said unto the princes of Balak, Get you into your land: for the LORD refuseth to give me leave to go with you.
        (Numbers 22:2-13)

The movement that the nation created was that of personally carrying the message of the God of Abraham to the entire world, or at least to the then known world around the nation of Israel. From these nations the message rippled to the remainder of the world.

Behold, I have taught you statutes and judgments, even as the LORD my God commanded me, that ye should do so in the land whither ye go to possess it. Keep therefore and do them; for this is your wisdom and your understanding in the sight of the nations, which shall hear all these statutes, and say, Surely this great nation is a wise and understanding people.
        (Deuteronomy 4:5-6)

Indeed based on the knowledge of the power of God in the midst of the children of Israel, pacts were formed with Israel by any means necessary. They were also willing to form these pacts under whatever conditions they were offered by the nation of Israel.

And when the inhabitants of Gibeon heard what Joshua had done unto Jericho and to Ai, They did work wilily, and went and made as if they had been ambassadors, and took old sacks upon their asses, and wine bottles, old, and rent, and bound up; And old shoes and clouted upon their feet, and old garments upon them; and all the bread of their provision was dry and mouldy. And they went to Joshua unto the camp at Gilgal, and said unto him, and to the men of Israel, We be come from a far country: now therefore make ye a league with us.

And the men of Israel said unto the Hivites, Peradventure ye dwell among us; and how shall we make a league with you?

And they said unto Joshua, We are thy servants.

And Joshua said unto them, Who are ye? and from whence come ye?

And they said unto him, From a very far country thy servants are come because of the name of the LORD thy God: for we have heard the fame of him, and all that he did in Egypt, And all that he did to the two kings of the Amorites, that were beyond Jordan, to Sihon king of Heshbon, and to Og king of Bashan, which was at Ashtaroth. Wherefore our elders and all the inhabitants of our country spake to us, saying, Take victuals with you for the journey, and go to meet them, and say unto them, We are your servants: therefore now make ye a league with us. This our bread we took hot for our provision out of our houses on the day we came forth to go unto you; but now, behold, it is dry, and it is mouldy: And these bottles of wine, which we filled, were new; and, behold, they be rent: and these our garments and our shoes are become old by reason of the very long journey. And the men took of their victuals, and asked not counsel at the mouth of the LORD.

And Joshua made peace with them, and made a league with them, to let them live: and the princes of the congregation sware unto them. And it came to pass at the end of three days after they had made a league with them, that they heard that they were their neighbours, and that they dwelt among them. And the children of Israel journeyed, and came unto their cities on the third day. Now their cities were Gibeon, and Chephirah, and Beeroth, and Kirjathjearim.

And the children of Israel smote them not, because the princes of the congregation had sworn unto them by the LORD God of Israel. And all the congregation murmured against the princes.

But all the princes said unto all the congregation, We have sworn unto them by the LORD God of Israel: now therefore we may not touch them. This we will do to them; we will even let them live, lest wrath be upon us, because of the oath which we sware unto them. And the princes said unto them, Let them live; but let them be hewers of wood and drawers of water unto all the congregation; as the princes had promised them.

And Joshua called for them, and he spake unto them, saying, Wherefore have ye beguiled us, saying, We are very far from you; when ye dwell among us? Now therefore ye are cursed, and there shall none of you be freed from being bondmen, and hewers of wood and drawers of water for the house of my God.

And they answered Joshua, and said, Because it was certainly told thy servants, how that the LORD thy God commanded his servant Moses to give you all the land, and to destroy all the inhabitants of the land from before you, therefore we were sore afraid of our lives because of you, and have done this thing. And now, behold, we are in thine hand: as it seemeth good and right unto thee to do unto us, do.

And so did he unto them, and delivered them out of the hand of the children of Israel, that they slew them not. And Joshua made them that day hewers of wood and drawers of water for the congregation, and for the altar of the LORD, even unto this day, in the place which he should choose.
    (Joshua 9:3-27)

It became so obvious to the nations around Israel that they were dealing with the power of God that they even formed alliances with one another to try to suppress the nation.

And it came to pass, when all the kings which were on this side Jordan, in the hills, and in the valleys, and in all the coasts of the great sea over against Lebanon, the Hittite, and the Amorite, the Canaanite, the Perizzite, the Hivite, and the Jebusite, heard thereof; That they gathered themselves together, to fight with Joshua and with Israel, with one accord.
    (Joshua 9:1-2)

Now it came to pass, when Adonizedek king of Jerusalem had heard how Joshua had taken Ai, and had utterly destroyed it; as he had done to Jericho and her king, so he had done to Ai and her king; and how the inhabitants of Gibeon had made peace with Israel, and were among them; That they feared greatly, because Gibeon was a great city, as one of the royal cities, and because it was greater than Ai, and all the men thereof were mighty.

Wherefore Adonizedek king of Jerusalem sent unto Hoham king of Hebron, and unto Piram king of Jarmuth, and unto Japhia king of Lachish, and unto Debir king of Eglon, saying, Come up unto me, and help me, that we may smite Gibeon: for it hath made peace with Joshua and with the children of Israel.

Therefore the five kings of the Amorites, the king of Jerusalem, the king of Hebron, the king of Jarmuth, the king of Lachish, the king of Eglon, gathered themselves together, and went up, they and all their hosts, and encamped before Gibeon, and made war against it. And the men of Gibeon sent unto Joshua to the camp to Gilgal, saying, Slack not thy hand from thy servants; come up to us quickly, and save us, and help us: for all the kings of the Amorites that dwell in the mountains are gathered together against us.

So Joshua ascended from Gilgal, he, and all the people of war with him, and all the mighty men of valour.

And the LORD said unto Joshua, Fear them not: for I have delivered them into thine hand; there shall not a man of them stand before thee.

Joshua therefore came unto them suddenly, and went up from Gilgal all night. And the LORD discomfited them before Israel, and slew them with a great slaughter at Gibeon, and chased them along the way that goeth up to Bethhoron, and smote them to Azekah, and unto Makkedah. And it came to pass, as they fled from before Israel, and were in the going down to Bethhoron, that the LORD cast down great stones from heaven upon them unto Azekah, and they died: they were more which died with hailstones than they whom the children of Israel slew with the sword.

Then spake Joshua to the LORD in the day when the LORD delivered up the Amorites before the children of Israel, and he said in the sight of Israel, Sun, stand thou still upon Gibeon; and thou, Moon, in the valley of Ajalon. And the sun stood still, and the moon stayed, until the people had avenged themselves upon their enemies. Is not this written in the book of Jasher? So the sun stood still in the midst of heaven, and hasted not to go down about a whole day. And there was no day like that before it or after it, that the LORD hearkened unto the voice of a man: for the LORD fought for Israel.
(Joshua 10:1-14)

Then finally the nation of Israel started a series of forced relocations and took the message of God along with them. The nation of Israel because of its constant loss of sight of the message of God that had been entrusted to it, was moved about among many nations; by a means known as captivity. This can be seen as a negative if we look at it from a microscopic level of the persons in captivity. However, if it is looked at from a macrocosmic level, we begin to see how it is beneficial. From this macroscopic level we see that by its movement, the nation of Israel was able to introduce the God of Abraham to many nations. This they did through Moses, Joshua and all the other prophets.

Though their being moved from one place to another may have seemed to an uninformed observer as a method of punishment and isolation by God, it was not. The message of God was being demonstrated, in great power, to all who came in contact with the children of Israel.

Could the other nations have understood the power of the God of the universe if Israel had stayed in one place and broadcast the requirement for all nations to bow to Him? Maybe. But it seems that like every other man, and particularly every other nation on this earth, there was a need for "demonstrations that would convince". This God provided by the history of the nation of Israel.

Would Israel have preferred to be spared being placed in this position? Maybe; but if it had been the nation would not have completed itself by getting the message out to the people of the region and eventually to the world. We can see this in the succeeding history of the nation of Israel. When left to its own and allowed to have its judges and kings and other earthly officials, the nation of Israel slipped into a complacency of peace. This complacency of peace would cause the people of the nation to justify melding into the remainder of the world and forsaking the mission of God to produce the kingdom of God on the earth as it is in heaven.

My brothers in Abraham in the nation of Israel, and thus my brothers in God, remember the message that God has entrusted to you. Return this day to the position of being the muscle of the body of mankind to move the message of God. Return this day to a position from which you will demonstrate the power of God. Return this day to proclaiming the kingdom of God with man.

Though God called you to develop a pure people of worship to God, He has never let you be isolated from the world. You have been carrying His message and you have carried it very far. This does not even include the tens of thousand of miles that the apostles of Christ, who are also of the nation of Israel, spent in spreading the message of the kingdom of God to the world.

You have a mission and it is well past time for you to return to God so that he can re-direct you in the mission that you are perfectly equipped to do. It is by the hand of God that you were crafted to perform this mission. His word will not return void; you will accomplish His mission. It is just a matter of how much additional pain you want to force Him to inflict on the muscles to develop them to the precision that He requires you to have. You know the way to Him; for you have shown so many people the way. Remember where you were and return there, for this is where you will find God and complete the message of God.

Jesus said, and the apostle of God in Christ preached, that which is now history; the destruction of the temple in Jerusalem around 70 AD.

> *And when ye shall see Jerusalem compassed with armies, then know that the desolation thereof is nigh. Then let them which are in Judaea flee to the mountains; and let them which are in the midst of it depart out; and let not them that are in the countries enter thereinto. For these be the days of vengeance, that all things which are written may be fulfilled. But woe unto them that are with child, and to them that give suck, in those days! for there shall be great*

distress in the land, and wrath upon this people. And
they shall fall by the edge of the sword, and shall be
led away captive into all nations: and Jerusalem shall
be trodden down of the Gentiles, until the times of the
Gentiles be fulfilled.
        (Luke 21:20-24)

According to this prophecy, the nation of Israel has a limited amount of time to sit on the sidelines (*until the times of the Gentiles be fulfilled*). Start now to prepare; for the call may come sooner than you want it to if you have not prepared yourself by returning to God.

If you've forgotten the way, remember the words of God.

Thus Solomon finished the house of the LORD, and the
king's house: and all that came into Solomon's heart to
make in the house of the LORD, and in his own house,
he prosperously effected.

And the LORD appeared to Solomon by night, and said
unto him, I have heard thy prayer, and have chosen this
place to myself for an house of sacrifice. If I shut up
heaven that there be no rain, or if I command the locusts
to devour the land, or if I send pestilence among my
people; If my people, which are called by my name, shall
humble themselves, and pray, and seek my face, and turn
from their wicked ways; then will I hear from heaven,
and will forgive their sin, and will heal their land.
        (2 Chronicles 7:11-14)

Hear further the words of the LORD to your fathers and the newly released nation of antiquity. This is a message that is still fresh for the children of the nation that moved at God's command; the command which was first given through the man Moses. Hear again God's promise to the nation.

Ye have seen what I did unto the Egyptians, and how
I bare you on eagles' wings, and brought you unto
myself. Now therefore, if ye will obey my voice indeed,
and keep my covenant, then ye shall be a peculiar
treasure unto me above all people: for all the earth is
mine: And ye shall be unto me a kingdom of priests,

and an holy nation. These are the words which thou shalt speak unto the children of Israel.
(Exodus 19:4 -6)

+=+
+=+

I will close by citing some more examples of the introduction of the God of Abraham to the kings of the nations of their captivity.

Egypt

Even when he had been subdued by the God of the universe Pharaoh was still well aware of the benefit of serving God. The following gives us an indication of the mind of Pharaoh on this matter. Pharaoh knew that the actions of God could accrue to him a blessing.

And Pharaoh rose up in the night, he, and all his servants, and all the Egyptians; and there was a great cry in Egypt; for there was not a house where there was not one dead. And he called for Moses and Aaron by night, and said, Rise up, and get you forth from among my people, both ye and the children of Israel; and go, serve the LORD, as ye have said. Also take your flocks and your herds, as ye have said, and be gone; and bless me also.
(Exodus 12:30-32)

+=+

Babylon

The kings looked to the children of Israel to provide them the word of God for their rule.

King Nebuchadezzar did so.

Forasmuch as thou sawest that the stone was cut out of the mountain without hands, and that it brake in pieces the iron, the brass, the clay, the silver, and the gold; the great God hath made known to the king what shall come to pass hereafter: and the dream is certain, and the interpretation thereof sure.

Then the king Nebuchadnezzar fell upon his face, and worshipped Daniel, and commanded that they should offer an oblation and sweet odours unto him. The king answered unto Daniel, and said, Of a truth it is, that your God is a God of gods, and a Lord of kings, and a revealer of secrets, seeing thou couldest reveal this secret.

Then the king made Daniel a great man, and gave him many great gifts, and made him ruler over the whole province of Babylon, and chief of the governors over all the wise men of Babylon. Then Daniel requested of the king, and he set Shadrach, Meshach, and Abednego, over the affairs of the province of Babylon: but Daniel sat in the gate of the king.
(Daniel 2:45-49)

Then Nebuchadnezzar came near to the mouth of the burning fiery furnace, and spake, and said, Shadrach, Meshach, and Abednego, ye servants of the most high God, come forth, and come hither. Then Shadrach, Meshach, and Abednego, came forth of the midst of the fire. And the princes, governors, and captains, and the king's counsellors, being gathered together, saw these men, upon whose bodies the fire had no power, nor was an hair of their head singed, neither were their coats changed, nor the smell of fire had passed on them.

Then Nebuchadnezzar spake, and said, Blessed be the God of Shadrach, Meshach, and Abednego, who hath sent his angel, and delivered his servants that trusted in him, and have changed the king's word, and yielded their bodies, that they might not serve nor worship any god, except their own God. Therefore I make a decree, That every people, nation, and language, which speak any thing amiss against the God of Shadrach, Meshach, and Abednego, shall be cut in pieces, and their houses shall be made a dunghill: because there is no other God that can deliver after this sort.

Then the king promoted Shadrach, Meshach, and Abednego, in the province of Babylon.
(Daniel 3:26-30)

King Belshazzar honored God and even accepted his own destruction without reprisal against the messenger of God. He did so because he knew that it was a justified retribution for the thing which he had done, and he knew that it was coming from God.

And thou his son, O Belshazzar, hast not humbled thine heart, though thou knewest all this; But hast lifted up thyself against the Lord of heaven; and they have brought the vessels of his house before thee, and thou, and thy lords, thy wives, and thy concubines, have drunk wine in them; and thou hast praised the gods of silver, and gold, of brass, iron, wood, and stone, which see not, nor hear, nor know: and the God in whose hand thy breath is, and whose are all thy ways, hast thou not glorified: Then was the part of the hand sent from him; and this writing was written. And this is the writing that was written, MENE, MENE, TEKEL, UPHARSIN.

This is the interpretation of the thing: MENE; God hath numbered thy kingdom, and finished it. TEKEL; Thou art weighed in the balances, and art found wanting. PERES; Thy kingdom is divided, and given to the Medes and Persians.

Then commanded Belshazzar, and they clothed Daniel with scarlet, and put a chain of gold about his neck, and made a proclamation concerning him, that he should be the third ruler in the kingdom.

In that night was Belshazzar the king of the Chaldeans slain. And Darius the Median took the kingdom, being about threescore and two years old.
(Daniel 5:22-31)

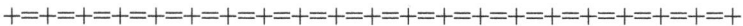

Medes

King Darius

Then the king arose very early in the morning, and went in haste unto the den of lions. And when he came to the den, he cried with a lamentable voice unto Daniel: and the king spake and said to Daniel, O Daniel, servant of the living God, is thy God, whom thou servest continually, able to deliver thee from the lions?

Then said Daniel unto the king, O king, live for ever. My God hath sent his angel, and hath shut the lions' mouths, that they have not hurt me: forasmuch as before him innocency was found in me; and also before thee, O king, have I done no hurt.

Then was the king exceeding glad for him, and commanded that they should take Daniel up out of the den. So Daniel was taken up out of the den, and no manner of hurt was found upon him, because he believed in his God. And the king commanded, and they brought those men which had accused Daniel, and they cast them into the den of lions, them, their children, and their wives; and the lions had the mastery of them, and brake all their bones in pieces or ever they came at the bottom of the den.

Then king Darius wrote unto all people, nations, and languages, that dwell in all the earth; Peace be multiplied unto you. I make a decree, That in every dominion of my kingdom men tremble and fear before the God of Daniel: for he is the living God, and stedfast for ever, and his kingdom that which shall not be destroyed, and his dominion shall be even unto the end. He delivereth and rescueth, and he worketh signs and wonders in heaven and in earth, who hath delivered Daniel from the power of the lions.
    (Daniel 6:19-27)

+=+

Persians

Cyrus

Now in the first year of Cyrus king of Persia, that the word of the LORD by the mouth of Jeremiah might be fulfilled, the LORD stirred up the spirit of Cyrus king of Persia, that he made a proclamation throughout all his kingdom, and put it also in writing, saying, Thus saith

Cyrus king of Persia, The LORD God of heaven hath given me all the kingdoms of the earth; and he hath charged me to build him an house at Jerusalem, which is in Judah. Who is there among you of all his people? his God be with him, and let him go up to Jerusalem, which is in Judah, and build the house of the LORD God of Israel, (he is the God,) which is in Jerusalem. And whosoever remaineth in any place where he sojourneth, let the men of his place help him with silver, and with gold, and with goods, and with beasts, beside the freewill offering for the house of God that is in Jerusalem.
    (Ezra 1:1-4)

+=+

The Word from the Bible

Exodus 19:3-8

And Moses went up unto God, and the LORD called unto him out of the mountain, saying, Thus shalt thou say to the house of Jacob, and tell the children of Israel; Ye have seen what I did unto the Egyptians, and how I bare you on eagles' wings, and brought you unto myself. Now therefore, if ye will obey my voice indeed, and keep my covenant, then ye shall be a peculiar treasure unto me above all people: for all the earth is mine: And ye shall be unto me a kingdom of priests, and an holy nation. These are the words which thou shalt speak unto the children of Israel.

And Moses came and called for the elders of the people, and laid before their faces all these words which the LORD commanded him.

And all the people answered together, and said, All that the LORD hath spoken we will do.

And Moses returned the words of the people unto the LORD.

1 Samuel 8:1-9

And it came to pass, when Samuel was old, that he made his sons judges over Israel. Now the name of his firstborn was Joel; and the name of his second, Abiah: they were judges in Beersheba. And his sons walked not in his ways, but turned aside after lucre, and took bribes, and perverted judgment.

Then all the elders of Israel gathered themselves together, and came to Samuel unto Ramah, And said unto him, Behold, thou art old, and thy sons walk not in thy ways: now make us a king to judge us like all the nations.

But the thing displeased Samuel, when they said, Give us a king to judge us. And Samuel prayed unto the LORD.

And the LORD said unto Samuel, Hearken unto the voice of the people in all that they say unto thee: for they have not rejected thee, but they have rejected me, that I should not reign over them. According to all the works which they have done since the day that I brought them up out of Egypt even unto this day, wherewith they have forsaken me, and served other gods, so do they also unto thee. Now therefore hearken unto their voice: howbeit yet protest solemnly unto them, and show them the manner of the king that shall reign over them.

Matthew 25:14-29

For the kingdom of heaven is as a man travelling into a far country, who called his own servants, and delivered unto them his goods. And unto one he gave five talents, to another two, and to another one; to every man according to his several ability; and straightway took his journey. Then he that had received the five talents went and traded with the same, and made them other five talents. And likewise he that had received two, he also gained other two. But he that had received one went and digged in the earth, and hid his lord's money. After a long time the lord of those servants cometh, and reckoneth with them.

And so he that had received five talents came and brought other five talents, saying, Lord, thou deliveredst unto me five talents: behold, I have gained beside them five talents more. His lord said unto him, Well done, thou good and faithful servant: thou hast been faithful over a few things, I will make thee ruler over many things: enter thou into the joy of thy lord.

He also that had received two talents came and said, Lord, thou deliveredst unto me two talents: behold, I have gained two other talents beside them. His lord said unto him, Well done, good and faithful servant; thou hast been faithful over a few things, I will make thee ruler over many things: enter thou into the joy of thy lord.

Then he which had received the one talent came and said, Lord, I knew thee that thou art an hard man, reaping where thou hast not sown, and gathering where thou hast not strawed: And I was afraid, and went and hid thy talent in the earth: lo, there thou hast that is thine.

His lord answered and said unto him, Thou wicked and slothful servant, thou knewest that I reap where I sowed not, and gather where I have not strawed: Thou oughtest therefore to have put my money to the exchangers, and then at my coming I should have received mine own with usury. Take therefore the talent from him, and give it unto him which hath ten talents. For unto every one that hath shall be given, and he shall have abundance: but from him that hath not shall be taken away even that which he hath.

Chapter Two

Distance from God
(a natural selection process)

From the beginning God has given mankind the message that He wants to personally relate to them. This is the lesson of the communication between God and Adam in the Garden of Eden. *"And the LORD God called unto Adam, and said unto him, Where art thou?"* (Genesis 3:9)

From the beginning God has allowed man to make the choice of following Him, sort of. It might be closer to the point of God's view to reverse this concept. God has presented to mankind that, even in disobedience, mankind will never be separated from Him. Even though, from a human perspective, Adam's sin made him eligible for immediate death, God did not execute this judgment. God took another route.

> *And unto Adam he said, Because thou hast hearkened unto the voice of thy wife, and hast eaten of the tree, of which I commanded thee, saying, Thou shalt not eat of it: cursed is the ground for thy sake; in sorrow shalt thou eat of it all the days of thy life;*
> (Genesis 3:17)

Think about it for a moment. Why would God create a being such as man just to destroy it? God made man with the desire to explore his boundaries. God also gave man the authority to expand his focus beyond his then current limitations. God invented the *question*: the why, the what, the wherefore and other similar concepts. Above all, God knew what man would do, and yes, even what Satan would do, before there was ever a man, or a Satan.

What is sometimes missed in looking at this early episode in mankind's existence is that God has a selection process. Though He will not utterly cut man off, He will restrict man's handling of His things.

And the LORD God said, Behold, the man is become as one of us, to know good and evil: and now, lest he put forth his hand, and take also of the tree of life, and eat, and live for ever: Therefore the LORD God sent him forth from the garden of Eden, to till the ground from whence he was taken. So he drove out the man; and he placed at the east of the garden of Eden Cherubims, and a flaming sword which turned every way, to keep the way of the tree of life.
(Genesis 3:22-24)

The distance that the members of mankind, men and women, place between themselves and God serves as a natural selection process for our being allowed to handle the things of God. It is rather human-centric for us to blame God for the distance; but this is what we do. A brief meditation on the magnitude of God will reveal to us that God cannot separate Himself from mankind; since God is everywhere. The only place that anything can go to separate itself from God is nowhere. He who hath an ear, let him hear.

This selection process was activated with Cain and Abel.

And in process of time it came to pass, that Cain brought of the fruit of the ground an offering unto the LORD. And Abel, he also brought of the firstlings of his flock and of the fat thereof. And the LORD had respect unto Abel and to his offering: But unto Cain and to his offering he had not respect. And Cain was very wroth, and his countenance fell. And the LORD said unto Cain, Why art thou wroth? and why is thy countenance fallen? If thou doest well, shalt thou not be accepted? and if thou doest not well, sin lieth at the door. And unto thee shall be his desire, and thou shalt rule over him.
(Genesis 4:3)

The selection process continues with Noah.

"And God saw that the wickedness of man was great in the earth, and that every imagination of the thoughts of his heart was only evil continually. And it repented the LORD that he had made man on the earth, and it grieved him at his heart. And the LORD said, I will destroy man whom I have created from the face of the earth; both

man, and beast, and the creeping thing, and the fowls of the air; for it repenteth me that I have made them. But Noah found grace in the eyes of the LORD."
    (Genesis 6:5-8)

The selection process goes forward to Abram.

Now the LORD had said unto Abram, Get thee out of thy country, and from thy kindred, and from thy father's house, unto a land that I will show thee: And I will make of thee a great nation, and I will bless thee, and make thy name great; and thou shalt be a blessing: And I will bless them that bless thee, and curse him that curseth thee: and in thee shall all families of the earth be blessed.

So Abram departed, as the LORD had spoken unto him; and Lot went with him: and Abram was seventy and five years old when he departed out of Haran.
    (Genesis 12:1-4)

Furthermore, God illustrated the strength of His selection of Abram, who had been renamed Abraham by God, when he quickened him thusly.

And it came to pass after these things, that God did tempt Abraham, and said unto him, Abraham: and he said, Behold, here I am. And he said, Take now thy son, thine only son Isaac, whom thou lovest, and get thee into the land of Moriah; and offer him there for a burnt offering upon one of the mountains which I will tell thee of.

And Abraham rose up early in the morning, and saddled his ass, and took two of his young men with him, and Isaac his son, and clave the wood for the burnt offering, and rose up, and went unto the place of which God had told him. Then on the third day Abraham lifted up his eyes, and saw the place afar off. And Abraham said unto his young men, Abide ye here with the ass; and I and the lad will go yonder and worship, and come again to you.

And Abraham took the wood of the burnt offering, and laid it upon Isaac his son; and he took the fire in his hand, and a knife; and they went both of them together.

And Isaac spake unto Abraham his father, and said, My father: and he said, Here am I, my son. And he said, Behold the fire and the wood: but where is the lamb for a burnt offering? And Abraham said, My son, God will provide himself a lamb for a burnt offering: so they went both of them together.

And they came to the place which God had told him of; and Abraham built an altar there, and laid the wood in order, and bound Isaac his son, and laid him on the altar upon the wood. And Abraham stretched forth his hand, and took the knife to slay his son.

And the angel of the LORD called unto him out of heaven, and said, Abraham, Abraham: and he said, Here am I. And he said, Lay not thine hand upon the lad, neither do thou any thing unto him: for now I know that thou fearest God, seeing thou hast not withheld thy son, thine only son from me.

And Abraham lifted up his eyes, and looked, and behold behind him a ram caught in a thicket by his horns: and Abraham went and took the ram, and offered him up for a burnt offering in the stead of his son. And Abraham called the name of that place Jehovahjireh: as it is said to this day, In the mount of the LORD it shall be seen.

And the angel of the LORD called unto Abraham out of heaven the second time, And said, By myself have I sworn, saith the LORD, for because thou hast done this thing, and hast not withheld thy son, thine only son: That in blessing I will bless thee, and in multiplying I will multiply thy seed as the stars of the heaven, and as the sand which is upon the sea shore; and thy seed shall possess the gate of his enemies; And in thy seed shall all the nations of the earth be blessed; because thou hast obeyed my voice. "

(Genesis 22:1-18)

We could continue the examples through Isaac and Ishmael, Jacob and Esau, David and Saul on to Judas and Jesus of Nazareth.

The flow of man's history shows that it is not God's distance from man that is the matter, but it is man's distance from God that drives the selection process. If you think about it, this only makes sense. If God cannot say of a man that *thou hast been faithful over a few things,* how can He ever say to that same man *I will make thee ruler over many things?* The handling of the things of God does not just affect man, it affects all of this our existence. There is a ripple effect for all existence, across time and space.

Therefore, consider wisely, O man, your concentration on the things of God. Choose to handle them properly and all of mankind benefits. If you choose to handle them improperly, God will not allow it; especially not when it hurts any of His servants; and this can be anyone. Remember, even the poorest child can be crafted by God to move the universe of man's potentialities. The only option for God when we choose against proper handling of His things is to *Take therefore the talent from him, and give it unto him which hath ten talents.*

Above all, please understand that these things are God's doing and not by the choice, and sometimes not even by the hand, of man. The reaction to any offense against the things of God is from the Kingdom of God and not from the kingdom of man.

When trouble comes, we say,
"God why weren't you there?"
How soon we forget
That He is everywhere.

Whether in peace we live
Or in sorrow we abide,
It is on His stream of grace
That we constantly ride;

The unmerited favor
That comes from above,
As the deepest expression
Of God's unchanging love:

A love so boundless
And constantly true,
Abiding with us
In all that we do.

There may come times
When we push it away,
And then see our lives
Enter moments of decay.

God has not left us,
It is we who did move,
In a vain attempt
To "find our groove".

If you look deep inside,
You will begin to see
That the distance from God
Has been created by thee.

When we rethink our actions
And reverse our course,
Pointing it back to Him;
He can remove remorse.

No more "what could have been"
Or "what I might have done",
For the battle of life,
Will surely be won.

The power of God
Is available to all;
It is up to us
To answer Its call.

Chapter 2a

Ishmael – Skeleton
(support)

As this book was being develop, it started to become ever more intensely obvious that God has a plan and a place for every nation on the earth. This book is an attempt to re-establish God-centered dialog among the children of Abraham. To accomplish the mission of the book it was essential for me to look to God for understanding. One area of especial need for me is in understanding where the children of Abraham in the children of Ishmael fit into the overall plan for the world.

<u>Retaining the Form</u>

My thoughts were directed to expanding the example of a body to describe the nations of the world in the body of mankind. Looking at all of mankind as a body, the nations of Ishmael seem to be of a skeletal nature. The purpose of the skeletal system is to assist in retaining the form of the body. In this case it is the total body of mankind.

The children of Ishmael, in the day in which I am living, are striving mightily to maintain a nation that directly honors God. It is called a theocracy. This is a government that has religion as its central control. The rules that control daily interactions in such a government are intended to be the same rules that were given to the nation by God. This does not say that the government is always successful in accomplishing this; only that this is the intention of the religious and secular leaders of the nation.

Children of Ishmael, please continue to struggle to retain the structure of a God-ruled government; which was the original for all mankind. However, there is one thing that I would request further. Please continue to seek the wisdom of God for the nations. In this way you will be better able to regulate your conduct in relation to the other nations which God created on this earth. This is so because all nations are created by God and only God has authority over them, including yours.

Some nations have decided to move away from a theocracy to a monarchy. God does allow us this freedom. He does, however, warn us of the pitfalls of this choice and He is grieved by this decision.

> *Then all the elders of Israel gathered themselves together, and came to Samuel unto Ramah, And said unto him, Behold, thou art old, and thy sons walk not in thy ways: now make us a king to judge us like all the nations.*
>
> *But the thing displeased Samuel, when they said, Give us a king to judge us. And Samuel prayed unto the LORD.*
>
> *And the LORD said unto Samuel, Hearken unto the voice of the people in all that they say unto thee: for they have not rejected thee, but they have rejected me, that I should not reign over them. According to all the works which they have done since the day that I brought them up out of Egypt even unto this day, wherewith they have forsaken me, and served other gods, so do they also unto thee. Now therefore hearken unto their voice: howbeit yet protest solemnly unto them, and show them the manner of the king that shall reign over them.*
>
> (1 Samuel 8:4-9)

The nations of Ishmael appear to be attempting to hold the course. This does not say that they are doing everything right, but simply that they have retained God as the central concentration of their government.

Some work needs to be done on understanding the way God has revealed to mankind that is the best way for it to structure itself under the new call to love.

> *And there shall come forth a rod out of the stem of Jesse, and a Branch shall grow out of his roots: And the spirit of the LORD shall rest upon him, the spirit of wisdom and understanding, the spirit of counsel and might, the spirit of knowledge and of the fear of the LORD; And shall make him of quick understanding in the fear of the LORD: and he shall not judge after the sight of his eyes, neither reprove after the hearing of his ears: But with righteousness shall he judge the poor, and reprove with equity for the meek of the earth: and he shall smite the earth with the rod of his mouth, and with the breath of his lips shall he slay the*

wicked. And righteousness shall be the girdle of his loins, and faithfulness the girdle of his reins.

The wolf also shall dwell with the lamb, and the leopard shall lie down with the kid; and the calf and the young lion and the fatling together; and a little child shall lead them. And the cow and the bear shall feed; their young ones shall lie down together: and the lion shall eat straw like the ox. And the sucking child shall play on the hole of the asp, and the weaned child shall put his hand on the cockatrice' den.

They shall not hurt nor destroy in all my holy mountain: for the earth shall be full of the knowledge of the LORD, as the waters cover the sea.

And in that day there shall be a root of Jesse, which shall stand for an ensign of the people; to it shall the Gentiles seek: and his rest shall be glorious.
(Isaiah 11: 1-10)

The revived emphasis on love allows nations to look to God to preserve their existence. This is the way things were back in the time of Adam, when man was first created. The renewed emphasis on love does not allow for the destruction of other nations.

Support for the Muscular System

The skeletal system is also called on to support the muscles. The muscles need the skeleton to provide a foundation for movement. The children of Israel can learn from the Godly children of Ishmael in moving again toward the reverence of God in all aspects of their lives. We can all learn much from the Godly children of Ishmael about placing God as the center of even our governments.

The children of Ishmael seem to be working to retain the form of a God-centered society that is closer to that of Moses' time. They are, of course, taking much criticism from the world for doing this. Some of the criticism comes from their brethren. To hold to such a form can be a good thing when God is constantly in the minds and hearts of the government officials. Such a position can be beneficial for any country. It does not, however, give any nation a mandate or a license to destroy others just to preserve this way of life. This is God's business.

Recall the lesson of the Edomites, who were the descendants of Esau who was the son of Isaac, the son of Abraham.

> *The vision of Obadiah. Thus saith the Lord GOD concerning Edom; We have heard a rumour from the LORD, and an ambassador is sent among the heathen, Arise ye, and let us rise up against her in battle. Behold, I have made thee small among the heathen: thou art greatly despised. The pride of thine heart hath deceived thee, thou that dwellest in the clefts of the rock, whose habitation is high; that saith in his heart, Who shall bring me down to the ground?*

> *Though thou exalt thyself as the eagle, and though thou set thy nest among the stars, thence will I bring thee down, saith the LORD. If thieves came to thee, if robbers by night, (how art thou cut off!) would they not have stolen till they had enough? if the grapegatherers came to thee, would they not leave some grapes?*

> *How are the things of Esau searched out! how are his hidden things sought up! All the men of thy confederacy have brought thee even to the border: the men that were at peace with thee have deceived thee, and prevailed against thee; they that eat thy bread have laid a wound under thee: there is none understanding in him.*

> *Shall I not in that day, saith the LORD, even destroy the wise men out of Edom, and understanding out of the mount of Esau? And thy mighty men, O Teman, shall be dismayed, to the end that every one of the mount of Esau may be cut off by slaughter.*

> *For thy violence against thy brother Jacob shame shall cover thee, and thou shalt be cut off for ever. In the day that thou stoodest on the other side, in the day that the strangers carried away captive his forces, and foreigners entered into his gates, and cast lots upon Jerusalem, even thou wast as one of them. But thou shouldest not have looked on the day of thy brother in the day that he became a stranger; neither shouldest thou have rejoiced over the children of Judah in the day of their destruction; neither*

shouldest thou have spoken proudly in the day of distress. Thou shouldest not have entered into the gate of my people in the day of their calamity; yea, thou shouldest not have looked on their affliction in the day of their calamity, nor have laid hands on their substance in the day of their calamity; Neither shouldest thou have stood in the crossway, to cut off those of his that did escape; neither shouldest thou have delivered up those of his that did remain in the day of distress.

For the day of the LORD is near upon all the heathen: as thou hast done, it shall be done unto thee: thy reward shall return upon thine own head. For as ye have drunk upon my holy mountain, so shall all the heathen drink continually, yea, they shall drink, and they shall swallow down, and they shall be as though they had not been.
(Obadiah 1:1-16)

Please don't place any of your nations in the position where God will have to once again deliver the same type of recompense for violations of His will and of His way. Don't stir Him to wrath by pursuing the path of going nation against nation, especially not those among God's chosen ones of your brothers. Furthermore, don't support such conducts by others outside of the nations of Ishmael against God's chosen among the nations of Abraham. This does not mean that you need mount a defense of these nations, just that you don't become a participant in their destruction. You are, of course, called to become a participant in their enhancement: this is only right for brothers.

Don't move against any nation, directly or indirectly, for good or for evil, without the ABSOLUTE commandment of God. In this matter He does not give hints or inferences, He gives direct commands. Always turn to Him first, to avenge any wrong that may be done to you. His way of recompense is far more effective than any we can ever deliver. It may also be that He is trying our nations, as iron is tried in the fire, to make us stronger. Not every offense needs an external answer; some are designed to produce internal strength.

Ishmael rose above anger and separation

We do not and cannot accept any statement of exclusivity by the children of Ishmael. These statements says that none other than they are good enough to worship God. It also sometimes says that none else is worshipping the true God. There is only one God to worship and this must be done by all righteous nations. The attitude of separation was foretold by God when he sent his angel to give Hagar the word of peace which proved to her that God had not forgotten her in her trials.

> *And the angel of the LORD found her by a fountain of water in the wilderness, by the fountain in the way to Shur. And he said, Hagar, Sarai's maid, whence camest thou? and whither wilt thou go?*
>
> *And she said, I flee from the face of my mistress Sarai.*
>
> *And the angel of the LORD said unto her, Return to thy mistress, and submit thyself under her hands. And the angel of the LORD said unto her, I will multiply thy seed exceedingly, that it shall not be numbered for multitude.*
>
> *And the angel of the LORD said unto her, Behold, thou art with child, and shalt bear a son, and shalt call his name Ishmael; because the LORD hath heard thy affliction. And he will be a wild man; his hand will be against every man, and every man's hand against him; and he shall dwell in the presence of all his brethren.*
>   (Genesis 16:7-12)

Hagar was also told that the angel of the LORD would not allow the death of Ishmael just because the two women could not get along with one another. He confirmed that Ishmael is a part of the family of Abraham.

> *And Sarah saw the son of Hagar the Egyptian, which she had born unto Abraham, mocking. Wherefore she said unto Abraham, Cast out this bondwoman and her son: for the son of this bondwoman shall not be heir with my son, even with Isaac.*
>
> *And the thing was very grievous in Abraham's sight because of his son.*
>
> *And God said unto Abraham, Let it not be grievous in thy sight because of the lad, and because of thy bondwoman; in all that Sarah hath said unto thee, hearken unto her voice; for in Isaac shall thy seed be called. And also of the son of the bondwoman will I make a nation, because he is thy seed.*

And Abraham rose up early in the morning, and took bread, and a bottle of water, and gave it unto Hagar, putting it on her shoulder, and the child, and sent her away: and she departed, and wandered in the wilderness of Beersheba.

And the water was spent in the bottle, and she cast the child under one of the shrubs. And she went, and sat her down over against him a good way off, as it were a bow shot: for she said, Let me not see the death of the child. And she sat over against him, and lift up her voice, and wept.

And God heard the voice of the lad; and the angel of God called to Hagar out of heaven, and said unto her, What aileth thee, Hagar? fear not; for God hath heard the voice of the lad where he is. Arise, lift up the lad, and hold him in thine hand; for I will make him a great nation.
    (Genesis 21:9-18)

This promise is confirmed after the death of Abraham. Ishmael is the root of a nation as the angel of the LORD said.

Now these are the generations of Ishmael, Abraham's son, whom Hagar the Egyptian, Sarah's handmaid, bare unto Abraham: And these are the names of the sons of Ishmael, by their names, according to their generations: the firstborn of Ishmael, Nebajoth; and Kedar, and Adbeel, and Mibsam, And Mishma, and Dumah, and Massa, Hadar, and Tema, Jetur, Naphish, and Kedemah: These are the sons of Ishmael, and these are their names, by their towns, and by their castles; twelve princes according to their nations.

And these are the years of the life of Ishmael, an hundred and thirty and seven years: and he gave up the ghost and died; and was gathered unto his people. And they dwelt from Havilah unto Shur, that is before Egypt, as thou goest toward Assyria: and he died in the presence of all his brethren.
    (Genesis 25:12-18)

There is no reason that the children of Abraham cannot learn how to coexist with one another. This is what Ishmael and Isaac did for their father Abraham in his day. The Scriptures record that it was both Isaac and Ishmael who buried their dad, Abraham.

> *And these are the days of the years of Abraham's life which he lived, an hundred threescore and fifteen years. Then Abraham gave up the ghost, and died in a good old age, an old man, and full of years; and was gathered to his people.*
>
> *And his sons Isaac and Ishmael buried him in the cave of Machpelah, in the field of Ephron the son of Zohar the Hittite, which is before Mamre; The field which Abraham purchased of the sons of Heth: there was Abraham buried, and Sarah his wife.*
> (Genesis 25:7-10)

I think it's time for the children of Ishmael to honor their first parent Abraham and the God of Abraham more than any other. The phrase "any other" includes any brother who has come since Abraham; even the one who set the pattern for Islam. So that I won't be accused of defaming the one who established Islam, by saying anything amiss about him, I will not mention his name here, but we all know who he was.

Explanation of terms

Let me digress for a moment. You will find that I use the term God to refer to the Most High One. This is not a matter of snubbing any righteous term that may be used by any other people to refer to the Almighty. It is only that for me it feels right to use the title God. This is because the title is embedded in the word Good; and God is Good. But this is a personal matter with me and I mention it only to ask your indulgence of my use of this title in reference to the Almighty, in this book.

I do not state, or imply, that God is the name of the Most High. It is only a feeble way man has of addressing such an extremely majestic One. I don't believe that any human could ever comprehend or express the Almighty's name, if He ever chose to have one. In fact the Almighty doesn't need a name.

There will be very few who will ever enter into direct conversation with the Almighty. Those who do, will not need to call Him by name. They will only receive from the Almighty blessed directions in what they are to do. The Almighty will call us by name, but we will not have such comfort in His presence as to call the Almighty by His; if He even has one. Enoch who walked and talked with Him and Moses who communed with Him only referred to Him by title.

I write this so you won't be offended if I don't call the Almighty by any persons stated name. Even if the Almighty were to tell me His name and even if I could phrase it properly, I would not willingly use it. I am too insignificant in comparison to the Almighty to ever speak His name. It would be my feeling that the very mention by me of His name would be a violation of His Law.

> *Thou shalt not take the name of the LORD thy God in vain; for the LORD will not hold him guiltless that taketh his name in vain.*
> (Exodus 20:7)

Indeed, it would take a direct command of the Almighty to cause me to say His name. And that command would only be active for me at the instant when He gave it. I would not store the permission for use at any other time.

I wrote this because in the time in which I am living people are being killed for not saying the *right* name of God. Indeed people are being killed for dishonoring the messengers of God. This seems to be a reversal of the ways of God, as I understand them: but it is the way things were, as of this writing.

God is above all

God, in times past, sent forth the prophets to give their lives where necessary for the mission of God. This was done so that they would understand that in delivering a message of life it would sometimes require that they have devotion unto death. God let His prophets know that their lives were subject to termination. Moses showed forth this true Spirit of God in the prophets when, on behalf of the children of Israel, he offered his life to God in exchange for theirs.

> *And it came to pass on the morrow, that Moses said unto the people, Ye have sinned a great sin: and now I will go up unto the LORD; peradventure I shall make an atonement for your sin. And Moses returned unto the LORD, and said, Oh, this people have sinned a great sin, and have made them gods of gold. Yet now, if thou wilt forgive their sin--; and if not, blot me, I pray thee, out of thy book which thou hast written.*
> (Exodus 32:30-32)

Of course God rejected this offer. It is the responsibility of every man to bear the consequences of his own sin.

> *And the LORD said unto Moses, Whosoever hath sinned against me, him will I blot out of my book. Therefore now go, lead the people unto the place of which I have spoken unto thee: behold, mine Angel shall go before thee: nevertheless in the day when I visit I will visit their sin upon them.*
>
> *And the LORD plagued the people, because they made the calf, which Aaron made.*
> (Exodus 32:33-35)

When Moses was rebuffed from outside his nation, he merely turned this aside and continued the mission of God.

> *And Moses sent messengers from Kadesh unto the king of Edom, Thus saith thy brother Israel, Thou knowest all the travail that hath befallen us: How our fathers went down into Egypt, and we have dwelt in Egypt a long time; and the Egyptians vexed us, and our fathers: And when we cried unto the LORD, he heard our voice, and sent an angel, and hath brought us forth out of Egypt: and, behold, we are in Kadesh, a city in the uttermost of thy border: Let us pass, I pray thee, through thy country: we will not pass through the fields, or through the vineyards, neither will we drink of the water of the wells: we will go by the king's high way, we will not turn to the right hand nor to the left, until we have passed thy borders.*
>
> *And Edom said unto him, Thou shalt not pass by me, lest I come out against thee with the sword.*
>
> *And the children of Israel said unto him, We will go by the high way: and if I and my cattle drink of thy water, then I will pay for it: I will only, without doing any thing else, go through on my feet.*
>
> *And he said, Thou shalt not go through. And Edom came out against him with much people, and with a strong hand. Thus Edom refused to give Israel passage through his border: wherefore Israel turned away from him.*
> (Deuteronomy 20:14-21)

It is God who notices the slight to His prophets and to His people; and it is God who recompenses the offender. This is seen very dramatically with Moses and his sister. God has no respect of persons.

And Miriam and Aaron spake against Moses because of the Ethiopian woman whom he had married: for he had married an Ethiopian woman. And they said, Hath the LORD indeed spoken only by Moses? hath he not spoken also by us? And the LORD heard it.

(Now the man Moses was very meek, above all the men which were upon the face of the earth.)

And the LORD spake suddenly unto Moses, and unto Aaron, and unto Miriam, Come out ye three unto the tabernacle of the congregation. And they three came out. And the LORD came down in the pillar of the cloud, and stood in the door of the tabernacle, and called Aaron and Miriam: and they both came forth. And he said, Hear now my words: If there be a prophet among you, I the LORD will make myself known unto him in a vision, and will speak unto him in a dream. My servant Moses is not so, who is faithful in all mine house. Who was faithful to him that appointed him, as also Moses was faithful in all his house. With him will I speak mouth to mouth, even apparently, and not in dark speeches; and the similitude of the LORD shall he behold: wherefore then were ye not afraid to speak against my servant Moses?

And the anger of the LORD was kindled against them; and he departed. And the cloud departed from off the tabernacle; and, behold, Miriam became leprous, white as snow: and Aaron looked upon Miriam, and, behold, she was leprous.

And Aaron said unto Moses, Alas, my lord, I beseech thee, lay not the sin upon us, wherein we have done foolishly, and wherein we have sinned. Let her not be as one dead, of whom the flesh is half consumed when he cometh out of his mother's womb.

And Moses cried unto the LORD, saying, Heal her now, O God, I beseech thee.

And the LORD said unto Moses, If her father had but spit in her face, should she not be ashamed seven days? let her be shut out from the camp seven days, and after that let her be received in again.

And Miriam was shut out from the camp seven days: and the people journeyed not till Miriam was brought in again.
(Numbers 12:1-15)

It is God who notices the abomination of the nations and recompenses them, in His time. Sometimes this results in total annihilation.

And the LORD spake unto Moses, saying, Vex the Midianites, and smite them: For they vex you with their wiles, wherewith they have beguiled you in the matter of Peor, and in the matter of Cozbi, the daughter of a prince of Midian, their sister, which was slain in the day of the plague for Peor's sake.
(Numbers 25:16-18)

Sometimes He stays His hand for a greater benefit.

Now these are the nations which the LORD left, to prove Israel by them, even as many of Israel as had not known all the wars of Canaan; Only that the generations of the children of Israel might know, to teach them war, at the least such as before knew nothing thereof; Namely, five lords of the Philistines, and all the Canaanites, and the Sidonians, and the Hivites that dwelt in mount Lebanon, from mount Baalhermon unto the entering in of Hamath. And they were to prove Israel by them, to know whether they would hearken unto the commandments of the LORD, which he commanded their fathers by the hand of Moses.
(Judges 3:1-4)

In all such discipline, it is God who decides; it is God who shows the way; it is God who leads the way. And He does so in such a fashion that there is no collateral damage or loss of uninvolved lives. Humans are not so precise when they veer away from God and attempt to take their own vengeance. Humans experience this kind of failure because they are overriding God's authority; they are entering into areas where they do not belong.

How should one chase a thousand, and two put ten thousand to flight, except their Rock had sold them, and the LORD had shut them up? For their rock is not as our Rock, even our enemies themselves being judges. For their vine is of the vine of Sodom, and of the fields of Gomorrah: their grapes are grapes of gall, their clusters are bitter: Their wine is the poison of dragons, and the cruel venom of asps. Is not this laid up in store with me, and sealed up among my treasures?

To me belongeth vengeance, and recompense; their foot shall slide in due time: for the day of their calamity is at hand, and the things that shall come upon them make haste.
(Deuteronomy 32:30-35)

The man Ishmael understood this about the God of his father Abraham. Ishmael accepted his place of unity with the family of Abraham. We must know that this unity takes precedence over the actions of any of Ishmael's children. Ishmael stood closer to the central will of God than most of us will ever have a chance to do on this earth. His was the mission to provide the skeletal structure for the kingdom of man. If you listen to any man of your nations, listen first to him and to the witness of his life. The price that can be exacted by God for taking on His work of vengeance is an unnecessary one to pay. Please believe that He will do what is written.

I say to the children of Ishmael "Stand strong in your allegiance and your search for the true God". However, don't assume that you are the only ones to whom God is revealed. Remember that Abraham had two sons, Ishmael and Isaac. Should one of the sons destroy the other, this will surely grieve the heart of Abraham. And as we all know, Abraham is not dead, but is resting in Heaven with the LORD.

As Abraham looks upon those of the children of Ishmael, don't let him see them trying to destroy the family; not for any reason. Abraham ranks among the greatest diplomats the world has ever seen. He practiced diplomacy for the sake of his family and God. Remember Lot.

And the LORD said, Because the cry of Sodom and Gomorrah is great, and because their sin is very grievous; I will go down now, and see whether they have done altogether according to the cry of it, which is come unto me; and if not, I will know. And the men turned their faces from thence, and went toward Sodom: but Abraham stood yet before the LORD.

And Abraham drew near, and said, Wilt thou also destroy the righteous with the wicked? Peradventure there be fifty righteous within the city: wilt thou also destroy and not spare the place for the fifty righteous that are therein? That be far from thee to do after this manner, to slay the righteous with the wicked: and that the righteous should be as the wicked, that be far from thee: Shall not the Judge of all the earth do right?

And the LORD said, If I find in Sodom fifty righteous within the city, then I will spare all the place for their sakes.

And Abraham answered and said, Behold now, I have taken upon me to speak unto the LORD, which am but dust and ashes: Peradventure there shall lack five of the fifty righteous: wilt thou destroy all the city for lack of five?

And he said, If I find there forty and five, I will not destroy it.

And he spake unto him yet again, and said, Peradventure there shall be forty found there. And he said, I will not do it for forty's sake. And he said unto him, Oh let not the LORD be angry, and I will speak: Peradventure there shall thirty be found there.

And he said, I will not do it, if I find thirty there. And he said, Behold now, I have taken upon me to speak unto the LORD: Peradventure there shall be twenty found there.

And he said, I will not destroy it for twenty's sake.

And he said, Oh let not the LORD be angry, and I will speak yet but this once: Peradventure ten shall be found there.

And he said, I will not destroy it for ten's sake.

And the LORD went his way, as soon as he had left communing with Abraham: and Abraham returned unto his place.

(Genesis 18:20-33)

Live up to the standard of Abraham and pursue diplomacy with your brothers. This is required for the sons of Ishmael. This must be done for the sons of Israel who is Jacob, the son of Isaac, who is the brother of Ishmael. According to the ways of Abraham and the God of Abraham, these are your brothers.

The Word from the Bible

Malachi 1:6-14

A son honoureth his father, and a servant his master: if then I be a father, where is mine honour? and if I be a master, where is my fear? saith the LORD of hosts unto you, O priests, that despise my name.

And ye say, Wherein have we despised thy name?

Ye offer polluted bread upon mine altar; and ye say, Wherein have we polluted thee? In that ye say, The table of the LORD is contemptible. And if ye offer the blind for sacrifice, is it not evil? and if ye offer the lame and sick, is it not evil? offer it now unto thy governor; will he be pleased with thee, or accept thy person? saith the LORD of hosts.

And now, I pray you, beseech God that he will be gracious unto us: this hath been by your means: will he regard your persons? saith the LORD of hosts. Who is there even among you that would shut the doors for nought? neither do ye kindle fire on mine altar for nought. I have no pleasure in you, saith the LORD of hosts, neither will I accept an offering at your hand.

For from the rising of the sun even unto the going down of the same my name shall be great among the Gentiles; and in every place incense shall be offered unto my name, and a pure offering: for my name shall be great among the heathen, saith the LORD of hosts. But ye have profaned it, in that ye say, The table of the LORD is polluted; and the fruit thereof, even his meat, is contemptible. Ye said also, Behold, what a weariness is it! and ye have snuffed at it, saith the LORD of hosts; and ye brought that which was torn, and the lame, and the sick; thus ye brought an offering: should I accept this of your hand? saith the LORD.

But cursed be the deceiver, which hath in his flock a male, and voweth, and sacrificeth unto the Lord a corrupt thing: for I am a great King, saith the LORD of hosts, and my name is dreadful among the heathen.

Romans 3:5-9

But if our unrighteousness commend the righteousness of God, what shall we say? Is God unrighteous who taketh vengeance? (I speak as a man) God forbid: for then how shall God judge the world?

For if the truth of God hath more abounded through my lie unto his glory; why yet am I also judged as a sinner? And not rather, (as we be slanderously reported, and as some affirm that we say,) Let us do evil, that good may come? whose damnation is just.

What then? are we better than they? No, in no wise: for we have before proved both Jews and Gentiles, that they are all under sin; As it is written, There is none righteous, no, not one: There is none that understandeth, there is none that seeketh after God. They are all gone out of the way, they are together become unprofitable; there is none that doeth good, no, not one. Their throat is an open sepulchre; with their tongues they have used deceit; the poison of asps is under their lips: Whose mouth is full of cursing and bitterness: Their feet are swift to shed blood: Destruction and misery are in their ways: And the way of peace have they not known: There is no fear of God before their eyes.

Romans 3:19-31

Now we know that what things soever the law saith, it saith to them who are under the law: that every mouth may be stopped, and all the world may become guilty before God. Therefore by the deeds of the law there shall no flesh be justified in his sight: for by the law is the knowledge of sin.

But now the righteousness of God without the law is manifested, being witnessed by the law and the prophets; Even the righteousness of God which is by faith of Jesus Christ unto all and upon all them that believe: for there is no difference: For all have sinned, and come short of the glory of God; Being justified freely by his grace through the redemption that is in Christ Jesus: Whom God hath set forth to be a propitiation through faith in his blood, to declare his righteousness for the remission of sins that are past, through the forbearance of God; To declare,

I say, at this time his righteousness: that he might be just, and the justifier of him which believeth in Jesus.

Where is boasting then? It is excluded. By what law? of works? Nay: but by the law of faith. Therefore we conclude that a man is justified by faith without the deeds of the law. Is he the God of the Jews only? is he not also of the Gentiles? Yes, of the Gentiles also: Seeing it is one God, which shall justify the circumcision by faith, and uncircumcision through faith. Do we then make void the law through faith? God forbid: yea, we establish the law.

Job 19:25-27

For I know that my redeemer liveth, and that he shall stand at the latter day upon the earth: And though after my skin worms destroy this body, yet in my flesh shall I see God: Whom I shall see for myself, and mine eyes shall behold, and not another; though my reins be consumed within me.

Malachi 3:1-3

Behold, I will send my messenger, and he shall prepare the way before me: and the Lord, whom ye seek, shall suddenly come to his temple, even the messenger of the covenant, whom ye delight in: behold, he shall come, saith the LORD of hosts.

But who may abide the day of his coming? and who shall stand when he appeareth? for he is like a refiner's fire, and like fullers' soap: And he shall sit as a refiner and purifier of silver: and he shall purify the sons of Levi, and purge them as gold and silver, that they may offer unto the LORD an offering in righteousness.

Chapter Three

We Need A Saviour

The Law of Moses started out as a collection of codes of conduct that gave clear directions about what was needed to rightly worship God. The children of Israel committed themselves to these Laws, at least in word.

> *And Moses came and told the people all the words of the LORD, and all the judgments: and all the people answered with one voice, and said, All the words which the LORD hath said will we do.*
>
> *And he took the book of the covenant, and read in the audience of the people: and they said, All that the LORD hath said will we do, and be obedient.*
>   (Exodus 24:3, 7)

When Israel was returning to the LORD after having drifted away from Him, they expressed their intention to stay the course with God.

> *Now therefore fear the LORD, and serve him in sincerity and in truth: and put away the gods which your fathers served on the other side of the flood, and in Egypt; and serve ye the LORD. And if it seem evil unto you to serve the LORD, choose you this day whom ye will serve; whether the gods which your fathers served that were on the other side of the flood, or the gods of the Amorites, in whose land ye dwell: but as for me and my house, we will serve the LORD.*
>
> *And the people answered and said, God forbid that we should forsake the LORD, to serve other gods; For the LORD our God, he it is that brought us up and our fathers out of the land of Egypt, from the house of bondage, and which did those great signs in our sight, and preserved us in all the way wherein we went, and*

among all the people through whom we passed: And the LORD drave out from before us all the people, even the Amorites which dwelt in the land: therefore will we also serve the LORD; for he is our God.
(Joshua 24:14-18)

However as time passed and as the Law started to highlight the fact that the nation of Israel has been selected to represent God through obedience to the Law, it also started to become more and more obvious that the average man could not do so.

There is, of course, the provision of the sacrifice to make up the difference between the abilities of man and the requirements of God. This was the means of acknowledgement to God of the insufficiency of man. God has always known the exact state of man, and it is for this reason that He created a way to make up for the shortfall, the hugely immense shortfall, between Him and man.

There were sacrifices for sins of the nation.

And if the whole congregation of Israel sin through ignorance, and the thing be hid from the eyes of the assembly, and they have done somewhat against any of the commandments of the LORD concerning things which should not be done, and are guilty; When the sin, which they have sinned against it, is known, then the congregation shall offer a young bullock for the sin, and bring him before the tabernacle of the congregation.
(Leviticus 4:13-14)

There were sacrifices for sins among the rulers.

When a ruler hath sinned, and done somewhat through ignorance against any of the commandments of the LORD his God concerning things which should not be done, and is guilty; Or if his sin, wherein he hath sinned, come to his knowledge; he shall bring his offering, a kid of the goats, a male without blemish: And he shall lay his hand upon the head of the goat, and kill it in the place where they kill the burnt offering before the LORD: it is a sin offering.
(Leviticus 4:22-24)

There were sacrifices for sins among the common people.

And if any one of the common people sin through ignorance, while he doeth somewhat against any of the commandments of the LORD concerning things which ought not to be done, and be guilty; Or if his sin, which he hath sinned, come to his knowledge: then he shall bring his offering, a kid of the goats, a female without blemish, for his sin which he hath sinned.
(Leviticus 4:27-28)

These are only the sin offerings for acts done in ignorance; there are several other offerings that the LORD established to bring the nation back into conformance with the ways of God. Even with all this, both the individuals and the representatives of the nation, the priests, fell short of the observance of the ordinances of God. They seemed to constantly lose sight of the need for their continual refreshing in His sight. The people and the nation seemed to view the sacrifice as an excuse for doing evil. They came to points in their history where they expected God to forgive them even when they willfully and systematically violated His commandments.

We who live in the present age know of many ways that a person or group can move away from the laws of the nations, especially in the United States. If we look, for example, at the system of taxation, we can see a form of sacrifice to the earthly god of government. With the tax code as it is there are many people who may violate the tax codes truly out of ignorance. However, there are many individuals who, even though they understand what is required, choose to defy the code anyway. There are even employers, who are the representatives of groups of individuals who also decide to bypass the tax laws.

Some may say that this is because the tax code is onerous and made by man. This, however, cannot be used as an excuse. To say this is similar to saying that when vendors exact a higher price for their goods and services, we can take it upon ourselves to ignore them. And since we can ignore the vendor's rules, we can pay the cashier whatever was the former price and walk away with the items anyway. This is unjust to the vendor; for if we want what the vendor offers, we must pay what the vendor asks, or we should seek out another vendor; or receive the vendor's permission to pay a lesser price. To do otherwise is a crime in most nations of the world.

In the case of God there is no excuse, or even hint of excuse. God is always just and God is always fair. When He asks for a certain thing of us, it is not just His *right*, (I use that term to refer to God for the sake of human understanding) but it is within His power to command it without recourse. The truth is that God is good and we know that those things which He establishes are also done for the good of mankind.

Even so, the nation of Israel, by the witness of the prophets, strayed far from the right execution of God's commandments; which were given to them for their prosperity. This is what the Law of Moses provided: a means to the prosperity of the nation within the blessings of God. These blessings were liberally spread to the common people and to the rulers and to the priests and to the representatives of the government.

Remember, God knows the condition of mankind. He knew what Adam would do before Adam did it. He knew what Cain would do to Abel before it happened. He has created man to be master over the things of the earth, and He has shown, in his benevolence, that He will allow man to do so. That is, he will allow man to do so up to the point where a man, group of men, or mankind as a whole is tending toward the destruction of the creation of God in mankind.

When mankind's survival is at stake, the bar has been raised to the heavens and God activates His already built methodologies to accomplish the redemption of mankind. An example of His intervention can be seen in the happening surrounding the events of 70 AD in Jerusalem.

> *When ye therefore shall see the abomination of desolation, spoken of by Daniel the prophet, stand in the holy place, (whoso readeth, let him understand:)*

> *Then let them which be in Judaea flee into the mountains: Let him which is on the housetop not come down to take any thing out of his house: Neither let him which is in the field return back to take his clothes. And woe unto them that are with child, and to them that give suck in those days!*

> *But pray ye that your flight be not in the winter, neither on the sabbath day: For then shall be great tribulation, such as was not since the beginning of the world to this time, no, nor ever shall be.*

And except those days should be shortened, there should no flesh be saved: but for the elect's sake those days shall be shortened.
      (Matthew 24:15-22)

The nation of Israel was created as a people who were to serve God.

Ye have seen what I did unto the Egyptians, and how I bare you on eagles' wings, and brought you unto myself. Now therefore, if ye will obey my voice indeed, and keep my covenant, then ye shall be a peculiar treasure unto me above all people: for all the earth is mine: And ye shall be unto me a kingdom of priests, and an holy nation. These are the words which thou shalt speak unto the children of Israel.
      (Exodus 19:4-6)

As the priests of God, they were the transport for the message of God; like they transported the tabernacle of God. They were the transport of the message of God not just within themselves. In this nation of priests, the people of this nation should have no need to be prodded to accept the message of God. No, the message was not just to this nation, but to the world. The nation of Israel is the son of God created to announce the presence of God in the world to all mankind. This they would do by their words, by their actions, and by their episodes in time (later to be referred to as their history). They did so in Egypt, they did so in Babylon and they did so in Persia, and they did so by report of their actions throughout the land. This report even went out by the will of God to the entire world. It is, therefore, not possible for this nation to *fall into disrepair*; God will not allow it. According to the everlasting covenant of God this nation will not fall over the precipice of existence and become merely an extinct historical note.

However, as the nation became more and more out of tune with the will of God, as presented in the Law of Moses, it became quite obvious that there is a need for a Saviour for the nation of Israel and for the world. To continually repeat the Law in their ears had not been effective: the people of the nation had shown that they were such a strong and proud people (whom God called stiffnecked). There even came a time when they willfully chose not to turn to God, even when He showed them the negative consequences of moving away from Him.

Indeed, the nation of Israel had found its own solution by forming alliances with other nations. At one point some of them even went to Egypt for help, where they were told not to return.

> *Woe to them that go down to Egypt for help; and stay on horses, and trust in chariots, because they are many; and in horsemen, because they are very strong; but they look not unto the Holy One of Israel, neither seek the LORD! Yet he also is wise, and will bring evil, and will not call back his words: but will arise against the house of the evildoers, and against the help of them that work iniquity. Now the Egyptians are men, and not God; and their horses flesh, and not spirit. When the LORD shall stretch out his hand, both he that helpeth shall fall, and he that is holpen shall fall down, and they all shall fail together.*
>
> (Isaiah 31:1-3)

Yes, it might be said that the people of the nation were just trying to survive under the yoke of conquest, but this is not a justification. Since they were no longer the dominant nation, they may have used the excuse that they had to conform to the ways of the nation of conquest. The individual Israelite Daniel presented a different and consistent face of devotion to God in rejecting the things that he believed were not of the LORD.

> *And the king appointed them a daily provision of the king's meat, and of the wine which he drank: so nourishing them three years, that at the end thereof they might stand before the king. Now among these were of the children of Judah, Daniel, Hananiah, Mishael, and Azariah: Unto whom the prince of the eunuchs gave names: for he gave unto Daniel the name of Belteshazzar; and to Hananiah, of Shadrach; and to Mishael, of Meshach; and to Azariah, of Abednego. But Daniel purposed in his heart that he would not defile himself with the portion of the king's meat, nor with the wine which he drank: therefore he requested of the prince of the eunuchs that he might not defile himself.*
>
> (Daniel 1:5-8)

This type of devotion to the things of God had been lost to the nation. The nation, in general, was no longer ready to stand up for God against all odds. They no longer believed in God's protection as did Shadrach, Meshach, and Abednego.

> *Nebuchadnezzar spake and said unto them, Is it true, O Shadrach, Meshach, and Abednego, do not ye serve my gods, nor worship the golden image which I have set up? Now if ye be ready that at what time ye hear the sound of the cornet, flute, harp, sackbut, psaltery, and dulcimer, and all kinds of music, ye fall down and worship the image which I have made; well: but if ye worship not, ye shall be cast the same hour into the midst of a burning fiery furnace; and who is that God that shall deliver you out of my hands?*

> *Shadrach, Meshach, and Abednego, answered and said to the king, O Nebuchadnezzar, we are not careful to answer thee in this matter. If it be so, our God whom we serve is able to deliver us from the burning fiery furnace, and he will deliver us out of thine hand, O king. But if not, be it known unto thee, O king, that we will not serve thy gods, nor worship the golden image which thou hast set up.*

(Daniel 3:14-18)

Most definitely, the message of Job had been dismissed as nonsense for the then *modem* man of Israel. There weren't very many, if any, left who were willing to stand fast for God in the face of physical torment and deprivation.

> *Wherefore do I take my flesh in my teeth, and put my life in mine hand? Though he slay me, yet will I trust in him: but I will maintain mine own ways before him. He also shall be my salvation: for an hypocrite shall not come before him.*

(Job 13:14-16)

There was a need for someone who could and would say just that on behalf of the nation of Israel. There was a need for a human lamb to serve as the sacrifice for sin.

The LORD hath made bare his holy arm in the eyes of all the nations; and all the ends of the earth shall see the salvation of our God. Depart ye, depart ye, go ye out from thence, touch no unclean thing; go ye out of the midst of her; be ye clean, that bear the vessels of the LORD. For ye shall not go out with haste, nor go by flight: for the LORD will go before you; and the God of Israel will be your rereward.

Behold, my servant shall deal prudently, he shall be exalted and extolled, and be very high. As many were astonied at thee; his visage was so marred more than any man, and his form more than the sons of men: So shall he sprinkle many nations; the kings shall shut their mouths at him: for that which had not been told them shall they see; and that which they had not heard shall they consider.

Who hath believed our report? and to whom is the arm of the LORD revealed? For he shall grow up before him as a tender plant, and as a root out of a dry ground: he hath no form nor comeliness; and when we shall see him, there is no beauty that we should desire him. He is despised and rejected of men; a man of sorrows, and acquainted with grief: and we hid as it were our faces from him; he was despised, and we esteemed him not. Surely he hath borne our griefs, and carried our sorrows: yet we did esteem him stricken, smitten of God, and afflicted. But he was wounded for our transgressions, he was bruised for our iniquities: the chastisement of our peace was upon him; and with his stripes we are healed.

All we like sheep have gone astray; we have turned every one to his own way; and the LORD hath laid on him the iniquity of us all. He was oppressed, and he was afflicted, yet he opened not his mouth: he is brought as a lamb to the slaughter, and as a sheep before her shearers is dumb, so he openeth not his mouth. He was taken from prison and from judgment: and who shall declare his generation? for he was cut off out of the land of the living: for the transgression of my people was he stricken. And he made his grave with the wicked, and with the rich in his death; because he had done no violence, neither was any deceit in his mouth.

Yet it pleased the LORD to bruise him; he hath put him to grief: when thou shalt make his soul an offering for sin, he shall see his seed, he shall prolong his days, and the pleasure of the LORD shall prosper in his hand. He shall see of the travail of his soul, and shall be satisfied: by his knowledge shall my righteous servant justify many; for he shall bear their iniquities. Therefore will I divide him a portion with the great, and he shall divide the spoil with the strong; because he hath poured out his soul unto death: and he was numbered with the transgressors; and he bare the sin of many, and made intercession for the transgressors.

(Isaiah 52:10-53:12)

But when God sent such a man, why should He just limit the sacrifice of this man to one nation on the earth? Why not make this sacrifice effective for all peoples of the earth? And while He was at it, why not make the benefits of this sacrifice eternal? Why continue to sacrifice and to sacrifice when God has the power to create a sacrifice that will pay the price for all, once and for all?

We need such a Saviour and only God can provide him. The promise of Scripture, as recorded by the prophets, is that God will provide such a one for us. This is the promise that was laid out in the writings of the prophets as being near at hand at the close of the Old Testament. This is the promise that is stated and believed to have been fulfilled in the record as written in the New Testament. At least it can be said that it is believed by billions of our fellow humans in this day.

Ask God to help you reach the understanding of its fulfillment. Stop searching for what has already come. With the help of God through the Holy Ghost, receive what He has already provided. Since only God could provide the Saviour, it seems reasonable to think as true that only God can reveal the Saviour to you. Seek His guidance to do so: He's waiting for you.

We try mightily
To follow the course
That will move God to us,
Our actions to endorse.

But no matter how we try,
We fall short of the mark;
We wallow in sin;
We stumble in the dark.

We look around us
For another man
To reach out
And lend us a hand.

We look at our neighbor,
The grass on the other side,
To find a set of habits
In which we can abide.

We join organizations
To match our goals,
But still we know
There are gapping holes

In our sense of satisfaction,
Our feeling of worth;
We even begin to despise
Our time on the earth.

The government can't help,
We know this is true;
They only want to take
More than what's due.

The favor of man,
No matter how it's formed,
Does not our soul provide
A feeling permanently warm.

We even look to the church
To provide the way
That will deliver us to God
To lighten our day.

No, none of this works
In whatever flavor.
To conquer this life,
We need a Saviour.

Chapter 3a

My 3 Dads

I was born; this is obvious. However what may not be obvious is that I have three dads. Don't think me so strange just yet. We all have three dads, with only three exceptions in the entire history of mankind. Let me describe our three dads and then I'll share information on the three exceptions.

Dad 1   God. Don't think that the egg and sperm that started you was allowed to interact in a positive fashion by anyone other than God. Don't forget that our being alive is because God still breathes into our nostrils the breath of life, and we become living souls. Life is under the authority of God to give or to withhold, not by some automatic natural force embedded in the physiology of man.

Dad 2   My biological parent, who was given the grace of God to be able to produce offspring. This is not to say that I am necessarily a worthy work of this creative force, but merely to say that it was activated by the work of my biological dad, and, oh by the way, my biological mother helped a *little* too.

Dad 3   Satan, who appears to us after we exit the womb to start the process of *instruction*. Satan delivers the instruction that we have "a right to..." This most interesting being is determined to have us believe that we don't have to humble ourselves for anyone or anything. His teachings tell us that we can take whatever we want from anyone we want to, sometimes even if we do get caught.

One of Satan's main lessons is centered on teaching us the proper use of guilt. Guilt is to be instilled in others but never taken on by us. We are to use guilt to force others to bend to our will. To do this we must tell them that they are not smart enough or cute enough or rich enough. Then we *share* with them that if they just do what we say, we'll show them how to take care of these deficiencies.

Satan will even quote Scripture to you. Satan's favorite is Proverbs 21:2: "*Every way of a man is right in his own eyes: but the LORD pondereth the hearts*", well part of it is. He is anxious to teach you that "*Every way of a man is right*". He leaves out the part that says "*in his own eyes*". And he is absolutely not interested in you knowing "*but the LORD pondereth the hearts*". It's a, me thing.

Exception #1

There is a man called Adam; who is the first man created on this earth. This man only had two dads.

> Dad 1   *And the LORD God formed man of the dust of the ground, and breathed into his nostrils the breath of life; and man became a living soul.*
> (Genesis 2:7)

> Dad 3   *Now the serpent was more subtle than any beast of the field which the LORD God had made. And he said unto the woman, Yea, hath God said, Ye shall not eat of every tree of the garden?*
>
> *And the woman said unto the serpent, We may eat of the fruit of the trees of the garden: But of the fruit of the tree which is in the midst of the garden, God hath said, Ye shall not eat of it, neither shall ye touch it, lest ye die.*
>
> *And the serpent said unto the woman, Ye shall not surely die: For God doth know that in the day ye eat thereof, then your eyes shall be opened, and ye shall be as gods, knowing good and evil.*
>
> *And when the woman saw that the tree was good for food, and that it was pleasant to the eyes, and a tree to be desired to make one wise,*

> *she took of the fruit thereof, and did eat, and*
> *gave also unto her husband with her; and he did*
> *eat. And the eyes of them both were opened, and*
> *they knew that they were naked; and they sewed*
> *fig leaves together, and made themselves aprons.*
> (Genesis 3:1-7).

It was a, me thing, then, too. Even though Adam was created by God, he yielded himself to dad #3 and thus became #3's child in his motivations and actions.

Exception #2

There is another man who appears much later in history. His dad #2 was old and had no children yet,

> *But the angel said unto him, Fear not, Zacharias: for thy*
> *prayer is heard; and thy wife Elisabeth shall bear thee*
> *a son, and thou shalt call his name John.*
> (Luke 1:13).

The angel of the LORD appeared to his dad #2 and told him that this would be a special child.

> *For he shall be great in the sight of the Lord, and shall*
> *drink neither wine nor strong drink; and he shall be*
> *filled with the Holy Ghost, even from his mother's womb.*
> (Luke 1:15)

His mission was revealed in prophecy before he was born: and he was diligent to perform the task assigned to him by God.

> *In those days came John the Baptist, preaching in the*
> *wilderness of Judaea, And saying, Repent ye: for the*
> *kingdom of heaven is at hand. For this is he that was*
> *spoken of by the prophet Esaias, saying, The voice of one*
> *crying in the wilderness, Prepare ye the way of the Lord,*
> *make his paths straight.*
> (Matthew 3:1-3)

So let's take a look at his dads.

Dad 1   God. Like the rest of us, He is the originator of the life of John the Baptist through the breath of life.

Dad 2 *There was in the days of Herod, the king of Judaea, a certain priest named Zacharias, of the course of Abia: and his wife was of the daughters of Aaron, and her name was Elisabeth. And they were both righteous before God, walking in all the commandments and ordinances of the Lord blameless.*

(Luke 1:5-6)

Dad 3 Satan was not really allowed to be very active, though he remained present and sent some of his ambassadors on occasion to try to sway John to the ways of The Demon of evil (which can be shortened to Devil). He still wanted to claim parental rights over John, but John was *filled with the Holy Ghost, even from his mother's womb.*

Sorry Satan (well I'm not really sorry for you; it's just a literary thing), this time there was no room for **you** in the *human inn.*

Exception #3

Finally, there is the man to whom all other men, including the two special ones above, have been striving to rise. All men have been striving to become like him even though they were not aware of his existence; for a time. This is the man that is the one that God created to show all other men what is His will. Furthermore, God introduced this man into reality before the foundation of the world. This is what all mankind can become and what all mankind must strive to become in order to be able to prosper in the eternity for which our souls are designed. This is the man Jesus of Nazareth, the Son of the Living God, who became the Messiah, the Christ. He, like the first man Adam, only has two dads, but his two dads are of one accord.

Dad 1 God. Like the rest of us, He is the originator of the life of Jesus of Nazareth through the breath of life.

Dad 2 His biological father is the Holy Ghost and the overshadowing of the power of God.

And in the sixth month the angel Gabriel was sent from God unto a city of Galilee, named

Nazareth, To a virgin espoused to a man whose name was Joseph, of the house of David; and the virgin's name was Mary. And the angel came in unto her, and said, Hail, thou that art highly favoured, the Lord is with thee: blessed art thou among women. And when she saw him, she was troubled at his saying, and cast in her mind what manner of salutation this should be.

And the angel said unto her, Fear not, Mary: for thou hast found favour with God. And, behold, thou shalt conceive in thy womb, and bring forth a son, and shalt call his name JESUS. He shall be great, and shall be called the Son of the Highest: and the Lord God shall give unto him the throne of his father David: And he shall reign over the house of Jacob for ever; and of his kingdom there shall be no end.

Then said Mary unto the angel, How shall this be, seeing I know not a man?

And the angel answered and said unto her, The Holy Ghost shall come upon thee, and the power of the Highest shall overshadow thee: therefore also that holy thing which shall be born of thee shall be called the Son of God.
(Luke 1:26-35)

The Heart of the Mater

The Lord Jesus Christ was sent to this earth to save man from his sin. A very important part of this is the way that he demonstrates, by his life, what I will become and to Whom I belong. Christ Jesus leads me to the Father and shows me that the Father has nullified the seed planted in my spirit by the things of the Devil and of any other devil. Through the sacrifice of Jesus Christ He has provided the *medicine* that will cleanse my soul and repair it after these evil things have been dissolved through his blood. His is the way to God and the promise of permanent residence before God, in His kingdom, as a full participant in the grace of God.

For we know that if our earthly house of this tabernacle were dissolved, we have a building of God, an house not made with hands, eternal in the heavens.

For in this we groan, earnestly desiring to be clothed upon with our house which is from heaven: If so be that being clothed we shall not be found naked. For we that are in this tabernacle do groan, being burdened: not for that we would be unclothed, but clothed upon, that mortality might be swallowed up of life. Now he that hath wrought us for the selfsame thing is God, who also hath given unto us the earnest of the Spirit.

Therefore we are always confident, knowing that, whilst we are at home in the body, we are absent from the Lord: (For we walk by faith, not by sight:) We are confident, I say, and willing rather to be absent from the body, and to be present with the Lord. Wherefore we labour, that, whether present or absent, we may be accepted of him.

For we must all appear before the judgment seat of Christ; that every one may receive the things done in his body, according to that he hath done, whether it be good or bad.
      (2 Corinthians 5:1-10)

The Word from the Bible

Genesis 1:26-30

And God said, Let us make man in our image, after our likeness: and let them have dominion over the fish of the sea, and over the fowl of the air, and over the cattle, and over all the earth, and over every creeping thing that creepeth upon the earth. So God created man in his own image, in the image of God created he him; male and female created he them. And God blessed them, and God said unto them, Be fruitful, and multiply, and replenish the earth, and subdue it: and have dominion over the fish of the sea, and over the fowl of the air, and over every living thing that moveth upon the earth.

And God said, Behold, I have given you every herb bearing seed, which is upon the face of all the earth, and every tree, in the which is the fruit of a tree yielding seed; to you it shall be for meat. And to every beast of the earth, and to every fowl of the air, and to every thing that creepeth upon the earth, wherein there is life, I have given every green herb for meat: and it was so.

Exodus 40:13-15

And thou shalt put upon Aaron the holy garments, and anoint him, and sanctify him; that he may minister unto me in the priest's office. And thou shalt bring his sons, and clothe them with coats: And thou shalt anoint them, as thou didst anoint their father, that they may minister unto me in the priest's office: for their anointing shall surely be an everlasting priesthood throughout their generations.

Numbers 11:26-30

But there remained two of the men in the camp, the name of the one was Eldad, and the name of the other Medad: and the spirit rested upon them; and they were of them that were written, but went not out unto the tabernacle: and they prophesied in the camp.

And there ran a young man, and told Moses, and said, Eldad and Medad do prophesy in the camp.

And Joshua the son of Nun, the servant of Moses, one of his young men, answered and said, My lord Moses, forbid them.

And Moses said unto him, Enviest thou for my sake? would God that all the LORD'S people were prophets, and that the LORD would put his spirit upon them! And Moses gat him into the camp, he and the elders of Israel.

Jeremiah 7:1-16

The word that came to Jeremiah from the LORD, saying, Stand in the gate of the Lord's house, and proclaim there this word, and say, Hear the word of the LORD, all ye of Judah, that enter in at these gates to worship the LORD. Thus saith the LORD of hosts, the God of Israel, Amend your ways and your doings, and I will cause you to dwell in this place. Trust ye not in lying words, saying, The temple of the LORD, The temple of the LORD, The temple of the LORD, are these. For if ye thoroughly amend your ways and your doings; if ye thoroughly execute judgment between a man and his neighbour; If ye oppress not the stranger, the fatherless, and the widow, and shed not innocent blood in this place, neither walk after other gods to your hurt: Then will I cause you to dwell in this place, in the land that I gave to your fathers, for ever and ever.

Behold, ye trust in lying words, that cannot profit. Will ye steal, murder, and commit adultery, and swear falsely, and burn incense unto Baal, and walk after other gods whom ye know not; And come and stand before me in this house, which is called by my name, and say, We are delivered to do all these abominations? Is this house, which is called by my name, become a den of robbers in your eyes? Behold, even I have seen it, saith the LORD. But go ye now unto my place which was in Shiloh, where I set my name at the first, and see what I did to it for the wickedness of my people Israel.

And now, because ye have done all these works, saith the LORD, and I spake unto you, rising up early and speaking, but ye heard not; and I called you, but ye answered not; Therefore will I do unto this house, which is called by my name, wherein ye trust, and unto the place which I gave to you and to your fathers, as I have done to Shiloh. And I will cast you out of my sight, as I have cast out all your brethren, even the whole seed of Ephraim. Therefore pray not thou for this people, neither lift up cry nor prayer for them, neither make intercession to me: for I will not hear thee.

Chapter Four

A Divine Occupation

From time to time I have been given the opportunity by God to supervise some of my fellow humans in the position of corporate manager. This is a most humbling honor for me. In performing this function I have tried to keep God at the forefront of my dealings with my charges. This allowed me to understand and promote the aims of my own manager, who placed me in this position. It also pushed me to understand the corporate structure and the place of my department and my position therein. I pray that I have returned at least full value for compensation given to all who trusted me in this regard.

As a manager, one of my functions was to direct individuals in certain positions in the company. To do an effective job at this it is necessary to evaluate job descriptions. I discovered that it is very difficult to work with a person without understanding their job description. I had to understand this not just for those who reported to me, but also for those to whom I reported.

It is extremely important that we understand our peers, those who are our manager(s), the peer of the manager, and so on up the entire organizational ladder. This is required because we must be ready, should conflicting orders come our way, to process those that have the backing of those most responsible for the success of the operation. This can sometimes cause us to have to give additional explanations of our actions to our manager; and we have to be ready for that as well. ***This is equally, if not more so, true in religious organizations***, such as churches and Bible schools.

Another of my duties was to select individuals for particular positions. This does not just mean hiring; it also involves promotion within the department. It is also a major part of lateral movement in the department, from one job function to another. The manager must understand the qualifications that are required in any individual that will fill the position. This understanding allows the manager to locate the candidate that best fits the position. Sometimes this is done directly and sometimes it means that an individual with potential is selected and tailored to fit the position.

This seems to be the point where God was when He highlighted the need for a Redeemer for the nation of Israel and for all mankind. We know that as He looked among the crop of mankind He saw the truly unfit condition of man.

> *And God saw that the wickedness of man was great in the earth, and that every imagination of the thoughts of his heart was only evil continually.*
> (Genesis 6:5).

This was the state in the time of Noah and it was the state when the man Jesus was born; and it is still the state, in general, of mankind today. So it was up to God to prepare a Redeemer.

God could either prepare a redeemer from Heaven, or develop one by a radical transformation of an individual on earth. To understand this I'd like to take you through how we might envision the position of excellence in the Kingdom of God known as Redeemer. And incidentally, the selection was done even before the creation of anything that is in this sphere, most time referred to as before the foundation of the world. God does like to be prepared in advance; always. And, yes, He knew how we will behave before we were.

But before we proceed, may we have a word of prayer.

> PRAYER: Father, You know that I am in no way trying to analyze what You have done, for this is impossible for a human, such as I am. I am, instead, trying to gain a grasp on the, most high concept of Redeemer, or as we also call him, the Messiah. This will be useful to me to prevent me from following false Christ's. *For there shall arise false Christs, and false prophets, and shall shew great signs and wonders; insomuch that, if it were possible, they shall deceive the very elect.* This is the message that is given to us in your Bible in Matthew 24:24

Please guide my spirit, my heart and my soul in this endeavor, as you immerse all in the Holy Ghost. Please let these words serve to instruct others besides myself in the recognition of Your majesty and far reaching love for all mankind. Let it be so that they move the undecided to see that You have indeed provided the Redeemer. My strong desire is that they move the seeker to clearly see the revealed Redeemer that You have already sent to mankind. To You, be all the glory.

Father, You have cast me in a certain mold on this earth with power that only depends on You. This is marvelous and wonderful to be. Therefore, I rest in Your creativity. Furthermore, I claim the promise of Your Son, the revealed Redeemer. He has said, *And whatsoever ye shall ask in my name, that will I do, that the Father may be glorified in the Son*, as recorded in John 14:13. I claim this promise and ask all this in the name of Jesus and for his sake. Amen.

Let us continue. We have previously read where mankind needed a Messiah to deliver it from itself. We will now share with you our insights into this position of excellence in the Kingdom of God. We will only put forth some qualifications at this time.

Job Description: The ideal candidate will have a keen knowledge of the things of Heaven and the things of earth. He will be able to provide mankind with a means to stay in fellowship with God. This means that he must be durable enough to remain active even without the cooperation of the recipient of the benefits. Furthermore, this means that he must have a good contingency plan to cover downtime of the primary operation or absence of the operator.

Qualifications: Not a novice to this operation. The ideal candidate must be one that has a great amount of experience in the operation of the job functions of this position. This candidate must possess maturity and a keen sense of purpose. The candidate must have a strong work ethic and be able to withstand long hours of effort under very stressful conditions. The ideal candidate will look to no one else to assist him in starting the operation. The candidate must be a good teacher, for he must train his staff in the workings of the department that he will lead. Ideally, the candidate will be willing to put his life into the position and to work until the job is complete; whatever it takes.

Let's continue by describing generally the way we will attempt to locate the Messiah using the list above. After this we will be able to search the Scriptures for a good candidate to fill this position. We only need to find one person who will fill this position, since the type of Messiah we are searching for is one that will perform the function forever. The minimum that we require is that the one who fills this position establish a procedure for continued deliverables from the work done for the total life span of all mankind. This will, of course, depend on our defining the position such that the deliverable covers all contingencies.

As with any job opening we must start with a clear description of the job to be performed. We also understand that in this search we have our limitations. We are limited to the same set of information that anyone in a position of decision about the qualifications of any other individual is limited. We must depend first on the statements of the person seeking the designation. Once we are comfortable with these statements, we can then find others who can confirm what we have received. This is done in an organization either through other employers or through objective witnesses of the person's performance. We will use the testimony of witnesses for our discussion of the selection process.

The person filling this position will in a sense work himself out of a job. It is their responsibility to create the structure and then pass it on to other humans to continue the process. In case we don't think this happens, I have a personal story to briefly recount. Earlier in my life I was charged with the project of merging two computer centers into one. This involved moving the equipment from the parent company to a company that had been acquired by the parent company. Along with the computers, of course, went the computer applications that ran the business processes. We were very successful in this project.

We accomplished this with my staff, with assistance from the new company's staff. Upon its completion, the data center was turned over to a combined staff; consisting of some members of my staff under my former leadership and members of the staff of the receiving data center. I was not a part of the new staff: I knew this would be the case when I started the project. It was then the responsibility of the new data center manager to train and nurture the collected group of individuals to produce the information that was required. I then got to sit down and rest, from a certain point of view, until the corporation delivered my final check and I got to enter into a new position in life.

With this experience behind me it was possible for me to better relate to the mission that is before he who is to fill the role of the Redeemer, the Messiah. This person will come to a group of people, the children of Israel to deliver a product. While there he will train a set of people in the working of the product. Once he has the new group trained he will leave them with the product and send them forth to maintain it. Theirs will also be the task of filling a multitude of positions with other individuals to further expand the impact of the product on mankind. This is the environment that the Redeemer will have to build.

This is not the definitive list of specifications. It is, however, enough for us to consider at this time. I will now let you take a moment to digest what we've covered thus far. Therefore, we will leave this topic for now. Later we will continue with the selection process for the Messiah: I promise.

The universe was planned,
The world was on the board,
All sat in readiness
In the Kingdom of the LORD.

Time had not begun,
It was waiting for the call
Of He who has the power
To start creation's ball

Rolling forward to make
All that would be,
In a world He created
For you and me.

The workers were set,
They were ready to go,
Each had been told
What they needed to know

To assist in the creation
Of this most noble thing;
Sounding for all time
With a most resounding ring.

All points had been plotted,
Nothing was left to chance;
All materials provided
Well in advance.

The field was prepped,
And it was quite dark;
In increasing anticipation
Of that first spark.

Yes, everything was ready,
Anxious to do its best
To allow the LORD of all
To return to His rest.

And all that was left
To complete the plan
Is to announce to all
The Son of man,

Who assists the LORD
And works with the host
To deliver a work for which
Only God can boast.

Chapter 4a

Son of Man

In Appendix A through E, you will find a list of the times that the phrase 'son of man' is used in the Bible. There are three forms of these words:

1. *son of man* found imbedded in sentences. This appears only in the Old Testament and is used to refer to a male.

2. *Son of man* found at the beginning of a sentence and capitalized according to standard sentence structure. These sentences are exclusively found in the book of Ezekiel and refer to the man Ezekiel. The expression occurs when the LORD addresses Ezekiel and gives him an assignment.

3. *Son of man* found anywhere in the sentence and capitalized to provide emphasis and distinction to the subject of the expression. This seems to be exclusively used in the New Testament to refer to Jesus of Nazareth.

"Why is this important," you ask. To start, let's go through some well-known rules of grammar. In constructing expressions, capitalization is very important. Typically, at least in the United States, the first letter of all proper names is capitalized. Also, the first letter of sentences is capitalized. Capitalization is also used to give an expression emphasis above its normal weight; such as when we write Catholic as opposed to catholic. The entire body of baptized believers belongs to the church catholic, but only approximately half of the professing believers belong to the Catholic Church. The same grammatical rule is used in the Bible where Jesus is referred to as the *Son of man* and not as the *son of man.* Ezekiel, however, refers to himself as the *son of man* almost exclusively in the book of Ezekiel.

The book of Ezekiel contains another example where the expression *Son of man* is used. It is not used to indicate any increased level of power, nor is it used for emphasis. In the book of Ezekiel, the expression is only used at the beginning of a sentence. Specifically, it is used at the beginning of a sentence in which God is referring to Ezekiel, most times in preparing him for an assignment.

Other than at the beginning of a sentence, according to proper grammatical rules, there is no place in the Bible where the expression *Son of man* is used to refer to a human; other than its use in the New Testament to refer to Jesus of Nazareth. This is necessary because, though Jesus is the only begotten son of God (John 3:16), he is not the only son of God.

> *Now there was a day when the sons of God came to present themselves before the LORD, and Satan came also among them.*
> (Job 1:6)

We will, therefore, consider the *Son of man* as more than a designation of a male born into the human race. This must be a unique title for a unique human. We will show you that this title only applies to one human. It is perfectly understandable if this is not a title that immediately makes sense, when it is not referring to just another male. There was the same confusion when it was applied to a human some time ago.

> *Now is the judgment of this world: now shall the prince of this world be cast out. And I, if I be lifted up from the earth, will draw all men unto me. This he said, signifying what death he should die.*
>
> *The people answered him, We have heard out of the law that Christ abideth for ever: and how sayest thou, The Son of man must be lifted up? who is this Son of man?*
> (John 12:31-34)

The title *Son of man* does not indicate a method of birth, for the Son of man was in existence before Jesus of Nazareth was born. Jesus said this while speaking as the Son of man.

> *Your father Abraham rejoiced to see my day: and he saw it, and was glad.*
>
> *Then said the Jews unto him, Thou art not yet fifty years old, and hast thou seen Abraham?*
>
> *Jesus said unto them, Verily, verily, I say unto you, Before Abraham was, I am.*
> (John 8:56-58)

The Son of man was not a mere man. The Son of man has tremendous power that was given to him to perform the works of God among men; among these is the power to forgive sin.

> *For whether is easier, to say, Thy sins be forgiven thee;*
> *or to say, Arise, and walk. But that ye may know that the*
> *Son of man hath power on earth to forgive sins, (then*
> *saith he to the sick of the palsy,) Arise, take up thy bed,*
> *and go unto thine house.*
> (Matthew 9:5-6)

There are several times in history where men have healed others, but there has never been a time before Jesus when a man could forgive sin. This indicates to us that the Son of man is more than mortal. From this we know that the Son of man is one who had received great authority from God. It was not the kind of temporary authority that was given to the priests who performed the sacrifices: this is an indwelling authority that is a part of the nature of the Son of man. God had imputed to him ownership rights in the powers so delegated.

When God established the priesthood, there were specific responsibilities that were given to the priests. They were not given license to invent reality as they saw fit, but they looked to God for the instructions on how to proceed. Even Jesus had a set of tasks to perform on God's behalf.

> *These words spake Jesus, and lifted up his eyes to*
> *heaven, and said, Father, the hour is come; glorify thy*
> *Son, that thy Son also may glorify thee: As thou hast*
> *given him power over all flesh, that he should give*
> *eternal life to as many as thou hast given him. And this is*
> *life eternal, that they might know thee the only true God,*
> *and Jesus Christ, whom thou hast sent. I have glorified*
> *thee on the earth: I have finished the work which thou*
> *gavest me to do.*
> (John 17:1-4)

But what we saw, during the approximately three and a half years of ministry of the Son of man on the earth, is not the full scope of his assignment; only that portion that pertained to that time in history. We know that he was learning before he was manifested in Jesus of Nazareth.

> *Then said Jesus unto them, When ye have lifted up the*
> *Son of man, then shall ye know that I am he, and that*
> *I do nothing of myself; but as my Father hath taught me,*
> *I speak these things. And he that sent me is with me: the*
> *Father hath not left me alone; for I do always those*
> *things that please him. As he spake these words, many*
> *believed on him.*
> (John 8:28-30)

Furthermore, we know that he had glory before he came to this earth.

> *And now, O Father, glorify thou me with thine own self*
> *with the glory which I had with thee before the world*
> *was. I have manifested thy name unto the men which*
> *thou gavest me out of the world: thine they were, and*
> *thou gavest them me; and they have kept thy word. Now*
> *they have known that all things whatsoever thou hast*
> *given me are of thee. For I have given unto them the*
> *words which thou gavest me; and they have received*
> *them, and have known surely that I came out from thee,*
> *and they have believed that thou didst send me.*
> (John 17:5-8)

The Son of man had this glory before he was manifested in the Messiah on earth. This glory activated by God to perform His will and His works. I think back to the beginning of the human race and I see what the Son of man did by the side of the Father with this great gift from God. In my mind I hear again those words of God where He said *let us make man*. The expression "*let us*" indicates that there were others in attendance at the creation of mankind, at least one. Furthermore, this other, or others, seems to have participated in the creation of mankind.

However, there is something even more curious about the events that unfold in the Bible at a later time. Even though God created all and owned all, He did not take direct controlling participative possession of all of mankind. In fact, at that time He did not do so for any of mankind. Adam illustrates this in that he was allowed to follow his own course in the garden. God did not make him obey, as one could with a possession. God's actions toward Adam were more of the actions of an earthly father to a child who is starting to mature. God warned him about the consequences of performing certain restricted actions, but did not force Adam to obey.

And the LORD God took the man, and put him into the Garden of Eden to dress it and to keep it. And the LORD God commanded the man, saying, Of every tree of the garden thou mayest freely eat: But of the tree of the knowledge of good and evil, thou shalt not eat of it: for in the day that thou eatest thereof thou shalt surely die.
(Genesis 2:15-17)

Moses told us that God established His inheritance in the children of Israel, and established His direct controlling participative possession of a nation among men.

I prayed therefore unto the LORD, and said, O Lord GOD, destroy not thy people and thine inheritance, which thou hast redeemed through thy greatness, which thou hast brought forth out of Egypt with a mighty hand. Remember thy servants, Abraham, Isaac, and Jacob; look not unto the stubbornness of this people, nor to their wickedness, nor to their sin: Lest the land whence thou broughtest us out say, Because the LORD was not able to bring them into the land which he promised them, and because he hated them, he hath brought them out to slay them in the wilderness. Yet they are thy people and thine inheritance, which thou broughtest out by thy mighty power and by thy stretched out arm.
(Deuteronomy 9:26-29)

The common definition of inheritance does not apply here. That is, the inheritance that has someone else giving a thing to another, cannot be implied in this passage. There is none from whom God can inherit anything for there is nothing more powerful than God, and this by definition as well as by reality. The word *inheritance* in this context means to set-aside for a unique relationship.

Then since God has established a unique relationship with the nation of Israel, is there any being that has a similar relationship with the remainder of mankind? Yes!

I will declare the decree: the LORD hath said unto me, Thou art my Son; this day have I begotten thee. Ask of me, and I shall give thee the heathen for thine inheritance, and the uttermost parts of the earth for thy possession.
(Psalm 2:7-8)

This being is the Redeemer, the Messiah, and the Christ (notice the capitalized *S* embedded in the sentence, a special person is set forth here). Christ is Jesus of Nazareth; who is also the Son of man; who is the Son of God. This is a very unique relationship with God. There have been other sons but there is only one Son. The nation of Israel is a son of God.

> *And thou shalt say unto Pharaoh, Thus saith the LORD,*
> *Israel is my son, even my firstborn: And I say unto thee,*
> *Let my son go, that he may serve me: and if thou refuse*
> *to let him go, behold, I will slay thy son, even thy*
> *firstborn.*
> (Exodus 4:22-23)

As the son of God, the nation of Israel received an assignment to serve God in a special way, because of this unique relationship with God.

> *And Moses went up unto God, and the LORD called unto*
> *him out of the mountain, saying, Thus shalt thou say to*
> *the house of Jacob, and tell the children of Israel; Ye*
> *have seen what I did unto the Egyptians, and how I bare*
> *you on eagles' wings, and brought you unto myself. Now*
> *therefore, if ye will obey my voice indeed, and keep my*
> *covenant, then ye shall be a peculiar treasure unto me*
> *above all people: for all the earth is mine: And ye shall*
> *be unto me a kingdom of priests, and an holy nation.*
> *These are the words which thou shalt speak unto the*
> *children of Israel.*
> (Exodus 19:3-6)

Might we find a similar assignment of duties by God to the Son of God? If so, what might that be? The answer is revealed in the Son's other title.

The Son of God is the Son of man. This means that as the Son of God he has responsibility for the whole of mankind and this includes Israel. Though Israel was selected to minister to God, it is still the Son of man's *job* to manifest excellence in all mankind. It is because the Son of man has performed his duties so well that the remainder of mankind is now his inheritance. He has nurtured them and is best fit in the entire universe, save for God Himself, to coordinate their activities on into eternity. For this purpose he has been given an eternal kingdom

And the seventh angel sounded; and there were great
voices in heaven, saying, The kingdoms of this world are
become the kingdoms of our Lord, and of his Christ; and
he shall reign for ever and ever. And the four and twenty
elders, which sat before God on their seats, fell upon
their faces, and worshipped God, Saying, We give thee
thanks, O Lord God Almighty, which art, and wast, and
art to come; because thou hast taken to thee thy great
power, and hast reigned.
                    (Revelation 11:15-17)

The nation of Israel was raised up as a full grown son. For this reason it was expected of them that they could follow orders and maintain allegiances. For this reason any deviation from the strict specifications could not be allowed. For this reason they were placed in a position of facing judgment for their actions on this earth. For them it is by their works that they are judged. To eliminate the sting of this judgment, animal sacrifices were established to make a way of escape. However, the effect of this sacrifice on the souls of Israel was only temporary.

The heathen, also called the Gentiles, on the other hand, are told specifically to approach God as children.

And Jesus called a little child unto him, and set him in
the midst of them, And said, Verily I say unto you, Except
ye be converted, and become as little children, ye shall
not enter into the kingdom of heaven.

Whosoever therefore shall humble himself as this little
child, the same is greatest in the kingdom of heaven. And
whoso shall receive one such little child in my name
receiveth me.

But whoso shall offend one of these little ones which
believe in me, it were better for him that a millstone were
hanged about his neck, and that he were drowned in the
depth of the sea. Woe unto the world because of
offences! for it must needs be that offences come; but
woe to that man by whom the offence cometh!
                    (Matthew 18:2-7)

Therefore, since we can *behave* as children, the Son of man uses forbearance and petition to move us to excellence. For this reason we see a shift from judgment to personal sacrifice. There was a personal sacrifice of the highest magnitude by the Son of man, who is the Son of God, who has been given tremendous power by God. Such a sacrifice is so potent that it need be done only once: it is permanent. The sacrifice was made and the price was paid, for all mankind, when Jesus hung on the cross and died. It was presented, by the will of God, first to the nation of Israel, and then extended through them to the Gentiles.

> *Jesus answered and said, This voice came not because of me, but for your sakes. Now is the judgment of this world: now shall the prince of this world be cast out. And I, if I be lifted up from the earth, will draw all men unto me. This he said, signifying what death he should die.*
> (John 12:30-33)

Therefore, because the Son of man is custodian over children, there is a need for a different set of instructions. This is the instruction to grace and forgiveness through his blood sacrifice on the cross. Children need a milder form of discipline than adults or their development can be seriously affected. This God knows and this the Son knows. The age of grace through the illustration of the love of God in the sacrifice of His Son is a gift that even a child can understand.

Which of us, if it became necessary would not sacrifice our life for those we truly love; especially our little brothers and little sisters? Furthermore, which one of us who truly love God wouldn't give all to Him, even our life? So those of us who think we are of an adult mind should find this illustration of pure love that much easier to accept. However, you might want to approach this from the simple faith of a child of God; not with an adult's skepticism: remember this, being a child has its benefits. Therefore be wise as an adult but obedient as a well-behaved child. In this way we become heirs to the forbearance of God for our errors and failings; the forbearance that is encased in His Son and in the Son's mission as the Son of man, from before the foundation of the world.

But what about the *old school* folks in Israel? I don't want to leave any loose ends hanging. As we read the Bible, specifically the Old Testament, we see that the nation of Israel didn't act very much like an adult. This does not mean that they are given up and tossed away.

The covenant they received is eternal: the LORD swore by Himself that it was so.

> *And Abram fell on his face: and God talked with him, saying, As for me, behold, my covenant is with thee, and thou shalt be a father of many nations. Neither shall thy name any more be called Abram, but thy name shall be Abraham; for a father of many nations have I made thee. And I will make thee exceeding fruitful, and I will make nations of thee, and kings shall come out of thee. And I will establish my covenant between me and thee and thy seed after thee in their generations for an everlasting covenant, to be a God unto thee, and to thy seed after thee.*
> (Genesis 17:3-7)

What it does mean, however, is that Israel may just want to admit that they are still children when it comes to the things of God. By doing so, they can accept the treatment that we Gentile children receive from the Son of man. By doing so, they can participate in the benefits of the eternal sacrifice that was made by the Lord Jesus Christ, the Son of God, and enter thereby into God's rest.

On behalf of God the Father and all the Father's children who have accepted the Son's offer of refreshing, I extend the Lord's invitation.

> *In the last day, that great day of the feast, Jesus stood and cried, saying, If any man thirst, let him come unto me, and drink. He that believeth on me, as the scripture hath said, out of his belly shall flow rivers of living water. (But this spake he of the Spirit, which they that believe on him should receive: for the Holy Ghost was not yet given; because that Jesus was not yet glorified.)*
> (John 7:37-39)

And, as they say in the movies, **"He's here!"**

> *And when the day of Pentecost was fully come, they were all with one accord in one place. And suddenly there came a sound from heaven as of a rushing mighty wind, and it filled all the house where they were sitting. And there appeared unto them cloven tongues like as of fire, and it sat upon each of them. And they were all filled*

with the Holy Ghost, and began to speak with other tongues, as the Spirit gave them utterance.

And there were dwelling at Jerusalem Jews, devout men, out of every nation under heaven. Now when this was noised abroad, the multitude came together, and were confounded, because that every man heard them speak in his own language. And they were all amazed and marvelled, saying one to another, Behold, are not all these which speak Galilaeans? And how hear we every man in our own tongue, wherein we were born? Parthians, and Medes, and Elamites, and the dwellers in Mesopotamia, and in Judaea, and Cappadocia, in Pontus, and Asia, Phrygia, and Pamphylia, in Egypt, and in the parts of Libya about Cyrene, and strangers of Rome, Jews and proselytes, Cretes and Arabians, we do hear them speak in our tongues the wonderful works of God.
(Acts 2:1-11)

I extend to you the Lord's welcome on his behalf and in his name. Amen.

The Word from the Bible

Daniel 9:24-27

Seventy weeks are determined upon thy people and upon thy holy city, to finish the transgression, and to make an end of sins, and to make reconciliation for iniquity, and to bring in everlasting righteousness, and to seal up the vision and prophecy, and to anoint the most Holy.

Know therefore and understand, that from the going forth of the commandment to restore and to build Jerusalem unto the Messiah the Prince shall be seven weeks, and threescore and two weeks: the street shall be built again, and the wall, even in troublous times.

And after threescore and two weeks shall Messiah be cut off, but not for himself: and the people of the prince that shall come shall destroy the city and the sanctuary; and the end thereof shall be with a flood, and unto the end of the war desolations are determined. And he shall confirm the covenant with many for one week: and in the midst of the week he shall cause the sacrifice and the oblation to cease, and for the overspreading of abominations he shall make it desolate, even until the consummation, and that determined shall be poured upon the desolate.

Job 19:25-27

For I know that my redeemer liveth, and that he shall stand at the latter day upon the earth: And though after my skin worms destroy this body, yet in my flesh shall I see God: Whom I shall see for myself, and mine eyes shall behold, and not another; though my reins be consumed within me.

Psalm 2:7-12

I will declare the decree: the LORD hath said unto me, Thou art my Son; this day have I begotten thee. Ask of me, and I shall give thee the heathen for thine inheritance, and the uttermost parts of the earth for thy possession. Thou shalt break them with a rod of iron; thou shalt dash them in pieces like a potter's vessel.

Be wise now therefore, O ye kings: be instructed, ye judges of the earth. Serve the LORD with fear, and rejoice with trembling. Kiss the Son, lest he be angry, and ye perish from the way, when his wrath is kindled but a little. Blessed are all they that put their trust in him.

Isaiah 8:18-9:7

Behold, I and the children whom the LORD hath given me are for signs and for wonders in Israel from the LORD of hosts, which dwelleth in mount Zion. And when they shall say unto you, Seek unto them that have familiar spirits, and unto wizards that peep, and that mutter: should not a people seek unto their God? for the living to the dead?

To the law and to the testimony: if they speak not according to this word, it is because there is no light in them. And they shall pass through it, hardly bestead and hungry: and it shall come to pass, that when they shall be hungry, they shall fret themselves, and curse their king and their God, and look upward. And they shall look unto the earth; and behold trouble and darkness, dimness of anguish; and they shall be driven to darkness. Nevertheless the dimness shall not be such as was in her vexation, when at the first he lightly afflicted the land of Zebulun and the land of Naphtali, and afterward did more grievously afflict her by the way of the sea, beyond Jordan, in Galilee of the nations.

The people that walked in darkness have seen a great light: they that dwell in the land of the shadow of death, upon them hath the light shined. Thou hast multiplied the nation, and not increased the joy: they joy before thee according to the joy in harvest, and as men rejoice when they divide the spoil. For thou hast broken the yoke of his burden, and the staff of his shoulder, the rod of his oppressor, as in the day of Midian. For every battle of the warrior is with confused noise, and garments rolled in blood; but this shall be with burning and fuel of fire.

For unto us a child is born, unto us a son is given: and the government shall be upon his shoulder: and his name shall be called Wonderful, Counsellor, The mighty God, The everlasting Father, The Prince of Peace. Of the increase of his government and peace there shall be no end, upon the throne of David, and upon his kingdom, to order it, and to establish it with judgment and with justice from henceforth even for ever. The zeal of the LORD of hosts will perform this.

Malachi 3:1-6

Behold, I will send my messenger, and he shall prepare the way before me: and the Lord, whom ye seek, shall suddenly come to his temple, even the messenger of the covenant, whom ye delight in: behold, he shall come, saith the LORD of hosts. But who may abide the day of his coming? and who shall stand when he appeareth? for he is like a refiner's fire, and like fullers' soap: And he shall sit as a refiner and purifier of silver: and he shall purify the sons of Levi, and purge them as gold and silver, that they may offer unto the LORD an offering in righteousness.

Then shall the offering of Judah and Jerusalem be pleasant unto the LORD, as in the days of old, and as in former years. And I will come near to you to judgment; and I will be a swift witness against the sorcerers, and against the adulterers, and against false swearers, and against those that oppress the hireling in his wages, the widow, and the fatherless, and that turn aside the stranger from his right, and fear not me, saith the LORD of hosts. For I am the LORD, I change not; therefore ye sons of Jacob are not consumed.

Luke 1:8-20

And it came to pass, that while he executed the priest's office before God in the order of his course, According to the custom of the priest's office, his lot was to burn incense when he went into the temple of the Lord. And the whole multitude of the people were praying without at the time of incense. And there appeared unto him an angel of the Lord standing on the right side of the altar of incense. And when Zacharias saw him, he was troubled, and fear fell upon him.

But the angel said unto him, Fear not, Zacharias: for thy prayer is heard; and thy wife Elisabeth shall bear thee a son, and thou shalt call his name John. And thou shalt have joy and gladness; and many shall rejoice at his birth. For he shall be great in the sight of the Lord, and shall drink neither wine nor strong drink; and he shall be filled with the Holy Ghost, even from his mother's womb. And many of the children of Israel shall he turn to the Lord their God. And he shall go before him in the spirit and power of Elias, to turn the hearts of the fathers to the children, and the disobedient to the wisdom of the just; to make ready a people prepared for the Lord.

And Zacharias said unto the angel, Whereby shall I know this? for I am an old man, and my wife well stricken in years.

And the angel answering said unto him, I am Gabriel, that stand in the presence of God; and am sent to speak unto thee, and to shew thee these glad tidings. And, behold, thou shalt be dumb, and not able to speak, until the day that these things shall be performed, because thou believest not my words, which shall be fulfilled in their season.

Luke 1:26-38

And in the sixth month the angel Gabriel was sent from God unto a city of Galilee, named Nazareth, To a virgin espoused to a man whose name was Joseph, of the house of David; and the virgin's name was Mary. And the angel came in unto her, and said, Hail, thou that art highly favoured, the Lord is with thee: blessed art thou among women. And when she saw him, she was troubled at his saying, and cast in her mind what manner of salutation this should be.

And the angel said unto her, Fear not, Mary: for thou hast found favour with God. And, behold, thou shalt conceive in thy womb, and bring forth a son, and shalt call his name JESUS. He shall be great, and shall be called the Son of the Highest: and the Lord God shall give unto him the throne of his father David: And he shall reign over the house of Jacob for ever; and of his kingdom there shall be no end.

Then said Mary unto the angel, How shall this be, seeing I know not a man?

And the angel answered and said unto her, The Holy Ghost shall come upon thee, and the power of the Highest shall overshadow thee: therefore also that holy thing which shall be born of thee shall be called the Son of God. And, behold, thy cousin Elisabeth, she hath also conceived a son in her old age: and this is the sixth month with her, who was called barren. For with God nothing shall be impossible.

And Mary said, Behold the handmaid of the Lord; be it unto me according to thy word. And the angel departed from her.

Genesis 14:18-20

And Melchizedek king of Salem brought forth bread and wine: and he was the priest of the most high God. And he blessed him, and said, Blessed be Abram of the most high God, possessor of heaven and earth: And blessed be the most high God, which hath delivered thine enemies into thy hand. And he gave him tithes of all.

Psalm 110

A Psalm of David.

The LORD said unto my Lord, Sit thou at my right hand, until I make thine enemies thy footstool.

The LORD shall send the rod of thy strength out of Zion: rule thou in the midst of thine enemies. Thy people shall be willing in the day of thy power, in the beauties of holiness from the womb of the morning: thou hast the dew of thy youth.

The LORD hath sworn, and will not repent, Thou art a priest for ever after the order of Melchizedek. The Lord at thy right hand shall strike through kings in the day of his wrath. He shall judge among the heathen, he shall fill the places with the dead bodies; he shall wound the heads over many countries. He shall drink of the brook in the way: therefore shall he lift up the head.

Chapter Five

Discovering the Messiah

In a prior discussion we prepared a *job description* and limited set of *qualifications* for the position of Messiah.

Job Description: The ideal candidate will have a keen knowledge of the things of Heaven and the things of earth. He will be able to provide mankind with a means to stay in fellowship with God. This means that he must be durable enough to remain active even without the cooperation of the recipient of the benefits. Furthermore, this means that he must have a good contingency plan to cover downtime of the primary operation or absence of the operator.

Qualifications: Not a novice to this operation. The ideal candidate must be one that has a great amount of experience in the operation of the job functions of this position. This candidate must possess maturity and a keen sense of purpose. The candidate must have a strong work ethic and be able to withstand long hours of effort under very stressful conditions. The ideal candidate will look to no one else to assist him in starting the operation. The candidate must be a good teacher, for he must train his staff in the workings of the department that he will lead. Ideally, the candidate will be

willing to put his life into the position
and to work until the job is complete;
whatever it takes.

We will continue our search for the Messiah here. First, however, we think that it is prudent to repeat our prayer to God relative to this matter.

PRAYER: Father, You know that I am in no way trying to analyze what You have done, for this is impossible for a human, such as I am. I am, instead, trying to gain a grasp on the, most high concept of Redeemer, or as we also call him, the Messiah. This will be useful to me to prevent me from following false Christ's. *For there shall arise false Christs, and false prophets, and shall shew great signs and wonders; insomuch that, if it were possible, they shall deceive the very elect.* This is the message that is given to us in your Bible in Matthew 24:24

Please guide my spirit, my heart and my soul in this endeavor, as You immerse all in the Holy Ghost. Please let these words serve to instruct others besides myself in the recognition of Your majesty and far reaching love for all mankind. Let it be so that they move the undecided to see that You have indeed provided the Redeemer. My strong desire is that they move the seeker to clearly see the revealed Redeemer that You have already sent to mankind. To You, be all the glory.

Father, You have cast me in a certain mold on this earth with power that only depends on You. This is marvelous and wonderful to be. Therefore, I rest in Your creativity. Furthermore, I claim the promise of Your Son, the revealed Redeemer. He has said,

And whatsoever ye shall ask in my name, that will I do, that the Father may be glorified in the Son, as recorded in John 14:13. I claim this promise and ask all this in the name of Jesus and for his sake. Amen.

Let us continue. This assignment requires someone who has first hand knowledge of both the things of Heaven and the things of earth. Our candidate must come from Heaven, or be one who is born of heavenly substances; or both. The prophets of old told us that this assignment is an everlasting one. Therefore, the person given to the task must have a portion of the nature of God. He must be one who will go with God *to everlasting.* It is not necessary that he come *from everlasting,* for only God is that.

Before the mountains were brought forth, or ever thou hadst formed the earth and the world, even from everlasting to everlasting, thou art God.
(Psalm 90:2)

The candidate's soul must be one that was in existence from before the foundation of the world. In this way he will fully understand the trials that mankind has faced during its existence. He will also understand the place in which God has situated the world and the other inanimate objects. This is an intricate thing; for we don't usually think of the earth as having any other function but to be here. However, in Genesis God tells us of an *earth with attitude.*

And the LORD said unto Cain, Where is Abel thy brother?

And he said, I know not: Am I my brother's keeper?

And he said, What hast thou done? the voice of thy brother's blood crieth unto me from the ground. And now art thou cursed from the earth, which hath opened her mouth to receive thy brother's blood from thy hand; When thou tillest the ground, it shall not henceforth yield unto thee her strength; a fugitive and a vagabond shalt thou be in the earth.
(Genesis 4:9-12)

Through the books of Moses, the LORD revealed to us that the earth had the ability to reject the people if they didn't follow righteousness.

> *And if ye will not yet for all this hearken unto me, then I will punish you seven times more for your sins. And I will break the pride of your power; and I will make your heaven as iron, and your earth as brass: And your strength shall be spent in vain: for your land shall not yield her increase, neither shall the trees of the land yield their fruits.*
> (Leviticus 26:18-20)

The candidate that has been around since before the foundation of the world will have an immense amount of understanding of the human condition. This understanding is gathered by observation, as well as by interaction. We have an example of the interaction of the Messiah, also known as the Son of man, in the history of the captive children of Israel.

> *Therefore because the king's commandment was urgent, and the furnace exceeding hot, the flame of the fire slew those men that took up Shadrach, Meshach, and Abednego. And these three men, Shadrach, Meshach, and Abednego, fell down bound into the midst of the burning fiery furnace.*
>
> *Then Nebuchadnezzar the king was astonied, and rose up in haste, and spake, and said unto his counsellors, Did not we cast three men bound into the midst of the fire? They answered and said unto the king, True, O king. He answered and said, Lo, I see four men loose, walking in the midst of the fire, and they have no hurt; and the form of the fourth is like the Son of God.*
> (Daniel 3:22-25)

Such a being (or spirit) will fully understand the task of mediation ascribed to him.

> *For there is one God, and one mediator between God and men, the man Christ Jesus; Who gave himself a ransom for all, to be testified in due time.*
> (1 Timothy 2:5-6)

It would also be helpful if he was of a spirit that had become accustomed to direct communication with God. It would be ideal if God was in fact his teacher.

> *Then said Jesus unto them, When ye have lifted up the*
> *Son of man, then shall ye know that I am he, and that*
> *I do nothing of myself; but as my Father hath taught me,*
> *I speak these things. And he that sent me is with me: the*
> *Father hath not left me alone; for I do always those*
> *things that please him. As he spake these words, many*
> *believed on him.*
> (John 8:28-30)

Finally, it would be extremely useful if he passed through life as we do. That is, was born, was raised, fought the internal battles that we face and was subject to the same temptations. In other words, that he fully understands the human condition, not just by observation and training, but by actual experience. He must also have prevailed over these human features and prospered even with this burden of humanity.

> *For we have not an high priest which cannot be touched*
> *with the feeling of our infirmities; but was in all points*
> *tempted like as we are, yet without sin.*
> (Hebrews 4:15)

We have given some pointers to a candidate for this position in some of the preceding discussion. Let's continue with a discussion of the person and personality of the Messiah. Let's start with things that we can see. According to the prophets, the child will be born in a very unique fashion.

> *Therefore the Lord himself shall give you a sign; Behold,*
> *a virgin shall conceive, and bear a son, and shall call his*
> *name Immanuel. Butter and honey shall he eat, that*
> *he may know to refuse the evil, and choose the good.*
> (Isaiah 7:14-15)

> *Now the birth of Jesus Christ was on this wise: When as*
> *his mother Mary was espoused to Joseph, before they*
> *came together, she was found with child of the Holy*
> *Ghost. Then Joseph her husband, being a just man, and*
> *not willing to make her a publick example, was minded*
> *to put her away privily. But while he thought on these*

things, behold, the angel of the LORD appeared unto him in a dream, saying,

Joseph, thou son of David, fear not to take unto thee Mary thy wife: for that which is conceived in her is of the Holy Ghost. And she shall bring forth a son, and thou shalt call his name JESUS: for he shall save his people from their sins.

Now all this was done, that it might be fulfilled which was spoken of the Lord by the prophet, saying, Behold, a virgin shall be with child, and shall bring forth a son, and they shall call his name Emmanuel, which being interpreted is, God with us.
(Matthew 1:18-23)

This catches my eye because at this time in history there is only one way that a virgin can be with child, and that is if some heavenly intervention takes place. Oh, I know you say that she could be artificially inseminated, but this science was not available at that time in history. Furthermore, the babies born by artificial insemination still have a limited, human spirit. Furthermore, as we, limited humans, grow, we will still have very little knowledge of the things of earth, and even less knowledge of the things of Heaven.

The child born to the virgin had to be a product of Heaven and created using heavenly substance. This was doable in that day because God did know about artificial insemination and God can create the materials necessary to perform conception in a virgin. And He did cause it to be done.

And the angel answered and said unto her, The Holy Ghost shall come upon thee, and the power of the Highest shall overshadow thee: therefore also that holy thing which shall be born of thee shall be called the Son of God.
(Luke 1:35)

We know that the genetics of this child is phenomenal; God doesn't skimp on his marvels and miracles. The male genetic packet containing the Y-chromosome, that was delivered from Heaven for conception must have had some really, really potent genetic potential built into it. This child of the Virgin Mary has the ability to learn at a phenomenal rate and to retain any information ever given to him.

*And there shall come forth a rod out of the stem of Jesse,
and a Branch shall grow out of his roots: And the spirit
of the LORD shall rest upon him, the spirit of wisdom
and understanding, the spirit of counsel and might, the
spirit of knowledge and of the fear of the LORD; And
shall make him of quick understanding in the fear of the
LORD: and he shall not judge after the sight of his eyes,
neither reprove after the hearing of his ears: But with
righteousness shall he judge the poor, and reprove with
equity for the meek of the earth: and he shall smite the
earth with the rod of his mouth, and with the breath of
his lips shall he slay the wicked.*
(Isaiah 11:1-4)

He might even have the ability to acquire information not as man
does, but directly as God does.

*But the LORD said unto Samuel, Look not on his
countenance, or on the height of his stature; because
I have refused him: for the LORD seeth not as man
seeth; for man looketh on the outward appearance, but
the LORD looketh on the heart.*
(1 Samuel 16:7)

We have also read about the actions of a good earthly father in
prior writings. A good earthly father's actions are an expression of the
nature of the Father. Thus, it seems reasonable to assume that God who
taught the earthly ones would, as one might say, practice what
He *preaches*. The child, therefore, would receive the benefit of training
in all matters of Heaven and of earth.

The child is born with no hindrances from containing within it all
knowledge. The only thing necessary for its completion would be the
maturation of the neural paths to withstand the weight of the information.
Indeed, we all have the potential for this kind of understanding: man has
indeed been created as a most marvelous work of God. Just think about it:
in our ideal state we will be able to retain all the information given to us
by God of both Heaven and earth. Wonderful!

The only man in history, past and present that fills these
requirements for the position is Jesus of Nazareth. We will draw upon
the writings that have been given to us by those of our ancestors who
witnessed his life. But history says he died on the cross in the time of

some of the other of our ancestors. Even so, let's see whether he fits the *job description* and then we can search for a solution to this *death* thing.

Job Description

A keen knowledge of the things of Heaven and the things of earth

> *And Jesus, when he was baptized, went up straightway out of the water: and, lo, the heavens were opened unto him, and he saw the Spirit of God descending like a dove, and lighting upon him: And lo a voice from heaven, saying, This is my beloved Son, in whom I am well pleased.*
> (Matthew 3:16-17)

> *And now, O Father, glorify thou me with thine own self with the glory which I had with thee before the world was.*
> (John 17:5)

> *For I have given unto them the words which thou gavest me; and they have received them, and have known surely that I came out from thee, and they have believed that thou didst send me.*
> (John 17:8)

Provide mankind with a means to stay in fellowship with God

> *Thomas saith unto him, Lord, we know not whither thou goest; and how can we know the way? Jesus saith unto him, I am the way, the truth, and the life: no man cometh unto the Father, but by me.*
> (John 14:5)

Durable enough to remain active even without cooperation of the recipients of the benefits

> *Behold, the hour cometh, yea, is now come, that ye shall be scattered, every man to his own, and shall leave me alone: and yet I am not alone, because the Father is with me.*
> (John 16:32)

Have a good contingency plan to cover downtime of the primary operation or absence of the operator

> *Therefore also said the wisdom of God, I will send them prophets and apostles, and some of them they shall slay*

and persecute: That the blood of all the prophets, which was shed from the foundation of the world, may be required of this generation; From the blood of Abel unto the blood of Zacharias, which perished between the altar and the temple: verily I say unto you, It shall be required of this generation.
    (Luke 11:49-51)

Now ye are the body of Christ, and members in particular. And God hath set some in the church, first apostles, secondarily prophets, thirdly teachers, after that miracles, then gifts of healings, helps, governments, diversities of tongues.
    (1 Corinthians 12:27-28)

And he gave some, apostles; and some, prophets; and some, evangelists; and some, pastors and teachers; For the perfecting of the saints, for the work of the ministry, for the edifying of the body of Christ:
    (Ephesians 4:11-12)

Establishing an operation's procedure or procedures

One final matter remains, which is the perpetuation of the process that he started on this earth.

The apostles and disciples surely could not do it alone. They were certain to run into the same problem that faced the priests and prophets of the past. In the case of the priests some of them became lazy about following the strict orders of God and decided to go their own way. In the case of some of the prophets, their brothers and sisters on the earth decided to kill them. The others of the prophets died, and their messages were eventually discarded by those who heard.

Such would be the fate of the disciples and apostles that were left to run the process as well, if they were left alone to do it. However, to solve the problems described above, Jesus sent an eternal *reminder*; a teacher for all time.

If ye love me, keep my commandments. And I will pray the Father, and he shall give you another Comforter, that he may abide with you for ever; Even the Spirit of truth; whom the world cannot receive, because it seeth

him not, neither knoweth him: but ye know him; for he dwelleth with you, and shall be in you.
(John 14:15-17)

Qualifications

Not a novice to this operation

Your father Abraham rejoiced to see my day: and he saw it, and was glad.

Then said the Jews unto him, Thou art not yet fifty years old, and hast thou seen Abraham?

Jesus said unto them, Verily, verily, I say unto you, Before Abraham was, I am.
(John 8:56-58)

Father, I will that they also, whom thou hast given me, be with me where I am; that they may behold my glory, which thou hast given me: for thou lovedst me before the foundation of the world.
(John 17:24)

Broad history of experience in the operation of the job functions of this position

I have glorified thee on the earth: I have finished the work which thou gavest me to do. And now, O Father, glorify thou me with thine own self with the glory which I had with thee before the world was. I have manifested thy name unto the men which thou gavest me out of the world: thine they were, and thou gavest them me; and they have kept thy word.
(John 17:4-6)

Maturity and a keen sense of purpose

And the child grew, and waxed strong in spirit, filled with wisdom: and the grace of God was upon him.

Now his parents went to Jerusalem every year at the feast of the passover. And when he was twelve years old, they went up to Jerusalem after the custom of the feast. And when they had fulfilled the days, as they returned, the child Jesus tarried behind in Jerusalem; and Joseph and his mother knew not of it. But they, supposing him to have been in the company, went a day's journey; and they sought him among their kinsfolk and acquaintance. And when they found him not, they turned back again to Jerusalem, seeking him.

And it came to pass, that after three days they found him in the temple, sitting in the midst of the doctors, both hearing them, and asking them questions. And all that heard him were astonished at his understanding and answers. And when they saw him, they were amazed: and his mother said unto him, Son, why hast thou thus dealt with us? behold, thy father and I have sought thee sorrowing.

And he said unto them, How is it that ye sought me? wist ye not that I must be about my Father's business?
(Luke 2:40-49)

Strong work ethic

Let this mind be in you, which was also in Christ Jesus: Who, being in the form of God, thought it not robbery to be equal with God: But made himself of no reputation, and took upon him the form of a servant, and was made in the likeness of men: And being found in fashion as a man, he humbled himself, and became obedient unto death, even the death of the cross.

Wherefore God also hath highly exalted him, and given him a name which is above every name: That at the name of Jesus every knee should bow, of things in heaven, and things in earth, and things under the earth; And that every tongue should confess that Jesus Christ is Lord, to the glory of God the Father.
(Philippians 2:5-11)

Able to withstand long hours of effort under very stressful conditions

And Jesus going up to Jerusalem took the twelve disciples apart in the way, and said unto them, Behold, we go up to Jerusalem; and the Son of man shall be

betrayed unto the chief priests and unto the scribes, and
they shall condemn him to death, And shall deliver him
to the Gentiles to mock, and to scourge, and to crucify
him: and the third day he shall rise again.

(Matthew 20:17-19)

Look to no one else to assist him in starting the operation

And I saw in the right hand of him that sat on the throne
a book written within and on the backside, sealed with
seven seals. And I saw a strong angel proclaiming with
a loud voice, Who is worthy to open the book, and to
loose the seals thereof? And no man in heaven, nor in
earth, neither under the earth, was able to open the
book, neither to look thereon.

And I wept much, because no man was found worthy to
open and to read the book, neither to look thereon.

And one of the elders saith unto me, Weep not: behold,
the Lion of the tribe of Juda, the Root of David, hath
prevailed to open the book, and to loose the seven seals
thereof.

And I beheld, and, lo, in the midst of the throne and of
the four beasts, and in the midst of the elders, stood
a Lamb as it had been slain, having seven horns and
seven eyes, which are the seven Spirits of God sent forth
into all the earth.

(Revelation 5:1-6)

A good teacher, for he must train his staff in the workings of the department that he will lead

I have manifested thy name unto the men which thou
gavest me out of the world: thine they were, and thou
gavest them me; and they have kept thy word. Now they
have known that all things whatsoever thou hast given
me are of thee. For I have given unto them the words
which thou gavest me; and they have received them, and
have known surely that I came out from thee, and they
have believed that thou didst send me.

(John 17:6-8)

<u>Willing to put his life into the position</u>

> *I am the good shepherd: the good shepherd giveth his*
> *life for the sheep.*
> (John 10:11)

<u>Work until the job is complete, whatever it takes.</u>

> *After this, Jesus knowing that all things were now*
> *accomplished, that the scripture might be fulfilled, saith,*
> *I thirst. Now there was set a vessel full of vinegar: and*
> *they filled a spunge with vinegar, and put it upon hyssop,*
> *and put it to his mouth. When Jesus therefore had*
> *received the vinegar, he said, It is finished: and*
> *he bowed his head, and gave up the ghost.*
> (John 19:28-30)

Post Process Review

Well, this is where the matter becomes very, very interesting. Unlike the prophets and priest before him, this Jesus of Nazareth decided that he didn't want to stay dead. I told you there was some potent stuff in that packet delivered from Heaven, to the virgin who gave birth.

He decided that he would take himself, and the total package of all that he had already received when he was absorbing knowledge, grace and truth in Heaven, and that which he now had from earth, and go to his temporary rest in Heaven. And the *Corporate Founder and Chief*, the LORD God delivered to him a benefit packet that would allow him to conduct whatever business he was assigned, in Heaven and in earth.

> *And Jesus came and spake unto them, saying, All power*
> *is given unto me in heaven and in earth.*
> (Matthew 28:18)

Mission Accomplished

So the position has been filled and the work completed. We also have a process that is ongoing and eternal. New people are being trained and the resources that are necessary for the continuation of the job are richly available. Mankind has been redeemed from the wages of his sin.

For when ye were the servants of sin, ye were free from righteousness. What fruit had ye then in those things whereof ye are now ashamed? for the end of those things is death. But now being made free from sin, and become servants to God, ye have your fruit unto holiness, and the end everlasting life. For the wages of sin is death; but the gift of God is eternal life through Jesus Christ our Lord.
(Romans 6:20-23)

And whenever the apostles and disciples get into a crunch, they just send an *e-mail* (short for eternal-mail) to Jesus for more resources.

Verily, verily, I say unto you, He that believeth on me, the works that I do shall he do also; and greater works than these shall he do; because I go unto my Father. And whatsoever ye shall ask in my name, that will I do, that the Father may be glorified in the Son. If ye shall ask any thing in my name, I will do it.
(John 14:12-14)

This Jesus can easily provide from his reservoir of *all power*.

I pray that you accept his invitation to join him as one of his followers. Then, he will show you the place selected for you. He will give you your assignment to be one of his apostles or prophets, or teachers, or any other of the designation in the body of the church of Christ, including just being a member. But please understand; there are different portions of the body of Christ which need service. Where you fit best cannot be forced on you by either yourself or anyone else; this is only from God.

I beseech you therefore, brethren, by the mercies of God, that ye present your bodies a living sacrifice, holy, acceptable unto God, which is your reasonable service. And be not conformed to this world: but be ye transformed by the renewing of your mind, that ye may prove what is that good, and acceptable, and perfect, will of God.

For I say, through the grace given unto me, to every man that is among you, not to think of himself more highly than he ought to think; but to think soberly, according as God hath dealt to every man the measure of faith. For as we have many members in one body, and all members have not the same office: So we, being many, are one body in Christ, and every one members one of another. Having then gifts differing according to the grace that is given to us, whether prophecy, let us prophesy according to the proportion of faith; Or ministry, let us wait on our ministering: or he that teacheth, on teaching; Or he that exhorteth, on exhortation: he that giveth, let him do it with simplicity; he that ruleth, with diligence; he that showeth mercy, with cheerfulness.

(Romans 12:1-8)

You can be sure that with the indwelling of the Holy Ghost, you will be conformable to the position in which you serve; to accomplish anything God asks of you.

I know both how to be abased, and I know how to abound: every where and in all things I am instructed both to be full and to be hungry, both to abound and to suffer need. I can do all things through Christ which strengtheneth me.

(Philippians 4:12-13)

I know that you're too intelligent to pass up such a marvelous opportunity, so just ask God to deliver it to you. There are no restrictions from entry into the rest of the Lord Jesus Christ.

I Jesus have sent mine angel to testify unto you these things in the churches. I am the root and the offspring of David, and the bright and morning star. And the Spirit and the bride say, Come. And let him that heareth say, Come. And let him that is athirst come. And whosoever will, let him take the water of life freely.

(Revelation 22:16-17)

All positions required,
The LORD did fill;
To bring about His
Most excellent will.

To create a place
In a brand new land,
The knowledge of God,
Its design, to expand.

In Heaven His will
Is served above all,
In every mansion,
Room and hall.

And, this Heaven is vast
With unlimited bounds
Through which His majesty
For ever and ever resounds.

But even though vast,
Heaven is a small place
When one considers God's
Glory, Power and Grace.

So, to expand His richness
Beyond the confines above,
God commissioned an extension
Of His boundless love.

The Son of God,
The Son of man,
Was well aware of
God's Holy plan;

Constantly learning
As creation unfolds,
And in God's hand
A universe He holds.

Standing with the Father,
He hears, "Let there be light;"
Watching darkness in the land
By the Word takes flight.

But the seal of Majesty
Was not yet done
Until the Father said,
"This is my beloved Son".

Chapter 5a

In Their Own Words

I am saddened by the rising tide of what is referred to as "suicide bombings" among the children of Abraham. This seems to me to be a case where someone else has told another person how to die. Something within me, I believe it to be the Holy Ghost sent from God, tells me that only God has the authority to tell me how to die. I know for sure that only He, through the Holy Ghost in me, has the authority to tell me how to live. It is past time for the children of Abraham to take a good look at who has the authority to tell them what to do.

Something that might help in this is to study examples of successes in God. It seems good for us, therefore, to look to some of the prominent names in the Bible in order to determine the measure of their success. This is very important in this day when so many people are trying to tell us how we should live, and die. Let us look to the Scripture and note the situations surrounding those who were successful in fulfilling God's requirements for their lives and their deaths.

We will look at the expected successes, and some unexpected ones. The list includes Noah, Job, Abraham, Pharaoh, Moses, Joshua, Daniel, Nebuchadnezzar and Belshazzar. Hopefully these names are well known to you and this will be just a review. So turn the page to learn more about the people in the Bible to whom God gave success of varying sorts.

Noah

And God saw that the wickedness of man was great in the earth, and that every imagination of the thoughts of his heart was only evil continually. And it repented the LORD that he had made man on the earth, and it grieved him at his heart. And the LORD said, I will destroy man whom I have created from the face of the earth; both man, and beast, and the creeping thing, and the fowls of the air; for it repenteth me that I have made them. But Noah found grace in the eyes of the LORD.

These are the generations of Noah: Noah was a just man and perfect in his generations, and Noah walked with God. And Noah begat three sons, Shem, Ham, and Japheth.

The earth also was corrupt before God, and the earth was filled with violence. And God looked upon the earth, and, behold, it was corrupt; for all flesh had corrupted his way upon the earth.

And God said unto Noah, The end of all flesh is come before me; for the earth is filled with violence through them; and, behold, I will destroy them with the earth. Make thee an ark of gopher wood; rooms shalt thou make in the ark, and shalt pitch it within and without with pitch. And this is the fashion which thou shalt make it of: The length of the ark shall be three hundred cubits, the breadth of it fifty cubits, and the height of it thirty cubits. A window shalt thou make to the ark, and in a cubit shalt thou finish it above; and the door of the ark shalt thou set in the side thereof; with lower, second, and third stories shalt thou make it.

And, behold, I, even I, do bring a flood of waters upon the earth, to destroy all flesh, wherein is the breath of life, from under heaven; and every thing that is in the earth shall die. But with thee will I establish my covenant; and thou shalt come into the ark, thou, and thy sons, and thy wife, and thy sons' wives with thee.

(Genesis 6:5-18)

And God blessed Noah and his sons, and said unto them, Be fruitful, and multiply, and replenish the earth. And the fear of you and the dread of you shall be upon every beast of the earth, and upon every fowl of the air, upon all that moveth upon the earth, and upon all the fishes of the sea; into your hand are they delivered. Every moving thing that liveth shall be meat for you; even as the green herb have I given you all things. But flesh with the life thereof, which is the blood thereof, shall ye not eat. And surely your blood of your lives will I require; at the hand of every beast will I require it, and at the hand of man; at the hand of every man's brother will I require the life of man. Whoso sheddeth man's blood, by man shall his blood be shed: for in the image of God made he man.

(Genesis 9:1-6)

Job

*And the LORD said unto Satan, Hast thou considered my
servant Job, that there is none like him in the earth,
a perfect and an upright man, one that feareth God, and
escheweth evil?*
(Job 1:8)

*What ye know, the same do I know also: I am not inferior
unto you. Surely I would speak to the Almighty, and
I desire to reason with God. But ye are forgers of lies, ye
are all physicians of no value. O that ye would
altogether hold your peace! and it should be your
wisdom. Hear now my reasoning, and hearken to the
pleadings of my lips. Will ye speak wickedly for God?
and talk deceitfully for him?*

*Will ye accept his person? will ye contend for God? Is it
good that he should search you out? or as one man
mocketh another, do ye so mock him? He will surely
reprove you, if ye do secretly accept persons. Shall not
his excellency make you afraid? and his dread fall upon
you? Your remembrances are like unto ashes, your
bodies to bodies of clay.*

*Hold your peace, let me alone, that I may speak, and let
come on me what will. Wherefore do I take my flesh in
my teeth, and put my life in mine hand? Though he slay
me, yet will I trust in him: but I will maintain mine own
ways before him.*
(Job 13:2-15)

*If a man die, shall he live again? all the days of my
appointed time will I wait, till my change come.*
(Job 14:14)

*For I know that my redeemer liveth, and that he shall stand
at the latter day upon the earth: And though after my skin
worms destroy this body, yet in my flesh shall I see God:
Whom I shall see for myself, and mine eyes shall behold,
and not another; though my reins be consumed within me.*
(Job 19:25-27)

__Abraham__

And there went out the king of Sodom, and the king of Gomorrah, and the king of Admah, and the king of Zeboiim, and the king of Bela (the same is Zoar;) and they joined battle with them in the vale of Siddim; With Chedorlaomer the king of Elam, and with Tidal king of nations, and Amraphel king of Shinar, and Arioch king of Ellasar; four kings with five.

And the vale of Siddim was full of slimepits; and the kings of Sodom and Gomorrah fled, and fell there; and they that remained fled to the mountain. And they took all the goods of Sodom and Gomorrah, and all their victuals, and went their way. And they took Lot, Abram's brother's son, who dwelt in Sodom, and his goods, and departed.

And there came one that had escaped, and told Abram the Hebrew; for he dwelt in the plain of Mamre the Amorite, brother of Eshcol, and brother of Aner: and these were confederate with Abram. And when Abram heard that his brother was taken captive, he armed his trained servants, born in his own house, three hundred and eighteen, and pursued them unto Dan. And he divided himself against them, he and his servants, by night, and smote them, and pursued them unto Hobah, which is on the left hand of Damascus. And he brought back all the goods, and also brought again his brother Lot, and his goods, and the women also, and the people. And the king of Sodom went out to meet him after his return from the slaughter of Chedorlaomer, and of the kings that were with him, at the valley of Shaveh, which is the king's dale.

And Melchizedek king of Salem brought forth bread and wine: and he was the priest of the most high God. And he blessed him, and said, Blessed be Abram of the most high God, possessor of heaven and earth: And blessed be the most high God, which hath delivered thine enemies into thy hand.

And he gave him tithes of all.

And the king of Sodom said unto Abram, Give me the persons, and take the goods to thyself.

And Abram said to the king of Sodom, I have lift up mine hand unto the LORD, the most high God, the possessor of heaven and earth, That I will not take from a thread even to a shoelatchet, and that I will not take any thing that is thine, lest thou shouldest say, I have made Abram rich: Save only that which the young men have eaten, and the portion of the men which went with me, Aner, Eshcol, and Mamre; let them take their portion.

(Genesis 14:8-24)

Pharaoh

Then Moses called for all the elders of Israel, and said unto them, Draw out and take you a lamb according to your families, and kill the passover. And ye shall take a bunch of hyssop, and dip it in the blood that is in the bason, and strike the lintel and the two side posts with the blood that is in the bason; and none of you shall go out at the door of his house until the morning. For the LORD will pass through to smite the Egyptians; and when he seeth the blood upon the lintel, and on the two side posts, the LORD will pass over the door, and will not suffer the destroyer to come in unto your houses to smite you.

And ye shall observe this thing for an ordinance to thee and to thy sons for ever. And it shall come to pass, when ye be come to the land which the LORD will give you, according as he hath promised, that ye shall keep this service.

And it shall come to pass, when your children shall say unto you, What mean ye by this service? That ye shall say, It is the sacrifice of the LORD's passover, who passed over the houses of the children of Israel in Egypt, when he smote the Egyptians, and delivered our houses.

And the people bowed the head and worshipped. And the children of Israel went away, and did as the LORD had commanded Moses and Aaron, so did they.

And it came to pass, that at midnight the LORD smote all the firstborn in the land of Egypt, from the firstborn of Pharaoh that sat on his throne unto the firstborn of the captive that was in the dungeon; and all the firstborn of cattle.

And Pharaoh rose up in the night, he, and all his servants, and all the Egyptians; and there was a great cry in Egypt; for there was not a house where there was not one dead. And he called for Moses and Aaron by night, and said, Rise up, and get you forth from among my people, both ye and the children of Israel; and go, serve the LORD, as ye have said. Also take your flocks and your herds, as ye have said, and be gone; and bless me also.

(Exodus 12:21-32)

Special Attention: *and bless me also*

Moses

And it came to pass on the morrow, that Moses said unto the people, Ye have sinned a great sin: and now I will go up unto the LORD; peradventure I shall make an atonement for your sin.

And Moses returned unto the LORD, and said, Oh, this people have sinned a great sin, and have made them gods of gold. Yet now, if thou wilt forgive their sin--; and if not, blot me, I pray thee, out of thy book which thou hast written.

And the LORD said unto Moses, Whosoever hath sinned against me, him will I blot out of my book.
  (Exodus 32:30-33)

And when the people complained, it displeased the LORD: and the LORD heard it; and his anger was kindled; and the fire of the LORD burnt among them, and consumed them that were in the uttermost parts of the camp.

And the people cried unto Moses; and when Moses prayed unto the LORD, the fire was quenched. And he called the name of the place Taberah: because the fire of the LORD burnt among them.
  (Numbers 11:1-3)

And Joshua the son of Nun, and Caleb the son of Jephunneh, which were of them that searched the land, rent their clothes: And they spake unto all the company of the children of Israel, saying, The land, which we passed through to search it, is an exceeding good land. If the LORD delight in us, then he will bring us into this land, and give it us; a land which floweth with milk and honey. Only rebel not ye against the LORD, neither fear ye the people of the land; for they are bread for us: their defence is departed from them, and the LORD is with us: fear them not.

But all the congregation bade stone them with stones.

And the glory of the LORD appeared in the tabernacle of the congregation before all the children of Israel. And the LORD said unto Moses, How long will this people provoke me? and how long will it be ere they believe me, for all the signs which I have showed among them? I will smite them with the pestilence, and disinherit them, and will make of thee a greater nation and mightier than they.

And Moses said unto the LORD, Then the Egyptians shall hear it, (for thou broughtest up this people in thy might from among them;) And they will tell it to the inhabitants of this land: for they have heard that thou LORD art among this people, that thou LORD art seen face to face, and that thy cloud standeth over them, and that thou goest before them, by day time in a pillar of a cloud, and in a pillar of fire by night. Now if thou shalt kill all this people as one man, then the nations which have heard the fame of thee will speak, saying, Because the LORD was not able to bring this people into the land which he sware unto them, therefore he hath slain them in the wilderness.

And now, I beseech thee, let the power of my LORD be great, according as thou hast spoken, saying, The LORD is longsuffering, and of great mercy, forgiving iniquity and transgression, and by no means clearing the guilty, visiting the iniquity of the fathers upon the children unto the third and fourth generation. Pardon, I beseech thee, the iniquity of this people according unto the greatness of thy mercy, and as thou hast forgiven this people, from Egypt even until now.

And the LORD said, I have pardoned according to thy word:

(Numbers 14:6-20)

Joshua

*Now it came to pass, when Adonizedek king of Jerusalem
had heard how Joshua had taken Ai, and had utterly
destroyed it; as he had done to Jericho and her king, so
he had done to Ai and her king; and how the inhabitants
of Gibeon had made peace with Israel, and were among
them; That they feared greatly, because Gibeon was
a great city, as one of the royal cities, and because it was
greater than Ai, and all the men thereof were mighty.
Wherefore Adonizedek king of Jerusalem sent unto
Hoham king of Hebron, and unto Piram king of Jarmuth,
and unto Japhia king of Lachish, and unto Debir king of
Eglon, saying, Come up unto me, and help me, that we
may smite Gibeon: for it hath made peace with Joshua
and with the children of Israel.*

*Therefore the five kings of the Amorites, the king of
Jerusalem, the king of Hebron, the king of Jarmuth, the
king of Lachish, the king of Eglon, gathered themselves
together, and went up, they and all their hosts, and
encamped before Gibeon, and made war against it.*

*And the men of Gibeon sent unto Joshua to the camp to
Gilgal, saying, Slack not thy hand from thy servants;
come up to us quickly, and save us, and help us: for all
the kings of the Amorites that dwell in the mountains are
gathered together against us. So Joshua ascended from
Gilgal, he, and all the people of war with him, and all the
mighty men of valour.*

*And the LORD said unto Joshua, Fear them not: for
I have delivered them into thine hand; there shall not
a man of them stand before thee.*

*Joshua therefore came unto them suddenly, and went up
from Gilgal all night. And the LORD discomfited them
before Israel, and slew them with a great slaughter at
Gibeon, and chased them along the way that goeth up to
Bethhoron, and smote them to Azekah, and unto
Makkedah.*

And it came to pass, as they fled from before Israel, and were in the going down to Bethhoron, that the LORD cast down great stones from heaven upon them unto Azekah, and they died: they were more which died with hailstones than they whom the children of Israel slew with the sword.

Then spake Joshua to the LORD in the day when the LORD delivered up the Amorites before the children of Israel, and he said in the sight of Israel, Sun, stand thou still upon Gibeon; and thou, Moon, in the valley of Ajalon. And the sun stood still, and the moon stayed, until the people had avenged themselves upon their enemies. Is not this written in the book of Jasher? So the sun stood still in the midst of heaven, and hasted not to go down about a whole day.

(Joshua 10:1-13)

Daniel

In the third year of the reign of Jehoiakim king of Judah came Nebuchadnezzar king of Babylon unto Jerusalem, and besieged it. And the Lord gave Jehoiakim king of Judah into his hand, with part of the vessels of the house of God: which he carried into the land of Shinar to the house of his god; and he brought the vessels into the treasure house of his god.

And the king spake unto Ashpenaz the master of his eunuchs, that he should bring certain of the children of Israel, and of the king's seed, and of the princes; Children in whom was no blemish, but well favoured, and skilful in all wisdom, and cunning in knowledge, and understanding science, and such as had ability in them to stand in the king's palace, and whom they might teach the learning and the tongue of the Chaldeans. And the king appointed them a daily provision of the king's meat, and of the wine which he drank: so nourishing them three years, that at the end thereof they might stand before the king.

Now among these were of the children of Judah, Daniel, Hananiah, Mishael, and Azariah: Unto whom the prince of the eunuchs gave names: for he gave unto Daniel the name of Belteshazzar; and to Hananiah, of Shadrach; and to Mishael, of Meshach; and to Azariah, of Abednego. But Daniel purposed in his heart that he would not defile himself with the portion of the king's meat, nor with the wine which he drank: therefore he requested of the prince of the eunuchs that he might not defile himself. Now God had brought Daniel into favour and tender love with the prince of the eunuchs.
(Daniel 1:1-9)

And the decree went forth that the wise men should be slain; and they sought Daniel and his fellows to be slain. Then Daniel answered with counsel and wisdom to Arioch the captain of the king's guard, which was gone forth to slay the wise men of Babylon: He answered and said to Arioch the king's captain, Why is the decree so hasty from the king? Then Arioch made the thing known to Daniel. Then Daniel went in, and desired of the king that he would give him time, and that he would show the king the interpretation.

Then Daniel went to his house, and made the thing known to Hananiah, Mishael, and Azariah, his companions: That they would desire mercies of the God of heaven concerning this secret; that Daniel and his fellows should not perish with the rest of the wise men of Babylon.

Then was the secret revealed unto Daniel in a night vision. Then Daniel blessed the God of heaven. Daniel answered and said, Blessed be the name of God for ever and ever: for wisdom and might are his: And he changeth the times and the seasons: he removeth kings, and setteth up kings: he giveth wisdom unto the wise, and knowledge to them that know understanding: He revealeth the deep and secret things: he knoweth what is in the darkness, and the light dwelleth with him. I thank thee, and praise thee, O thou God of my fathers, who hast given me wisdom and might, and hast made known unto me now what we desired of thee: for thou hast now made known unto us the king's matter.

Therefore Daniel went in unto Arioch, whom the king had ordained to destroy the wise men of Babylon: he went and said thus unto him; Destroy not the wise men of Babylon: bring me in before the king, and I will show unto the king the interpretation.

Then Arioch brought in Daniel before the king in haste, and said thus unto him, I have found a man of the captives of Judah, that will make known unto the king the interpretation.

The king answered and said to Daniel, whose name was Belteshazzar, Art thou able to make known unto me the dream which I have seen, and the interpretation thereof?

*Daniel answered in the presence of the king, and said,
The secret which the king hath demanded cannot the
wise men, the astrologers, the magicians, the
soothsayers, show unto the king; But there is a God in
heaven that revealeth secrets, and maketh known to the
king Nebuchadnezzar what shall be in the latter days.
Thy dream, and the visions of thy head upon thy bed, are
these; As for thee, O king, thy thoughts came into thy
mind upon thy bed, what should come to pass hereafter:
and he that revealeth secrets maketh known to thee what
shall come to pass. But as for me, this secret is not
revealed to me for any wisdom that I have more than any
living, but for their sakes that shall make known the
interpretation to the king, and that thou mightest know
the thoughts of thy heart.*
     (Daniel 2:13-30)

*Then said these men, We shall not find any occasion
against this Daniel, except we find it against him
concerning the law of his God. Then these presidents
and princes assembled together to the king, and said
thus unto him, King Darius, live for ever. All the
presidents of the kingdom, the governors, and the
princes, the counsellors, and the captains, have
consulted together to establish a royal statute, and to
make a firm decree, that whosoever shall ask a petition
of any God or man for thirty days, save of thee, O king,
he shall be cast into the den of lions. Now, O king,
establish the decree, and sign the writing, that it be not
changed, according to the law of the Medes and
Persians, which altereth not.*

*Wherefore king Darius signed the writing and the
decree.*

*Now when Daniel knew that the writing was signed,
he went into his house; and his windows being open in
his chamber toward Jerusalem, he kneeled upon his
knees three times a day, and prayed, and gave thanks
before his God, as he did aforetime. Then these men
assembled, and found Daniel praying and making*

supplication before his God. Then they came near, and spake before the king concerning the king's decree; Hast thou not signed a decree, that every man that shall ask a petition of any God or man within thirty days, save of thee, O king, shall be cast into the den of lions?

The king answered and said, The thing is true, according to the law of the Medes and Persians, which altereth not.

Then answered they and said before the king, That Daniel, which is of the children of the captivity of Judah, regardeth not thee, O king, nor the decree that thou hast signed, but maketh his petition three times a day.

Then the king, when he heard these words, was sore displeased with himself, and set his heart on Daniel to deliver him: and he laboured till the going down of the sun to deliver him.

Then these men assembled unto the king, and said unto the king, Know, O king, that the law of the Medes and Persians is, That no decree nor statute which the king establisheth may be changed.

Then the king commanded, and they brought Daniel, and cast him into the den of lions. Now the king spake and said unto Daniel, Thy God whom thou servest continually, he will deliver thee. And a stone was brought, and laid upon the mouth of the den; and the king sealed it with his own signet, and with the signet of his lords; that the purpose might not be changed concerning Daniel. Then the king went to his palace, and passed the night fasting: neither were instruments of music brought before him: and his sleep went from him.

Then the king arose very early in the morning, and went in haste unto the den of lions. And when he came to the den, he cried with a lamentable voice unto Daniel: and the king spake and said to Daniel, O Daniel, servant of the living God, is thy God, whom thou servest continually, able to deliver thee from the lions?

Then said Daniel unto the king, O king, live for ever. My God hath sent his angel, and hath shut the lions' mouths, that they have not hurt me: forasmuch as before him innocency was found in me; and also before thee, O king, have I done no hurt.

Then was the king exceeding glad for him, and commanded that they should take Daniel up out of the den. So Daniel was taken up out of the den, and no manner of hurt was found upon him, because he believed in his God. And the king commanded, and they brought those men which had accused Daniel, and they cast them into the den of lions, them, their children, and their wives; and the lions had the mastery of them, and brake all their bones in pieces or ever they came at the bottom of the den.

Then king Darius wrote unto all people, nations, and languages, that dwell in all the earth; Peace be multiplied unto you. I make a decree, That in every dominion of my kingdom men tremble and fear before the God of Daniel: for he is the living God, and stedfast for ever, and his kingdom that which shall not be destroyed, and his dominion shall be even unto the end. He delivereth and rescueth, and he worketh signs and wonders in heaven and in earth, who hath delivered Daniel from the power of the lions.

So this Daniel prospered in the reign of Darius, and in the reign of Cyrus the Persian
        (Daniel 6:5-28)

Nebuchadnezzar

Nebuchadnezzar the king, unto all people, nations, and languages, that dwell in all the earth; Peace be multiplied unto you. I thought it good to show the signs and wonders that the high God hath wrought toward me. How great are his signs! and how mighty are his wonders! his kingdom is an everlasting kingdom, and his dominion is from generation to generation.

I Nebuchadnezzar was at rest in mine house, and flourishing in my palace: I saw a dream which made me afraid, and the thoughts upon my bed and the visions of my head troubled me. Therefore made I a decree to bring in all the wise men of Babylon before me, that they might make known unto me the interpretation of the dream.

Then came in the magicians, the astrologers, the Chaldeans, and the soothsayers: and I told the dream before them; but they did not make known unto me the interpretation thereof. But at the last Daniel came in before me, whose name was Belteshazzar, according to the name of my god, and in whom is the spirit of the holy gods: and before him I told the dream, saying, O Belteshazzar, master of the magicians, because I know that the spirit of the holy gods is in thee, and no secret troubleth thee, tell me the visions of my dream that I have seen, and the interpretation thereof.

Thus were the visions of mine head in my bed; I saw, and behold, a tree in the midst of the earth, and the height thereof was great. The tree grew, and was strong, and the height thereof reached unto heaven, and the sight thereof to the end of all the earth: The leaves thereof were fair, and the fruit thereof much, and in it was meat for all: the beasts of the field had shadow under it, and the fowls of the heaven dwelt in the boughs thereof, and all flesh was fed of it. I saw in the visions of my head upon my bed, and, behold, a watcher and an holy one came down from heaven; He cried aloud, and said thus,

Hew down the tree, and cut off his branches, shake off his leaves, and scatter his fruit: let the beasts get away from under it, and the fowls from his branches: Nevertheless leave the stump of his roots in the earth, even with a band of iron and brass, in the tender grass of the field; and let it be wet with the dew of heaven, and let his portion be with the beasts in the grass of the earth: Let his heart be changed from man's, and let a beast's heart be given unto him: and let seven times pass over him.

This matter is by the decree of the watchers, and the demand by the word of the holy ones: to the intent that the living may know that the most High ruleth in the kingdom of men, and giveth it to whomsoever he will, and setteth up over it the basest of men.

This dream I king Nebuchadnezzar have seen. Now thou, O Belteshazzar, declare the interpretation thereof, forasmuch as all the wise men of my kingdom are not able to make known unto me the interpretation: but thou art able; for the spirit of the holy gods is in thee.

Then Daniel, whose name was Belteshazzar, was astonied for one hour, and his thoughts troubled him.

The king spake, and said, Belteshazzar, let not the dream, or the interpretation thereof, trouble thee.

Belteshazzar answered and said, My lord, the dream be to them that hate thee, and the interpretation thereof to thine enemies. The tree that thou sawest, which grew, and was strong, whose height reached unto the heaven, and the sight thereof to all the earth; Whose leaves were fair, and the fruit thereof much, and in it was meat for all; under which the beasts of the field dwelt, and upon whose branches the fowls of the heaven had their habitation: It is thou, O king, that art grown and become strong: for thy greatness is grown, and reacheth unto heaven, and thy dominion to the end of the earth.

And whereas the king saw a watcher and an holy one coming down from heaven, and saying, Hew the tree down, and destroy it; yet leave the stump of the roots thereof in the earth, even with a band of iron and brass, in the tender grass of the field; and let it be wet with the dew of heaven, and let his portion be with the beasts of the field, till seven times pass over him; This is the interpretation, O king, and this is the decree of the most High, which is come upon my lord the king: That they shall drive thee from men, and thy dwelling shall be with the beasts of the field, and they shall make thee to eat grass as oxen, and they shall wet thee with the dew of heaven, and seven times shall pass over thee, till thou know that the most High ruleth in the kingdom of men, and giveth it to whomsoever he will.

And whereas they commanded to leave the stump of the tree roots; thy kingdom shall be sure unto thee, after that thou shalt have known that the heavens do rule. Wherefore, O king, let my counsel be acceptable unto thee, and break off thy sins by righteousness, and thine iniquities by showing mercy to the poor; if it may be a lengthening of thy tranquillity.

All this came upon the king Nebuchadnezzar. At the end of twelve months he walked in the palace of the kingdom of Babylon. The king spake, and said, Is not this great Babylon, that I have built for the house of the kingdom by the might of my power, and for the honour of my majesty? While the word was in the king's mouth, there fell a voice from heaven, saying, O king Nebuchadnezzar, to thee it is spoken; The kingdom is departed from thee. And they shall drive thee from men, and thy dwelling shall be with the beasts of the field: they shall make thee to eat grass as oxen, and seven times shall pass over thee, until thou know that the most High ruleth in the kingdom of men, and giveth it to whomsoever he will.

The same hour was the thing fulfilled upon Nebuchadnezzar: and he was driven from men, and did eat grass as oxen, and his body was wet with the dew of heaven, till his hairs were grown like eagles' feathers, and his nails like birds' claws.

And at the end of the days I Nebuchadnezzar lifted up mine eyes unto heaven, and mine understanding returned unto me, and I blessed the most High, and I praised and honoured him that liveth for ever, whose dominion is an everlasting dominion, and his kingdom is from generation to generation: And all the inhabitants of the earth are reputed as nothing: and he doeth according to his will in the army of heaven, and among the inhabitants of the earth: and none can stay his hand, or say unto him, What doest thou? At the same time my reason returned unto me; and for the glory of my kingdom, mine honour and brightness returned unto me; and my counsellors and my lords sought unto me; and I was established in my kingdom, and excellent majesty was added unto me.

Now I Nebuchadnezzar praise and extol and honour the King of heaven, all whose works are truth, and his ways judgment: and those that walk in pride he is able to abase.
(Daniel 4:1-37)

NOTE: Even those who do not consistently revere God will be used by Him to accomplish His will. It is not for them to try to go around God or to try to set themselves above God. God will be honored even in those who have imperfect knowledge of His ways. Furthermore, the blessings of God will be bestowed on those who honor His way and His people, even though they may seem to be outsiders.

Belshazzar

Belshazzar the king made a great feast to a thousand of his lords, and drank wine before the thousand. Belshazzar, whiles he tasted the wine, commanded to bring the golden and silver vessels which his father Nebuchadnezzar had taken out of the temple which was in Jerusalem; that the king, and his princes, his wives, and his concubines, might drink therein.

Then they brought the golden vessels that were taken out of the temple of the house of God which was at Jerusalem; and the king, and his princes, his wives, and his concubines, drank in them. They drank wine, and praised the gods of gold, and of silver, of brass, of iron, of wood, and of stone.

In the same hour came forth fingers of a man's hand, and wrote over against the candlestick upon the plaster of the wall of the king's palace: and the king saw the part of the hand that wrote.

Then the king's countenance was changed, and his thoughts troubled him, so that the joints of his loins were loosed, and his knees smote one against another. The king cried aloud to bring in the astrologers, the Chaldeans, and the soothsayers. And the king spake, and said to the wise men of Babylon, Whosoever shall read this writing, and show me the interpretation thereof, shall be clothed with scarlet, and have a chain of gold about his neck, and shall be the third ruler in the kingdom.

Then came in all the king's wise men: but they could not read the writing, nor make known to the king the interpretation thereof. Then was king Belshazzar greatly troubled, and his countenance was changed in him, and his lords were astonied.

Now the queen by reason of the words of the king and his lords came into the banquet house: and the queen spake

*and said, O king, live for ever: let not thy thoughts
trouble thee, nor let thy countenance be changed: There
is a man in thy kingdom, in whom is the spirit of the holy
gods; and in the days of thy father light and
understanding and wisdom, like the wisdom of the gods,
was found in him; whom the king Nebuchadnezzar thy
father, the king, I say, thy father, made master of the
magicians, astrologers, Chaldeans, and soothsayers;
Forasmuch as an excellent spirit, and knowledge, and
understanding, interpreting of dreams, and showing of
hard sentences, and dissolving of doubts, were found in
the same Daniel, whom the king named Belteshazzar:
now let Daniel be called, and he will show the
interpretation.*

*Then was Daniel brought in before the king. And the
king spake and said unto Daniel, Art thou that Daniel,
which art of the children of the captivity of Judah, whom
the king my father brought out of Jewry? I have even
heard of thee, that the spirit of the gods is in thee, and
that light and understanding and excellent wisdom is
found in thee. And now the wise men, the astrologers,
have been brought in before me, that they should read
this writing, and make known unto me the interpretation
thereof: but they could not show the interpretation of the
thing: And I have heard of thee, that thou canst make
interpretations, and dissolve doubts: now if thou canst
read the writing, and make known to me the
interpretation thereof, thou shalt be clothed with scarlet,
and have a chain of gold about thy neck, and shalt be the
third ruler in the kingdom.*

*Then Daniel answered and said before the king, Let thy
gifts be to thyself, and give thy rewards to another; yet
I will read the writing unto the king, and make known to
him the interpretation. O thou king, the most high God
gave Nebuchadnezzar thy father a kingdom, and
majesty, and glory, and honour: And for the majesty that
he gave him, all people, nations, and languages,
trembled and feared before him: whom he would*

he slew; and whom he would he kept alive; and whom he would he set up; and whom he would he put down. But when his heart was lifted up, and his mind hardened in pride, he was deposed from his kingly throne, and they took his glory from him: And he was driven from the sons of men; and his heart was made like the beasts, and his dwelling was with the wild asses: they fed him with grass like oxen, and his body was wet with the dew of heaven; till he knew that the most high God ruled in the kingdom of men, and that he appointeth over it whomsoever he will.

And thou his son, O Belshazzar, hast not humbled thine heart, though thou knewest all this; But hast lifted up thyself against the Lord of heaven; and they have brought the vessels of his house before thee, and thou, and thy lords, thy wives, and thy concubines, have drunk wine in them; and thou hast praised the gods of silver, and gold, of brass, iron, wood, and stone, which see not, nor hear, nor know: and the God in whose hand thy breath is, and whose are all thy ways, hast thou not glorified: Then was the part of the hand sent from him; and this writing was written.

And this is the writing that was written,

MENE, MENE, TEKEL, UPHARSIN.

This is the interpretation of the thing:

MENE; God hath numbered thy kingdom, and finished it.

TEKEL; Thou art weighed in the balances, and art found wanting.

PERES; Thy kingdom is divided, and given to the Medes and Persians

Then commanded Belshazzar, and they clothed Daniel with scarlet, and put a chain of gold about his neck, and made a proclamation concerning him, that he should be the third ruler in the kingdom.

(Daniel 5:1-29)

NOTE: Even when God pronounces a sentence of death on a person, the promises made by that person are still binding. Furthermore, a man who is placed under burden by God and who fears God will not try to revenge himself against another because of the burden given to them.

Some observations

Let's now do an evaluation of some of the messages contained in the lives of these men.

It is wise to respect our rulers.

> *Obey them that have the rule over you, and submit yourselves: for they watch for your souls, as they that must give account, that they may do it with joy, and not with grief: for that is unprofitable for you.*
> (Hebrews 13:17)

> *And Joseph was brought down to Egypt; and Potiphar, an officer of Pharaoh, captain of the guard, an Egyptian, bought him of the hands of the Ishmeelites, which had brought him down thither.*

> *And the LORD was with Joseph, and he was a prosperous man; and he was in the house of his master the Egyptian. And his master saw that the LORD was with him, and that the LORD made all that he did to prosper in his hand. And Joseph found grace in his sight, and he served him: and he made him overseer over his house, and all that he had he put into his hand.*

> *And it came to pass from the time that he had made him overseer in his house, and over all that he had, that the LORD blessed the Egyptian's house for Joseph's sake; and the blessing of the LORD was upon all that he had in the house, and in the field. And he left all that he had in Joseph's hand; and he knew not ought he had, save the bread which he did eat.*

> *And Joseph was a goodly person, and well favoured.*
> (Genesis 39:1-6)

Only God establishes kings, kingdoms, power and principalities.

This is stated in the Old Testament.

> *Daniel answered and said, Blessed be the name of God for ever and ever: for wisdom and might are his: And he changeth the times and the seasons: he removeth kings, and setteth up kings: he giveth wisdom unto the*

wise, and knowledge to them that know understanding:
He revealeth the deep and secret things: he knoweth
what is in the darkness, and the light dwelleth with him.
(Daniel 2:20-22)

It is also revealed in the New Testament.

Let every soul be subject unto the higher powers. For
there is no power but of God: the powers that be are
ordained of God. Whosoever therefore resisteth the
power, resisteth the ordinance of God: and they that
resist shall receive to themselves damnation. For rulers
are not a terror to good works, but to the evil. Wilt thou
then not be afraid of the power? do that which is good,
and thou shalt have praise of the same: For he is the
minister of God to thee for good. But if thou do that which
is evil, be afraid; for he beareth not the sword in vain: for
he is the minister of God, a revenger to execute wrath
upon him that doeth evil. Wherefore ye must needs be
subject, not only for wrath, but also for conscience sake.
(Romans 13:1-5)

God controls the destiny of a kingdom.

In the Old Testament it is often done through the direct
intervention of the LORD.

Behold, I send an Angel before thee, to keep thee in the
way, and to bring thee into the place which I have
prepared. Beware of him, and obey his voice, provoke
him not; for he will not pardon your transgressions: for
my name is in him.

But if thou shalt indeed obey his voice, and do all that
I speak; then I will be an enemy unto thine enemies, and
an adversary unto thine adversaries. For mine Angel
shall go before thee, and bring thee in unto the Amorites,
and the Hittites, and the Perizzites, and the Canaanites,
the Hivites, and the Jebusites: and I will cut them off.
Thou shalt not bow down to their gods, nor serve them,
nor do after their works: but thou shalt utterly overthrow
them, and quite break down their images.
(Exodus 23:20-24)

Under the Law of Love, manifested in the New Testament, destruction of a kingdom is eliminated as an option, at this time.

> *And it came to pass, when the time was come that he should be received up, he stedfastly set his face to go to Jerusalem, And sent messengers before his face: and they went, and entered into a village of the Samaritans, to make ready for him. And they did not receive him, because his face was as though he would go to Jerusalem.*
>
> *And when his disciples James and John saw this, they said, Lord, wilt thou that we command fire to come down from heaven, and consume them, even as Elias did?*
>
> *But he turned, and rebuked them, and said, Ye know not what manner of spirit ye are of. For the Son of man is not come to destroy men's lives, but to save them.*
>
> *And they went to another village.*
> (Luke 9:51-56)

However, the Messiah, also known as the Son of man, has received a promise from the Father that his is the eventual rule over the earth, in the fullness of time.

> *When the Son of man shall come in his glory, and all the holy angels with him, then shall he sit upon the throne of his glory: And before him shall be gathered all nations: and he shall separate them one from another, as a shepherd divideth his sheep from the goats: And he shall set the sheep on his right hand, but the goats on the left.*
>
> *Then shall the King say unto them on his right hand, Come, ye blessed of my Father, inherit the kingdom prepared for you from the foundation of the world: For I was an hungred, and ye gave me meat: I was thirsty, and ye gave me drink: I was a stranger, and ye took me in: Naked, and ye clothed me: I was sick, and ye visited me: I was in prison, and ye came unto me.*
>
> *Then shall the righteous answer him, saying, Lord, when saw we thee an hungred, and fed thee? or thirsty, and gave thee drink? When saw we thee a stranger, and took*

thee in? or naked, and clothed thee? Or when saw we thee sick, or in prison, and came unto thee?

And the King shall answer and say unto them, Verily I say unto you, Inasmuch as ye have done it unto one of the least of these my brethren, ye have done it unto me.

Then shall he say also unto them on the left hand, Depart from me, ye cursed, into everlasting fire, prepared for the devil and his angels: For I was an hungred, and ye gave me no meat: I was thirsty, and ye gave me no drink: I was a stranger, and ye took me not in: naked, and ye clothed me not: sick, and in prison, and ye visited me not.

Then shall they also answer him, saying, Lord, when saw we thee an hungred, or athirst, or a stranger, or naked, or sick, or in prison, and did not minister unto thee?

Then shall he answer them, saying, Verily I say unto you, Inasmuch as ye did it not to one of the least of these, ye did it not to me.

And these shall go away into everlasting punishment: but the righteous into life eternal.
(Matthew 25:31-46)

What does all this mean?

I have recently been reading about some of the children of Abraham who want to destroy the nation of others of the children of Abraham. From the Old Testament perspective, this requires a direct intervention by God. The proclamation of God's will may come through his prophets. If it is truly in the fashion of olden times, there will be many signs and wonders that will demonstrate to even the average servant of God that this is what must be. We have, however, moved into a new time, under a new dispensation. We have moved into the time that the prophet wrote about.

Behold, I will send my messenger, and he shall prepare the way before me: and the Lord, whom ye seek, shall suddenly come to his temple, even the messenger of the covenant, whom ye delight in: behold, he shall come, saith the LORD of hosts. But who may abide the day of his

coming? and who shall stand when he appeareth? for he is
like a refiner's fire, and like fullers' soap: And he shall sit
as a refiner and purifier of silver: and he shall purify the
sons of Levi, and purge them as gold and silver, that they
may offer unto the LORD an offering in righteousness.
(Malachi 3:1-3)

God has always been accessible to you through the witness of His prophets. He is now accessible to you directly; He does not send His commands through the prophets: they are already contained in His word. You are, therefore, without excuse if you blindly follow the orders of anyone to terminate any other human's life. The words of a single man, claiming to speak for God is not sufficient to eliminate your punishment from God for not turning to Him for His will. You have a responsibility to ask God for guidance by looking into His word. This is His word that is written in the Bible, but most motivating is that it is His word written on your heart.

But this shall be the covenant that I will make with the
house of Israel; After those days, saith the LORD, I will put
my law in their inward parts, and write it in their hearts;
and will be their God, and they shall be my people. And
they shall teach no more every man his neighbour, and
every man his brother, saying, Know the LORD: for they
shall all know me, from the least of them unto the greatest
of them, saith the LORD: for I will forgive their iniquity,
and I will remember their sin no more.
(Jeremiah 31:33-34)

And if that is too confusing, then go to Him in prayer. In this matter it is the life of your soul that is at stake, and this is far more important than your physical life.

The law cannot be a blind guide. The light of God's word and presence must be invoked. Consider the conflict that arose over one woman's sin and the resolution provided by the Law of Love. This resolution was an augmentation of the Law of Moses; following the spirit, not just the letter.

And the scribes and Pharisees brought unto him
a woman taken in adultery; and when they had set her in
the midst, They say unto him, Master, this woman was

taken in adultery, in the very act. Now Moses in the law commanded us, that such should be stoned: but what sayest thou? This they said, tempting him, that they might have to accuse him.

But Jesus stooped down, and with his finger wrote on the ground, as though he heard them not. So when they continued asking him, he lifted up himself, and said unto them, He that is without sin among you, let him first cast a stone at her. And again he stooped down, and wrote on the ground.

And they which heard it, being convicted by their own conscience, went out one by one, beginning at the eldest, even unto the last: and Jesus was left alone, and the woman standing in the midst.

When Jesus had lifted up himself, and saw none but the woman, he said unto her, Woman, where are those thine accusers? hath no man condemned thee?

She said, No man, Lord.

And Jesus said unto her, Neither do I condemn thee: go, and sin no more.
(John 8:3-11)

If you believe that Jesus was a prophet, at a minimum, then you must believe that he came with the message of God. As you read his message mentioned above about the conduct of the man of God in the human race, you will note that he cancelled any hint of holy wars, suicide bombings or other such methods of removing the enemy.

Ye have heard that it hath been said, An eye for an eye, and a tooth for a tooth: But I say unto you, That ye resist not evil: but whosoever shall smite thee on thy right cheek, turn to him the other also. And if any man will sue thee at the law, and take away thy coat, let him have thy cloak also. And whosoever shall compel thee to go a mile, go with him twain. Give to him that asketh thee, and from him that would borrow of thee turn not thou away.

Ye have heard that it hath been said, Thou shalt love thy neighbour, and hate thine enemy. But I say unto you,

Love your enemies, bless them that curse you, do good to them that hate you, and pray for them which despitefully use you, and persecute you; That ye may be the children of your Father which is in heaven: for he maketh his sun to rise on the evil and on the good, and sendeth rain on the just and on the unjust. For if ye love them which love you, what reward have ye? do not even the publicans the same? And if ye salute your brethren only, what do ye more than others? do not even the publicans so?

Be ye therefore perfect, even as your Father which is in heaven is perfect.
(Matthew 5:38-48)

Likewise, if you believe the prophets of the Old Testament you will realize that God is leading the world toward a time when there will be no more wars.

And there shall come forth a rod out of the stem of Jesse, and a Branch shall grow out of his roots: And the spirit of the LORD shall rest upon him, the spirit of wisdom and understanding, the spirit of counsel and might, the spirit of knowledge and of the fear of the LORD; And shall make him of quick understanding in the fear of the LORD: and he shall not judge after the sight of his eyes, neither reprove after the hearing of his ears: But with righteousness shall he judge the poor, and reprove with equity for the meek of the earth: and he shall smite the earth with the rod of his mouth, and with the breath of his lips shall he slay the wicked. And righteousness shall be the girdle of his loins, and faithfulness the girdle of his reins.

The wolf also shall dwell with the lamb, and the leopard shall lie down with the kid; and the calf and the young lion and the fatling together; and a little child shall lead them. And the cow and the bear shall feed; their young ones shall lie down together: and the lion shall eat straw like the ox. And the sucking child shall play on the hole of the asp, and the weaned child shall put his hand on the cockatrice' den.

They shall not hurt nor destroy in all my holy mountain: for the earth shall be full of the knowledge of the LORD, as the

waters cover the sea. And in that day there shall be a root of
Jesse, which shall stand for an ensign of the people; to it
shall the Gentiles seek: and his rest shall be glorious.
(Isaiah 11:1-10)

The messengers of God have spoken. Your choice now is to live according to human dictations, or to go directly to God and ask for guidance. Many religious leaders of today will have you sacrifice your well-being and your life for a matter that they *say* is from God. However, when the political climate changes and they are then at peace with a former enemy, the message changes. God does not change. If you want your enemies to be removed from your life, you have the power to do this by petitioning God for peace within yourself. No external force can overrule God in you.

And fear not them which kill the body, but are not able to
kill the soul: but rather fear him which is able to destroy
both soul and body in hell.
(Matthew 10:28)

Judas saith unto him, not Iscariot, Lord, how is it that
thou wilt manifest thyself unto us, and not unto the world?

Jesus answered and said unto him, If a man love me,
he will keep my words: and my Father will love him, and
we will come unto him, and make our abode with him.
He that loveth me not keepeth not my sayings: and the
word which ye hear is not mine, but the Father's which
sent me. These things have I spoken unto you, being yet
present with you. But the Comforter, which is the Holy
Ghost, whom the Father will send in my name, he shall
teach you all things, and bring all things to your
remembrance, whatsoever I have said unto you.

Peace I leave with you, my peace I give unto you: not as
the world giveth, give I unto you. Let not your heart be
troubled, neither let it be afraid.
(John 14:22-27)

The Word from the Bible

Habakkuk 2:18-20

What profiteth the graven image that the maker thereof hath graven it; the molten image, and a teacher of lies, that the maker of his work trusteth therein, to make dumb idols?

Woe unto him that saith to the wood, Awake; to the dumb stone, Arise, it shall teach! Behold, it is laid over with gold and silver, and there is no breath at all in the midst of it.

But the LORD is in his holy temple: let all the earth keep silence before him.

Psalm 4:1-8

To the chief Musician on Neginoth, A Psalm of David.

Hear me when I call, O God of my righteousness: thou hast enlarged me when I was in distress; have mercy upon me, and hear my prayer.

O ye sons of men, how long will ye turn my glory into shame? how long will ye love vanity, and seek after leasing? Selah.

But know that the LORD hath set apart him that is godly for himself: the LORD will hear when I call unto him. Stand in awe, and sin not: commune with your own heart upon your bed, and be still. Selah.

Offer the sacrifices of righteousness, and put your trust in the LORD. There be many that say, Who will show us any good?

LORD, lift thou up the light of thy countenance upon us. Thou hast put gladness in my heart, more than in the time that their corn and their wine increased. I will both lay me down in peace, and sleep: for thou, LORD, only makest me dwell in safety.

Malachi 4:1-6

For, behold, the day cometh, that shall burn as an oven; and all the proud, yea, and all that do wickedly, shall be stubble: and the day that cometh shall burn them up, saith the LORD of hosts, that it shall leave them neither root nor branch. But unto you that fear my name shall the Sun of righteousness arise with healing in his wings; and ye shall go forth, and grow up as calves of the stall. And ye shall tread down the wicked; for they shall be ashes under the soles of your feet in the day that I shall do this, saith the LORD of hosts. Remember ye the law of Moses my servant, which I commanded unto him in Horeb for all Israel, with the statutes and judgments.

Behold, I will send you Elijah the prophet before the coming of the great and dreadful day of the LORD: And he shall turn the heart of the fathers to the children, and the heart of the children to their fathers, lest I come and smite the earth with a curse.

Isaiah 11:1-9

And there shall come forth a rod out of the stem of Jesse, and a Branch shall grow out of his roots: And the spirit of the LORD shall rest upon him, the spirit of wisdom and understanding, the spirit of counsel and might, the spirit of knowledge and of the fear of the LORD; And shall make him of quick understanding in the fear of the LORD: and he shall not judge after the sight of his eyes, neither reprove after the hearing of his ears: But with righteousness shall he judge the poor, and reprove with equity for the meek of the earth: and he shall smite the earth with the rod of his mouth, and with the breath of his lips shall he slay the wicked. And righteousness shall be the girdle of his loins, and faithfulness the girdle of his reins.

The wolf also shall dwell with the lamb, and the leopard shall lie down with the kid; and the calf and the young lion and the fatling together; and a little child shall lead them. And the cow and the bear shall feed; their young ones shall lie down together: and the lion shall eat straw like the ox. And the sucking child shall play on the hole of the asp, and the weaned child shall put his hand on the cockatrice' den. They shall not hurt nor destroy in all my holy mountain: for the earth shall be full of the knowledge of the LORD, as the waters cover the sea.

Chapter Six

The Church Is In You

Many nations; one world.

The nations of the world seem to feel that they have each established the best way to live. Alliances have been formed of like-minded governments, for the most part, and life seems to be crystal clear. However, the people of the nations are not as sure as the governments of these same nations that this is so. There is unrest in all spheres of humanity. Some of this unrest is tolerated as the normal course of human existence. Some of this unrest is squashed as a threat to the continued form of the given government. In each case there are justifications for these attitudes. What, however, does God have to say about this?

To answer this question we will carry out a study of some of the phase of the development of mankind. We will look primarily at the collections of men that we mentioned above, the government. How has the government progressed over the years, and how has this been seen in the light of the Most High?

Phase 1 - Recognizing the existence of the Creator.

> *And Adam knew his wife again; and she bare a son, and called his name Seth: For God, said she, hath appointed me another seed instead of Abel, whom Cain slew. And to Seth, to him also there was born a son; and he called his name Enos: then began men to call upon the name of the LORD.*
> (Genesis 4:25-26)

At this point in mankind's history it became obvious, some may say necessary, that mankind discover the God of the universe. As more and more people were born there must have been some thought about the matters of origin and order: origin in the sense of man's search for the Creator. Order in the sense of knowing what forces had come into play to make the things that were seen around him.

The search for the Creator was the easiest part of it. Man was still young enough and localized enough to have heard the accounts of Adam and the contacts made by God with him. In this environment it was very easy to know who the Creator is; for there was a first hand, reliable account of the maker of the Universe's presence.

Knowing that God is the Creator of the universe is one of the key factors in mankind's turn to calling upon His name. They knew that there was none other who had done for them what he had done. If asked, they would have given an answer like unto that found in the New Testament. During this episode in Scripture, the apostles had just witnessed the desertion of many, so called, disciples. Jesus used this time to affirm their dedication to the mission of God. It is this affirmation that provides the similarity with those who were calling on the name of the LORD in the early history of our existence.

Then said Jesus unto the twelve, Will ye also go away?

Then Simon Peter answered him, Lord, to whom shall we go? thou hast the words of eternal life. And we believe and are sure that thou art that Christ, the Son of the living God.
(John 6:67-69)

So also might the children of Adam-extended have said to God: "To whom else shall we turn, thou alone hast the words of **natural** life".

As interactions between man and man started to increase, there were probably some differences of opinion that crept in. These differences of opinion, sometimes even arguments, must have led them to seek a system of ordering the life that they had been given. Again it was time to turn to the Creator.

God had indeed told them to *Be fruitful, and multiply, and replenish the earth, and subdue it: and have dominion over the fish of the sea, and over the fowl of the air, and over every living thing that moveth upon the earth.* (Genesis 1:28) However, how were they supposed to do this? To find the answer, *then began men to call upon the name of the LORD.*

Phase 2 - Conquer the animals (leviathan) - Theocracy

I will send my fear before thee, and will destroy all the people to whom thou shalt come, and I will make all thine enemies turn their backs unto thee. And I will send hornets before thee, which shall drive out the Hivite, the Canaanite, and the Hittite, from before thee. I will not drive them out from before thee in one year; lest the land become desolate, and the beast of the field multiply against thee. By little and little I will drive them out from before thee, until thou be increased, and inherit the land.
(Exodus 23:27-30)

When mankind began to recognize the Creator they also remembered the instructions that God had given to them. Other than being fruitful, man is to *have dominion over the fish of the sea, and over the fowl of the air, and over every living thing that moveth upon the earth.* This, however, started to slip because of mankind's drifting away from the central principle of relationship with God.

After the great falling away of the sons of God that occurred in the time of Noah, God had begun to establish a people who would serve Him. The major part of this service is to be a good steward over the world in which mankind is housed. God performed His part by establishing a covenant with man.

And God spake unto Noah, and to his sons with him, saying, And I, behold, I establish my covenant with you, and with your seed after you; And with every living creature that is with you, of the fowl, of the cattle, and of every beast of the earth with you; from all that go out of the ark, to every beast of the earth.
(Genesis 9:8-10)

That God establishes covenants with mankind doesn't seem to carry through in the minds of man to cause man to honor their side of the covenant with God. Therefore, God started a process that will illustrate to all mankind that they should indeed honor God. This process started by the selection of a man (Jacob) to be the father of a nation (Israel) whose only mission is to serve God.

Israel was not called forth to change the world directly, but only to serve God directly. We can see now, after the fact, that by serving God directly, this new nation was also able to point the way back to God.

This was done by example and by the spread of the message of God to the world.

This message of God is called the good news, or Gospel, of the Kingdom. It was spread to other lands by Israel when they were residents of these nations. As Israel entered these nations, in various ways, the message of God took on life in the midst of the other peoples. The first of these was Egypt under the Pharaohs. At first they entered Egypt as an honored guest. After a while, however, they were seen as a commodity to be exploited. In both cases, Israel was pushed to remember God. Their captivity did not escape His notice.

Before God took them to the point of being ready to carry the fully composed message, He gave them a place to call home. His provision of this *Promised Land* showed just how far mankind had slipped from the standard of Noah's day. For in this provision it was God who had to prepare the way. God had to wean man slowly back into digesting the meat of His purpose for mankind on the earth. God performed this weaning through various trying times for the nation of Israel; as examples for all mankind.

As we continue to list additional stages that God took the nation of Israel and the world through, our intention is to reveal God's provision for the time when all mankind is calling on the name of the LORD. A bonus that we will receive when this occurs is that the world will truly be *one nation under God*.

Phase 3 - Conquer one another, the establishment of principalities - Rulers

The nation of Israel finds itself at a point where it no longer respects God's ability to provide leadership for them. This was not totally unfounded since some of the rulers were not living up to their calling in God. However, instead of petitioning God for His intervention to provide righteous leaders, they decided to take matters into their own hands. They wanted a ruler that would be a representative for them to the nations around them. They wanted to have the same bragging rights that all the other nations had about the stature of their rulers. In this way they would establish themselves as a principality among the nations. They could then conquer in their own name and for their own purposes. God's way was placed on the back burner.

> *And it came to pass, when Samuel was old, that he made his sons judges over Israel. Now the name of his*

firstborn was Joel; and the name of his second, Abiah: they were judges in Beersheba. And his sons walked not in his ways, but turned aside after lucre, and took bribes, and perverted judgment.

Then all the elders of Israel gathered themselves together, and came to Samuel unto Ramah, And said unto him, Behold, thou art old, and thy sons walk not in thy ways: now make us a king to judge us like all the nations.

But the thing displeased Samuel, when they said, Give us a king to judge us. And Samuel prayed unto the LORD.
(1 Samuel 8:1-6)

It was no longer sufficient that they had a ruler who could not be seen; even though God spoke often in their midst.

And the LORD said unto Samuel, Hearken unto the voice of the people in all that they say unto thee: for they have not rejected thee, but they have rejected me, that I should not reign over them. According to all the works which they have done since the day that I brought them up out of Egypt even unto this day, wherewith they have forsaken me, and served other gods, so do they also unto thee. Now therefore hearken unto their voice: howbeit yet protest solemnly unto them, and show them the manner of the king that shall reign over them.
(1 Samuel 8:7-9)

Phase 4 - Humanitarian principles established for the nations - Leaders

After years of exploitation by the kings, God exalted a king who would establish the concept of fair dealing with the people of God. This king was not developed from the nation of Israel, but from one of the surrounding nations. In fact, the nation of Israel was under control of this king and his nation. Again God was delivering a message to the people of God and to the world at large. The message to the nation of Israel is that God has control over all nations. The message to the world at large is that God has control over all nations. (Yes, they are the same.)

The king that rose up, though he was not of the nation of Israel, acknowledged the grace that had been given to him by God. This is a very public example of God using the Gentile to establish his word. It set the stage for the participative forms of government that we now have, where the people have more of a place in the minds of the rulers. Conquering and being conquered was now giving way to a sense of responsibility for the conquered.

> *Now in the first year of Cyrus king of Persia, that the word of the LORD spoken by the mouth of Jeremiah might be accomplished, the LORD stirred up the spirit of Cyrus king of Persia, that he made a proclamation throughout all his kingdom, and put it also in writing, saying, Thus saith Cyrus king of Persia, All the kingdoms of the earth hath the LORD God of heaven given me; and he hath charged me to build him an house in Jerusalem, which is in Judah. Who is there among you of all his people? The LORD his God be with him, and let him go up.*
>
>   (2 Chronicles 36:22-23)

> *Now in the first year of Cyrus king of Persia, that the word of the LORD by the mouth of Jeremiah might be fulfilled, the LORD stirred up the spirit of Cyrus king of Persia, that he made a proclamation throughout all his kingdom, and put it also in writing, saying, Thus saith Cyrus king of Persia, The LORD God of heaven hath given me all the kingdoms of the earth; and he hath charged me to build him an house at Jerusalem, which is in Judah. Who is there among you of all his people? his God be with him, and let him go up to Jerusalem, which is in Judah, and build the house of the LORD God of Israel, (he is the God,) which is in Jerusalem.*

> *And whosoever remaineth in any place where he sojourneth, let the men of his place help him with silver, and with gold, and with goods, and with beasts, beside the freewill offering for the house of God that is in Jerusalem.*

> *Then rose up the chief of the fathers of Judah and Benjamin, and the priests, and the Levites, with all them whose spirit God had raised, to go up to build the house of the LORD which is in Jerusalem.*

> *And all they that were about them strengthened their hands with vessels of silver, with gold, with goods, and*

with beasts, and with precious things, beside all that was willingly offered. Also Cyrus the king brought forth the vessels of the house of the LORD, which Nebuchadnezzar had brought forth out of Jerusalem, and had put them in the house of his gods; Even those did Cyrus king of Persia bring forth by the hand of Mithredath the treasurer, and numbered them unto Sheshbazzar, the prince of Judah.

(Ezra 1:18)

And it came to pass in the month Nisan, in the twentieth year of Artaxerxes the king, that wine was before him: and I took up the wine, and gave it unto the king. Now I had not been beforetime sad in his presence. Wherefore the king said unto me, Why is thy countenance sad, seeing thou art not sick? this is nothing else but sorrow of heart.

Then I was very sore afraid, And said unto the king, Let the king live for ever: why should not my countenance be sad, when the city, the place of my fathers' sepulchres, lieth waste, and the gates thereof are consumed with fire?

Then the king said unto me, For what dost thou make request?

So I prayed to the God of heaven. And I said unto the king, If it please the king, and if thy servant have found favour in thy sight, that thou wouldest send me unto Judah, unto the city of my fathers' sepulchres, that I may build it.

And the king said unto me, (the queen also sitting by him,) For how long shall thy journey be? and when wilt thou return?

So it pleased the king to send me; and I set him a time. Moreover I said unto the king, If it please the king, let letters be given me to the governors beyond the river, that they may convey me over till I come into Judah; And a letter unto Asaph the keeper of the king's forest, that he may give me timber to make beams for the gates of the palace which appertained to the house, and for the wall of the city, and for the house that I shall enter into.

And the king granted me, according to the good hand of my God upon me.
        (Nehemiah 2:1-8)

Phase 5 - Roman model of government - Democracy

The participative form of government was extended during the time of the Roman Empire. In this era the rulers opened themselves up to audiences with the common people. They, of course, expected respect, but they also gave respect. Their rule over their nation no longer depended on just a show of power, but the concept of diplomacy became much more important. This is reflected in the pronouncements of God through His people. These pronouncements required that honor be paid to the rulers for their service. Indeed, the service of a ruler was once again revered as being specifically ordained by God. However, the service to God is still to be observed and that above the service to the rulers.

Then went the Pharisees, and took counsel how they might entangle him in his talk. And they sent out unto him their disciples with the Herodians, saying, Master, we know that thou art true, and teachest the way of God in truth, neither carest thou for any man: for thou regardest not the person of men. Tell us therefore, What thinkest thou? Is it lawful to give tribute unto Caesar, or not?

But Jesus perceived their wickedness, and said, Why tempt ye me, ye hypocrites? Shew me the tribute money.

And they brought unto him a penny.

And he saith unto them, Whose is this image and superscription?

They say unto him, Caesar's.

Then saith he unto them, Render therefore unto Caesar the things which are Caesar's; and unto God the things that are God's.

When they had heard these words, they marvelled, and left him, and went their way.
        (Matthew 22:15-22)

Let every soul be subject unto the higher powers. For there is no power but of God: the powers that be are ordained of God. Whosoever therefore resisteth the power, resisteth the ordinance of God: and they that resist shall receive to themselves damnation. For rulers are not a terror to good works, but to the evil. Wilt thou then not be afraid of the power? do that which is good, and thou shalt have praise of the same: For he is the minister of God to thee for good. But if thou do that which is evil, be afraid; for he beareth not the sword in vain: for he is the minister of God, a revenger to execute wrath upon him that doeth evil. Wherefore ye must needs be subject, not only for wrath, but also for conscience sake.

For for this cause pay ye tribute also: for they are God's ministers, attending continually upon this very thing. Render therefore to all their dues: tribute to whom tribute is due; custom to whom custom; fear to whom fear; honour to whom honour.

Owe no man any thing, but to love one another: for he that loveth another hath fulfilled the law.
        (Romans 13:1-8)

Phase 6 - Opening the door of Heaven - Messianic era (YOU ARE HERE)

This also paved the way for what is known as the Messianic era. Jesus came into a world where loyalty to rulers had been re-established as the norm in society. It had been codified in certain nations as a due service from those being ruled. It was not difficult for them to give this loyalty since the *new* ruler knew how to listen to the people he ruled. There were organizations in place, such as the Senate of the Roman Empire, which could keep the ruler informed of the needs of the people, or at least some of the people. Into this world Jesus came with the message of the Gospel.

God had prepared the world to receive the message of direct participation by the God of the universe in the affairs of man. The former methods of using an unlike substitute, as was done in the animal sacrifices, was about to be replaced. God was revealing to man that He had always been an active part of their existence. He now sent His servant to dwell as God with them and to partake of their life. No longer would man be able to say that the God of the universe is one of distant understanding. No longer could man claim that the things of God were impossible for a mere mortal man. The Ruler of the Universe is entering the Message of mankind's renewal, through his Ambassador.

This was the perfect way of intervening on behalf of the *common man,* with the ruler. Though God still maintains His lofty status and is far, far above man, there is now no longer an excuse. A man has been sent among men to represent and present God in full. This man is the mediator between man and God. Like the man Moses, this man would go to talk with God on our behalf. However, going even beyond Moses, this man showed us how we also may talk to God. The fear that held the children of Israel when God came into their midst was no longer an excuse. This type of fear would soon be unnecessary; and soon again, not tolerated: but this is ahead in our discovery path.

Through direct conversations with the man Jesus, God showed that He is accessible to all of us. We, however, have to remember to petition Him as did His Son Jesus. And we are told how to do that.

> *After this manner therefore pray ye: Our Father which art in heaven, Hallowed be thy name. Thy kingdom come, Thy will be done in earth, as it is in heaven. Give us this day our daily bread. And forgive us our debts, as we forgive our debtors. And lead us not into temptation, but deliver us from evil: For thine is the kingdom, and the power, and the glory, for ever. Amen.*
> (Matthew 6:9-13)

> *Seeing then that we have a great high priest, that is passed into the heavens, Jesus the Son of God, let us hold fast our profession. For we have not an high priest which cannot be touched with the feeling of our infirmities; but was in all points tempted like as we are, yet without sin. Let us therefore come boldly unto the throne of grace, that we may obtain mercy, and find grace to help in time of need.*
> (Hebrews 4:14)

> *At the same time came the disciples unto Jesus, saying, Who is the greatest in the kingdom of heaven?*

> *And Jesus called a little child unto him, and set him in the midst of them, And said, Verily I say unto you, Except ye be converted, and become as little children, ye shall*

not enter into the kingdom of heaven. Whosoever therefore shall humble himself as this little child, the same is greatest in the kingdom of heaven.
(Matthew 18:1-4)

Again I say unto you, That if two of you shall agree on earth as touching any thing that they shall ask, it shall be done for them of my Father which is in heaven. For where two or three are gathered together in my name, there am I in the midst of them.
(Matthew 18:19-20)

Phase 7 - God in you - Indwelling Spirit (WHERE WE NEED TO GO)

We have received a new challenge. This challenge is to incorporate the fullness of God within ourselves as did Jesus of Nazareth. True, we start at a later time than he did; for he started his journey to the provision of one of God's richest blessings to mankind at conception. In scientific terms, the life of Jesus of Nazareth, the Son of God, started with the fertilization of the egg. At this time he was given the spark of life from God and started to develop into a special vessel of God. We who are otherwise born are given the spark of life from our earthly father through our earthly mother. The earliest that we can activate the spark of God for a special calling is after birth. This was the case with John the Baptist.

However, no matter when we start, once we do start we receive the full power of the potentiality of God. This is not just a change of mind but a new force dwelling within. This force is called the Comforter. It is this force that places the church within each of us; and not just as a structure that is to be visited on occasion. We are the church and thus we are *in* church at all times. This adds a new responsibility to rightly deal with the body which is the church, which now reflects God.

We have an opportunity to petition God for full activation of the Comforter. Because of our limitations, this will most likely be done *by little and little*, but I am not prepared to limit the hand of God in your life to this method. If you seek it, and if it conforms to His will, you might just see the full activation in an instant in time. This is between you and God.

Jesus saith unto him, Have I been so long time with you, and yet hast thou not known me, Philip? he that hath seen me hath seen the Father; and how sayest thou then,

Show us the Father? Believest thou not that I am in the Father, and the Father in me? the words that I speak unto you I speak not of myself: but the Father that dwelleth in me, he doeth the works. Believe me that I am in the Father, and the Father in me: or else believe me for the very works' sake.

Verily, verily, I say unto you, He that believeth on me, the works that I do shall he do also; and greater works than these shall he do; because I go unto my Father. And whatsoever ye shall ask in my name, that will I do, that the Father may be glorified in the Son. If ye shall ask any thing in my name, I will do it.

If ye love me, keep my commandments. And I will pray the Father, and he shall give you another Comforter, that he may abide with you for ever; Even the Spirit of truth; whom the world cannot receive, because it seeth him not, neither knoweth him: but ye know him; for he dwelleth with you, and shall be in you.
(John 14:9-17)

Jesus answered and said unto him, If a man love me, he will keep my words: and my Father will love him, and we will come unto him, and make our abode with him. He that loveth me not keepeth not my sayings: and the word which ye hear is not mine, but the Father's which sent me.

These things have I spoken unto you, being yet present with you. But the Comforter, which is the Holy Ghost, whom the Father will send in my name, he shall teach you all things, and bring all things to your remembrance, whatsoever I have said unto you. Peace I leave with you, my peace I give unto you: not as the world giveth, give I unto you. Let not your heart be troubled, neither let it be afraid.
(John 14:23-27)

If I had not done among them the works which none other man did, they had not had sin: but now have they both seen and hated both me and my Father. But this cometh to pass, that the word might be fulfilled that is

written in their law, They hated me without a cause. But when the Comforter is come, whom I will send unto you from the Father, even the Spirit of truth, which proceedeth from the Father, he shall testify of me: And ye also shall bear witness, because ye have been with me from the beginning.
(John 15:24-27)

For other foundation can no man lay than that is laid, which is Jesus Christ. Now if any man build upon this foundation gold, silver, precious stones, wood, hay, stubble; Every man's work shall be made manifest: for the day shall declare it, because it shall be revealed by fire; and the fire shall try every man's work of what sort it is. If any man's work abide which he hath built thereupon, he shall receive a reward. If any man's work shall be burned, he shall suffer loss: but he himself shall be saved; yet so as by fire.

Know ye not that ye are the temple of God, and that the Spirit of God dwelleth in you? If any man defile the temple of God, him shall God destroy; for the temple of God is holy, which temple ye are.
(1 Corinthians3:11-17)

Final Phase - One Christian nation in God

For thus saith the LORD that created the heavens; God himself that formed the earth and made it; he hath established it, he created it not in vain, he formed it to be inhabited: I am the LORD; and there is none else. I have not spoken in secret, in a dark place of the earth: I said not unto the seed of Jacob, Seek ye me in vain: I the LORD speak righteousness, I declare things that are right. Assemble yourselves and come; draw near together, ye that are escaped of the nations: they have no knowledge that set up the wood of their graven image, and pray unto a god that cannot save. Tell ye, and bring them near; yea, let them take counsel together: who hath declared this from ancient time? who hath told it from that time? have not I the LORD? and there is no God else beside me; a just God and a Saviour; there is none beside me.

Look unto me, and be ye saved, all the ends of the earth: for I am God, and there is none else. I have sworn by myself, the word is gone out of my mouth in righteousness, and shall not return, That unto me every knee shall bow, every tongue shall swear. Surely, shall one say, in the LORD have I righteousness and strength: even to him shall men come; and all that are incensed against him shall be ashamed. In the LORD shall all the seed of Israel be justified, and shall glory.
        (Isaiah 45:18-25)

Let this mind be in you, which was also in Christ Jesus: Who, being in the form of God, thought it not robbery to be equal with God: But made himself of no reputation, and took upon him the form of a servant, and was made in the likeness of men: And being found in fashion as a man, he humbled himself, and became obedient unto death, even the death of the cross. Wherefore God also hath highly exalted him, and given him a name which is above every name: That at the name of Jesus every knee should bow, of things in heaven, and things in earth, and things under the earth; And that every tongue should confess that Jesus Christ is Lord, to the glory of God the Father.
        (Philippians 2:5-11)

For those who are currently of a different theological mindset than Christianity, let's look at the ending of this message: *to the glory of God the Father*. No matter what you wish to call yourself, even agnostic and atheist, your final existence will be *to the glory of God the Father*. You may have different views of God than Christians do, but you will all bow to God in the final wrap-up. I am not pointing the way to one nation under gods, but to one nation in God.

For those who are agnostics and those who call themselves atheists, your god will be death. This applies also to those who don't believe that man is eternal, or who think that this earth is all there is. This is the one thing that will rule over all, no matter who we are. But what then happens if death is also subject to another? What is the outcome when death is subject to God?

For all others, there is a personal being that will usher them into the final state that they will stay in for eternity. Death may be viewed as an eternal state for those who don't believe in a personal God. However, since there is a personal Creator of the universe, there is a God. Furthermore, since all that is, came from the being that preceded it; ultimately coming from God who preceded it all, I choose to call Him the Most High God.

This leaves one point for exploration. This is the question: when will you come to grips with the limitations of mankind and succumb to the rule of love? When will we all understand that just as happens in childhood disputes, so is happening in the world today? For those who have forgotten their childhood, let me refresh your recollection. A child gets into a fight with another child and loses. The child then goes to tell his big brother (uncle, friend, fellow gang member or some other person) and vengeance is sought. And indeed vengeance may be achieved. Then there is another loser. This loser goes to his big brother (uncle, friend, fellow gang member, etc.) and vengeance is again sought. There is again another loser; so the cycle continues.

This cycle will continue creating more and more losers as it goes on. The objective of this cycle is to continue until all are losers. The *winners* think that the objective is for them to win, but for them to win someone else must lose. And the loser will not quit until they have beat the winners, thus creating more losers. With this cycle there will be mounds of losers but only one real winner. This winner may be a person or group of persons, but there are tons of other persons or groups that will be the losers.

Only someone outside of the circle of spite can make the difference. This someone must have a superior solution that will remove the desire for victory and that will quench the fire of loss. As man moves up the chain from community to city to state to province to country to nation, there will be only one who can provide such a solution. There is only one who is outside of the cycle. This one is God.

The gift that God will bestow on those who are ready to reach the highest level that mankind will reach is to provide them with the power to replicate the solution that He gives. This will come through placing in them a portion of the intelligence (some like to call it Spirit) that powers the Divine. God gave an example of this process in the Bible with his servant Moses.

And Moses said, The people, among whom I am, are six hundred thousand footmen; and thou hast said, I will give them flesh, that they may eat a whole month. Shall the flocks and the herds be slain for them, to suffice them? or shall all the fish of the sea be gathered together for them, to suffice them?

And the LORD said unto Moses, Is the LORD'S hand waxed short? thou shalt see now whether my word shall come to pass unto thee or not.

And Moses went out, and told the people the words of the LORD, and gathered the seventy men of the elders of the people, and set them round about the tabernacle. And the LORD came down in a cloud, and spake unto him, and took of the spirit that was upon him, and gave it unto the seventy elders: and it came to pass, that, when the spirit rested upon them, they prophesied, and did not cease.

But there remained two of the men in the camp, the name of the one was Eldad, and the name of the other Medad: and the spirit rested upon them; and they were of them that were written, but went not out unto the tabernacle: and they prophesied in the camp. And there ran a young man, and told Moses, and said, Eldad and Medad do prophesy in the camp. And Joshua the son of Nun, the servant of Moses, one of his young men, answered and said, My lord Moses, forbid them.

And Moses said unto him, Enviest thou for my sake? would God that all the LORD'S people were prophets, and that the LORD would put his spirit upon them! And Moses gat him into the camp, he and the elders of Israel.
(Number 11:21-30)

There is another example with the prophets Elijah and Elisha.

And Elijah took his mantle, and wrapped it together, and smote the waters, and they were divided hither and thither, so that they two went over on dry ground. And it came to pass, when they were gone over, that Elijah said unto Elisha, Ask what I shall do for thee, before I be taken away from thee. And Elisha said, I pray thee, let

a double portion of thy spirit be upon me. And he said,
Thou hast asked a hard thing: nevertheless, if thou see
me when I am taken from thee, it shall be so unto thee;
but if not, it shall not be so.
       (2 Kings 2:8-10)

Both Moses and Elijah were humans. There is a potent Spirit that is available to all mankind. This was revealed by His Son, Jesus Christ.

If ye love me, keep my commandments. And I will pray
the Father, and he shall give you another Comforter,
that he may abide with you for ever; Even the Spirit of
truth; whom the world cannot receive, because it seeth
him not, neither knoweth him: but ye know him; for
he dwelleth with you, and shall be in you.
       (John 14:15-17)

The quest for oneness with the Spirit of God is the journey on which all mankind should place itself. But this is not really a quest, for the Creator has issued it as a gift. This gift is housed in the spirit of man as it connects to the Holy Ghost. This is the time when the church will be in you. This is the time when we will be able to truly see victory on a global scale. There is only one other alternative and that is to continue the cycle until there is total destruction of mankind.

But fear not, the Creator that I serve will not allow his creation to be destroyed by mankind just to prove a point. His request is for you to accept the gift of His and His Son's church, and for it to reside in you. However, like a good Father, He will invoke the "for your own good" scenario one day and the church will be in you all. This may be for some a very nasty medicine, but it will definitely be for our own good.

When I was young I learned that if I took my medicine quickly, my mother would give me a treat that made the taste of the medicine disappear. God is prepared to give the world the treat of peace for taking its medicine. This is the medicine that produces the healing of acceptance of one another and the understanding of all mankind, person to person, through Him. I've taken the medicine and it's really not yucky at all. Please join me in service to God rather than man.

Fear not, O land; be glad and rejoice: for the LORD will
do great things. Be not afraid, ye beasts of the field: for
the pastures of the wilderness do spring, for the tree
beareth her fruit, the fig tree and the vine do yield their

strength. Be glad then, ye children of Zion, and rejoice in the LORD your God: for he hath given you the former rain moderately, and he will cause to come down for you the rain, the former rain, and the latter rain in the first month. And the floors shall be full of wheat, and the vats shall overflow with wine and oil. And I will restore to you the years that the locust hath eaten, the cankerworm, and the caterpillar, and the palmerworm, my great army which I sent among you. And ye shall eat in plenty, and be satisfied, and praise the name of the LORD your God, that hath dealt wondrously with you: and my people shall never be ashamed. And ye shall know that I am in the midst of Israel, and that I am the LORD your God, and none else: and my people shall never be ashamed.

And it shall come to pass afterward, that I will pour out my spirit upon all flesh; and your sons and your daughters shall prophesy, your old men shall dream dreams, your young men shall see visions: And also upon the servants and upon the handmaids in those days will I pour out my spirit.

And I will show wonders in the heavens and in the earth, blood, and fire, and pillars of smoke. The sun shall be turned into darkness, and the moon into blood, before the great and the terrible day of the LORD come.

And it shall come to pass, that whosoever shall call on the name of the LORD shall be delivered: for in mount Zion and in Jerusalem shall be deliverance, as the LORD hath said, and in the remnant whom the LORD shall call.

(Joel 2:21-32)

We've come a long way,
So we'd like to think;
Starting way back
At the missing link.

Each civilization
Is proud of the stride
That propelled it along
On God's planned ride

To positions of power
According to His command,
With a place of authority
In each ones land.

We look back and see
All that we've done,
We proclaim to our brothers
That we are now one.

We think "game over"
Let's count our winnings,
But there's still much work,
Some undiscovered beginnings.

We need to ask ourselves
If we're really satisfied
With the place in life
At which we now abide?

Or, is there more
For us to strive to obtain;
Are there challenges
That for us still remain?

The answer for most
Is a resounding, "YES".
We're nowhere near
Being our best

Until that day when we've
Asked the Lord Most High
To grant us a place
In His infinite sky;

When each has accomplished
What God wants you to do;
By making sure
That the church is in you.

Chapter 6a

No Need of Teachers

The Scriptures tells of the time when God's presence is powerfully manifest among men. First the house of Israel is given the opportunity to experience this *new beginning*.

> *Behold, the days come, saith the LORD, that I will make a new covenant with the house of Israel, and with the house of Judah: Not according to the covenant that I made with their fathers in the day that I took them by the hand to bring them out of the land of Egypt; which my covenant they brake, although I was an husband unto them, saith the LORD: But this shall be the covenant that I will make with the house of Israel; After those days, saith the LORD, I will put my law in their inward parts, and write it in their hearts; and will be their God, and they shall be my people.*

> *And they shall teach no more every man his neighbour, and every man his brother, saying, Know the LORD: for they shall all know me, from the least of them unto the greatest of them, saith the LORD: for I will forgive their iniquity, and I will remember their sin no more.*
> (Jeremiah 31:31-32)

> *And it shall come to pass afterward, that I will pour out my spirit upon all flesh; and your sons and your daughters shall prophesy, your old men shall dream dreams, your young men shall see visions: And also upon the servants and upon the handmaids in those days will I pour out my spirit. And I will show wonders in the heavens and in the earth, blood, and fire, and pillars of smoke. The sun shall be turned into darkness, and the moon into blood, before the great and the terrible day of the LORD come.*

*And it shall come to pass, that whosoever shall call on the
name of the LORD shall be delivered: for in mount Zion
and in Jerusalem shall be deliverance, as the LORD hath
said, and in the remnant whom the LORD shall call.*
(Joel 2:28-32)

Then the Gentiles will have their chance to share the
understanding of God that leads to worship.

*For from the rising of the sun even unto the going down
of the same my name shall be great among the Gentiles;
and in every place incense shall be offered unto my
name, and a pure offering: for my name shall be great
among the heathen, saith the LORD of hosts.*
(Malachi 1:11)

At this time God delivered to man a state of the highest spiritual
and intellectual awareness of His presence. He did this through an
emissary who understands God and shares that understanding with all
mankind; Jew and Gentile.

*And there shall come forth a rod out of the stem of Jesse,
and a Branch shall grow out of his roots: And the spirit
of the LORD shall rest upon him, the spirit of wisdom
and understanding, the spirit of counsel and might, the
spirit of knowledge and of the fear of the LORD; And
shall make him of quick understanding in the fear of the
LORD: and he shall not judge after the sight of his eyes,
neither reprove after the hearing of his ears: But with
righteousness shall he judge the poor, and reprove with
equity for the meek of the earth: and he shall smite the
earth with the rod of his mouth, and with the breath of
his lips shall he slay the wicked. And righteousness shall
be the girdle of his loins, and faithfulness the girdle of
his reins.*

*The wolf also shall dwell with the lamb, and the leopard
shall lie down with the kid; and the calf and the young
lion and the fatling together; and a little child shall lead
them. And the cow and the bear shall feed; their young
ones shall lie down together: and the lion shall eat straw
like the ox. And the sucking child shall play on the hole*

of the asp, and the weaned child shall put his hand on the cockatrice' den. They shall not hurt nor destroy in all my holy mountain: for the earth shall be full of the knowledge of the LORD, as the waters cover the sea.

And in that day there shall be a root of Jesse, which shall stand for an ensign of the people; to it shall the Gentiles seek: and his rest shall be glorious.
(Isaiah 11:1-10)

There is, however, some preparation that mankind must endure in order to enter into this state of spiritual and intellectual bliss. This is where the challenge lies. The first part of the challenge is the recognition and acceptance of the one who comes *out of the stem of Jesse*. This one is Jesus of Nazareth, who is the Christ. The reason it is necessary for us to accept the provisions for us that were made through Jesus Christ is because it is he who provided the way for us to enter into the state of high spiritual and intellectual bliss in God. This is done by our receiving a new part of our being called the Comforter. The Comforter takes over several important function in our life; but only if we yield them thereto.

And I will pray the Father, and he shall give you another Comforter, that he may abide with you for ever; Even the Spirit of truth; whom the world cannot receive, because it seeth him not, neither knoweth him: but ye know him; for he dwelleth with you, and shall be in you.
(John 14:16-17)

the Comforter, which is the Holy Ghost, whom the Father will send in my name, he shall teach you all things, and bring all things to your remembrance, whatsoever I have said unto you.
(John 14:26)

But when the Comforter is come, whom I will send unto you from the Father, even the Spirit of truth, which proceedeth from the Father, he shall testify of me: And ye also shall bear witness, because ye have been with me from the beginning.
(John 15:26-27)

Since the people of God already have the availability of this status, what are all these other human functions that still exist? Why do we have apostles, prophets, and other gifts of the Spirit? Are these only for those who have not yet been convinced of the truth of the Gospel, or are they for the church as well?

Yes, some of the functions of the body of Christ are for the introduction of the Gospel, to the world; but, principally they are for the edification of the church.

> *Now ye are the body of Christ, and members in particular. And God hath set some in the church, first apostles, secondarily prophets, thirdly teachers, after that miracles, then gifts of healings, helps, governments, diversities of tongues. Are all apostles? are all prophets? are all teachers? are all workers of miracles? Have all the gifts of healing? do all speak with tongues? do all interpret? But covet earnestly the best gifts: and yet show I unto you a more excellent way.*
> (1 Corinthians 12:12-31)

Looking back at the nation of Israel, we see that they too had the representatives of God in their midst. However, it is all too easy to lose sight of the purpose of God, even when it is right in front of our faces. The children of Israel had the voice of God in direct communication with them on many occasions. However, memory is very, very short. Even when they had the constant reminders of the prophets, such as Samuel, they still made their own way. This is why we need these voices in the church. By sharing the wonders of God through His working in their lives, they present the constant face of God to the church. This leaves the church with no excuse for straying from the things of God. That is not to say that they won't, but it is to say that they will do so without excuse.

There are many in this world who are unsure about their relationship with God; some of whom are in the church. These are the ones who will need to have someone show them, by word and by example, the way to harness the promises of God. To say that there is no need for teachers is not to say that there won't be a use for them. The folks who don't need a teacher are those who yield to the presence of the Comforter within them. All mankind has not fully tapped into the gift of the Holy Ghost that God places in those who request it of Him. There are some, even those who gather with the children of God, who would sow doubt among the people of God. There must be representatives of God to present again and again the truth of God to quiet any doubts that may be raised from inside or outside a person.

> *All scripture is given by inspiration of God, and is profitable for doctrine, for reproof, for correction, for instruction in righteousness: That the man of God may be perfect, thoroughly furnished unto all good works.*
> (2 Timothy 3:16-17)

The words of these individuals or organizations, which would sow doubt, have to be silenced by a sound refreshing of the Word of God in the lives of the people of God. This is the function of the apostles, preachers and other elect of God. It is not their mission to give new Scripture, but rather to pronounce the good news in the Scripture that has been given. To do this the man of God must be prepared through the working of the truth of the Scriptures in his life.

> *Study to show thyself approved unto God, a workman that needeth not to be ashamed, rightly dividing the word of truth. But shun profane and vain babblings: for they will increase unto more ungodliness.*
> (2 Timothy 2:15-16)

Furthermore, we who are of the house and family of God must be very careful. This care starts with a proper mindset about who we honor as a messenger of God.

> *For whosoever shall call upon the name of the Lord shall be saved. How then shall they call on him in whom they have not believed? and how shall they believe in him of whom they have not heard? and how shall they hear without a preacher? And how shall they preach, except they be sent? as it is written, How beautiful are the feet of them that preach the gospel of peace, and bring glad tidings of good things! But they have not all obeyed the gospel. For Esaias saith, Lord, who hath believed our report? So then faith cometh by hearing, and hearing by the word of God.*
> (Romans 10:13-17)

The one *sent* does not depend on any authority derived from man. Training in a religious institution or attendance at a particular church or sitting under a particular teacher does not, by itself, mean the same as being sent. This sending is by the Spirit of God.

Christ told his disciples to wait for the promise that was to come; which is now here. This promise is the Comforter. This is the promise that equips us to act in the service of God.

> *If ye love me, keep my commandments. And I will pray the Father, and he shall give you another Comforter, that he may abide with you for ever; Even the Spirit of truth; whom the world cannot receive, because it seeth him not, neither knoweth him: but ye know him; for he dwelleth with you, and shall be in you.*
> (John 14:15-17)

Once we are in right standing with God through Jesus Christ and have entered into His presence, we can proceed to present the Gospel among men. The power we need to do this is provided by God.

> *But ye shall receive power, after that the Holy Ghost is come upon you: and ye shall be witnesses unto me both in Jerusalem, and in all Judaea, and in Samaria, and unto the uttermost part of the earth.*
> (Acts 1:8)

This is the power that goes along with the men who are sent. This is the power that you must feel flowing in and from those who you will trust to deliver to you the message of God. You do not have to judge, for the evidence is obvious. This evidence will be given freely to those who truly seek God.

> *Either make the tree good, and his fruit good; or else make the tree corrupt, and his fruit corrupt: for the tree is known by his fruit. O generation of vipers, how can ye, being evil, speak good things? for out of the abundance of the heart the mouth speaketh. A good man out of the good treasure of the heart bringeth forth good things: and an evil man out of the evil treasure bringeth forth evil things. But I say unto you, That every idle word that men shall speak, they shall give account thereof in the*

day of judgment. For by thy words thou shalt be justified,
and by thy words thou shalt be condemned.
(Matthew 12:33-37)

If we do not receive this power, we will be intruding where we ought not to be. Furthermore, even when we do receive a calling from God, we must operate in a God-centered fashion.

Brethren, if a man be overtaken in a fault, ye which are
spiritual, restore such an one in the spirit of meekness;
considering thyself, lest thou also be tempted. Bear ye
one another's burdens, and so fulfil the law of Christ.
For if a man think himself to be something, when he is
nothing, he deceiveth himself. But let every man prove
his own work, and then shall he have rejoicing in himself
alone, and not in another. For every man shall bear his
own burden.
(Galatians 6:1-5)

We must also do so in the love of God. The failure to perform our duties in love makes them worthless and our efforts are in vain.

Though I speak with the tongues of men and of angels,
and have not charity, I am become as sounding brass, or
a tinkling cymbal. And though I have the gift of
prophecy, and understand all mysteries, and all
knowledge; and though I have all faith, so that I could
remove mountains, and have not charity, I am nothing.
And though I bestow all my goods to feed the poor, and
though I give my body to be burned, and have not
charity, it profiteth me nothing.

Charity suffereth long, and is kind; charity envieth not;
charity vaunteth not itself, is not puffed up, Doth not
behave itself unseemly, seeketh not her own, is not easily
provoked, thinketh no evil; Rejoiceth not in iniquity, but
rejoiceth in the truth; Beareth all things, believeth all
things, hopeth all things, endureth all things. Charity
never faileth: but whether there be prophecies, they shall
fail; whether there be tongues, they shall cease; whether
there be knowledge, it shall vanish away.
(1 Corinthians 13:1-8)

Even though there are messengers of God, it is still better that each individual come to the point where they can directly learn from the Comforter. This is the message of those who have come into a true knowledge of the full potential of those who are in God.

The servant of God, Moses, said it very well when God placed a measure of his spirit on others of the children of Israel.

> *And the LORD said unto Moses, Gather unto me seventy men of the elders of Israel, whom thou knowest to be the elders of the people, and officers over them; and bring them unto the tabernacle of the congregation, that they may stand there with thee. And I will come down and talk with thee there: and I will take of the spirit which is upon thee, and will put it upon them; and they shall bear the burden of the people with thee, that thou bear it not thyself alone.*
> (Numbers 11:16-17)

> *And Moses went out, and told the people the words of the LORD, and gathered the seventy men of the elders of the people, and set them round about the tabernacle. And the LORD came down in a cloud, and spake unto him, and took of the spirit that was upon him, and gave it unto the seventy elders: and it came to pass, that, when the spirit rested upon them, they prophesied, and did not cease.*

> *But there remained two of the men in the camp, the name of the one was Eldad, and the name of the other Medad: and the spirit rested upon them; and they were of them that were written, but went not out unto the tabernacle: and they prophesied in the camp. And there ran a young man, and told Moses, and said, Eldad and Medad do prophesy in the camp.*

> *And Joshua the son of Nun, the servant of Moses, one of his young men, answered and said, My lord Moses, forbid them.*

> *And Moses said unto him, Enviest thou for my sake? would God that all the LORD'S people were prophets, and that the LORD would put his spirit upon them!*
> (Numbers 11:24-29)

The apostle Paul reinforced this desire in God.

But if all prophesy, and there come in one that believeth not, or one unlearned, he is convinced of all, he is judged of all: And thus are the secrets of his heart made manifest; and so falling down on his face he will worship God, and report that God is in you of a truth.
(1 Corinthians 14:24-25)

Saving the best for last, as they say, we have the promise of God. This is for those who say to Moses and Paul, "It's nice that you want this, but we can't always have what we want." To them God would say that they can indeed have what they want, because He will provide it.

And it shall come to pass afterward, that I will pour out my spirit upon all flesh; and your sons and your daughters shall prophesy, your old men shall dream dreams, your young men shall see visions: And also upon the servants and upon the handmaids in those days will I pour out my spirit.
(Joel 2:28-29)

To depend on human messengers for a time is okay for proselytes, those who are *babes* in Christ. It is not okay for those who are seasoned warriors of the LORD. Those who want to say that their actions are controlled by God and are done for the glory of God must have a personal relationship with the God for whom they are acting. To say that a man told you that your actions are for the benefit of God will not impress God. God want to be the sole focus of your devotion.

It is too easy to give our devotion to some person who has helped us. Stories abound about patients falling in love with nurses and students falling in love with teachers. This, however, is not sufficient in the kingdom of God. The following is an amazing passage of Scripture.

Take heed to thyself, lest thou make a covenant with the inhabitants of the land whither thou goest, lest it be for a snare in the midst of thee: But ye shall destroy their altars, break their images, and cut down their groves: For thou shalt worship no other god: for the LORD, whose name is Jealous, is a jealous God: Lest thou make a covenant with the inhabitants of the land, and they go a whoring after their gods, and do sacrifice unto their

gods, and one call thee, and thou eat of his sacrifice;
And thou take of their daughters unto thy sons, and their
daughters go a whoring after their gods, and make thy
sons go a whoring after their gods.
(Exodus 34:12-16)

God must be the source of our inspiration so that we will always make him the focus of our worship. No man, other than the Christ, is worthy of our devotion. Blind acceptance of any man is to reject God. To reject God is to practice unrighteousness. To practice unrighteousness is to cheat ourselves out of the blessing of God. To cheat ourselves out of the blessing of God is to cheat all of those around us out of the bountiful goodness that comes from our Godly interactions with others. To cheat others out of this bountiful goodness will lead to war within our organization and even among nations.

From whence come wars and fightings among you?
come they not hence, even of your lusts that war in your
members? Ye lust, and have not: ye kill, and desire to
have, and cannot obtain: ye fight and war, yet ye have
not, because ye ask not. Ye ask, and receive not, because
ye ask amiss, that ye may consume it upon your lusts.

Ye adulterers and adulteresses, know ye not that the
friendship of the world is enmity with God? whosoever
therefore will be a friend of the world is the enemy of
God. Do ye think that the scripture saith in vain, The
spirit that dwelleth in us lusteth to envy? But he giveth
more grace. Wherefore he saith, God resisteth the
proud, but giveth grace unto the humble.

Submit yourselves therefore to God. Resist the devil, and
he will flee from you. Draw nigh to God, and he will
draw nigh to you. Cleanse your hands, ye sinners; and
purify your hearts, ye double minded.
(James 4:1-8)

There is a lot at stake in our rejecting the absolute authority of the Holy Ghost to lead the people of God. It is time for many more of us to grow up and stop acting as babes in the kingdom of God. It is time for more of us to begin to act like men of God.

For we know in part, and we prophesy in part. But when that which is perfect is come, then that which is in part shall be done away. When I was a child, I spake as a child, I understood as a child, I thought as a child: but when I became a man, I put away childish things. For now we see through a glass, darkly; but then face to face: now I know in part; but then shall I know even as also I am known. And now abideth faith, hope, charity, these three; but the greatest of these is charity.
(1 Corinthians 13:9-13)

Dependence on anything other than the best, the Holy Ghost sent by God, is a childish thing. Put it away.

And Elijah came unto all the people, and said, How long halt ye between two opinions? if the LORD be God, follow him: but if Baal, then follow him. And the people answered him not a word.
(1 Kings 18:21)

The Word from the Bible

Exodus 34:8-10

And Moses made haste, and bowed his head toward the earth, and worshipped. And he said, If now I have found grace in thy sight, O LORD, let my LORD, I pray thee, go among us; for it is a stiffnecked people; and pardon our iniquity and our sin, and take us for thine inheritance.

And he said, Behold, I make a covenant: before all thy people I will do marvels, such as have not been done in all the earth, nor in any nation: and all the people among which thou art shall see the work of the LORD: for it is a terrible thing that I will do with thee.

Isaiah 19:24-25

In that day shall Israel be the third with Egypt and with Assyria, even a blessing in the midst of the land: Whom the LORD of hosts shall bless, saying, Blessed be Egypt my people, and Assyria the work of my hands, and Israel mine inheritance.

Psalm 2:7-8

I will declare the decree: the LORD hath said unto me, Thou art my Son; this day have I begotten thee. Ask of me, and I shall give thee the heathen for thine inheritance, and the uttermost parts of the earth for thy possession.

Matthew 3:1-2

In those days came John the Baptist, preaching in the wilderness of Judaea, And saying, Repent ye: for the kingdom of heaven is at hand.

Matthew 4:12-17

Now when Jesus had heard that John was cast into prison, he departed into Galilee; And leaving Nazareth, he came and dwelt in Capernaum, which is upon the sea coast, in the borders of Zabulon and Nephthalim: That it might be fulfilled which was spoken by Esaias the prophet, saying, The land of Zabulon, and the land of Nephthalim, by the way of the sea, beyond Jordan, Galilee of the Gentiles; The people which sat in darkness saw great light; and to them which sat in the region and shadow of death light is sprung up. From that time Jesus began to preach, and to say, Repent: for the kingdom of heaven is at hand.

Matthew 10:1-7

And when he had called unto him his twelve disciples, he gave them power against unclean spirits, to cast them out, and to heal all manner of sickness and all manner of disease. Now the names of the twelve apostles are these; The first, Simon, who is called Peter, and Andrew his brother; James the son of Zebedee, and John his brother; Philip, and Bartholomew; Thomas, and Matthew the publican; James the son of Alphaeus, and Lebbaeus, whose surname was Thaddaeus; Simon the Canaanite, and Judas Iscariot, who also betrayed him. These twelve Jesus sent forth, and commanded them, saying, Go not into the way of the Gentiles, and into any city of the Samaritans enter ye not: But go rather to the lost sheep of the house of Israel. And as ye go, preach, saying, The kingdom of heaven is at hand.

Matthew 12-24-28

But when the Pharisees heard it, they said, This fellow doth not cast out devils, but by Beelzebub the prince of the devils. And Jesus knew their thoughts, and said unto them, Every kingdom divided against itself is brought to desolation; and every city or house divided against itself shall not stand: And if Satan cast out Satan, he is divided against himself; how shall then his kingdom stand? And if I by Beelzebub cast out devils, by whom do your children cast them out? therefore they shall be your judges. But if I cast out devils by the Spirit of God, then the kingdom of God is come unto you.

Matthew 16:27

For the Son of man shall come in the glory of his Father with his angels; and then he shall reward every man according to his works. Verily I say unto you, There be some standing here, which shall not taste of death, till they see the Son of man coming in his kingdom.

Mark 8:38-9:1

Whosoever therefore shall be ashamed of me and of my words in this adulterous and sinful generation; of him also shall the Son of man be ashamed, when he cometh in the glory of his Father with the holy angels. And he said unto them, Verily I say unto you, That there be some of them that stand here, which shall not taste of death, till they have seen the kingdom of God come with power.

Luke 9:26

For whosoever shall be ashamed of me and of my words, of him shall the Son of man be ashamed, when he shall come in his own glory, and in his Father's, and of the holy angels. But I tell you of a truth, there be some standing here, which shall not taste of death, till they see the kingdom of God.

Chapter Seven

Some of You Shall Not Die

You know, sometimes I have a very difficult time with the idea that Jesus was really totally straightforward in what he said. Do you sometimes feel the same way? It's not that I don't believe that he did what the apostles said he did, but there's this thing about timing. Sometimes we read things in the Scriptures and some of us don't really seem to be able to get a handle on this timing thing.

One matter that comes immediately to mind is the last week of Daniel.

> *Seventy weeks are determined upon thy people and upon thy holy city, to finish the transgression, and to make an end of sins, and to make reconciliation for iniquity, and to bring in everlasting righteousness, and to seal up the vision and prophecy, and to anoint the most Holy. Know therefore and understand, that from the going forth of the commandment to restore and to build Jerusalem unto the Messiah the Prince shall be seven weeks, and threescore and two weeks: the street shall be built again, and the wall, even in troublous times.*
>
> *And after threescore and two weeks shall Messiah be cut off, but not for himself: and the people of the prince that shall come shall destroy the city and the sanctuary; and the end thereof shall be with a flood, and unto the end of the war desolations are determined. And he shall confirm the covenant with many for one week: and in the midst of the week he shall cause the sacrifice and the oblation to cease, and for the overspreading of abominations he shall make it desolate, even until the consummation, and that determined shall be poured upon the desolate.*
>
> (Daniel 9:24-27)

There are some who feel that it passed right after all the other weeks. There are others who feel that it is suspended and waiting for some time that is to come, which only the Father knows. This is an example of what I mean by that timing thing.

Let's take a look at that last week. There is no place that I have discovered in Scripture where is written that Daniel said that all the other week would pass and then the last week would wait. Maybe he was told that, but there is nowhere in Scripture where this is revealed. On second thought, if it's not in Scripture, I don't think it happened.

There are a lot of very, very smart and some very, very devout folks who believe that there is something that is between the lines of this message. It is this matter of between the line messages that can cause *outsiders* to doubt the veracity of our Lord. We, of course, know that he is perfect and cannot lie. But there's this thing of appearances, about which we must be careful.

> *Rejoice evermore.*
>
> *Pray without ceasing.*
>
> *In every thing give thanks: for this is the will of God in Christ Jesus concerning you.*
>
> *Quench not the Spirit.*
>
> *Despise not prophesyings.*
>
> *Prove all things; hold fast that which is good.*
>
> *Abstain from all appearance of evil.*
>
> *And the very God of peace sanctify you wholly; and I pray God your whole spirit and soul and body be preserved blameless unto the coming of our Lord Jesus Christ.*
> (1 Thessalonians 5:16-23)

To give incomplete information in some cases is a sin; we like to call it the sin of omission. We are told that, as people of God, our answers should be succinct and precise.

> *But above all things, my brethren, swear not, neither by heaven, neither by the earth, neither by any other oath: but let your yea be yea; and your nay, nay; lest ye fall into condemnation.*
> (James 5:12)

This is, to me, very sound counsel and from a very reputable source. It is a technique that is not limited to persons of God: in testimony in courts in the United States this principle is applied to the framing of the majority of the questions and answers. However, there are some who have stated that the Bible has given a message that is either to be ignored or it must be re-interpreted using the technique of the Pharisees.

> *Woe unto you, scribes and Pharisees, hypocrites! for ye pay tithe of mint and anise and cummin, and have omitted the weightier matters of the law, judgment, mercy, and faith: these ought ye to have done, and not to leave the other undone. Ye blind guides, which strain at a gnat, and swallow a camel.*
> (Matthew 23:23-24)

I just don't think that is right.

"What in the world," you say, "is he talking about"?

Well, I hope you read the title to this topic, for in it is the clue to the dilemma. But before we explore this further, let's determine why this is important.

There are some who feel that Jesus was a good man, and that's nice. Other will admit this and go so far as to say that he was even one of the prophets of God. However, among these are some who believe that we can't believe everything he says. Others say that we can't believe that he said everything that the Bible says he said. Some others say we can't believe everything that is written about him. However, let's use the method given by God to the nation of Israel.

> *At the mouth of two witnesses, or three witnesses, shall he that is worthy of death be put to death; but at the mouth of one witness he shall not be put to death.*
> (Deuteronomy 17:6)

> *One witness shall not rise up against a man for any iniquity, or for any sin, in any sin that he sinneth: at the mouth of two witnesses, or at the mouth of three witnesses, shall the matter be established.*
> (Deuteronomy 19:15)

To all people God gives the assurance that Jesus is indeed more than *just* a prophet. To all, God states that everything written about him in the Bible is true; by the mouth of two or three witnesses.

> *And Jesus, when he was baptized, went up straightway out of the water: and, lo, the heavens were opened unto him, and he saw the Spirit of God descending like a dove, and lighting upon him: And lo a voice from heaven, saying, This is my beloved Son, in whom I am well pleased.*
> (Matthew 3:16-17)

> *And after six days Jesus taketh Peter, James, and John his brother, and bringeth them up into an high mountain apart, And was transfigured before them: and his face did shine as the sun, and his raiment was white as the light. And, behold, there appeared unto them Moses and Elias talking with him.*

> *Then answered Peter, and said unto Jesus, Lord, it is good for us to be here: if thou wilt, let us make here three tabernacles; one for thee, and one for Moses, and one for Elias.*

> *While he yet spake, behold, a bright cloud overshadowed them: and behold a voice out of the cloud, which said, This is my beloved Son, in whom I am well pleased; hear ye him.*
> (Matthew 17:1-5)

> *And it came to pass in those days, that Jesus came from Nazareth of Galilee, and was baptized of John in Jordan. And straightway coming up out of the water, he saw the heavens opened, and the Spirit like a dove descending upon him: And there came a voice from heaven, saying, Thou art my beloved Son, in whom I am well pleased.*
> (Mark 1:9-11)

> *And after six days Jesus taketh with him Peter, and James, and John, and leadeth them up into an high mountain apart by themselves: and he was transfigured before them. And his raiment became shining, exceeding white as snow; so as no fuller on earth can white them.*

And there appeared unto them Elias with Moses: and they were talking with Jesus.

And Peter answered and said to Jesus, Master, it is good for us to be here: and let us make three tabernacles; one for thee, and one for Moses, and one for Elias. For he wist not what to say; for they were sore afraid.

And there was a cloud that overshadowed them: and a voice came out of the cloud, saying, This is my beloved Son: hear him.
(Mark 9:2-7)

Now when all the people were baptized, it came to pass, that Jesus also being baptized, and praying, the heaven was opened, And the Holy Ghost descended in a bodily shape like a dove upon him, and a voice came from heaven, which said, Thou art my beloved Son; in thee I am well pleased.
(Luke 3:21-22)

And it came to pass about an eight days after these sayings, he took Peter and John and James, and went up into a mountain to pray. And as he prayed, the fashion of his countenance was altered, and his raiment was white and glistering. And, behold, there talked with him two men, which were Moses and Elias: Who appeared in glory, and spake of his decease which he should accomplish at Jerusalem.

But Peter and they that were with him were heavy with sleep: and when they were awake, they saw his glory, and the two men that stood with him. And it came to pass, as they departed from him, Peter said unto Jesus, Master, it is good for us to be here: and let us make three tabernacles; one for thee, and one for Moses, and one for Elias: not knowing what he said.

While he thus spake, there came a cloud, and overshadowed them: and they feared as they entered into the cloud. And there came a voice out of the cloud, saying, This is my beloved Son: hear him.
(Luke 9:28-33)

God said: *This is my beloved Son, in whom I am well pleased; hear ye him.* Therefore, let's do that, hear him. Jesus said that the words he delivered were not his own, but that they came from God. Thus, by listening to him we are in actuality listening to God.

> *I have glorified thee on the earth: I have finished the work which thou gavest me to do. And now, O Father, glorify thou me with thine own self with the glory which I had with thee before the world was. I have manifested thy name unto the men which thou gavest me out of the world: thine they were, and thou gavest them me; and they have kept thy word. Now they have known that all things whatsoever thou hast given me are of thee. For I have given unto them the words which thou gavest me; and they have received them, and have known surely that I came out from thee, and they have believed that thou didst send me.*
>
> (John 17:4-8)

Listening to Jesus is listening to God; that is an ideal thing and very easy, therefore, to follow his pronouncements and live thereby. Jesus says that the Comforter, who has been sent by the Father at his request, will share with us even more of his words, and that these too are the things of the Father. He told us that the Father confirmed his message.

> *I can of mine own self do nothing: as I hear, I judge: and my judgment is just; because I seek not mine own will, but the will of the Father which hath sent me. If I bear witness of myself, my witness is not true. There is another that beareth witness of me; and I know that the witness which he witnesseth of me is true.*
>
> *Ye sent unto John, and he bare witness unto the truth. But I receive not testimony from man: but these things I say, that ye might be saved. He was a burning and a shining light: and ye were willing for a season to rejoice in his light. But I have greater witness than that of John: for the works which the Father hath given me to finish, the same works that I do, bear witness of me, that the Father hath sent me. And the Father himself, which hath sent me, hath borne witness of me. Ye have neither*

*heard his voice at any time, nor seen his shape. And ye
have not his word abiding in you: for whom he hath sent,
him ye believe not.*

*Search the scriptures; for in them ye think ye have
eternal life: and they are they which testify of me.*
(John 5:30-39)

*Philip saith unto him, Lord, show us the Father, and it
sufficeth us. Jesus saith unto him, Have I been so long
time with you, and yet hast thou not known me, Philip?
he that hath seen me hath seen the Father; and how
sayest thou then, Show us the Father? Believest thou not
that I am in the Father, and the Father in me? the words
that I speak unto you I speak not of myself: but the
Father that dwelleth in me, he doeth the works. Believe
me that I am in the Father, and the Father in me: or else
believe me for the very works' sake.*
(John 14:8-11)

For many, however, even Jesus' statement about the Father is
called into question.

Please let me digress for a moment and speak to the Father before
I continue. Thanks.

"Father in Heaven, I in no way doubt Your working in
the world through Jesus of Nazareth who is the Christ,
the Son of the Living God, who You are. I only write
these things to those who need a further evidence of
Your working in the earth. Even though I have not seen
these things, I believe them because I have been *shown*
them through the power of the Holy Ghost. Therefore,
I communicate in this fashion to those who need to have
further evidences of the power of Jesus, even before
he received all power. My desire is that through reading
this, they can see Your hand in his life.

My desire is that through reading this, they will see Your
seal on the truth that he uttered. May they through this
come to fully understand why You said of Jesus, '*This is
my beloved Son in whom I am well pleased*'. And by
seeing Your seal, it is my prayer that they will heed Your

command to '*Hear ye him*'. This is my desire in Jesus name. Amen."

Thank you for your indulgence.

There is indeed a blessing for those who are able to capture the truth of the Gospel writers, and turn to God.

> *But Thomas, one of the twelve, called Didymus, was not with them when Jesus came. The other disciples therefore said unto him, We have seen the LORD. But he said unto them, Except I shall see in his hands the print of the nails, and put my finger into the print of the nails, and thrust my hand into his side, I will not believe.*
>
> *And after eight days again his disciples were within, and Thomas with them: then came Jesus, the doors being shut, and stood in the midst, and said, Peace be unto you. Then saith he to Thomas, Reach hither thy finger, and behold my hands; and reach hither thy hand, and thrust it into my side: and be not faithless, but believing.*
>
> *And Thomas answered and said unto him, My LORD and my God.*
>
> *Jesus saith unto him, Thomas, because thou hast seen me, thou hast believed: blessed are they that have not seen, and yet have believed.*
> (John 20:24-29)

However, if you don't yet have the faith to send your request for faith directly to God, let me try to help. Do you know that you can ask God directly for edification on this matter? Yes, you can!

> *If any of you lack wisdom, let him ask of God, that giveth to all men liberally, and upbraideth not; and it shall be given him. But let him ask in faith, nothing wavering. For he that wavereth is like a wave of the sea driven with the wind and tossed. For let not that man think that he shall receive any thing of the Lord. A double minded man is unstable in all his ways.*
> (James 1:5-8)
>
> *Ask, and it shall be given you; seek, and ye shall find; knock, and it shall be opened unto you: For every one*

that asketh receiveth; and he that seeketh findeth; and to him that knocketh it shall be opened. Or what man is there of you, whom if his son ask bread, will he give him a stone? Or if he ask a fish, will he give him a serpent? If ye then, being evil, know how to give good gifts unto your children, how much more shall your Father which is in heaven give good things to them that ask him?
(Matthew 7:7-11)

The Bible tells of a prophet who is to come as a special messenger of God, with a special message. Moses spoke of this prophet to the children of Israel.

The LORD thy God will raise up unto thee a Prophet from the midst of thee, of thy brethren, like unto me; unto him ye shall hearken; According to all that thou desiredst of the LORD thy God in Horeb in the day of the assembly, saying, Let me not hear again the voice of the LORD my God, neither let me see this great fire any more, that I die not.

And the LORD said unto me, They have well spoken that which they have spoken. I will raise them up a Prophet from among their brethren, like unto thee, and will put my words in his mouth; and he shall speak unto them all that I shall command him. And it shall come to pass, that whosoever will not hearken unto my words which he shall speak in my name, I will require it of him.
(Deuteronomy 18:15-19)

Jesus is that Prophet and he gave a prophecy of things to come during his time in history as a man on earth.

And Jesus went out, and departed from the temple: and his disciples came to him for to shew him the buildings of the temple. And Jesus said unto them, See ye not all these things? verily I say unto you, There shall not be left here one stone upon another, that shall not be thrown down.
(Matthew 24:1-2)

When ye therefore shall see the abomination of desolation, spoken of by Daniel the prophet, stand in the holy place, (whoso readeth, let him understand:) Then let them which be in Judaea flee into the mountains: Let him which is on the housetop not come down to take any thing out of his house: Neither let him which is in the field return back to take his clothes.

And woe unto them that are with child, and to them that give suck in those days! But pray ye that your flight be not in the winter, neither on the sabbath day: For then shall be great tribulation, such as was not since the beginning of the world to this time, no, nor ever shall be. And except those days should be shortened, there should no flesh be saved: but for the elect's sake those days shall be shortened.

(Matthew 24:15-22)

This message was given a few decades before it happened; and it did happen. Those of the children of Abraham who are also the children of Israel will remember this historic event, with much pain. It is the destruction at Jerusalem in around 70 AD.

The events that Jesus said would happen did happen exactly as he said they would. These include the method of attack, the forewarning to flee, the escape of the Christians, and the behavior of the inhabitants, particularly those who gave suck in that day. It is a fulfilled prophecy. It establishes Jesus as a prophet of God. But we can go further than that, if you will believe the record of those who were living during his time. Some of the messages they left us are indicated in a section at the end of this topic. They describe Jesus as not just a prophet but as The Prophet, and the Messiah, and the Son of God.

This brings us, finally, to the matter that is most important. Since Jesus is a prophet, at least, and since he showed forth extreme power in his ministry on earth, we can say that the hand of God was mighty upon him. Therefore, it is not unreasonable to think that God has imbued him with power of a tremendous nature. This *qualifies* him as a prophet of the highest order. For the works sake, he is most likely the Prophet of the Highest Order, the Messiah. Since he is, at least, a prophet of the highest order then it is not unreasonable for us to think that God would allow him to have a kingdom. David is also considered to be a prophet and it is well known that God gave him a kingdom. The works that Jesus did are far beyond those that were done by any man, even those done by David. But his kingdom is not limited to the physical world.

Jesus answered, My kingdom is not of this world: if my kingdom were of this world, then would my servants fight, that I should not be delivered to the Jews: but now is my kingdom not from hence.
(John 18:36)

If you are able to believe that Jesus is a prophet of God, then believe his words.

For the Son of man shall come in the glory of his Father with his angels; and then he shall reward every man according to his works. Verily I say unto you, There be some standing here, which shall not taste of death, till they see the Son of man coming in his kingdom.
(Matthew 16:27-28)

This is, unfortunately, the matter that is in some contention in the Christian world: the matter of when this kingdom will reach fruition. Well, I hope that we have established the truthfulness of Jesus. Furthermore, I hope that we have established the completeness of the message of Jesus. Please don't get caught up in these words of Jesus.

Nevertheless I tell you the truth; It is expedient for you that I go away: for if I go not away, the Comforter will not come unto you; but if I depart, I will send him unto you. And when he is come, he will reprove the world of sin, and of righteousness, and of judgment: Of sin, because they believe not on me; Of righteousness, because I go to my Father, and ye see me no more; Of judgment, because the prince of this world is judged.

I have yet many things to say unto you, but ye cannot bear them now. Howbeit when he, the Spirit of truth, is come, he will guide you into all truth: for he shall not speak of himself; but whatsoever he shall hear, that shall he speak: and he will shew you things to come. He shall glorify me: for he shall receive of mine, and shall shew it unto you.
(John 16:7-14)

These words do not mean that the Spirit will revise the things that have already been presented. Rather this tells us that there are so many other things that we can know about the kingdom of God, that the minds of the twelve apostles, and of the disciples at that time, were not ready to retain. I take as truth that "... some of you will not die...", and I am fairly certain that all have died that were around when this message was given. This applies even when we consider the disciple whom Jesus loved and the rumors about his living forever.

Then Peter, turning about, seeth the disciple whom Jesus loved following; which also leaned on his breast at supper, and said, Lord, which is he that betrayeth thee? Peter seeing him saith to Jesus, Lord, and what shall this man do?

Jesus saith unto him, If I will that he tarry till I come, what is that to thee? follow thou me.

Then went this saying abroad among the brethren, that that disciple should not die: yet Jesus said not unto him, He shall not die; but, If I will that he tarry till I come, what is that to thee?
(John 21:20 -23)

As *that disciple whom Jesus loved* noted, he did not mean that this disciple would live forever. And even if we accept the rumor we must understand that, one, does not make, some.

Now before anybody gets all mad about this thing, known as the second coming, let me make one statement. I am not, at this point addressing the second coming directly. That Jesus will one day return physically to this earth is not the subject of this discussion. That there will be an actual physical end to the earth as we know it is also not the direct discussion at this time.

The matter at hand is this, "When is the message given by Christ activated?"

The answer is this: "At the time when the signs that he mentioned have taken place."

These signs took place around 70 AD and thus heralded the completion of the prophecy of Jesus of Nazareth for the world. It also completed one other matter.

A Psalm of David. The LORD said unto my Lord, Sit thou at my right hand, until I make thine enemies thy footstool.
(Psalm 110:1)

This is also complete. The enemies of the Lord have been made his footstool. This does not mean what is often thought. The LORD did not say "until I destroy your enemies": the Lord said *until I make thine enemies thy footstool*. This is done.

Let me explain by way of a dialogue.

Assumption 1: God the Father is *the LORD* written in the Psalm.

Assumption 2: Jesus is the, *my Lord,* written in the Psalm.

Question 1:   Who were Jesus' enemies?

Answer 1:   The folk who condemned him to be crucified? This Jesus told us.

> *He that hateth me hateth my Father also. If I had not done among them the works which none other man did, they had not had sin: but now have they both seen and hated both me and my Father. But this cometh to pass, that the word might be fulfilled that is written in their law, They hated me without a cause.*
> (John 15:23-25)

These are the ones who indicted themselves before man and before God.

> *When Pilate saw that he could prevail nothing, but that rather a tumult was made, he took water, and washed his hands before the multitude, saying, I am innocent of the blood of this just person: see ye to it. Then answered all the people, and said, His blood be on us, and on our children.*
> (Matthew 27:24-25)

Addendum: They were eligible for forgiveness for this, by accepting the power of the request made by Jesus to the Father.

> *And when they were come to the place, which is called Calvary, there they*

crucified him, and the malefactors, one on the right hand, and the other on the left. Then said Jesus, Father, forgive them; for they know not what they do. And they parted his raiment, and cast lots.
(Luke 23:33-34)

Question 2:   Who were not Jesus' enemies?

Answer 2:   Anybody other than those mentioned by Jesus and who indicted themselves. Yes, the Roman government did perform the action they were directed to perform by those who wanted him crucified. They did not defend him, but they were not his enemies. At worst they were disinterested in him; disinterest, however, does not rise to the status of enmity without additional factors. Some of the things done by the government officials about Jesus are described below.

When Pilate saw that he could prevail nothing, but that rather a tumult was made, he took water, and washed his hands before the multitude, saying, I am innocent of the blood of this just person: see ye to it.
(Matthew 27:24)

And so Pilate, willing to content the people, released Barabbas unto them, and delivered Jesus, when he had scourged him, to be crucified.
(Mark 15:15)

Then said Pilate to the chief priests and to the people, I find no fault in this man. And they were the more fierce, saying, He stirreth up the people, teaching throughout all Jewry, beginning from Galilee to this place. When Pilate heard of Galilee, he asked whether the man were a Galilaean. And as soon as he knew that he belonged unto Herod's jurisdiction, he sent him to Herod, who himself also was at Jerusalem at that time.

(Luke 23:4-7)

And when Herod saw Jesus, he was exceeding glad: for he was desirous to see him of a long season, because he had heard many things of him; and he hoped to have seen some miracle done by him. Then he questioned with him in many words; but he answered him nothing. And the chief priests and scribes stood and vehemently accused him. And Herod with his men of war set him at nought, and mocked him, and arrayed him in a gorgeous robe, and sent him again to Pilate. And the same day Pilate and Herod were made friends together: for before they were at enmity between themselves.

(Luke 23:8-12)

And Pilate, when he had called together the chief priests and the rulers and the people, Said unto them, Ye have brought this man unto me, as one that perverteth the people: and, behold, I, having examined him before you, have found no fault in this man touching those things whereof ye accuse him: No, nor yet Herod: for I sent you to him; and, lo, nothing worthy of death is done unto him. I will therefore chastise him, and release him. (For of necessity he must release one unto them at the feast.)

And they cried out all at once, saying, Away with this man, and release unto us Barabbas: (Who for a certain sedition made in the city, and for murder, was cast into prison.)

Pilate therefore, willing to release Jesus, spake again to them. But they cried, saying, Crucify him, crucify him. And he said unto them the third time, Why, what evil hath he done? I have found no cause of death in him: I will therefore chastise him, and let him go. And they were instant with loud voices, requiring that he might be crucified. And the voices of them and of the chief priests prevailed.

And Pilate gave sentence that it should be as they required.
(Luke 23:13-24)

In 70 AD, Jesus' enemies were made his footstool by being subjected to his pronouncement for the temple and the city. And this was done by the authority of God the Father. Jesus is able to rest on the footstool of those who nailed him to the cross. They are now under his dominion and they are awaiting his pleasure to use them as he sees fit. Of course, as he see fit will be for their benefit. We don't usually tear up our footstools, but we take care of them so that they can provide us with years of service. Such is also the mind of the Lord.

Bottom line: the Messiah has come. Those who would deny his power in the world have been neutralized as a force to combat him. In fact they are the ones who will be the force that provide for his relaxed re-entry into the world. His kingdom is now. His Gospel is to be understood and followed in the current time. We must look to him to continue to manifest God as we were told to.

After this manner therefore pray ye: Our Father which art in heaven, Hallowed be thy name. Thy kingdom come, Thy will be done in earth, as it is in heaven. Give us this day our daily bread. And forgive us our debts, as we forgive our debtors. And lead us not into temptation, but deliver us from evil: For thine is the kingdom, and the power, and the glory, for ever. Amen.
(Matthew 6:9-13)

This also calls us to participate in the human enterprise as Jesus has directed us to do. As a matter of fact, it is considered a sign of a civilized society to do so. This participation is that of loving our neighbor as ourselves. This participation calls us to honor our brothers in the kingdom of God with man. This participation is especially critical for the children of Abraham, for they are without excuse. Abraham set the standard, by his actions of living at peace in a world that was in turmoil. We are not the first ones to see strife among nations. Let us, however, be the last ones to give an eye for an eye or a tooth for a tooth.

> *But I say unto you which hear, Love your enemies, do good to them which hate you, Bless them that curse you, and pray for them which despitefully use you. And unto him that smiteth thee on the one cheek offer also the other; and him that taketh away thy cloke forbid not to take thy coat also. Give to every man that asketh of thee; and of him that taketh away thy goods ask them not again. And as ye would that men should do to you, do ye also to them likewise.*

> *For if ye love them which love you, what thank have ye? for sinners also love those that love them. And if ye do good to them which do good to you, what thank have ye? for sinners also do even the same. And if ye lend to them of whom ye hope to receive, what thank have ye? for sinners also lend to sinners, to receive as much again. But love ye your enemies, and do good, and lend, hoping for nothing again; and your reward shall be great, and ye shall be the children of the Highest: for he is kind unto the unthankful and to the evil. Be ye therefore merciful, as your Father also is merciful.*
>   (Luke 6:27-36)

We who are the children of Abraham, and those who join us, are a noble people. We are a tolerant people. We are a Godly people. Let us begin and continue to act and react as ones who know the true and only Living God. Remember, please, that He was first the God of Abraham before He announced any other title for Himself. Let us honor one another as befits children of this noble servant and friend of God.

There is much talk
Of waiting for the day
When Jesus will return
And seal for us the way.

Much time is spent trying
To determine when
The Lord Jesus Christ
Will all reality amend.

The day of the event
No one will know
But the Father in Heaven,
Who did not bestow

The knowledge of the matter
Even on His blessed Son
While he was on earth,
Our lives to make one

With his Father God
In a bond most dear,
Which Jesus said
Was surely near.

The kingdom of God
On earth with men,
A time of great rejoicing,
Reconciling us to Him.

Bringing all back to He,
Who made us all;
Overshadowing the example
Of Adam's fall.

We must believe the words
Of Jesus the Lord,
And with him, now
Come on board.

For Christ rules now
In his kingdom on earth;
From the spiritual realm
He is surely perched

To pull all mankind
Together by his might;
So step boldly now
Into his marvelous Light.

Jesus the Messiah and Prophet

Matthew 28:1-8

In the end of the sabbath, as it began to dawn toward the first day of the week, came Mary Magdalene and the other Mary to see the sepulchre. And, behold, there was a great earthquake: for the angel of the Lord descended from heaven, and came and rolled back the stone from the door, and sat upon it. His countenance was like lightning, and his raiment white as snow: And for fear of him the keepers did shake, and became as dead men.

And the angel answered and said unto the women, Fear not ye: for I know that ye seek Jesus, which was crucified. He is not here: for he is risen, as he said. Come, see the place where the Lord lay. And go quickly, and tell his disciples that he is risen from the dead; and, behold, he goeth before you into Galilee; there shall ye see him: lo, I have told you.

And they departed quickly from the sepulchre with fear and great joy; and did run to bring his disciples word.

Matthew 28:16-18

Then the eleven disciples went away into Galilee, into a mountain where Jesus had appointed them. And when they saw him, they worshipped him: but some doubted. And Jesus came and spake unto them, saying, All power is given unto me in heaven and in earth.

Luke 16:14-17

And the Pharisees also, who were covetous, heard all these things: and they derided him.

And he said unto them, Ye are they which justify yourselves before men; but God knoweth your hearts: for that which is highly esteemed among men is abomination in the sight of God. The law and the prophets were until John: since that time the kingdom of God is preached, and every man presseth into it. And it is easier for heaven and earth to pass, than one tittle of the law to fail.

Luke 17:20-37

And when he was demanded of the Pharisees, when the kingdom of God should come, he answered them and said, The kingdom of God cometh not with observation: Neither shall they say, Lo here! or, lo there! for, behold, the kingdom of God is within you.

And he said unto the disciples, The days will come, when ye shall desire to see one of the days of the Son of man, and ye shall not see it. And they shall say to you, See here; or, see there: go not after them, nor follow them. For as the lightning, that lighteneth out of the one part under heaven, shineth unto the other part under heaven; so shall also the Son of man be in his day. But first must he suffer many things, and be rejected of this generation.

And as it was in the days of Noe, so shall it be also in the days of the Son of man. They did eat, they drank, they married wives, they were given in marriage, until the day that Noe entered into the ark, and the flood came, and destroyed them all. Likewise also as it was in the days of Lot; they did eat, they drank, they bought, they sold, they planted, they builded; But the same day that Lot went out of Sodom it rained fire and brimstone from heaven, and destroyed them all. Even thus shall it be in the day when the Son of man is revealed.

In that day, he which shall be upon the housetop, and his stuff in the house, let him not come down to take it away: and he that is in the field, let him likewise not return back. Remember Lot's wife. Whosoever shall seek to save his life shall lose it; and whosoever shall lose his life shall preserve it. I tell you, in that night there shall be two men in one bed; the one shall be taken, and the other shall be left. Two women shall be grinding together; the one shall be taken, and the other left. Two men shall be in the field; the one shall be taken, and the other left.

And they answered and said unto him, Where, Lord? And he said unto them, Wheresoever the body is, thither will the eagles be gathered together.

Luke 22:14-18

And when the hour was come, he sat down, and the twelve apostles with him. And he said unto them, With desire I have desired to eat this passover with you before I suffer: For I say unto you, I will not any more eat thereof, until it be fulfilled in the kingdom of God. And he took the cup, and gave thanks, and said, Take this, and divide it among yourselves: For I say unto you, I will not drink of the fruit of the vine, until the kingdom of God shall come.

Luke 22:66-69

And as soon as it was day, the elders of the people and the chief priests and the scribes came together, and led him into their council, saying, Art thou the Christ? tell us.

And he said unto them, If I tell you, ye will not believe: And if I also ask you, ye will not answer me, nor let me go. Hereafter shall the Son of man sit on the right hand of the power of God.

Luke 24:35-53

And they told what things were done in the way, and how he was known of them in breaking of bread. And as they thus spake, Jesus himself stood in the midst of them, and saith unto them, Peace be unto you. But they were terrified and affrighted, and supposed that they had seen a spirit.

And he said unto them, Why are ye troubled? and why do thoughts arise in your hearts? Behold my hands and my feet, that it is I myself: handle me, and see; for a spirit hath not flesh and bones, as ye see me have. And when he had thus spoken, he shewed them his hands and his feet. And while they yet believed not for joy, and wondered, he said unto them, Have ye here any meat?

And they gave him a piece of a broiled fish, and of an honeycomb. And he took it, and did eat before them.

And he said unto them, These are the words which I spake unto you, while I was yet with you, that all things must be fulfilled, which were written in the law of Moses, and in the prophets, and in the psalms, concerning me. Then opened he their understanding, that they might understand the scriptures, And said unto them, Thus it is written, and thus it behoved Christ to suffer, and to rise from the dead the third day: And that repentance and remission of sins should be preached in his name among all nations, beginning at Jerusalem. And ye are witnesses of these things.

And, behold, I send the promise of my Father upon you: but tarry ye in the city of Jerusalem, until ye be endued with power from on high.

And he led them out as far as to Bethany, and he lifted up his hands, and blessed them. And it came to pass, while he blessed them, he was parted from them, and carried up into heaven. And they worshipped him, and returned to Jerusalem with great joy: And were continually in the temple, praising and blessing God. Amen.

John 17:1-26

These words spake Jesus, and lifted up his eyes to heaven, and said, Father, the hour is come; glorify thy Son, that thy Son also may glorify thee: As thou hast given him power over all flesh, that he should give eternal life to as many as thou hast given him. And this is life eternal, that they might know thee the only true God, and Jesus Christ, whom thou hast sent.

I have glorified thee on the earth: I have finished the work which thou gavest me to do. And now, O Father, glorify thou me with thine own self with the glory which I had with thee before the world was. I have manifested thy name unto the men which thou gavest me out of the world: thine they were, and thou gavest them me; and they have kept thy word. Now they have known that all things whatsoever thou hast given me are of thee. For I have given unto them the words which thou gavest me; and they have received them, and have known surely that I came out from thee, and they have believed that thou didst send me.

I pray for them: I pray not for the world, but for them which thou hast given me; for they are thine. And all mine are thine, and thine are mine; and I am glorified in them. And now I am no more in the world, but these are in the world, and I come to thee. Holy Father, keep through thine own name those whom thou hast given me, that they may be one, as we are. While I was with them in the world, I kept them in thy name: those that thou gavest me I have kept, and none of them is lost, but the son of perdition; that the scripture might be fulfilled.

And now come I to thee; and these things I speak in the world, that they might have my joy fulfilled in themselves. I have given them thy word; and the world hath hated them, because they are not of the world, even as I am not of the world. I pray not that thou shouldest take them out of the world, but that thou shouldest keep them from the evil. They are not of the world, even as I am not of the world. Sanctify them through thy truth: thy word is truth.

As thou hast sent me into the world, even so have I also sent them into the world. And for their sakes I sanctify myself, that they also might be sanctified through the truth.

Neither pray I for these alone, but for them also which shall believe on me through their word; That they all may be one; as thou, Father, art in me, and I in thee, that they also may be one in us: that the world may believe that thou hast sent me. And the glory which thou gavest me I have given them; that they may be one, even as we are one: I in them, and thou in me, that they may be made perfect in one; and that the world may know that thou hast sent me, and hast loved them, as thou hast loved me.

Father, I will that they also, whom thou hast given me, be with me where I am; that they may behold my glory, which thou hast given me: for thou lovedst me before the foundation of the world. O righteous Father, the world hath not known thee: but I have known thee, and these have known that thou hast sent me. And I have declared unto them thy name, and will declare it: that the love wherewith thou hast loved me may be in them, and I in them.

Chapter 7a

Say Not Who Shall

Romans 10:1-13

Brethren, my heart's desire and prayer to God for Israel is, that they might be saved. For I bear them record that they have a zeal of God, but not according to knowledge. For they being ignorant of God's righteousness, and going about to establish their own righteousness, have not submitted themselves unto the righteousness of God. For Christ is the end of the law for righteousness to every one that believeth.

For Moses describeth the righteousness which is of the law, That the man which doeth those things shall live by them. But the righteousness which is of faith speaketh on this wise, Say not in thine heart, Who shall ascend into heaven? (that is, to bring Christ down from above:) Or, Who shall descend into the deep? (that is, to bring up Christ again from the dead.)

But what saith it? The word is nigh thee, even in thy mouth, and in thy heart: that is, the word of faith, which we preach; That if thou shalt confess with thy mouth the Lord Jesus, and shalt believe in thine heart that God hath raised him from the dead, thou shalt be saved. For with the heart man believeth unto righteousness; and with the mouth confession is made unto salvation. For the scripture saith, Whosoever believeth on him shall not be ashamed. For there is no difference between the Jew and the Greek: for the same Lord over all is rich unto all that call upon him. For whosoever shall call upon the name of the Lord shall be saved.

+=+

I would not say that there are none; but I will say that there are very few people who, just by looking at another person, can say for sure that they have cancer on the inside. It might be true to say that there are none, but I will leave some room for doubt in that area. However, there is no room for doubt about the fact that there is none who can, just by looking at a person, say that they are or are not a child of God. This fact does not seem to stop some people from attempting to so categorize other individuals. Sometimes they use the concept that "*by their fruits ye shall know them*" as stated in Matthew 7:16 and 7:20. However, this is referring specifically to the actions that come forth. It is an indicator of the state of the heart and spirit toward God. It is not a diagnostic tool for the status of the soul. One example of the use of this is in our interactions with false prophets.

> *Beware of false prophets, which come to you in sheep's clothing, but inwardly they are ravening wolves. Ye shall know them by their fruits. Do men gather grapes of thorns, or figs of thistles? Even so every good tree bringeth forth good fruit; but a corrupt tree bringeth forth evil fruit. A good tree cannot bring forth evil fruit, neither can a corrupt tree bring forth good fruit. Every tree that bringeth not forth good fruit is hewn down, and cast into the fire. Wherefore by their fruits ye shall know them.*

> *Not every one that saith unto me, Lord, Lord, shall enter into the kingdom of heaven; but he that doeth the will of my Father which is in heaven. Many will say to me in that day, Lord, Lord, have we not prophesied in thy name? and in thy name have cast out devils? and in thy name done many wonderful works? And then will I profess unto them, I never knew you: depart from me, ye that work iniquity.*
> (Matthew 7:15-23)

The difficulty of expanding this to all humans is because we cannot know for sure what challenges God is working others through in life. That which seems to us to be a clear matter of sin, may to God be a work in process; a transformation that is not yet complete. We, therefore, should never use a single incident or even a pattern of external incidents to diagnose the internal state of "believer or not".

Saul of Tarsus is a prime example. As a devout Jew, he felt that he was protecting the things of God by the persecution of the Christian. However, after being *educated* by Christ on the Damascus road, he was transformed into the apostle Paul. God does not work on our timetable of condemnation.

Transformation can occur in an instant. Someone who was formerly *obviously* headed to hell may in the next few minutes be transformed, by a renewing experience of Christ, into a power wielding servant of God. The route to Heaven, or the route to hell, is not one that any man can map for another. Consider the following passage of Scripture:

> *Verily I say unto you, All sins shall be forgiven unto the sons of men, and blasphemies wherewith soever they shall blaspheme: But he that shall blaspheme against the Holy Ghost hath never forgiveness, but is in danger of eternal damnation.*
> (Mark 3:28-29)

Notice that in this passage, Jesus left room for hope even in this most serious of sins. Please note the phrase *"is in danger of eternal damnation"*. This does not say that they will surely receive eternal condemnation, but that they are heading in that direction. And I think it is safe to say that if anyone would know what type of person will or will not receive such a punishment it would be Jesus of Nazareth. This is the same Jesus, who is the Christ, who did pay the price for the salvation of those who might be in such danger. He paid this price doubly with his life: he did so by the way he lived unto death and by giving his life on the cross. He also ushered in a new kind of life, eternal life, when he rose from the dead.

Jesus did not concentrate his words on saying who would go to hell. He was only interested in making all men ready to enter the kingdom of God. Here's an example of his drive in that direction.

> *And one of the scribes came, and having heard them reasoning together, and perceiving that he had answered them well, asked him, Which is the first commandment of all?*
>
> *And Jesus answered him, The first of all the commandments is, Hear, O Israel; The Lord our God is one Lord: And thou shalt love the Lord thy God with all thy heart, and with all thy soul, and with all thy mind,*

and with all thy strength: this is the first commandment. And the second is like, namely this, Thou shalt love thy neighbour as thyself. There is none other commandment greater than these.

And the scribe said unto him, Well, Master, thou hast said the truth: for there is one God; and there is none other but he: And to love him with all the heart, and with all the understanding, and with all the soul, and with all the strength, and to love his neighbour as himself, is more than all whole burnt offerings and sacrifices.

And when Jesus saw that he answered discreetly, he said unto him, Thou art not far from the kingdom of God.

And no man after that durst ask him any question.
(Mark 12:28-34)

This contains a specific statement to a specific person about their status relative to being accepted by God. It shows Jesus' concentration on reconciliation, and not condemnation. On the rare occasions that the glass is not totally full, it is partially full for Jesus, not partially empty.

Here is another passage that shows Jesus Christ's keen sense of concentration on the things of Heaven, and not the things of any other place.

Then said Jesus, Father, forgive them; for they know not what they do. And they parted his raiment, and cast lots.

And the people stood beholding. And the rulers also with them derided him, saying, He saved others; let him save himself, if he be Christ, the chosen of God. And the soldiers also mocked him, coming to him, and offering him vinegar, And saying, If thou be the king of the Jews, save thyself. And a superscription also was written over him in letters of Greek, and Latin, and Hebrew, THIS IS THE KING OF THE JEWS.

And one of the malefactors which were hanged railed on him, saying, If thou be Christ, save thyself and us. But the other answering rebuked him, saying, Dost not thou fear God, seeing thou art in the same condemnation? And we indeed justly; for we receive the due reward of our deeds: but this man hath done nothing amiss. And he said unto Jesus, Lord, remember me when thou comest into thy kingdom.

And Jesus said unto him, Verily I say unto thee, To day shalt thou be with me in paradise.
(Luke 23:34-43)

In this passage he did not indict the other thief as one who, because of his railing against him, was surely going to hell, or in any other way surely be separated from God. Jesus' concentration is on the provision of a place with God for anyone who seeks to have a right relationship with Him.

There is a statement made by Jesus that highlights his focus on God and His kingdom.

And as Moses lifted up the serpent in the wilderness, even so must the Son of man be lifted up: That whosoever believeth in him should not perish, but have eternal life. For God so loved the world, that he gave his only begotten Son, that whosoever believeth in him should not perish, but have everlasting life. For God sent not his Son into the world to condemn the world; but that the world through him might be saved.

He that believeth on him is not condemned: but he that believeth not is condemned already, because he hath not believed in the name of the only begotten Son of God. And this is the condemnation, that light is come into the world, and men loved darkness rather than light, because their deeds were evil. For every one that doeth evil hateth the light, neither cometh to the light, lest his deeds should be reproved. But he that doeth truth cometh to the light, that his deeds may be made manifest, that they are wrought in God.
(John 3:14-21)

A review of some of the final moments of the patriarchs of the Old Testament can shed some light on the difficulty of diagnosing who will go where in the kingdom of God. Let's start with Enoch.

And Jared lived after he begat Enoch eight hundred years, and begat sons and daughters: And all the days of

Jared were nine hundred sixty and two years: and he died.

And Enoch lived sixty and five years, and begat Methuselah: And Enoch walked with God after he begat Methuselah three hundred years, and begat sons and daughters: And all the days of Enoch were three hundred sixty and five years: And Enoch walked with God: and he was not; for God took him.
(Genesis 5:19-24)

This is the first man who was stated as being given entry directly into a place with God away from earth. It may or may not be true that he went to Heaven, but it is definitely true that he did not die the death as we know it. The exact phrase is that "*he was not*". From this passage alone, we don't really know what this means as pertains to Heaven, only that he was not anymore on this earth.

We read in the account of the final rest of Abraham that he was buried. But keep an open mind on this for now.

And these are the days of the years of Abraham's life which he lived, an hundred threescore and fifteen years. Then Abraham gave up the ghost, and died in a good old age, an old man, and full of years; and was gathered to his people. And his sons Isaac and Ishmael buried him in the cave of Machpelah, in the field of Ephron the son of Zohar the Hittite, which is before Mamre; The field which Abraham purchased of the sons of Heth: there was Abraham buried, and Sarah his wife.
(Genesis 25:7-10)

However, there is more, in this respect, to the final destination of the soul of Abraham. Even though he died and was buried, he still seems to have been in a place where he retained a form of consciousness. Furthermore, it is a place where others who are of a deserving nature before God can join Abraham. Scripture records a warning given by Jesus to those who cherish the things of this earth and NOT the things of God which sheds further light on the place of Abraham.

There was a certain rich man, which was clothed in purple and fine linen, and fared sumptuously every day: And there was a certain beggar named Lazarus, which was laid at his gate, full of sores, And desiring to be fed with the crumbs which fell from the rich man's table: moreover the dogs came and licked his sores.

And it came to pass, that the beggar died, and was carried by the angels into Abraham's bosom: the rich man also died, and was buried; And in hell he lift up his eyes, being in torments, and seeth Abraham afar off, and Lazarus in his bosom. And he cried and said, Father Abraham, have mercy on me, and send Lazarus, that he may dip the tip of his finger in water, and cool my tongue; for I am tormented in this flame.

But Abraham said, Son, remember that thou in thy lifetime receivedst thy good things, and likewise Lazarus evil things: but now he is comforted, and thou art tormented. And beside all this, between us and you there is a great gulf fixed: so that they which would pass from hence to you cannot; neither can they pass to us, that would come from thence.

Then he said, I pray thee therefore, father, that thou wouldest send him to my father's house: For I have five brethren; that he may testify unto them, lest they also come into this place of torment.

Abraham saith unto him, They have Moses and the prophets; let them hear them.

And he said, Nay, father Abraham: but if one went unto them from the dead, they will repent.

And he said unto him, If they hear not Moses and the prophets, neither will they be persuaded, though one rose from the dead.

(Luke 16:19-31)

The resting place of Moses in the time of Moses is apparently, from the reading of Scripture, in a grave.

And Moses went up from the plains of Moab unto the mountain of Nebo, to the top of Pisgah, that is over against Jericho. And the LORD showed him all the land of Gilead, unto Dan, And all Naphtali, and the land of

Ephraim, and Manasseh, and all the land of Judah, unto the utmost sea, And the south, and the plain of the valley of Jericho, the city of palm trees, unto Zoar. And the LORD said unto him, This is the land which I sware unto Abraham, unto Isaac, and unto Jacob, saying, I will give it unto thy seed: I have caused thee to see it with thine eyes, but thou shalt not go over thither.

So Moses the servant of the LORD died there in the land of Moab, according to the word of the LORD. And he buried him in a valley in the land of Moab, over against Bethpeor: but no man knoweth of his sepulchre unto this day.

And Moses was an hundred and twenty years old when he died: his eye was not dim, nor his natural force abated. And the children of Israel wept for Moses in the plains of Moab thirty days: so the days of weeping and mourning for Moses were ended.
(Deuteronomy 34:1-8)

David's final resting place is in the grave also, as written in the Scriptures. With David we see the term *slept* being used. This seems to indicate that the consciousness of David was suspended for a time. It does not say how long, but it seems apparent that David was not, as they say, "absent from the body and present with the Lord"; at least not instantaneously.

So David slept with his fathers, and was buried in the city of David. And the days that David reigned over Israel were forty years: seven years reigned he in Hebron, and thirty and three years reigned he in Jerusalem. Then sat Solomon upon the throne of David his father; and his kingdom was established greatly.
(1 Kings 2:10-12)

Finally, we have Elijah, who as is written *went up by a whirlwind into heaven.* When we read the account of his departure from earth, we can say that Elijah is definitely going toward the heavens.

And it came to pass, when the LORD would take up Elijah into heaven by a whirlwind, that Elijah went with Elisha from Gilgal. And Elijah said unto Elisha, Tarry here, I pray thee; for the LORD hath sent me to Bethel.

And Elisha said unto him, As the LORD liveth, and as thy soul liveth, I will not leave thee.

So they went down to Bethel. And the sons of the prophets that were at Bethel came forth to Elisha, and said unto him, Knowest thou that the LORD will take away thy master from thy head to day? And he said, Yea, I know it; hold ye your peace.

And Elijah said unto him, Elisha, tarry here, I pray thee; for the LORD hath sent me to Jericho.

And he said, As the LORD liveth, and as thy soul liveth, I will not leave thee. So they came to Jericho.

And the sons of the prophets that were at Jericho came to Elisha, and said unto him, Knowest thou that the LORD will take away thy master from thy head to day?

And he answered, Yea, I know it; hold ye your peace.

And Elijah said unto him, Tarry, I pray thee, here; for the LORD hath sent me to Jordan.

And he said, As the LORD liveth, and as thy soul liveth, I will not leave thee. And they two went on.

And fifty men of the sons of the prophets went, and stood to view afar off: and they two stood by Jordan. And Elijah took his mantle, and wrapped it together, and smote the waters, and they were divided hither and thither, so that they two went over on dry ground.

And it came to pass, when they were gone over, that Elijah said unto Elisha, Ask what I shall do for thee, before I be taken away from thee.

And Elisha said, I pray thee, let a double portion of thy spirit be upon me.

And he said, Thou hast asked a hard thing: nevertheless, if thou see me when I am taken from thee, it shall be so unto thee; but if not, it shall not be so.

And it came to pass, as they still went on, and talked, that, behold, there appeared a chariot of fire, and horses of fire, and parted them both asunder; and Elijah went up by a whirlwind into heaven. And Elisha saw it, and he cried, My father, my father, the chariot of Israel, and the horsemen thereof. And he saw him no more: and he took hold of his own clothes, and rent them in two pieces. He took up also the mantle of Elijah that fell from him, and went back, and stood by the bank of Jordan; And he took the mantle of Elijah that fell from him, and smote the waters, and said, Where is the LORD God of Elijah? and when he also had smitten the waters, they parted hither and thither: and Elisha went over.

And when the sons of the prophets which were to view at Jericho saw him, they said, The spirit of Elijah doth rest on Elisha. And they came to meet him, and bowed themselves to the ground before him.

And they said unto him, Behold now, there be with thy servants fifty strong men; let them go, we pray thee, and seek thy master: lest peradventure the spirit of the LORD hath taken him up, and cast him upon some mountain, or into some valley.

And he said, Ye shall not send. And when they urged him till he was ashamed, he said, Send.

They sent therefore fifty men; and they sought three days, but found him not.

And when they came again to him, (for he tarried at Jericho,) he said unto them, Did I not say unto you, Go not?
(2 Kings 2:1-2:18)

Say what?

But the righteousness which is of faith speaketh on this wise, Say not in thine heart, Who shall ascend into heaven? (that is, to bring Christ down from above:) Or, Who shall descend into the deep? (that is, to bring up Christ again from the dead.)
(Romans 10:6-7)

Why is this so?

A good question: I'm glad you asked it. Let's go to Scripture to find our answer; specifically, let's study the words of Jesus Christ.

> *Verily, verily, I say unto thee, We speak that we do know, and testify that we have seen; and ye receive not our witness. If I have told you earthly things, and ye believe not, how shall ye believe, if I tell you of heavenly things? And no man hath ascended up to heaven, but he that came down from heaven, even the Son of man which is in heaven.*
> (John 3:11-13)

This may seem on its face to be inaccurate, because Enoch, Abraham and Elijah are presumed to be there. Let us, however, take a look at this in detail.

For Abraham we have no scriptural reference as to how he got there. For Enoch we may deduce that God took him there. Of course we know that Jesus as a devout member of the nation of Israel knew of these Scriptures. There must be something more to Jesus' statement about ascending into Heaven. What is it?

The more to the statement is this: Jesus was not speaking of the end result of the event, but of the power behind the event. Jesus was saying that only the Son of man has ascended on his own power into Heaven.

God is aware of the meanings that the human mind will impute to His pronouncements and to those of His Son. For this reason He and His Son are very precise in their wording. We may not always understand what is being said, but this does not diminish the precision. Since Jesus is not yet crucified and he has not risen from the dead at this time his ascension must have a broader meaning than just the time of the crucifixion. His ascension must have already occurred at a time before the statement, from a human perspective.

The broader meaning is that the Son of man spans history. He had ascended in Jesus' past and he would do so after the crucifixion.

> *When they therefore were come together, they asked of him, saying, Lord, wilt thou at this time restore again the kingdom to Israel?*
>
> *And he said unto them, It is not for you to know the times or the seasons, which the Father hath put in his own power. But ye shall receive power, after that the Holy Ghost is come upon you: and ye shall be witnesses unto*

me both in Jerusalem, and in all Judaea, and in Samaria, and unto the uttermost part of the earth.

And when he had spoken these things, while they beheld, he was taken up; and a cloud received him out of their sight.
(Acts 1:6-9)

One of the past events that tell of his ascension is given to us in the book of Daniel. We know from Scripture that he was on the earth for the event recorded in Daniel.

Then was Nebuchadnezzar full of fury, and the form of his visage was changed against Shadrach, Meshach, and Abednego: therefore he spake, and commanded that they should heat the furnace one seven times more than it was wont to be heated. And he commanded the most mighty men that were in his army to bind Shadrach, Meshach, and Abednego, and to cast them into the burning fiery furnace. Then these men were bound in their coats, their hosen, and their hats, and their other garments, and were cast into the midst of the burning fiery furnace. Therefore because the king's commandment was urgent, and the furnace exceeding hot, the flame of the fire slew those men that took up Shadrach, Meshach, and Abednego. And these three men, Shadrach, Meshach, and Abednego, fell down bound into the midst of the burning fiery furnace.

Then Nebuchadnezzar the king was astonied, and rose up in haste, and spake, and said unto his counsellors, Did not we cast three men bound into the midst of the fire?

They answered and said unto the king, True, O king.

He answered and said, Lo, I see four men loose, walking in the midst of the fire, and they have no hurt; and the form of the fourth is like the Son of God.
(Daniel 3:19-25)

He was seen back in Heaven in the time of Daniel; and he came back to earth with the clouds of Heaven.

I saw in the night visions, and, behold, one like the Son of man came with the clouds of heaven, and came to the Ancient of days, and they brought him near before him. And there was given him dominion, and glory, and a kingdom, that all people, nations, and languages, should serve him: his dominion is an everlasting dominion, which shall not pass away, and his kingdom that which shall not be destroyed.

(Daniel 7:13-14)

There are other scriptural passages that tell of the Son of man descending from Heaven to earth. The one that set the stage for the ministry of Jesus of Nazareth and started the redemption of mankind is listed in the books of Matthew, Mark and John.

Then cometh Jesus from Galilee to Jordan unto John, to be baptized of him.

But John forbad him, saying, I have need to be baptized of thee, and comest thou to me?

And Jesus answering said unto him, Suffer it to be so now: for thus it becometh us to fulfil all righteousness.

Then he suffered him.

And Jesus, when he was baptized, went up straightway out of the water: and, lo, the heavens were opened unto him, and he saw the Spirit of God descending like a dove, and lighting upon him: And lo a voice from heaven, saying, This is my beloved Son, in whom I am well pleased.

(Matthew 3:13-17)

And it came to pass in those days, that Jesus came from Nazareth of Galilee, and was baptized of John in Jordan. And straightway coming up out of the water, he saw the heavens opened, and the Spirit like a dove descending upon him: And there came a voice from heaven, saying, Thou art my beloved Son, in whom I am well pleased.

(Mark 1:9-11)

The next day John seeth Jesus coming unto him, and saith, Behold the Lamb of God, which taketh away the sin of the world. This is he of whom I said, After me cometh a man which is preferred before me: for he was before me. And I knew him not: but that he should be made manifest to Israel, therefore am I come baptizing with water.

And John bare record, saying, I saw the Spirit descending from heaven like a dove, and it abode upon him. And I knew him not: but he that sent me to baptize with water, the same said unto me, Upon whom thou shalt see the Spirit descending, and remaining on him, the same is he which baptizeth with the Holy Ghost. And I saw, and bare record that this is the Son of God.

Again the next day after John stood, and two of his disciples; And looking upon Jesus as he walked, he saith, Behold the Lamb of God!
(John 1:29-36)

So when Paul writes *that is, to bring Christ down from above*, he is letting us know that this is the only way we can know who is in Heaven. For a man to have this kind of knowledge he would have to possess the power to bring Christ down so that he could be told this. No man should ever try to command Christ in any manner. No man needs that kind of information in order to *preach Jesus and him crucified*. There is no mention in the Scriptures that Christ would provide such information. Furthermore, there is no mention in the Scriptures that the Holy Ghost has been told to do so either.

But what of prophecy? Can we get this kind of information as a form of prophecy?

No!

It has always been of some interest to me that the apostles were not called prophets. We are given insight by Jesus as to why this is. Jesus said, *The law and the prophets were until John: since that time the kingdom of God is preached, and every man presseth into it.* (Luke 16:16)

After John we are past the time when the prophets come primarily from one section of the earth. God is pouring his spirit on all flesh, and many shall prophesy. From the time of John forward we will receive information from Christ during his time here, and from the Holy Ghost from the time of Pentecost to ---.

And it shall come to pass afterward, that I will pour out my spirit upon all flesh; and your sons and your daughters shall prophesy, your old men shall dream dreams, your young men shall see visions: And also upon the servants and upon the handmaids in those days will I pour out my spirit.

And I will show wonders in the heavens and in the earth, blood, and fire, and pillars of smoke. The sun shall be turned into darkness, and the moon into blood, before the great and the terrible day of the LORD come.

And it shall come to pass, that whosoever shall call on the name of the LORD shall be delivered: for in mount Zion and in Jerusalem shall be deliverance, as the LORD hath said, and in the remnant whom the LORD shall call.

(Joel 2:28-32)

Some may say

Some may say that Jesus has appeared unto them in a dream or vision. Be very careful about this one as well. The Psalmist writes: *The LORD said unto my Lord, Sit thou at my right hand, until I make thine enemies thy footstool* (Psalm 110:1). This means that Jesus the Lord is at the right hand of the Father. There are also several Scriptures in the New Testament where some of the apostles and prophets record that Jesus is seated at the right hand of the Father.

Furthermore, if we are to take the text literally, as in this case we can, Jesus is *resting* until his enemies are made his footstool by the LORD. Two matters to investigate on this subject (I'll let you do this for yourself):

1. Have all the enemies of the Lord been made his footstool?

2. Would someone who resides in Heaven leave there without the Father's command for them to do so? The Son of man only has one other scheduled departure time from Heaven, according to the Scriptures. This is what we call the *second coming of Christ*. At that time there will be absolutely no need for thinking about who is or is not in Heaven.

Maybe some have been visited by angels.

> *Let brotherly love continue. Be not forgetful to entertain strangers: for thereby some have entertained angels unawares.*
>
>   (Hebrews 13:1-2)

Christ, however, has not come down to reveal who is in Heaven, and no man can, or should, ever try to make him do so. To bring Christ down is to usher in the final events of our reality as we know it and to eliminate all chances for us to preach Jesus and him crucified. Let's not be too quick about asking God to deliver on this matter. Some of our earthly relatives may be collateral damage at this time.

The other side of the coin

On the other side of the equation is the statement about the deep, "*that is to bring Christ again from the dead*". We know that the Lord has knowledge of who is in Heaven because he was there, but what of the deep (we will call it hell) and how does it relate to Christ having died?

First, from the example of Abraham, Lazarus and the rich man we know that there are views from hell to Heaven, and from Heaven to hell. Thus, the Son of man can easily see from Heaven that which is in hell. But let's go a little deeper. The Son of man, the Messiah, the Son of God, is taught by the Father all things. The Father definitely knows who is in hell.

> *Whither shall I go from thy spirit? or whither shall I flee from thy presence? If I ascend up into heaven, thou art there: if I make my bed in hell, behold, thou art there. If I take the wings of the morning, and dwell in the uttermost parts of the sea; Even there shall thy hand lead me, and thy right hand shall hold me. If I say, Surely the darkness shall cover me; even the night shall be light about me. Yea, the darkness hideth not from thee; but the night shineth as the day: the darkness and the light are both alike to thee. For thou hast possessed my reins: thou hast covered me in my mother's womb.*
>
> *I will praise thee; for I am fearfully and wonderfully made: marvellous are thy works; and that my soul knoweth right well. My substance was not hid from thee, when I was made in secret, and curiously wrought in the lowest parts of the earth. Thine eyes did see my*

substance, yet being unperfect; and in thy book all my members were written, which in continuance were fashioned, when as yet there was none of them.
(Psalm 139:7-16)

Jesus likened his death and resurrection to the prophet Jonah's experience (who is also called Jonas).

Then certain of the scribes and of the Pharisees answered, saying, Master, we would see a sign from thee.

But he answered and said unto them, An evil and adulterous generation seeketh after a sign; and there shall no sign be given to it, but the sign of the prophet Jonas: For as Jonas was three days and three nights in the whale's belly; so shall the Son of man be three days and three nights in the heart of the earth.
(Matthew 12:38-40)

Jonah learned quite a bit about the nature of hell in that fish. Let us therefore learn from Jonah.

Then Jonah prayed unto the LORD his God out of the fish's belly, And said, I cried by reason of mine affliction unto the LORD, and he heard me; out of the belly of hell cried I, and thou heardest my voice. For thou hadst cast me into the deep, in the midst of the seas; and the floods compassed me about: all thy billows and thy waves passed over me.

Then I said, I am cast out of thy sight; yet I will look again toward thy holy temple. The waters compassed me about, even to the soul: the depth closed me round about, the weeds were wrapped about my head. I went down to the bottoms of the mountains; the earth with her bars was about me for ever: yet hast thou brought up my life from corruption, O LORD my God. When my soul fainted within me I remembered the LORD: and my prayer came in unto thee, into thine holy temple.
(Jonah 2:1-7)

It therefore seems reasonable to say that Christ absorbed quite a bit about that place while he was waiting for the days to pass. He wasn't just laying there counting the minutes.

Some feel, and I am among them, that his mission included delivering the Gospel to the captives in hell, also. After all this is the place that has the most desperate of captives. And it was for the sins of the world that he died; the sins of those living and dead, in Heaven and on earth; and even in hell.

> *And Jesus returned in the power of the Spirit into Galilee: and there went out a fame of him through all the region round about. And he taught in their synagogues, being glorified of all. And he came to Nazareth, where he had been brought up: and, as his custom was, he went into the synagogue on the sabbath day, and stood up for to read. And there was delivered unto him the book of the prophet Esaias. And when he had opened the book, he found the place where it was written, The Spirit of the Lord is upon me, because he hath anointed me to preach the gospel to the poor; he hath sent me to heal the brokenhearted, to preach deliverance to the captives, and recovering of sight to the blind, to set at liberty them that are bruised, To preach the acceptable year of the Lord. And he closed the book, and he gave it again to the minister, and sat down. And the eyes of all them that were in the synagogue were fastened on him.*
>
> *And he began to say unto them, This day is this scripture fulfilled in your ears.*
> (Luke 4:14-21)

Going even further, let's think about the sin that he collected and carried away from the world. What do you think happened to all the sin? Since he carried it away it was no longer on earth. The penalty has been lifted from the kingdom of man. The sin was not with him when he rose from the grave in his glorified body. He definitely did not take it to Heaven. There is only one other place that qualifies for this deposit at the time of his death. This place is hell: this seems, after all, to be an excellent storage place for such material. While he was visiting the captives there he could have easily found a *corner* to store it in.

It also seems reasonable that since he was there anyway preaching deliverance to the captives, he would also fulfill his mission. Jesus stated that his mission was to the lost sheep of Israel. (He did, however, still provide solace and healing for anyone with the faith to receive it. Israel was his primary mission, but not his only one.)

> *And, behold, a woman of Canaan came out of the same coasts, and cried unto him, saying, Have mercy on me, O Lord, thou son of David; my daughter is grievously vexed with a devil.*
>
> *But he answered her not a word. And his disciples came and besought him, saying, Send her away; for she crieth after us.*
>
> *But he answered and said, I am not sent but unto the lost sheep of the house of Israel.*
>
> *Then came she and worshipped him, saying, Lord, help me.*
>
> *But he answered and said, It is not meet to take the children's bread, and to cast it to dogs.*
>
> *And she said, Truth, Lord: yet the dogs eat of the crumbs which fall from their masters' table.*
>
> *Then Jesus answered and said unto her, O woman, great is thy faith: be it unto thee even as thou wilt. And her daughter was made whole from that very hour.*
> (Matthew 15:22-28)

If there were any lost sheep of Israel there, he could give them the hope of the gospel of the Kingdom of God. This seems to be absolutely within the character of the Son of man, as we see him revealed. No matter how tense the situation, he was always up to whatever came his way, and he was always ready to preach the Gospel to anyone, anywhere in the nation of Israel; or anywhere else.

Therefore Christ rose from the dead with full knowledge of who is descended into the deep. However, again there is no reason for him to share this information with anyone on earth. We here have no use for this kind of information. As a matter of fact, such information could lead us into a severe case of pride. This is the kind of pride that easily kills ministries of any magnitude.

To call upon Christ to reveal such information is to "*bring Christ up from the dead*". To review why this will never be revealed to anyone on this earth, please look back at the start of the section titled "Some may say".

So what?

"And so", you say, "What does all this mean?"

It means that we should not be so quick about condemning others to that terrible place called hell. We should not do so because we just don't know what trial a person may be facing that is masking a formerly strong relationship with God. As David went through his ups and down, so do many, if not all, men and women. Even some of those who would indicate that they, because of their actions, are lost to God may just be reacting to the problem of the moment. We, as people of God have no right to aggravate a situation by making diagnoses for which we have been given no authority.

Whole nations have been condemned because of the excesses of their rulers. This is God's decision to make. Yes, God has indicated through His word in the Bible that there will be nations that will be purged from existence because of their waywardness toward God. But in this purging of the nations, there will be many individuals who are saved "as by fire". Though the works of the nations are purged from the record of existence, the people of that nation can still be saved.

So when you plot to condemn either a person or a nation to final damnation by God, be very careful. The people of a nation are not all judged as worthy of the same judgment as the leaders of the nation, nor as the nation itself. This is an unusual thought for some of us to accept. We usually see the nation as the people, in the form of what is called government by the people and for the people. This is a nice statement, but is very far from the truth, even in those nations that have it as their credo. The nations are controlled by the individuals who are allowed the power from God. There is no nation controlled by all the people of that nation.

Therefore, there is no nation where all the people will receive the same treatment from God because of being a member of the nation. Each person will receive the measure of judgment that fits their relationship to the Father or to His Son Jesus Christ. And this measure of judgment is only fully known by the Father and His Son Jesus Christ.

Let's leave the designation of who goes where to the Godhead. Let's return to the time when we listened to the Scripture which says

Another parable put he forth unto them, saying, The kingdom of heaven is likened unto a man which sowed good seed in his field: But while men slept, his enemy came and sowed tares among the wheat, and went his way. But when the blade was sprung up, and brought forth fruit, then appeared the tares also.

So the servants of the householder came and said unto him, Sir, didst not thou sow good seed in thy field? from whence then hath it tares?

He said unto them, An enemy hath done this.

The servants said unto him, Wilt thou then that we go and gather them up?

But he said, Nay; lest while ye gather up the tares, ye root up also the wheat with them. Let both grow together until the harvest: and in the time of harvest I will say to the reapers, Gather ye together first the tares, and bind them in bundles to burn them: but gather the wheat into my barn.

(Matthew 13:24-30)

The Word from the Bible

Psalm 139:7-12

Whither shall I go from thy spirit? or whither shall I flee from thy presence? If I ascend up into heaven, thou art there: if I make my bed in hell, behold, thou art there. If I take the wings of the morning, and dwell in the uttermost parts of the sea; Even there shall thy hand lead me, and thy right hand shall hold me. If I say, Surely the darkness shall cover me; even the night shall be light about me. Yea, the darkness hideth not from thee; but the night shineth as the day: the darkness and the light are both alike to thee.

Psalm 16:8-10

I have set the LORD always before me: because he is at my right hand, I shall not be moved. Therefore my heart is glad, and my glory rejoiceth: my flesh also shall rest in hope. For thou wilt not leave my soul in hell; neither wilt thou suffer thine Holy One to see corruption.

Genesis 4:3-12

And in process of time it came to pass, that Cain brought of the fruit of the ground an offering unto the LORD. And Abel, he also brought of the firstlings of his flock and of the fat thereof. And the LORD had respect unto Abel and to his offering: But unto Cain and to his offering he had not respect. And Cain was very wroth, and his countenance fell.

And the LORD said unto Cain, Why art thou wroth? and why is thy countenance fallen? If thou doest well, shalt thou not be accepted? and if thou doest not well, sin lieth at the door. And unto thee shall be his desire, and thou shalt rule over him.

And Cain talked with Abel his brother: and it came to pass, when they were in the field, that Cain rose up against Abel his brother, and slew him.

And the LORD said unto Cain, Where is Abel thy brother?

And he said, I know not: Am I my brother's keeper?

And he said, What hast thou done? the voice of thy brother's blood crieth unto me from the ground. And now art thou cursed from the earth, which hath opened her mouth to receive thy brother's blood from thy hand; When thou tillest the ground, it shall not henceforth yield unto thee her strength; a fugitive and a vagabond shalt thou be in the earth.

Deuteronomy 31:16-17

And the LORD said unto Moses, Behold, thou shalt sleep with thy fathers; and this people will rise up, and go a whoring after the gods of the strangers of the land, whither they go to be among them, and will forsake me, and break my covenant which I have made with them. Then my anger shall be kindled against them in that day, and I will forsake them, and I will hide my face from them, and they shall be devoured, and many evils and troubles shall befall them; so that they will say in that day, Are not these evils come upon us, because our God is not among us?

1 Samuel 25:1

And Samuel died; and all the Israelites were gathered together, and lamented him, and buried him in his house at Ramah. And David arose, and went down to the wilderness of Paran.

1 Samuel 28:3-19

Now Samuel was dead, and all Israel had lamented him, and buried him in Ramah, even in his own city. And Saul had put away those that had familiar spirits, and the wizards, out of the land.

And the Philistines gathered themselves together, and came and pitched in Shunem: and Saul gathered all Israel together, and they pitched in Gilboa. And when Saul saw the host of the Philistines, he was afraid, and his heart greatly trembled. And when Saul inquired of the LORD, the LORD answered him not, neither by dreams, nor by Urim, nor by prophets.

Then said Saul unto his servants, Seek me a woman that hath a familiar spirit, that I may go to her, and inquire of her.

And his servants said to him, Behold, there is a woman that hath a familiar spirit at Endor.

And Saul disguised himself, and put on other raiment, and he went, and two men with him, and they came to the woman by night: and he said, I pray thee, divine unto me by the familiar spirit, and bring me him up, whom I shall name unto thee.

And the woman said unto him, Behold, thou knowest what Saul hath done, how he hath cut off those that have familiar spirits, and the wizards, out of the land: wherefore then layest thou a snare for my life, to cause me to die?

And Saul sware to her by the LORD, saying, As the LORD liveth, there shall no punishment happen to thee for this thing.

Then said the woman, Whom shall I bring up unto thee?

And he said, Bring me up Samuel.

And when the woman saw Samuel, she cried with a loud voice: and the woman spake to Saul, saying, Why hast thou deceived me? for thou art Saul.

And the king said unto her, Be not afraid: for what sawest thou? And the woman said unto Saul, I saw gods ascending out of the earth.

And he said unto her, What form is he of?

And she said, An old man cometh up; and he is covered with a mantle. And Saul perceived that it was Samuel, and he stooped with his face to the ground, and bowed himself.

And Samuel said to Saul, Why hast thou disquieted me, to bring me up?

And Saul answered, I am sore distressed; for the Philistines make war against me, and God is departed from me, and answereth me no more, neither by prophets, nor by dreams: therefore I have called thee, that thou mayest make known unto me what I shall do.

Then said Samuel, Wherefore then dost thou ask of me, seeing the LORD is departed from thee, and is become thine enemy?

And the LORD hath done to him, as he spake by me: for the LORD hath rent the kingdom out of thine hand, and given it to thy neighbour, even to David: Because thou obeyedst not the voice of the LORD, nor executedst his fierce wrath upon Amalek, therefore hath the LORD done this thing unto thee this day. Moreover the LORD will also deliver Israel with thee into the hand of the Philistines: and to morrow shalt thou and thy sons be with me: the LORD also shall deliver the host of Israel into the hand of the Philistines.

Then Saul fell straightway all along on the earth, and was sore afraid, because of the words of Samuel: and there was no strength in him; for he had eaten no bread all the day, nor all the night.

Chapter Eight

The Dead Rise

There are a number of groups training individuals to give up their lives in an attempt to inflict damage on other humans. I believe this goes by the name *suicide bombing*, among some others. This is not a new thing among men, nor was it created by those who now use it in earnest.

Among those in history that also used such techniques were the Japanese during the *world war*. They even had bigger tools to accomplish their mission: theirs was the airplane. This technique was tried again earlier in this century. These would be used to do suicide bombings of military targets. This is, however, where the two uses start to drift seriously apart. The latter use of this technique was primarily employed against military targets. There was, however, that one *little* matter or Pearl Harbor. In this one there were innocent people killed. I believe this is called collateral damage.

The current use of this technique is filled with collateral damage. It is being done in a fashion where those who are targeting others can't even tell if they have gained any military advantage at all. It seems like they don't just want to gain a military advantage. They say that they want to do the will of God, or Allah, or Jehovah, or any of the other titles given by man to the LORD of the universe. This is an excuse which is sometimes used in an attempt to take control of the LORD for some selfish purpose or for a special collection of humans. Once this excuse is in place, it is often extended to justify the atrocities against one another in His name. This is an abomination to God.

The folk who are being drawn into service in this enterprise are sometimes referred to as martyrs. This is an interesting, and somewhat troubling, thing to me, the whole concept of martyrdom. It only makes sense if those who are being martyred can rise from the dead. To become a martyr where there is no resurrection from the dead is to say that God would command humans to throw away their lives. This will never be my view of God. This is not the God of the universe who created such beautiful and beautifully functional entities as men and women. No, to suggest martyrdom without resurrection is to insult God.

So let us explore God's resurrection. We will explore two types of resurrection: the glorious rising and the judgmental rising.

The glorious rising

The glorious rising occurs when God has established a person or persons who are worthy of righteous treatment. An image of a glorious rising is illustrated below.

> *The hand of the LORD was upon me, and carried me out in the spirit of the LORD, and set me down in the midst of the valley which was full of bones, And caused me to pass by them round about: and, behold, there were very many in the open valley; and, lo, they were very dry.*
>
> *And he said unto me, Son of man, can these bones live?*
>
> *And I answered, O Lord GOD, thou knowest.*
>
> *Again he said unto me, Prophesy upon these bones, and say unto them, O ye dry bones, hear the word of the LORD. Thus saith the Lord GOD unto these bones; Behold, I will cause breath to enter into you, and ye shall live: And I will lay sinews upon you, and will bring up flesh upon you, and cover you with skin, and put breath in you, and ye shall live; and ye shall know that I am the LORD.*
>
> *So I prophesied as I was commanded: and as I prophesied, there was a noise, and behold a shaking, and the bones came together, bone to his bone. And when I beheld, lo, the sinews and the flesh came up upon them, and the skin covered them above: but there was no breath in them.*
>
> *Then said he unto me, Prophesy unto the wind, prophesy, son of man, and say to the wind, Thus saith the Lord GOD; Come from the four winds, O breath, and breathe upon these slain, that they may live.*

So I prophesied as he commanded me, and the breath
came into them, and they lived, and stood up upon their
feet, an exceeding great army.

Then he said unto me, Son of man, these bones are the
whole house of Israel: behold, they say, Our bones are
dried, and our hope is lost: we are cut off for our parts.
Therefore prophesy and say unto them, Thus saith the
Lord GOD; Behold, O my people, I will open your
graves, and cause you to come up out of your graves,
and bring you into the land of Israel. And ye shall know
that I am the LORD, when I have opened your graves, O
my people, and brought you up out of your graves, And
shall put my spirit in you, and ye shall live, and I shall
place you in your own land: then shall ye know that I the
LORD have spoken it, and performed it, saith the LORD.
(Ezekiel 37:1-14)

Note that in this rising, it is done by the will of God. God also gives
forth the reasons that He is causing the rising. God states that there is
worthiness in the one resurrected to receive such treatment from Him. It
is done when God has judged that the behavior of the person, or even an
entire nation, has been toward Him. The action that causes the
resurrection is the call of a people to devotion to God.

Resurrection is not earned because of performing a certain action
for or against mankind. There is nothing in the message above that
indicates that there was an earthly action that was done that caused the
resurrection. The ones resurrected received this honor from God for the
purpose of worshipping Him. In this case, it is done only by God and
His non-human agents; not by any agency of man.

The next example sheds light on the method God uses to announce
that a resurrection is imminent. The elements will be made to move so
that even those who didn't believe before in the things of God will be
moved to acknowledge that this must have been of God. Again there are
not human-to-human actions that announce the coming of
a resurrection.

Now from the sixth hour there was darkness over all the
land unto the ninth hour. And about the ninth hour Jesus
cried with a loud voice, saying, Eli, Eli, lama

sabachthani? that is to say, My God, my God, why hast thou forsaken me?

Some of them that stood there, when they heard that, said, This man calleth for Elias. And straightway one of them ran, and took a spunge, and filled it with vinegar, and put it on a reed, and gave him to drink. The rest said, Let be, let us see whether Elias will come to save him.

Jesus, when he had cried again with a loud voice, yielded up the ghost. And, behold, the veil of the temple was rent in twain from the top to the bottom; and the earth did quake, and the rocks rent; And the graves were opened; and many bodies of the saints which slept arose, And came out of the graves after his resurrection, and went into the holy city, and appeared unto many.

Now when the centurion, and they that were with him, watching Jesus, saw the earthquake, and those things that were done, they feared greatly, saying, Truly this was the Son of God.
(Matthew 27:45-54)

To announce the resurrection of the just individual, God sent some of those who had formerly been dead. He resurrected some folk who were easily recognized, and known to be dead. In this way those who were witness to the event would know that this was of God and would know that the power of resurrection was filling the air surrounding the event.

What signs do we have from God that His power is at work in the actions done by those who terminate their lives in a suicide bombing? Where is God's presence evident in these actions that kill--more correctly, murder--innocent individuals? If there are no signs, then it is not of God. God is not silent about His works: indeed He cannot be. We are reminded of this by His Prophet, Jesus of Nazareth.

And when he was come nigh, even now at the descent of the mount of Olives, the whole multitude of the disciples began to rejoice and praise God with a loud voice for all the mighty works that they had seen; Saying, Blessed be the King that cometh in the name of the Lord: peace in heaven, and glory in the highest.

And some of the Pharisees from among the multitude said unto him, Master, rebuke thy disciples.

And he answered and said unto them, I tell you that, if these should hold their peace, the stones would immediately cry out.
(Luke 19:37-40)

The judgmental rising

There is another kind of resurrection. This type of resurrection is one that is reserved for those who lack faith in God AND perform unrighteous acts and actions. To stay out of this class, we must do at least this much for God: we must have faith in God *far above* any that we might have in man.

Now faith is the substance of things hoped for, the evidence of things not seen. For by it the elders obtained a good report. Through faith we understand that the worlds were framed by the word of God, so that things which are seen were not made of things which do appear.

By faith Abel offered unto God a more excellent sacrifice than Cain, by which he obtained witness that he was righteous, God testifying of his gifts: and by it he being dead yet speaketh. By faith Enoch was translated that he should not see death; and was not found, because God had translated him: for before his translation he had this testimony, that he pleased God.

But without faith it is impossible to please him: for he that cometh to God must believe that he is, and that he is a rewarder of them that diligently seek him.
(Hebrews 11:1-6)

This does not say that we can please God by killing those who we choose to call His enemies. We can only please God when we diligently seek him. And I would maintain that if you diligently seek Him, you will discover another powerful alternative to destruction.

Dearly beloved, avenge not yourselves, but rather give place unto wrath: for it is written, Vengeance is mine; I will repay, saith the Lord.

Therefore if thine enemy hunger, feed him; if he thirst, give him drink: for in so doing thou shalt heap coals of fire on his head. Be not overcome of evil, but overcome evil with good.
(Romans 12:19-21)

When we are diligently seeking God and we pray that change happens, it happens; in His own time, it happens. Oh, you want change **right now**? Well, what extreme level of wisdom have you risen to that you can say to yourself, to God and to the world that you know better than God does when change must come?

Our prayer must be modeled after that of Jesus of Nazareth in order to fulfill God's requirements. This is the same way the prophets prayed, and it is the way all in Heaven petition God for the benefit of mankind. This is the way those in Heaven acknowledge God, when they're not involved in doing other works, according to His will, for the sake of the universe which was created by God and in which we live.

But when ye pray, use not vain repetitions, as the heathen do: for they think that they shall be heard for their much speaking. Be not ye therefore like unto them: for your Father knoweth what things ye have need of, before ye ask him.

After this manner therefore pray ye: Our Father which art in heaven, Hallowed be thy name. Thy kingdom come, Thy will be done in earth, as it is in heaven. Give us this day our daily bread. And forgive us our debts, as we forgive our debtors. And lead us not into temptation, but deliver us from evil: For thine is the kingdom, and the power, and the glory, for ever. Amen.

For if ye forgive men their trespasses, your heavenly Father will also forgive you: But if ye forgive not men their trespasses, neither will your Father forgive your trespasses.
(Matthew 6:7-15)

Forgive me for being cynical, but I do see something missing there. I don't see the part where it says, "And give us the power to destroy our fellow humans today". Even by saying this I am being generous to those who use the technique of *suicide bombing*. For them it should actually read, "And give us the power to **indiscriminately destroy** our fellow humans today".

Know ye not that when you destroy innocent life, you may have prevented someone from coming to a saving knowledge of the Lord. Rest assured though, God will not require their lapse from them, but their blood will be on your hands. God will recompense you according to the blood that you have kept from serving Him.

So, let's stop listening to me ramble and take a look at some Scripture on the matter.

> *And I saw an angel come down from heaven, having the key of the bottomless pit and a great chain in his hand. And he laid hold on the dragon, that old serpent, which is the Devil, and Satan, and bound him a thousand years, And cast him into the bottomless pit, and shut him up, and set a seal upon him, that he should deceive the nations no more, till the thousand years should be fulfilled: and after that he must be loosed a little season.*

> *And I saw thrones, and they sat upon them, and judgment was given unto them: and I saw the souls of them that were beheaded for the witness of Jesus, and for the word of God, and which had not worshipped the beast, neither his image, neither had received his mark upon their foreheads, or in their hands; and they lived and reigned with Christ a thousand years. But the rest of the dead lived not again until the thousand years were finished. This is the first resurrection. Blessed and holy is he that hath part in the first resurrection: on such the second death hath no power, but they shall be priests of God and of Christ, and shall reign with him a thousand years.*

> *And when the thousand years are expired, Satan shall be loosed out of his prison, And shall go out to deceive the nations which are in the four quarters of the earth, Gog and Magog, to gather them together to battle: the*

number of whom is as the sand of the sea. And they went up on the breadth of the earth, and compassed the camp of the saints about, and the beloved city: and fire came down from God out of heaven, and devoured them. And the devil that deceived them was cast into the lake of fire and brimstone, where the beast and the false prophet are, and shall be tormented day and night for ever and ever.

And I saw a great white throne, and him that sat on it, from whose face the earth and the heaven fled away; and there was found no place for them.

And I saw the dead, small and great, stand before God; and the books were opened: and another book was opened, which is the book of life: and the dead were judged out of those things which were written in the books, according to their works. And the sea gave up the dead which were in it; and death and hell delivered up the dead which were in them: and they were judged every man according to their works.

And death and hell were cast into the lake of fire. This is the second death. And whosoever was not found written in the book of life was cast into the lake of fire.
(Revelation 20:1-15)

The bottom line

Thought One: If you have worshipped God in truth, you will experience the glorious rising.

Thought Two: If you have done things that were not ordained by God, you might find yourself subject to the judgmental rising.

Thought Three: If others have done things by your command that were not ordained by God, both you and they will find yourselves subject to the judgmental rising.

All things are subject to the will of God. It is He who determines who must live and who will die. Nowhere does God relinquish His power to determine the fate of nations. Nowhere does His Son relinquish the power to determine the fate of individuals.

A better way

There is one other alternative. This is the one referred to as "absent from the body and present with the Lord".

> *For we know that if our earthly house of this tabernacle were dissolved, we have a building of God, an house not made with hands, eternal in the heavens. For in this we groan, earnestly desiring to be clothed upon with our house which is from heaven: If so be that being clothed we shall not be found naked. For we that are in this tabernacle do groan, being burdened: not for that we would be unclothed, but clothed upon, that mortality might be swallowed up of life. Now he that hath wrought us for the selfsame thing is God, who also hath given unto us the earnest of the Spirit.*

> *Therefore we are always confident, knowing that, whilst we are at home in the body, we are absent from the Lord: (For we walk by faith, not by sight:) We are confident, I say, and willing rather to be absent from the body, and to be present with the Lord. Wherefore we labour, that, whether present or absent, we may be accepted of him. For we must all appear before the judgment seat of Christ; that every one may receive the things done in his body, according to that he hath done, whether it be good or bad.*
> (2 Corinthians 5:1-10)

This is the dispensation of the dead; a rising that was put in place by Jesus of Nazareth and proclaimed by his disciples. It is indeed a unique approach not found in the Old Covenant. It is a method of resurrection that is actually not resurrection at all. There is not even a fraction of a second between the death of those who have access to this approach and their presentation before God for eternity.

However, to establish oneself in this most marvelous position before God, there is a requirement of faith. To take advantage of the blessings offered by God therein, one must believe in the life and message of Jesus of Nazareth. This is a tall order for many.

When Jesus came into the coasts of Caesarea Philippi, he asked his disciples, saying, Whom do men say that I the Son of man am?

And they said, Some say that thou art John the Baptist: some, Elias; and others, Jeremias, or one of the prophets.

He saith unto them, But whom say ye that I am?

And Simon Peter answered and said, Thou art the Christ, the Son of the living God.

And Jesus answered and said unto him, Blessed art thou, Simon Barjona: for flesh and blood hath not revealed it unto thee, but my Father which is in heaven. And I say also unto thee, That thou art Peter, and upon this rock I will build my church; and the gates of hell shall not prevail against it.
                    (Matthew 16:13-18)

I admonish everyone to believe in the Gospel of Jesus Christ. However, I will also let you know that by believing in the Gospel of Jesus Christ you will have to subject yourself to his teachings. This means that instead of destroying your enemies, you operate with a new set of parameters.

Ye have heard that it hath been said, Thou shalt love thy neighbour, and hate thine enemy. But I say unto you, Love your enemies, bless them that curse you, do good to them that hate you, and pray for them which despitefully use you, and persecute you; That ye may be the children of your Father which is in heaven: for he maketh his sun to rise on the evil and on the good, and sendeth rain on the just and on the unjust.

For if ye love them which love you, what reward have ye? do not even the publicans the same? And if ye salute your brethren only, what do ye more than others? do not even the publicans so?

Be ye therefore perfect, even as your Father which is in heaven is perfect.
                    (Matthew 5:43-48)

But you ask, "How stupid can this be? Enemies are to be destroyed, aren't they?"

No, it's not really necessary for us to do that. First, because we must believe that God can do all things for us if we just ask Him.

Is any among you afflicted? let him pray. Is any merry? let him sing psalms. Is any sick among you? let him call for the elders of the church; and let them pray over him, anointing him with oil in the name of the Lord: And the prayer of faith shall save the sick, and the Lord shall raise him up; and if he have committed sins, they shall be forgiven him.

Confess your faults one to another, and pray one for another, that ye may be healed. The effectual fervent prayer of a righteous man availeth much. Elias was a man subject to like passions as we are, and he prayed earnestly that it might not rain: and it rained not on the earth by the space of three years and six months. And he prayed again, and the heaven gave rain, and the earth brought forth her fruit.
     (James 5:13-18)

To get to this kind of prayer life we must place ourselves in a right relationship with God.

Judge not, that ye be not judged. For with what judgment ye judge, ye shall be judged: and with what measure ye mete, it shall be measured to you again.

And why beholdest thou the mote that is in thy brother's eye, but considerest not the beam that is in thine own eye? Or how wilt thou say to thy brother, Let me pull out the mote out of thine eye; and, behold, a beam is in thine own eye? Thou hypocrite, first cast out the beam out of thine own eye; and then shalt thou see clearly to cast out the mote out of thy brother's eye.
     (Matthew 7:1-5)

Until we are PERFECTLY doing the will of God, we have no means of persuading God that what we are about to do is righteous. Besides that, we all know that God knows who is and who is not righteous. If we are not righteous, our work is in vain. It doesn't matter that a religious leader pronounces us righteous; this they do not have the power to do. Only God has the power to declare righteousness or unrighteousness. However, those who are unrighteous know that they are.

One of the greatest examples of a demonstration of the power of God on behalf of His message, is through the prophet Elijah (called Elias in the New Testament of the Bible).

And it came to pass, when Ahab saw Elijah, that Ahab said unto him, Art thou he that troubleth Israel?

And he answered, I have not troubled Israel; but thou, and thy father's house, in that ye have forsaken the commandments of the LORD, and thou hast followed Baalim. Now therefore send, and gather to me all Israel unto mount Carmel, and the prophets of Baal four hundred and fifty, and the prophets of the groves four hundred, which eat at Jezebel's table.

So Ahab sent unto all the children of Israel, and gathered the prophets together unto mount Carmel.

And Elijah came unto all the people, and said, How long halt ye between two opinions? if the LORD be God, follow him: but if Baal, then follow him.

And the people answered him not a word.

Then said Elijah unto the people, I, even I only, remain a prophet of the LORD; but Baal's prophets are four hundred and fifty men. Let them therefore give us two bullocks; and let them choose one bullock for themselves, and cut it in pieces, and lay it on wood, and put no fire under: and I will dress the other bullock, and lay it on wood, and put no fire under: And call ye on the name of your gods, and I will call on the name of the LORD: and the God that answereth by fire, let him be God.

And all the people answered and said, It is well spoken.

And Elijah said unto the prophets of Baal, Choose you one bullock for yourselves, and dress it first; for ye are many; and call on the name of your gods, but put no fire under.

And they took the bullock which was given them, and they dressed it, and called on the name of Baal from morning even until noon, saying, O Baal, hear us. But there was no voice, nor any that answered. And they leaped upon the altar which was made.

And it came to pass at noon, that Elijah mocked them, and said, Cry aloud: for he is a god; either he is talking, or he is pursuing, or he is in a journey, or peradventure he sleepeth, and must be awaked.

And they cried aloud, and cut themselves after their manner with knives and lancets, till the blood gushed out upon them. And it came to pass, when midday was past, and they prophesied until the time of the offering of the evening sacrifice, that there was neither voice, nor any to answer, nor any that regarded.

And Elijah said unto all the people, Come near unto me. And all the people came near unto him. And he repaired the altar of the LORD that was broken down. And Elijah took twelve stones, according to the number of the tribes of the sons of Jacob, unto whom the word of the LORD came, saying, Israel shall be thy name: And with the stones he built an altar in the name of the LORD: and he made a trench about the altar, as great as would contain two measures of seed. And he put the wood in order, and cut the bullock in pieces, and laid him on the wood, and said, Fill four barrels with water, and pour it on the burnt sacrifice, and on the wood. And he said, Do it the second time. And they did it the second time. And he said, Do it the third time. And they did it the third time. And the water ran round about the altar; and he filled the trench also with water.

And it came to pass at the time of the offering of the evening sacrifice, that Elijah the prophet came near, and said, LORD God of Abraham, Isaac, and of Israel, let it be known this day that thou art God in Israel, and that I am thy servant, and that I have done all these things at thy word. Hear me, O LORD, hear me, that this people may know that thou art the LORD God, and that thou hast turned their heart back again.

Then the fire of the LORD fell, and consumed the burnt sacrifice, and the wood, and the stones, and the dust, and licked up the water that was in the trench.

And when all the people saw it, they fell on their faces: and they said, The LORD, he is the God; the LORD, he is the God.

(1 Kings 18:17-39)

The same man Elijah also participated in one of the most dazzling displays of God instantaneous ability to show His power, **without the use of man made instruments or structures**.

And it came to pass, when they were gone over, that Elijah said unto Elisha, Ask what I shall do for thee, before I be taken away from thee.

And Elisha said, I pray thee, let a double portion of thy spirit be upon me.

And he said, Thou hast asked a hard thing: nevertheless, if thou see me when I am taken from thee, it shall be so unto thee; but if not, it shall not be so.

And it came to pass, as they still went on, and talked, that, behold, there appeared a chariot of fire, and horses of fire, and parted them both asunder; and <u>Elijah went up by a whirlwind into heaven</u>.

And Elisha saw it, and he cried, My father, my father, the chariot of Israel, and the horsemen thereof. And he saw him no more: and he took hold of his own clothes, and rent them in two pieces.

(2 Kings 2:9-12)

It is also Elijah who gives us the direct illustration of what kind of rising from the dead is available for those who are righteous before God. His is one of the risings that skip the dead part. There was not for Elijah a fraction of a second between his leaving the confines of the kingdom of man, and joining God in the eternal life in Heaven. This is the kind of transference that is preached by the Gospel of Jesus Christ and is still being spread by his representatives today.

However, in the image of Elijah, this type of *resurrection* is available only to those who are willing to forego military action on their part. These are they who believe God so strongly that they are willing to honor him by standing still.

> *Come, behold the works of the LORD, what desolations he hath made in the earth. He maketh wars to cease unto the end of the earth; he breaketh the bow, and cutteth the spear in sunder; he burneth the chariot in the fire.*
>
> *Be still, and know that I am God: I will be exalted among the heathen, I will be exalted in the earth.*
> (Psalm 46:8-10)

We are therefore left with choices about how we want to serve God. However, since there is only one God, there is also only one right way to serve Him. We can try to serve Him in one or more of the myriad of wrong ways; none of which will be accepted by Him.

> *Enter ye in at the strait gate: for wide is the gate, and broad is the way, that leadeth to destruction, and many there be which go in thereat: Because strait is the gate, and narrow is the way, which leadeth unto life, and few there be that find it.*
>
> *Beware of false prophets, which come to you in sheep's clothing, but inwardly they are ravening wolves.*
> (Matthew 7:13-15)

Thus, we must serve Him in the only right way. The right way is to allow God to show forth his glory and presence among men through the acts that He performs. Today is the time to give control of your life to God.

> *Even from the days of your fathers ye are gone away from mine ordinances, and have not kept them. Return unto me, and I will return unto you, saith the LORD of hosts. But ye said, Wherein shall we return?*
> (Malachi 3:7)

Let's take a look again at the message of Joshua, the chosen leader of Israel after the passing of Moses. This time, though, let's actually make a decision. Let's make the decision to stop our interference by these vain acts of defiance against one another, and to let God make the difference in what is done. Listen to the man of God; at least by doing that you are following the advice of someone who achieved success through his devotion to God. And isn't everyone interested in following a successful man to the prize that waits at the end of this life and is grasped at the beginning of eternity?

> *Now therefore fear the LORD, and serve him in sincerity and in truth: and put away the gods which your fathers served on the other side of the flood, and in Egypt; and serve ye the LORD. And if it seem evil unto you to serve the LORD, choose you this day whom ye will serve; whether the gods which your fathers served that were on the other side of the flood, or the gods of the Amorites, in whose land ye dwell: but as for me and my house, we will serve the LORD.*
> (Joshua 24:14-15)

I would feel totally negligent were I to not mention one other matter. When a child is indiscriminately destroyed in this or any other fashion, who do you think gets the first audience with God? Is it the destroyer or is it the child?

The answer is: the child.

It is the child because before the killing device has finished the abomination of the destroyer, the advocate for the child has already spoken. Before the body of the destroyer has finished its fragmentation, heavenly forces have already been set in motion. Before the destroyer gets to give the excuse for their actions, the advocate for the child has already condemned them before God. Consider this well before you act.

> *Take heed that ye despise not one of these little ones; for I say unto you, That in heaven their angels do always behold the face of my Father which is in heaven.*
> (Matthew 18:10)

Some think they can order others
To indiscriminately kill,
In an attempt to cause nations
To bend to their will;

And those who are willing
To inflict on others such ill,
Hide behind the leaders
With whom they deal.

They strive for a title,
Which they call martyr;
To be used in some way
With God to barter

For a better position
In His Holy realm
Or some ship that allows
Them to take the helm,

To steer a course
Into eternity bright
And cause their enemies
To thus take flight.

But the work *that they do*
Is not limited to one,
And the damage that occurs
Can never be undone.

They trigger the promise
Of God to his nation
That he will visit their sin
To the fourth generation.

An act of vengeance which
Destroys ones they should love,
In a misguided attempt
To sway God above,

By an action that
He surely views as most coarse,
Which nowhere in His Mission
Did He ever endorse.

Arbitrary and sinful killing
Of even one child or man
Receives a recompense from
God's Strong Right Hand.

Chapter 8a

Tying the Hands of Jesus

Much of our talk about the Messiah and his mission to the earth is elitist. Some of us feel that we have the right to say who he should and who he should not accept. We even use some of his words in an attempt to shackle him to our concept of vengeance. This representation of vengeance we say we are doing on behalf of God. Sometimes we even manipulate Scripture to force the point. However, our view of vengeance is irrelevant.

> *Recompense to no man evil for evil. Provide things honest in the sight of all men. If it be possible, as much as lieth in you, live peaceably with all men.*
>
> *Dearly beloved, avenge not yourselves, but rather give place unto wrath: for it is written, Vengeance is mine; I will repay, saith the Lord. Therefore if thine enemy hunger, feed him; if he thirst, give him drink: for in so doing thou shalt heap coals of fire on his head. Be not overcome of evil, but overcome evil with good.*
> (Romans 12:17-21)

We have no right to manipulate vengeance in any way. The Scripture does not include a footnote, with a tickler to mankind which designates mankind as the agent to remind God of the need for vengeance. Furthermore, it definitely did not include any provision for man to tell God when and how and to whom vengeance is to be measured out. The same limitations apply to the associated concepts of justice and judgment.

On the matter of retribution, the LORD needs no reminders from we who are human. Furthermore, He does not require our assistance to accomplish this action. We who serve God need to move back into the love of God. We need to stop advertising to the world what bad things God will do to them.

In the olden days telling the *bad news* was the assignments of the prophets. Not all those who are advertising destruction to the world today are His prophets. To the children of Abraham I say, "Unless you have been called by God to be his prophet of destruction, don't step on this holy ground".

Since I am most familiar with the children of Abraham known as Christians, I will use the instructions given to them. And in case you wonder; yes, if I had been born in olden times, I would be among those called a prophet of God. Being a Christian, however, I prefer the title apostle.

> *The law and the prophets were until John: since that time the kingdom of God is preached, and every man presseth into it. And it is easier for heaven and earth to pass, than one tittle of the law to fail.*
> (Luke 16:16-17)

Therefore, let me help you untie the hands of Christ, the Messiah, in your mind.

My understanding of the current state of being in God is that we are now in the era when we must preach the love of God and leave vengeance, judgment and justice to God. Jesus Christ represented himself to us with this limitation in mind.

> *Ye judge after the flesh; I judge no man. And yet if I judge, my judgment is true: for I am not alone, but I and the Father that sent me. It is also written in your law, that the testimony of two men is true.*
> (John 8:15-17)

God has His time set for judgment. This includes current judgment as well as final judgment. At the final judgment it will be God, His Son, and those who have been specially selected for this assignment, which will do the judging.

Please understand; the words that are written here are not only for Christians. These words are for all the children of Abraham, as well as all who will hear from the remainder of the world. Let's begin with some very powerful Scripture passages.

> *The Lord is not slack concerning his promise, as some men count slackness; but is longsuffering to us-ward, not*

willing that any should perish, but that all should come to repentance.
(2 Peter 3:9)

And as it is appointed unto men once to die, but after this the judgment: So Christ was once offered to bear the sins of many; and unto them that look for him shall he appear the second time without sin unto salvation.
(Hebrews 9:27-28)

For the law having a shadow of good things to come, and not the very image of the things, can never with those sacrifices which they offered year by year continually make the comers thereunto perfect. For then would they not have ceased to be offered? because that the worshippers once purged should have had no more conscience of sins. But in those sacrifices there is a remembrance again made of sins every year. For it is not possible that the blood of bulls and of goats should take away sins.

Wherefore when he cometh into the world, he saith, Sacrifice and offering thou wouldest not, but a body hast thou prepared me: In burnt offerings and sacrifices for sin thou hast had no pleasure. Then said I, Lo, I come (in the volume of the book it is written of me,) to do thy will, O God.

Above when he said, Sacrifice and offering and burnt offerings and offering for sin thou wouldest not, neither hadst pleasure therein; which are offered by the law; Then said he, Lo, I come to do thy will, O God. He taketh away the first, that he may establish the second. By the which will we are sanctified through the offering of the body of Jesus Christ once for all.
(Hebrews 10:1-10)

The passages listed above give us an introduction to what the Messiah is assigned to do for mankind. This, however, is not sufficient for many people. They would take it upon themselves to tell God how he should operate in the theatre of mankind. This is particularly true among those Christians who want to restrict the message of the Messiah to the discussion of judgment. They, thereby, greatly reduce, if not eliminate, the message of mercy.

Our mission is not to pronounce judgment, it is to preach the Gospel.

> *And he said unto them, Go ye into all the world, and preach the gospel to every creature.*
> (Mark 16:15)

There is much discussion about God's judgment and how at the end of the world, whatever that fully means, God will HAVE to execute judgment. Yes, I'm sure God will execute judgment at the end of the world, just as He executes judgment all the time. However, the judgment He executes may astonish some of those who feel that they know what judgment He should execute.

One of the common expressions of judgment indicts the rotten unbelievers and seals their entry into hell and the lake that burns with fire and brimstone. This often misses the point that these are two different places with two different functions. Only one of them is an eternal repository. (*Study to shew thyself approved.*) These self-appointed judges, are quick to highlight the benefits of joining their cause.

This is most often emphasized by highlighting the giving of crowns to those who have endured. Thus, they give the notion that some will be debased relative to others, even among those who are a part of God's people. This only attempts to resurrect the dead theology of salvation through works. This was not just killed by the death and resurrection of Jesus Christ; it was made of no effect in all of reality and history.

The twelve disciples were given the assignment of one day judging the twelve tribes of Israel.

> *Ye are they which have continued with me in my temptations. And I appoint unto you a kingdom, as my Father hath appointed unto me; That ye may eat and drink at my table in my kingdom, and sit on thrones judging the twelve tribes of Israel.*
> (Luke 22:28-30)

Consider the following when you think about the matter of judgment. Maybe because Paul was the apostle to the Gentiles, he will be given the task of assisting in judging the remainder of the nations; that is, if there is any remainder of nations at that time, to be judged.

What would happen if the entire world were deemed to be a part of the nation of Israel as God views this nation: or all people were seen to be children of Abraham?

Jesus was a member of the nation of Israel, and he calls us brothers. The apostle Paul mentions that there was a revision in the participants in the family of Abraham to include the believers in Jesus Christ. And we really don't know how many of us have a lineage that leads back to King David and the original tribes of Israel. With the amount of intermarriage that went on even in the Bible days, it will be extremely difficult for man to sort out the extended nation of Abraham, Isaac and Jacob. By the way, did you know that Abraham had children of an Egyptian (Hagar - Genesis 16:1-4) and Moses married and Ethiopian (Numbers 12:1)?

> *And when Abram was ninety years old and nine, the LORD appeared to Abram, and said unto him, I am the Almighty God; walk before me, and be thou perfect. And I will make my covenant between me and thee, and will multiply thee exceedingly. And Abram fell on his face: and God talked with him, saying, As for me, behold, my covenant is with thee, and thou shalt be a father of many nations. Neither shall thy name any more be called Abram, but thy name shall be Abraham; for a father of many nations have I made thee. And I will make thee exceeding fruitful, and I will make nations of thee, and kings shall come out of thee.*
> (Genesis 17:1-6)

> *And there was a famine in the land, beside the first famine that was in the days of Abraham. And Isaac went unto Abimelech king of the Philistines unto Gerar. And the LORD appeared unto him, and said, Go not down into Egypt; dwell in the land which I shall tell thee of: Sojourn in this land, and I will be with thee, and will bless thee; for unto thee, and unto thy seed, I will give all these countries, and I will perform the oath which I sware unto Abraham thy father; And I will make thy seed to multiply as the stars of heaven, and will give unto thy seed all these countries; and in thy seed shall all the nations of the earth be blessed; Because that Abraham obeyed my voice, and*

kept my charge, my commandments, my statutes, and my laws.
(Genesis 26:1-5)

This could take in a fairly large chunk of the human race, if not all of us.

On a governmental note, we are told that there will be individuals who will reign with the Messiah. And if they are to reign with the Messiah then there must be others who will be subject to them.

And when he had taken the book, the four beasts and four and twenty elders fell down before the Lamb, having every one of them harps, and golden vials full of odours, which are the prayers of saints. And they sung a new song, saying, Thou art worthy to take the book, and to open the seals thereof: for thou wast slain, and hast redeemed us to God by thy blood out of every kindred, and tongue, and people, and nation; And hast made us unto our God kings and priests: and we shall reign on the earth.
(Revelation 5:8-10)

And lest you make the dangerous leap, don't read the word *reign* to imply *better*. A different calling only makes one unique, not better or worse than others who have another calling. Furthermore, if only the *Christians* exist in the world when the Messiah returns to take control of the government, there will be no one subject to anyone, only to the Father and His Son.

However, a world with only Christians is not the picture that is given in the Scripture. The Scripture reveals to us the state of reality at the time of time of the establishment of the kingdom of God on the earth. It tells us of the *duties* of the Messiah, sent from God: the Messiah controls all government, and it is only through him that some will reign with him.

For unto us a child is born, unto us a son is given: and the government shall be upon his shoulder: and his name shall be called Wonderful, Counsellor, The mighty God, The everlasting Father, The Prince of Peace. Of the increase of his government and peace there shall be no end, upon the throne of David, and upon his kingdom, to

order it, and to establish it with judgment and with justice from henceforth even for ever. The zeal of the LORD of hosts will perform this.
        (Isaiah 9:6-7)

We who believe in the Messiah are promised that those who believe in the Messiah are heirs to the promise. There must, therefore, be others who occupy the realm of God under the rule of the Messiah. There must be some in the realm who are the occupants of the new earth outside of the holy city. For this is where the Messiah comes to reign forever and ever.

And there came unto me one of the seven angels which had the seven vials full of the seven last plagues, and talked with me, saying, Come hither, I will show thee the bride, the Lamb's wife. And he carried me away in the spirit to a great and high mountain, and showed me that great city, the holy Jerusalem, descending out of heaven from God, Having the glory of God: and her light was like unto a stone most precious, even like a jasper stone, clear as crystal; And had a wall great and high, and had twelve gates, and at the gates twelve angels, and names written thereon, which are the names of the twelve tribes of the children of Israel: On the east three gates; on the north three gates; on the south three gates; and on the west three gates. And the wall of the city had twelve foundations, and in them the names of the twelve apostles of the Lamb.
        (Revelation 21:9-14)

And I saw no temple therein: for the Lord God Almighty and the Lamb are the temple of it. And the city had no need of the sun, neither of the moon, to shine in it: for the glory of God did lighten it, and the Lamb is the light thereof. And the nations of them which are saved shall walk in the light of it: and the kings of the earth do bring their glory and honour into it. And the gates of it shall not be shut at all by day: for there shall be no night there. And they shall bring the glory and honour of the nations into it. And there shall in no wise enter into it any thing that defileth, neither

whatsoever worketh abomination, or maketh a lie: but they
which are written in the Lamb's book of life.
(Revelation 21:22-27)

As I read the Scriptures from a purely logical perspective, believing that God is pure logic and then some, I see an opening for others besides the followers of the Messiah to occupy the earth after the time of his final return to take over all government. Since death, hell and the sea have given up their dead at that time, these others must include not just those who are alive at the time of his return, but also those who have died as well.

This is a worthy crowd, for the King of kings and Lord of lord, to be the master and ruler over. Make no mistake about it, at the time of his return, the Messiah will be recognized, for the glory of God, by ALL, as the legitimate ruler of the world.

Look unto me, and be ye saved, all the ends of the earth:
for I am God, and there is none else. I have sworn by
myself, the word is gone out of my mouth in
righteousness, and shall not return, That unto me every
knee shall bow, every tongue shall swear. Surely, shall
one say, in the LORD have I righteousness and strength:
even to him shall men come; and all that are incensed
against him shall be ashamed. In the LORD shall all the
seed of Israel be justified, and shall glory.
(Isaiah 45:22-25)

Many of these knees will not have thought about bowing to him before. Among those will be they who have chosen to turn their backs on him, for various and sundry reasons. But at this time there will be no escaping his presence and his Authority, as given to him by God the Father. This is different from the view of many other religious students and scholars. The predominant view across the children of Abraham is that God will dismiss the ones that have not already bowed the knee, into the nether region of extreme suffering; and this suffering will last for an eternity.

When I read the Bible I take it, as they say, at its word. The lake that burns with fire and brimstone is for the devil and his angels. The word *angels* means, at its highest; beings that were created in a divine state for an eternal existence in the same form in which they were created. At its most liberal, it means those who are agents of, in this case, Satan. Let us go one step further and evaluate the term *angel*. This title is a very powerful one. It does not fit those who are deceived by the enemy.

> *And as he sat upon the mount of Olives, the disciples came unto him privately, saying, Tell us, when shall these things be? and what shall be the sign of thy coming, and of the end of the world? And Jesus answered and said unto them, Take heed that no man deceive you. For many shall come in my name, saying, I am Christ; and shall deceive many.*
>
> (Matthew 24:3-5)

> *And many false prophets shall rise, and shall deceive many. And because iniquity shall abound, the love of many shall wax cold. But he that shall endure unto the end, the same shall be saved.*
>
> (Matthew 24:11-13)

> *And there was war in heaven: Michael and his angels fought against the dragon; and the dragon fought and his angels, And prevailed not; neither was their place found any more in heaven. And the great dragon was cast out, that old serpent, called the Devil, and Satan, which deceiveth the whole world: he was cast out into the earth, and his angels were cast out with him.*
>
> (Revelation 12:7-9)

> *And I beheld another beast coming up out of the earth; and he had two horns like a lamb, and he spake as a dragon. And he exerciseth all the power of the first beast before him, and causeth the earth and them which dwell therein to worship the first beast, whose deadly wound was healed. And he doeth great wonders, so that he maketh fire come down from heaven on the earth in the sight of men, And deceiveth them that dwell on the earth by the means of those miracles which he had power to do in the sight of the beast; saying to them that dwell on the earth, that they should make an image to the beast, which had the wound by a sword, and did live.*
>
> (Revelation 13:11-14)

The term *angel* only fits those who understand both the true nature of God and His Son, and the true nature of the satanic forces. Furthermore, as far as eternal punishment, it only fits those who, having such understanding, choose to take a stand for the satanic forces. This is not a coincidental matter, but a matter of the will and of evil choice. Most, if not all, humans are subject to their nature and are not masters of it. This is clearly stated by the apostle Paul, who even though he was devoted to God through Christ, still had battles within himself against evil. Satan is a powerful force that has the benefit of many, many years of experience in doing its job. Man is just beginning the fight. No man has any hope of winning by his power alone, or even in the entire group called mankind; and, yes, this applies to women as well.

> *For we know that the law is spiritual: but I am carnal, sold under sin. For that which I do I allow not: for what I would, that do I not; but what I hate, that do I. If then I do that which I would not, I consent unto the law that it is good.*

> *Now then it is no more I that do it, but sin that dwelleth in me. For I know that in me (that is, in my flesh,) dwelleth no good thing: for to will is present with me; but how to perform that which is good I find not. For the good that I would I do not: but the evil which I would not, that I do. Now if I do that I would not, it is no more I that do it, but sin that dwelleth in me.*

> *I find then a law, that, when I would do good, evil is present with me. For I delight in the law of God after the inward man: But I see another law in my members, warring against the law of my mind, and bringing me into captivity to the law of sin which is in my members.*

> *O wretched man that I am! who shall deliver me from the body of this death? I thank God through Jesus Christ our Lord. So then with the mind I myself serve the law of God; but with the flesh the law of sin.*
> (Romans 7:14-25)

I am reminded of a passage in the book of Jonah where God explained why he spared the Ninevites.

So Jonah went out of the city, and sat on the east side of the city, and there made him a booth, and sat under it in the shadow, till he might see what would become of the city. And the LORD God prepared a gourd, and made it to come up over Jonah, that it might be a shadow over his head, to deliver him from his grief. So Jonah was exceeding glad of the gourd. But God prepared a worm when the morning rose the next day, and it smote the gourd that it withered.

And it came to pass, when the sun did arise, that God prepared a vehement east wind; and the sun beat upon the head of Jonah, that he fainted, and wished in himself to die, and said, It is better for me to die than to live. And God said to Jonah, Doest thou well to be angry for the gourd?

And he said, I do well to be angry, even unto death.

Then said the LORD, Thou hast had pity on the gourd, for the which thou hast not laboured, neither madest it grow; which came up in a night, and perished in a night: And should not I spare Nineveh, that great city, wherein are more than sixscore thousand persons that cannot discern between their right hand and their left hand; and also much cattle?

(Jonah 4:5-11)

The state of the Ninevites is the same as that of much of the world at this present point in time. So many of the people who label themselves religious don't know the left hand of God from his powerful right hand (where sits the Messiah). So why shouldn't God apply the blessing which He gave to the Ninevites, as described in the book of Jonah, to the entire world. Oh, my, it seems that he already did.

Then certain of the scribes and of the Pharisees answered, saying, Master, we would see a sign from thee. But he answered and said unto them, An evil and adulterous generation seeketh after a sign; and there shall no sign be given to it, but the sign of the prophet Jonas: For as Jonas was three days and three nights in the whale's belly; so shall the Son of man be three days and three nights in the heart of the earth.

The men of Nineveh shall rise in judgment with this generation, and shall condemn it: because they repented at the preaching of Jonas; and, behold, a greater than Jonas is here.
(Matthew 12:38-41)

The power of God is shared with the Son. Specifically, this gift was given after the Messiah had performed all that God required of him, including the death on the cross.

And Jesus came and spake unto them, saying, All power is given unto me in heaven and in earth. Go ye therefore, and teach all nations, baptizing them in the name of the Father, and of the Son, and of the Holy Ghost: Teaching them to observe all things whatsoever I have commanded you: and, lo, I am with you alway, even unto the end of the world. Amen.
(Matthew 28:18-20)

Yes, those who choose for Christ will be saved. They will be saved from the destructive forces of life.

Come unto me, all ye that labour and are heavy laden, and I will give you rest. Take my yoke upon you, and learn of me; for I am meek and lowly in heart: and ye shall find rest unto your souls. For my yoke is easy, and my burden is light.
(Matthew 11:28-30)

They will be saved from a death that includes the wailing and gnashing of teeth until the end of the world.

Then Martha, as soon as she heard that Jesus was coming, went and met him: but Mary sat still in the house. Then said Martha unto Jesus, Lord, if thou hadst been here, my brother had not died. But I know, that even now, whatsoever thou wilt ask of God, God will give it thee.

Jesus saith unto her, Thy brother shall rise again.

Martha saith unto him, I know that he shall rise again in the resurrection at the last day.

Jesus said unto her, I am the resurrection, and the life: he that believeth in me, though he were dead, yet shall he live: And whosoever liveth and believeth in me shall never die. Believest thou this?

She saith unto him, Yea, Lord: I believe that thou art the Christ, the Son of God, which should come into the world.
(John 11:20-27)

And if they are alive when the Messiah returns, they will be saved from the destruction of all of their works. They will be saved from the destruction of much of their personality. With the help of the Holy Ghost they will have already started being conformed to the image of God in Christ, while they are still alive.

For other foundation can no man lay than that is laid, which is Jesus Christ. Now if any man build upon this foundation gold, silver, precious stones, wood, hay, stubble; Every man's work shall be made manifest: for the day shall declare it, because it shall be revealed by fire; and the fire shall try every man's work of what sort it is. If any man's work abide which he hath built thereupon, he shall receive a reward. If any man's work shall be burned, he shall suffer loss: but he himself shall be saved; yet so as by fire.
(1 Corinthians 3:11-15)

Those who are saved by Christ will enter into eternity, renewed in him. As such they will have a place with him in the presence of God for an eternity. The promise has already been made and cannot be undone.

Let not your heart be troubled: ye believe in God, believe also in me. In my Father's house are many mansions: if it were not so, I would have told you. I go to prepare a place for you. And if I go and prepare a place for you, I will come again, and receive you unto myself; that where I am, there ye may be also. And whither I go ye know, and the way ye know.

Thomas saith unto him, Lord, we know not whither thou goest; and how can we know the way?

Jesus saith unto him, I am the way, the truth, and the life:
no man cometh unto the Father, but by me.
    (John 14:1-6)

Never forget that every soul is created by the Word of God. Souls are eternal and are not expendable. There are other expendable things that God has made. Among these are concepts such as evil, malice, corrupt thoughts, evolution, thermodynamics, and inertia. These things have no authority in the kingdom of God. Many of them will have no place in the kingdom of God. They are not operative in Heaven, and they will not be required in the new heaven or on the new earth. Such are these that are also candidates for the lake.

And whosoever was not found written in the book of life
was cast into the lake of fire.
    (Revelation 20:15)

It is my prayer that when God and His Son are at the judgment seat, that they will forgive all who have not become angels of Satan among the humans. I pray this because I know that it is only because of their ignorance of the nature of His being that they have not become servants of the only Living God.

Their lack of conversion will in some case be accounted to our own inept statements about the nature of God. These are the statements that serve as stumbling blocks to others. This I pray is not the case with you, and I plead with God to conform me so that it is not the case for me. For me to ask for less than the salvation of the entire world is to make the sacrifice of Christ weak and of only little effect. This I will not do, nor will I ever allow that anyone has a right to do so.

The sacrifice of Christ is for all mankind and is for all persons on the earth; past, present and future; wherever they reside. To think otherwise dilutes the sacrifice significantly and may place us back at a position of not knowing for sure that any of us merits continuous existence, as our souls were made to be. All shall come to repentance; whether they do it on this earth or on the new earth is a choice that they make. But the fact is that they WILL do it on one or the other.

The Messiah, Christ, was sent on his mission by God the Father and having completed it he now wields all power *in heaven and in earth.* Jesus Christ can transform everyone. The following statement, from a representative of the Lord Jesus Christ, which I hold as a promise, on the matter of repentance, will forever reverberate in my mind and fill my heart.

> *The Lord is not slack concerning his promise, as some men count slackness; but is longsuffering to us-ward, not willing that any should perish, but that all should come to repentance.*
>
> (2 Peter 3:9)

To think otherwise is to give place to Satan to have power that is exempt from the influence of the sacrifice made on the cross. God has already shown that he does not punish those who act against Him in ignorance. Yes, he requires a penance from them, but this does not rise to the level of eternal punishment.

Let me stress this once more. Those who make the choice for Christ on this earth forego an uncomfortable waiting period between death and the final coming of the Lord Jesus Christ. Those who do it on this earth, go directly from death into life. Those who died under the promise to Abraham went into a sleep, called death, waiting for the resurrection. Those who were party to the time of the flood went into the sea waiting for Christ's return. The others will not see sleep but will enter the **uncomfortable** *place* that is described as hell: and there they stay until Christ's return to release them for judgment. This may be a year, a day, or it may be thousand upon thousands of years. The soul is immortal and will continue beyond death in one of these states. It is now your choice.

> *Thus saith the LORD, the Redeemer of Israel, and his Holy One, to him whom man despiseth, to him whom the nation abhorreth, to a servant of rulers, Kings shall see and arise, princes also shall worship, because of the LORD that is faithful, and the Holy One of Israel, and he shall choose thee.*
>
> *Thus saith the LORD, In an acceptable time have I heard thee, and in a day of salvation have I helped thee: and I will preserve thee, and give thee for a covenant of the people, to establish the earth, to cause to inherit the desolate heritages; That thou mayest say to the prisoners, Go forth; to them that are in darkness, Show yourselves. They shall feed in the ways, and their pastures shall be in all high places. They shall not hunger nor thirst; neither shall the heat nor sun smite*

them: for he that hath mercy on them shall lead them, even by the springs of water shall he guide them. And I will make all my mountains a way, and my highways shall be exalted. Behold, these shall come from far: and, lo, these from the north and from the west; and these from the land of Sinim. Sing, O heavens; and be joyful, O earth; and break forth into singing, O mountains: for the LORD hath comforted his people, and will have mercy upon his afflicted.

(Isaiah 49:7-13)

Now then we are ambassadors for Christ, as though God did beseech you by us: we pray you in Christ's stead, be ye reconciled to God. For he hath made him to be sin for us, who knew no sin; that we might be made the righteousness of God in him.

(2 Corinthians 5:20-21)

We then, as workers together with him, beseech you also that ye receive not the grace of God in vain. (For he saith, I have heard thee in a time accepted, and in the day of salvation have I succoured thee: behold, now is the accepted time; behold, now is the day of salvation.)

(2 Corinthians 6:1-2)

The Word from the Bible

John 18:33-36

Then Pilate entered into the judgment hall again, and called Jesus, and said unto him, Art thou the King of the Jews?

Jesus answered him, Sayest thou this thing of thyself, or did others tell it thee of me?

Pilate answered, Am I a Jew? Thine own nation and the chief priests have delivered thee unto me: what hast thou done?

Jesus answered, My kingdom is not of this world: if my kingdom were of this world, then would my servants fight, that I should not be delivered to the Jews: but now is my kingdom not from hence.

Matthew 6:19-21

Lay not up for yourselves treasures upon earth, where moth and rust doth corrupt, and where thieves break through and steal: But lay up for yourselves treasures in heaven, where neither moth nor rust doth corrupt, and where thieves do not break through nor steal: For where your treasure is, there will your heart be also.

Daniel 5:17-21

Then Daniel answered and said before the king, Let thy gifts be to thyself, and give thy rewards to another; yet I will read the writing unto the king, and make known to him the interpretation.

O thou king, the most high God gave Nebuchadnezzar thy father a kingdom, and majesty, and glory, and honour: And for the majesty that he gave him, all people, nations, and languages, trembled and feared before him: whom he would he slew; and whom he would he kept alive; and whom he would he set up; and whom he would he put down. But when his heart was lifted up, and his mind hardened in pride, he was deposed from his kingly throne, and they took his glory from him: And he was driven from the sons of men; and his heart was made like the beasts, and his dwelling was with the wild asses: they fed him with grass like oxen, and his body was wet with the dew of heaven; till he knew that the most high God ruled in the kingdom of men, and that he appointeth over it whomsoever he will.

John 1:1-3

In the beginning was the Word, and the Word was with God, and the Word was God. The same was in the beginning with God. All things were made by him; and without him was not any thing made that was made.

Matthew 24:4-14

And Jesus answered and said unto them, Take heed that no man deceive you. For many shall come in my name, saying, I am Christ; and shall deceive many.

And ye shall hear of wars and rumours of wars: see that ye be not troubled: for all these things must come to pass, but the end is not yet. For nation shall rise against nation, and kingdom against kingdom: and there shall be famines, and pestilences, and earthquakes, in divers places. All these are the beginning of sorrows.

Then shall they deliver you up to be afflicted, and shall kill you: and ye shall be hated of all nations for my name's sake. And then shall many be offended, and shall betray one another, and shall hate one another. And many false prophets shall rise, and shall deceive many. And because iniquity shall abound, the love of many shall wax cold.

But he that shall endure unto the end, the same shall be saved. And this gospel of the kingdom shall be preached in all the world for a witness unto all nations; and then shall the end come.

Isaiah 65:8-17

Thus saith the LORD, As the new wine is found in the cluster, and one saith, Destroy it not; for a blessing is in it: so will I do for my servants' sakes, that I may not destroy them all. And I will bring forth a seed out of Jacob, and out of Judah an inheritor of my mountains: and mine elect shall inherit it, and my servants shall dwell there. And Sharon shall be a fold of flocks, and the valley of Achor a place for the herds to lie down in, for my people that have sought me. But ye are they that forsake the LORD, that forget my holy mountain, that prepare a table for that troop, and that furnish the drink offering unto that number. Therefore will I number you to the sword, and ye shall all bow down to the slaughter: because when I called, ye did not answer; when I spake, ye did not hear; but did evil before mine eyes, and did choose that wherein I delighted not.

Therefore thus saith the Lord GOD, Behold, my servants shall eat, but ye shall be hungry: behold, my servants shall drink, but ye shall be thirsty: behold, my servants shall rejoice, but ye shall be ashamed: Behold, my servants shall sing for joy of heart, but ye shall cry for sorrow of heart, and shall howl for vexation of spirit. And ye shall leave your name for a curse unto my chosen: for the Lord GOD shall slay thee, and call his servants by another name: That he who blesseth himself in the earth shall bless himself in the God of truth; and he that sweareth in the earth shall swear by the God of truth; because the former troubles are forgotten, and because they are hid from mine eyes.

For, behold, I create new heavens and a new earth: and the former shall not be remembered, nor come into mind.

Isaiah 65:18-25

But be ye glad and rejoice for ever in that which I create: for, behold, I create Jerusalem a rejoicing, and her people a joy. And I will rejoice in Jerusalem, and joy in my people: and the voice of weeping shall be no more heard in her, nor the voice of crying. There shall be no more thence an infant of days, nor an old man that hath not filled his days: for the child shall die an hundred years old; but the sinner being an hundred years old shall be accursed. And they shall build houses, and inhabit them; and they shall plant vineyards, and eat the fruit of them. They shall not build, and another inhabit; they shall not plant, and another eat: for as the days of a tree are the days of my people, and mine elect shall long enjoy the work of their hands. They shall not labour in vain, nor bring forth for trouble; for they are the seed of the blessed of the LORD, and their offspring with them. And it shall come to pass, that before they call, I will answer; and while they are yet speaking, I will hear. The wolf and the lamb shall feed together, and the lion shall eat straw like the bullock: and dust shall be the serpent's meat. They shall not hurt nor destroy in all my holy mountain, saith the LORD.

Chapter Nine

My Kingdom

All this talk about what we own and how we intend to preserve our little niche in the world. Wars break out between nations over who should rule within a region. Wars break out within nations about which group of people should have authority over which other group.

This might be something that would be understandable if we were only referring to those who don't know God. Those who don't know God also don't know that it is God who establishes nations. They don't know that it is God who selects and empowers rulers. They don't know that it is only God who has the total view of the needs of all of mankind. So within the nations of those who don't know God, this might be understandable. But there aren't any nations that don't know God.

Now settle down for a moment. There are many nations that may not know **your** god. However, there is not a single nation that does not know of the existence of God. There are of course many in every nation who attempt to deny the existence of that god which is being portrayed by others. They do so because they recognize in the message of the servants of that god a hidden agenda. The agenda that they see there is one that attempts to manipulate others for the benefit of the servants of that god, but not for the benefit of God. They are actually rebelling against man, and in this case it is right to do.

The God of the Universe is not restricted to the boundaries of any religion. The God of the Universe has His own Kingdom. Even the universe and all its religions are held within the God of the Universe. In fact, the God of the Universe is not constrained by the bounds of the universe. He is the Creator thereof, and as such He is much, much bigger than the creation. So let's open up our minds to the God of the Universe and let Him instill within us an additional awareness of His universe.

First, understand that the God of the Universe did not create the universe and then go on vacation. He did not unleash forces that can then run rampant and transform the universe in any way that they see fit. He didn't unleash *accidents* that together will make a reality. The God of this universe is very much in control of this universe. The processes that He put in place are to a large degree self-executing. This does not mean, however, that they are executing outside of His plan.

As you read in the Words from the Bible, the powers of this earth are ordained by God: king Nebuchadnezzar knew that *the most high God ruled in the kingdom of men, and that he appointeth over it whomsoever he will* (Daniel 5:21). In fact, the very creation of the concept of authority was done at His hand: All things were made by him; and without him was not any thing made that was made (John 1:3). Therefore, it really doesn't matter whether you think you show great determination in your quest for power; if you are not the ones selected to hold that power, you will not receive it. Does this mean that the political process should be null and void? No, it does not.

What it does mean is that the political process must yield to the divine design that forms it. Those political leaders who want to capture the best information for their constituencies must tap into the source of this information. Those who are outside the political process, and wish to get in, must seek out the information from the Creator of the process, the God of the universe.

It may even be necessary for some of us to petition the God of the universe to make us ready for the position of power that He has set aside for us. At a minimum, the request will reduce frustration. This is especially true when seeking out the God of the universe; we receive the enlightenment that tells us when we are not ready to be part of the process. Maybe even for some of us, we will never be a power player in the political process; this is for God to reveal; He has long ago ordained the outcome.

Even those who are destined for leadership must understand that their position therein is only temporary. There is this small matter of death that interferes with the longest of tenures in politics. It is still just as definite as it has always been. For this reason be very careful about what you revere as your treasure or your contribution. *Lay not up for yourselves treasures upon earth, where moth and rust doth corrupt, and where thieves break through and steal* (Matthew 6:19).

The real power on this earth is not contained in earthen substance. Think about the number of people who were more powerful after death than they were in life. In life someone may be a very prominent proponent of the rights of man. This same person may also serve only in a single specialty area or region, such as minority rights in the United States. In death that same person could very well become the symbol of the struggle for freedom across many areas covering many peoples of the world. Such a person would be among the first to tell you that their kingdom is not of this earth. Let me explain.

The concept of the struggle for freedom transcends the bounds of any nation and even the bounds of mankind. It is the fuel for many other activities in this world beside the liberation of humans. It is also the fuel for the proper management of our environment. It also serves to remind us of our responsibility to treat our fellow creatures on this earth with some dignity; those creatures in what is called the animal kingdom, for instance. The struggle for freedom touches every area of life and not just the political arena. It goes far beyond even dismissal of the powerful segregation of who can sit where to be served what meal by whom.

It should be no wonder then that *Jesus answered, My kingdom is not of this world* (John 18:36). Furthermore, he requires of us that we prepare our minds for the realm that exists beyond our current horizon. This concept, of course, only makes sense to those who understand that every man has an immortal part: the soul. The soul will outlast the body of the man. This is the piece created by God to make us unique. It works in concert with the spirit of man. The soul is the piece that is given to each of us as a direct gift from God. It is the very essence of God imparted to mankind.

> *These are the generations of the heavens and of the earth when they were created, in the day that the LORD God made the earth and the heavens, And every plant of the field before it was in the earth, and every herb of the field before it grew: for the LORD God had not caused it to rain upon the earth, and there was not a man to till the ground. But there went up a mist from the earth, and watered the whole face of the ground. And the LORD God formed man of the dust of the ground, and breathed into his nostrils the breath of life; and man became a living soul.*
> (Genesis 2:4-7)

Therefore you must be diligent to *lay up for yourselves treasures in heaven, where neither moth nor rust doth corrupt, and where thieves do not break through nor steal* (Matthew 6:20). This is the level at which our true treasure lies.

Yes, even those who serve God will continue to be a part of the earthly striving that is happening now. This Jesus told us.

> *And ye shall hear of wars and rumours of wars: see that ye be not troubled: for all these things must come to pass, but the end is not yet. For nation shall rise against nation, and kingdom against kingdom: and there shall be famines, and pestilences, and earthquakes, in divers places. All these are the beginning of sorrows.*
> (Matthew 24:6

Mankind will try, for the full cycle of its existence, to determine what the will of God is. Mankind will continue its efforts to skirt around the limitations placed on it by God: those limitations which were placed there for mankind's protection. Yes, it would be better if every political leader sought the will of God before proceeding. However, for this to happen all would have to do so. For where there is one who does not yield to God, there is also fear on the part of the others. This is the fear that the one who does not yield will take advantage of the others who are yielded. The end result is: no one is in conformance with another. The end result is the world as we know it today.

There will come a day when God will reset the environment by His absolute will and ultimate power.

> *For, behold, I create new heavens and a new earth: and the former shall not be remembered, nor come into mind.*
> (Isaiah 65:17)

There was a similar time, which foreshadowed the time to come, in the time preceding the destruction of Jerusalem around 70 AD. At this time God intervened to correct the situation that was set against the good news of His transition of mankind from the rule of Law to the rule of love. He preserved the people of His Son Jesus Christ by giving them a warning.

> *When ye therefore shall see the abomination of desolation, spoken of by Daniel the prophet, stand in the holy place, (whoso readeth, let him understand:) Then let them which be in Judaea flee into the mountains: Let him which is on the housetop not come down to take any*

thing out of his house: Neither let him which is in the field return back to take his clothes. And woe unto them that are with child, and to them that give suck in those days!

But pray ye that your flight be not in the winter, neither on the sabbath day: For then shall be great tribulation, such as was not since the beginning of the world to this time, no, nor ever shall be. And except those days should be shortened, there should no flesh be saved: but for the elect's sake those days shall be shortened.
(Matthew 24:15-22)

The end result of the new *My kingdom* of the Messiah and of God the Father is repeated in the book of Revelation in the Bible.

And I saw a new heaven and a new earth: for the first heaven and the first earth were passed away; and there was no more sea.

And I John saw the holy city, new Jerusalem, coming down from God out of heaven, prepared as a bride adorned for her husband. And I heard a great voice out of heaven saying, Behold, the tabernacle of God is with men, and he will dwell with them, and they shall be his people, and God himself shall be with them, and be their God. And God shall wipe away all tears from their eyes; and there shall be no more death, neither sorrow, nor crying, neither shall there be any more pain: for the former things are passed away.

And he that sat upon the throne said, Behold, I make all things new. And he said unto me, Write: for these words are true and faithful.
(Revelation 21:1-5)

This is the day in which God sees that it is necessary for Him to send a divine representative visibly once again to the front of the journey of man to eternity. This is the time when if He does not, none of us will survive. One day, God will return mankind to the state it was in before yielding to the "me first, my pleasure above all" philosophy. One day we will live as Adam did when he was first created in the Garden of Eden. God did not destroy Eden.

And the LORD God said, Behold, the man is become as one of us, to know good and evil: and now, lest he put forth his hand, and take also of the tree of life, and eat, and live for ever: Therefore the LORD God sent him forth from the garden of Eden, to till the ground from whence he was taken. So he drove out the man; and he placed at the east of the garden of Eden Cherubims, and a flaming sword which turned every way, to keep the way of the tree of life.
(Genesis 3:22-24)

There must have been a reason that Eden was left intact. Might it be that the day will come, and already is, when God will re-open paradise to mankind? This day is the day of the Gospel of the Kingdom of God through Jesus of Nazareth, the Son of God. The first of these transactions was seen between Jesus and the thief as they both hung on the cross.

And one of the malefactors which were hanged railed on him, saying, If thou be Christ, save thyself and us.

But the other answering rebuked him, saying, Dost not thou fear God, seeing thou art in the same condemnation? And we indeed justly; for we receive the due reward of our deeds: but this man hath done nothing amiss. And he said unto Jesus, Lord, remember me when thou comest into thy kingdom.

And Jesus said unto him, Verily I say unto thee, To day shalt thou be with me in paradise.
(Luke 23:39-43)

It's now your turn to move in that direction. Jesus is the way.

The word goes out
Throughout the land,
Of the kingdom built
That forever will stand.

To all who seek it
Christ shows the way
That they must follow
From day to day.

Follow the path
That is in his decree
So pain and suffering
You will not see.

"Not so", some declare,
"God's on our side,
And with us alone
Doth He abide.

Your former thoughts
You must now discard,
Only our nation
Must you now regard.

On behalf of God,
And in His name,
We suppress all others
Until they are tame.

Our position with God
Is not at all new,
Our nation is powerful,
It is surely our due.

To God in His heavens
We have made our case
Against all other nations,
Most decadent and base."

Meanwhile God in His Heaven,
Measured this people's course,
And has marked this nation
To suffer great remorse.

For only God's kingdom
Is worthy of this high price;
Obedience to His name
And the giving of your life.

Chapter 9a

The Ultimate Time-out

Those who have children, or even those who have ever watched parents for any length of time, know what a *time-out* is. For those who don't, let me explain. A time-out is that period in a child's life when they must stop their negative behavior and sit in a state of quiet repose. This is a time given to them to ponder the consequences of their actions. It is intended by the parent to be for the good of the child. It is viewed by the child as an undeserved punishment: after all they were only being a child.

Time-outs are not an option, they are a necessity. This is something that every parental toolkit must have. God is a parent. God is a good parent. Time-outs are beneficial for the child. Therefore, He must be the originator of the time-out. Of course He is. All things were created by Him; and the time-out is among them. God also sets the standard for good parenting; after all He is The Father.

> *Ask, and it shall be given you; seek, and ye shall find; knock, and it shall be opened unto you: For every one that asketh receiveth; and he that seeketh findeth; and to him that knocketh it shall be opened.*
>
> *Or what man is there of you, whom if his son ask bread, will he give him a stone? Or if he ask a fish, will he give him a serpent? If ye then, being evil, know how to give good gifts unto your children, how much more shall your Father which is in heaven give good things to them that ask him? Therefore all things whatsoever ye would that men should do to you, do ye even so to them: for this is the law and the prophets.*
> (Matthew 7:7-12)

God loves everyone, even the so-called degenerate sinners among us. This should not be a surprise to anyone.

Beloved, let us love one another: for love is of God; and every one that loveth is born of God, and knoweth God. He that loveth not knoweth not God; for God is love. In this was manifested the love of God toward us, because that God sent his only begotten Son into the world, that we might live through him. Herein is love, not that we loved God, but that he loved us, and sent his Son to be the propitiation for our sins. Beloved, if God so loved us, we ought also to love one another.
(1 John 4:7-11)

And the grace of our Lord was exceeding abundant with faith and love which is in Christ Jesus. This is a faithful saying, and worthy of all acceptation, that Christ Jesus came into the world to save sinners; of whom I am chief. Howbeit for this cause I obtained mercy, that in me first Jesus Christ might show forth all longsuffering, for a pattern to them which should hereafter believe on him to life everlasting. Now unto the King eternal, immortal, invisible, the only wise God, be honour and glory forever and ever. Amen.
(1 Timothy 1:14-17)

All people on the earth are the children of God, for all people were made according to God's purposes. This is the good news of the availability of God to all mankind. It is good news to know of His all encompassing love for all mankind. This is the message of Jesus of Nazareth, the Christ: that all men have a place in the will of God. This is the good news of the kingdom of God.

For when we were yet without strength, in due time Christ died for the ungodly. For scarcely for a righteous man will one die: yet peradventure for a good man some would even dare to die. But God commendeth his love toward us, in that, while we were yet sinners, Christ died for us. Much more then, being now justified by his blood, we shall be saved from wrath through him. For if, when we were enemies, we were reconciled to God by the death of his Son, much more, being reconciled, we shall be saved by his life.
(Romans 5:6-10)

The bad news of the kingdom of God, from a human perspective, is the same as the good news: that we are all children of God. As children of God, no matter what state we are in relative to obedience to God, we are subject to His chastisement. Our being subject to his chastisement means that we will receive His time-outs when we are disobedient.

Many of us are comfortable with the thoughts of the time-outs that God gives to His children; well somewhat comfortable.

> *My son, despise not the chastening of the LORD; neither be weary of his correction: For whom the LORD loveth he correcteth; even as a father the son in whom he delighteth.*
>
> (Proverbs 3:11-12)

> *And ye have forgotten the exhortation which speaketh unto you as unto children, My son, despise not thou the chastening of the Lord, nor faint when thou art rebuked of him: For whom the Lord loveth he chasteneth, and scourgeth every son whom he receiveth. If ye endure chastening, God dealeth with you as with sons; for what son is he whom the father chasteneth not? But if ye be without chastisement, whereof all are partakers, then are ye bastards, and not sons. Furthermore we have had fathers of our flesh which corrected us, and we gave them reverence: shall we not much rather be in subjection unto the Father of spirits, and live?*
>
> (Hebrews 12:5-9)

> *And Miriam and Aaron spake against Moses because of the Ethiopian woman whom he had married: for he had married an Ethiopian woman. And they said, Hath the LORD indeed spoken only by Moses? hath he not spoken also by us? And the LORD heard it.*
>
> *(Now the man Moses was very meek, above all the men which were upon the face of the earth.)*
>
> *And the LORD spake suddenly unto Moses, and unto Aaron, and unto Miriam, Come out ye three unto the tabernacle of the congregation.*
>
> *And they three came out.*

And the LORD came down in the pillar of the cloud, and stood in the door of the tabernacle, and called Aaron and Miriam: and they both came forth. And he said, Hear now my words: If there be a prophet among you, I the LORD will make myself known unto him in a vision, and will speak unto him in a dream. My servant Moses is not so, who is faithful in all mine house. With him will I speak mouth to mouth, even apparently, and not in dark speeches; and the similitude of the LORD shall he behold: wherefore then were ye not afraid to speak against my servant Moses?

And the anger of the LORD was kindled against them; and he departed. And the cloud departed from off the tabernacle; and, behold, Miriam became leprous, white as snow: and Aaron looked upon Miriam, and, behold, she was leprous.

And Aaron said unto Moses, Alas, my lord, I beseech thee, lay not the sin upon us, wherein we have done foolishly, and wherein we have sinned. Let her not be as one dead, of whom the flesh is half consumed when he cometh out of his mother's womb.

And Moses cried unto the LORD, saying, Heal her now, O God, I beseech thee.

And the LORD said unto Moses, If her father had but spit in her face, should she not be ashamed seven days? let her be shut out from the camp seven days, and after that let her be received in again.

And Miriam was shut out from the camp seven days: and the people journeyed not till Miriam was brought in again. And afterward the people removed from Hazeroth, and pitched in the wilderness of Paran.
        (Numbers 12:1-16)

To some it may come as a surprise that He also chastens those who are not listed among His people, according to mankind. Let us take a look at some time-outs dispensed from the Father in Heaven. Let's look at a few examples of those who were considered by man to be outside the family of God and yet received a time-out from Him.

Pharaoh's time-out prevented him from sinning against God by taking another man's wife for his own.

And there was a famine in the land: and Abram went down into Egypt to sojourn there; for the famine was grievous in the land. And it came to pass, when he was come near to enter into Egypt, that he said unto Sarai his wife, Behold now, I know that thou art a fair woman to look upon: Therefore it shall come to pass, when the Egyptians shall see thee, that they shall say, This is his wife: and they will kill me, but they will save thee alive. Say, I pray thee, thou art my sister: that it may be well with me for thy sake; and my soul shall live because of thee.

And it came to pass, that, when Abram was come into Egypt, the Egyptians beheld the woman that she was very fair. The princes also of Pharaoh saw her, and commended her before Pharaoh: and the woman was taken into Pharaoh's house. And he entreated Abram well for her sake: and he had sheep, and oxen, and he asses, and menservants, and maidservants, and she asses, and camels.

And the LORD plagued Pharaoh and his house with great plagues because of Sarai Abram's wife.

And Pharaoh called Abram, and said, What is this that thou hast done unto me? why didst thou not tell me that she was thy wife? Why saidst thou, She is my sister? so I might have taken her to me to wife: now therefore behold thy wife, take her, and go thy way. And Pharaoh commanded his men concerning him: and they sent him away, and his wife, and all that he had.
(Genesis 12:10-20)

Let's look at a similar time-out given by God to *an outsider*, king Abimelech.

And Abraham journeyed from thence toward the south country, and dwelled between Kadesh and Shur, and sojourned in Gerar. And Abraham said of Sarah his wife, She is my sister: and Abimelech king of Gerar sent, and took Sarah.

But God came to Abimelech in a dream by night, and said to him, Behold, thou art but a dead man, for the woman which thou hast taken; for she is a man's wife.

But Abimelech had not come near her: and he said, LORD, wilt thou slay also a righteous nation? Said he not unto me, She is my sister? and she, even she herself said, He is my brother: in the integrity of my heart and innocency of my hands have I done this.

And God said unto him in a dream, Yea, I know that thou didst this in the integrity of thy heart; for I also withheld thee from sinning against me: therefore suffered I thee not to touch her. Now therefore restore the man his wife; for he is a prophet, and he shall pray for thee, and thou shalt live: and if thou restore her not, know thou that thou shalt surely die, thou, and all that are thine.

Therefore Abimelech rose early in the morning, and called all his servants, and told all these things in their ears: and the men were sore afraid. Then Abimelech called Abraham, and said unto him, What hast thou done unto us? and what have I offended thee, that thou hast brought on me and on my kingdom a great sin? thou hast done deeds unto me that ought not to be done. And Abimelech said unto Abraham, What sawest thou, that thou hast done this thing?

And Abraham said, Because I thought, Surely the fear of God is not in this place; and they will slay me for my wife's sake. And yet indeed she is my sister; she is the daughter of my father, but not the daughter of my mother; and she became my wife. And it came to pass, when God caused me to wander from my father's house, that I said unto her, This is thy kindness which thou shalt shew unto me; at every place whither we shall come, say of me, He is my brother.

And Abimelech took sheep, and oxen, and menservants, and womenservants, and gave them unto Abraham, and

restored him Sarah his wife. And Abimelech said,
Behold, my land is before thee: dwell where it pleaseth
thee. And unto Sarah he said, Behold, I have given thy
brother a thousand pieces of silver: behold, he is to thee
a covering of the eyes, unto all that are with thee, and
with all other: thus she was reproved.

So Abraham prayed unto God: and God healed
Abimelech, and his wife, and his maidservants; and they
bare children. For the LORD had fast closed up all the
wombs of the house of Abimelech, because of Sarah
Abraham's wife.
(Genesis 20:1-18)

There are other powerful time-outs given in the book of Daniel, involving kings Nebuchadnezzar (Daniel 4) and Belshazzar (Daniel 5). From the multitudes of time-outs and restoration that are listed in the Bible we can clearly see that God is the God of all people. As such He has to have a place for the serious time-outs of mankind. This place cannot be limited by time and space, for God is the God of all, alive, as we know it, or not. There are time-outs in life and there is an ultimate time-out at death for those who need such a time-out.

Once we pass from life into death and if we have not learned to live according to God's command there is still another training ground that awaits us. However, this is the most unpleasant of training grounds. It is called hell.

For the redeemed, Jesus promised that they would not have to be partakers of that time-out; for he will vouch for them to the Father.

My sheep hear my voice, and I know them, and they
follow me: And I give unto them eternal life; and they
shall never perish, neither shall any man pluck them out
of my hand. My Father, which gave them me, is greater
than all; and no man is able to pluck them out of my
Father's hand. I and my Father are one.
(John 10:27-30)

Jesus has been given responsibility for chastening and training those who follow him. This he does through his representative, sent by the Father at his request.

Believe me that I am in the Father, and the Father in me: or else believe me for the very works' sake. Verily, verily, I say unto you, He that believeth on me, the works that I do shall he do also; and greater works than these shall he do; because I go unto my Father.

And whatsoever ye shall ask in my name, that will I do, that the Father may be glorified in the Son. If ye shall ask any thing in my name, I will do it.

If ye love me, keep my commandments. And I will pray the Father, and he shall give you another Comforter, that he may abide with you for ever; Even the Spirit of truth; whom the world cannot receive, because it seeth him not, neither knoweth him: but ye know him; for he dwelleth with you, and shall be in you.
(John 14:11-17)

These things have I spoken unto you, being yet present with you. But the Comforter, which is the Holy Ghost, whom the Father will send in my name, he shall teach you all things, and bring all things to your remembrance, whatsoever I have said unto you.
(John 14:25-26)

For the others they will have to depend on their faith in God and any righteousness that this may give them before God. This is a very, very difficult way to bypass the ultimate time-out. I do not say that it is impossible, but only that it is a very difficult thing to do. Abraham did it, Moses did it, and others of the Old Testament patriarchs did it. But that was then and this is now. Jesus established a much easier and sure way.

To get a clearer view of the stakes involved, let's take a look at the glimpse that Jesus Christ gave of the state of the inhabitants.

There was a certain rich man, which was clothed in purple and fine linen, and fared sumptuously every day: And there was a certain beggar named Lazarus, which was laid at his gate, full of sores, And desiring to be fed with the crumbs which fell from the rich man's table: moreover the dogs came and licked his sores. And it came to pass, that the beggar died, and was carried by the angels into Abraham's bosom: the rich man also died, and was buried; And in hell he lift up his eyes, being in torments, and seeth Abraham afar off, and Lazarus in his bosom. And he cried and said, Father Abraham, have mercy on me, and send Lazarus, that he may dip the tip of his finger in water, and cool my tongue; for I am tormented in this flame.

But Abraham said, Son, remember that thou in thy lifetime receivedst thy good things, and likewise Lazarus evil things: but now he is comforted, and thou art tormented. And beside all this, between us and you there is a great gulf fixed: so that they which would pass from hence to you cannot; neither can they pass to us, that would come from thence.

Then he said, I pray thee therefore, father, that thou wouldest send him to my father's house: For I have five brethren; that he may testify unto them, lest they also come into this place of torment.

Abraham saith unto him, They have Moses and the prophets; let them hear them.

And he said, Nay, father Abraham: but if one went unto them from the dead, they will repent.

And he said unto him, If they hear not Moses and the prophets, neither will they be persuaded, though one rose from the dead.
(Luke 16:19-31)

One lesson from this is that if one is assigned to hell, because of the life that was NOT lived here on earth, one can clearly see that there is a Heaven, and that there are souls inhabiting this domain. Furthermore, those in hell can clearly see that those people in Heaven were, like them, formerly on the earth. In this way they can't ever say that it was impossible for them to achieve Heaven.

According to the glimpse given of hell by Jesus, those who are there have a strong desire to be in a better place. The account of the rich man and Lazarus also teaches us that by evaluating the things of Heaven, one who is in hell can gain additional information. They can come to a definite understanding that only through God can one come to a saving knowledge.

The way to righteousness with God was illustrated in the statement to the rich man. In this statement, the rich man was told that his relatives would have to depend on the messages from God through the prophets for their salvation. This was the way revealed by God before the good news of the kingdom God entered the world through Jesus Christ. Indeed, in the message of the prophets is contained the good news of the kingdom of God in Jesus Christ.

> *And he said unto them, Ye are they which justify*
> *yourselves before men; but God knoweth your hearts:*
> *for that which is highly esteemed among men is*
> *abomination in the sight of God. The law and the*
> *prophets were until John: since that time the kingdom of*
> *God is preached, and every man presseth into it.*
> (Luke 16:15)

Another interesting thing about those in hell, if we take the rich man as being an example, is that they have a renewed burden for souls. They come into a full knowledge of the sovereignty of God in the universe: that only by an act in Heaven can they obtain relief. They are very anxious to receive the benefit (relief of parched lips) that comes from prostrating oneself before God, if it were possible. The message is beginning to sink in.

From the rich man we gain some significant understanding of the transformation that the inhabitants of hell experience. They want desperately to have some solace and are instant in their petitions to the inhabitants of Heaven, requesting that intervene on their behalf. With this knowledge it is my perception that if they are ever released from this state, they will be **EXTREMELY** grateful and **EXTREMELY** anxious to follow the way of God, and even anxious to accept the Lordship of Christ. If they could only obtain release they would surely be ready to take their place in the eternal kingdom, even if only as a gnat on the wall. They will be the *poster boys* for the message in the lesson of the prodigal son: they will *be* the Samaritan.

> *And, behold, a certain lawyer stood up, and tempted*
> *him, saying, Master, what shall I do to inherit eternal*
> *life?*

He said unto him, What is written in the law? how readest thou?

And he answering said, Thou shalt love the Lord thy God with all thy heart, and with all thy soul, and with all thy strength, and with all thy mind; and thy neighbour as thyself.

And he said unto him, Thou hast answered right: this do, and thou shalt live.

But he, willing to justify himself, said unto Jesus, And who is my neighbour?

And Jesus answering said, A certain man went down from Jerusalem to Jericho, and fell among thieves, which stripped him of his raiment, and wounded him, and departed, leaving him half dead. And by chance there came down a certain priest that way: and when he saw him, he passed by on the other side. And likewise a Levite, when he was at the place, came and looked on him, and passed by on the other side. But a certain Samaritan, as he journeyed, came where he was: and when he saw him, he had compassion on him, And went to him, and bound up his wounds, pouring in oil and wine, and set him on his own beast, and brought him to an inn, and took care of him. And on the morrow when he departed, he took out two pence, and gave them to the host, and said unto him, Take care of him; and whatsoever thou spendest more, when I come again, I will repay thee.

Which now of these three, thinkest thou, was neighbour unto him that fell among the thieves?

And he said, He that shewed mercy on him.

Then said Jesus unto him, Go, and do thou likewise.
      (Luke 10:25-37)

Fortunately, hell is only a way-station between destinies. The Bible tells us that there is a time when it is emptied of its inhabitants.

And I saw a great white throne, and him that sat on it, from whose face the earth and the heaven fled away; and there was found no place for them. And I saw the dead, small and great, stand before God; and the books were opened: and another book was opened, which is the book of life: and the dead were judged out of those things which were written in the books, according to their works. And the sea gave up the dead which were in it; and death and hell delivered up the dead which were in them: and they were judged every man according to their works.
(Revelation 20:11-13)

Fortunately, hell is a temporary place. The Bible tells us that there will come a time when it will be no more.

And death and hell were cast into the lake of fire. This is the second death.
(Revelation 20:14)

Fortunately, hell can be the ultimate time-out and lessons can be learned there, so that understanding of and obedience to God can come in time.

Look unto me, and be ye saved, all the ends of the earth: for I am God, and there is none else. I have sworn by myself, the word is gone out of my mouth in righteousness, and shall not return, That unto me every knee shall bow, every tongue shall swear. Surely, shall one say, in the LORD have I righteousness and strength: even to him shall men come; and all that are incensed against him shall be ashamed. In the LORD shall all the seed of Israel be justified, and shall glory.
(Isaiah 45:22-25)

But why would you want to go to this extreme to learn a lesson that is available to you now? Turn to God and follow Him.

"How," you ask.

Now faith is the substance of things hoped for, the evidence of things not seen. For by it the elders obtained a good report. Through faith we understand that the worlds were framed by the word of God, so that things which are seen were not made of things which do appear. By faith Abel offered unto God a more excellent sacrifice than Cain, by which he obtained witness that he was righteous, God testifying of his gifts: and by it he being dead yet speaketh. By faith Enoch was translated that he should not see death; and was not found, because God had translated him: for before his translation he had this testimony, that he pleased God.

But without faith it is impossible to please him: for he that cometh to God must believe that he is, and that he is a rewarder of them that diligently seek him.
(Hebrews 11:1-6)

You must open your mind to the God of the universe; Who you can see in the world around you, even if you are missing His presence when you look within. With this belief in place, then turn to God and ask Him to direct you in the path you should go.

If any of you lack wisdom, let him ask of God, that giveth to all men liberally, and upbraideth not; and it shall be given him. But let him ask in faith, nothing wavering. For he that wavereth is like a wave of the sea driven with the wind and tossed. For let not that man think that he shall receive any thing of the Lord. A double minded man is unstable in all his ways.
(James 1:5-8)

The time is now.

And Elijah came unto all the people, and said, How long halt ye between two opinions? if the LORD be God, follow him: but if Baal, then follow him. And the people answered him not a word.
(1 Kings 18:21)

Now therefore fear the LORD, and serve him in sincerity and in truth: and put away the gods which your fathers served on the other side of the flood, and in Egypt; and serve ye the LORD. And if it seem evil unto you to serve the LORD, choose you this day whom ye will serve; whether the gods which your fathers served that were on the other side of the flood, or the gods of the Amorites, in

whose land ye dwell: but as for me and my house, we will
serve the LORD.
(Joshua 24:14-15)

Lest I be accused of providing an incomplete path, let me continue. I wouldn't want to leave you even one inch outside paradise. Indeed, I don't want to leave you even one micron away from having access to God's presence; you must enter fully therein.

There is a definitive way given to bridge this gap. Read here the final message you **must** hear. Once you do, please let God and His Son fill in the details.

Let not your heart be troubled: ye believe in God, believe
also in me. In my Father's house are many mansions: if it
were not so, I would have told you. I go to prepare
a place for you. And if I go and prepare a place for you,
I will come again, and receive you unto myself; that
where I am, there ye may be also. And whither I go ye
know, and the way ye know.

Thomas saith unto him, Lord, we know not whither thou
goest; and how can we know the way?

Jesus saith unto him, I am the way, the truth, and the life:
no man cometh unto the Father, but by me.
(John 14:1-6)

But don't think that I and others like me are finished yet. We may be a part of the full solution that God provides for you in your walk with Him. It is one thing to have access to the presence of God; it is another to know what to do once you gain such access. Yes, this does mean that I, and others like me, intend to intercede on your journey. But you can be sure that we will only do so as directed by God and His Son and the Holy Ghost, for your benefit.

The Word from the Bible

Genesis 13:14-18

And the LORD said unto Abram, after that Lot was separated from him, Lift up now thine eyes, and look from the place where thou art northward, and southward, and eastward, and westward: For all the land which thou seest, to thee will I give it, and to thy seed for ever. And I will make thy seed as the dust of the earth: so that if a man can number the dust of the earth, then shall thy seed also be numbered.

Arise, walk through the land in the length of it and in the breadth of it; for I will give it unto thee.

Then Abram removed his tent, and came and dwelt in the plain of Mamre, which is in Hebron, and built there an altar unto the LORD.

Genesis 15:1-18

After these things the word of the LORD came unto Abram in a vision, saying, Fear not, Abram: I am thy shield, and thy exceeding great reward.

And Abram said, Lord GOD, what wilt thou give me, seeing I go childless, and the steward of my house is this Eliezer of Damascus? And Abram said, Behold, to me thou hast given no seed: and, lo, one born in my house is mine heir.

And, behold, the word of the LORD came unto him, saying, This shall not be thine heir; but he that shall come forth out of thine own bowels shall be thine heir. And he brought him forth abroad, and said, Look now toward heaven, and tell the stars, if thou be able to number them: and he said unto him, So shall thy seed be.

And he believed in the LORD; and he counted it to him for righteousness.

And he said unto him, I am the LORD that brought thee out of Ur of the Chaldees, to give thee this land to inherit it.

And he said, Lord GOD, whereby shall I know that I shall inherit it?

And he said unto him, Take me an heifer of three years old, and a she goat of three years old, and a ram of three years old, and a turtledove, and a young pigeon. And he took unto him all these, and divided them in the midst, and laid each piece one against another: but the birds divided he not. And when the fowls came down upon the carcases, Abram drove them away.

And when the sun was going down, a deep sleep fell upon Abram; and, lo, an horror of great darkness fell upon him. And he said unto Abram, Know of a surety that thy seed shall be a stranger in a land that is not theirs, and shall serve them; and they shall afflict them four hundred years; And also that nation, whom they shall serve, will I judge: and afterward shall they come out with great substance. And thou shalt go to thy fathers in peace; thou shalt be buried in a good old age. But in the fourth generation they shall come hither again: for the iniquity of the Amorites is not yet full.

And it came to pass, that, when the sun went down, and it was dark, behold a smoking furnace, and a burning lamp that passed between those pieces. In the same day the LORD made a covenant with Abram, saying, Unto thy seed have I given this land, from the river of Egypt unto the great river, the river Euphrates:

Genesis 17:1-16

And when Abram was ninety years old and nine, the LORD appeared to Abram, and said unto him, I am the Almighty God; walk before me, and be thou perfect. And I will make my covenant between me and thee, and will multiply thee exceedingly.

And Abram fell on his face: and God talked with him, saying, As for me, behold, my covenant is with thee, and thou shalt be a father of many nations. Neither shall thy name any more be called Abram, but thy name shall be Abraham; for a father of many nations have I made thee. And I will make thee exceeding fruitful, and I will make nations of thee, and kings shall come out of thee. And I will establish my covenant between me and thee and thy seed after thee in their generations for an everlasting covenant, to be a God unto thee, and to thy seed after thee. And I will give unto thee, and to thy seed after thee, the land wherein thou art a stranger, all the land of Canaan, for an everlasting possession; and I will be their God.

And God said unto Abraham, Thou shalt keep my covenant therefore, thou, and thy seed after thee in their generations. This is my covenant, which ye shall keep, between me and you and thy seed after thee; Every man child among you shall be circumcised. And ye shall circumcise the flesh of your foreskin; and it shall be a token of the covenant betwixt me and you. And he that is eight days old shall be circumcised among you, every man child in your generations, he that is born in the house, or bought with money of any stranger, which is not of thy seed. He that is born in thy house, and he that is bought with thy money, must needs be circumcised: and my covenant shall be in your flesh for an everlasting covenant. And the uncircumcised man child whose flesh of his foreskin is not circumcised, that soul shall be cut off from his people; he hath broken my covenant.

And God said unto Abraham, As for Sarai thy wife, thou shalt not call her name Sarai, but Sarah shall her name be. And I will bless her, and give thee a son also of her: yea, I will bless her, and she shall be a mother of nations; kings of people shall be of her.

Genesis 21:8-21

And the child grew, and was weaned: and Abraham made a great feast the same day that Isaac was weaned. And Sarah saw the son of Hagar the Egyptian, which she had born unto Abraham, mocking. Wherefore she said unto Abraham, Cast out this bondwoman and her son: for the son of this bondwoman shall not be heir with my son, even with Isaac.

And the thing was very grievous in Abraham's sight because of his son.

And God said unto Abraham, Let it not be grievous in thy sight because of the lad, and because of thy bondwoman; in all that Sarah hath said unto thee, hearken unto her voice; for in Isaac shall thy seed be called. And also of the son of the bondwoman will I make a nation, because he is thy seed.

And Abraham rose up early in the morning, and took bread, and a bottle of water, and gave it unto Hagar, putting it on her shoulder, and the child, and sent her away: and she departed, and wandered in the wilderness of Beersheba.

And the water was spent in the bottle, and she cast the child under one of the shrubs. And she went, and sat her down over against him a good way off, as it were a bow shot: for she said, Let me not see the death of the child. And she sat over against him, and lift up her voice, and wept.

And God heard the voice of the lad; and the angel of God called to Hagar out of heaven, and said unto her, What aileth thee, Hagar? fear not; for God hath heard the voice of the lad where he is. Arise, lift up the lad, and hold him in thine hand; for I will make him a great nation.

And God opened her eyes, and she saw a well of water; and she went, and filled the bottle with water, and gave the lad drink.

And God was with the lad; and he grew, and dwelt in the wilderness, and became an archer. And he dwelt in the wilderness of Paran: and his mother took him a wife out of the land of Egypt.

Genesis 26:1-6

And there was a famine in the land, beside the first famine that was in the days of Abraham. And Isaac went unto Abimelech king of the Philistines unto Gerar. And the LORD appeared unto him, and said, Go not down into Egypt; dwell in the land which I shall tell thee of: Sojourn in this land, and I will be with thee, and will bless thee; for unto thee, and unto thy seed, I will give all these countries, and I will perform the oath which I sware unto Abraham thy father; And I will make thy seed to multiply as the stars of heaven, and will give unto thy seed all these countries; and in thy seed shall all the nations of the earth be blessed; Because that Abraham obeyed my voice, and kept my charge, my commandments, my statutes, and my laws.

And Isaac dwelt in Gerar:

Chapter Ten

Why live in unity?
Abraham!

What is unity? It is an allowance of diversity, with an understanding of the place of each in the whole.

Unity is not total acceptance of all qualities of the other. In modern times it is framed as finding a diplomatic solution.

Abraham is the key to the promise. The descendants of Abraham inherit the promise. They are only "entitled" to the promise as given to them by the original heir. They will only receive the promise if allowed to do so by the one who made the promise: God.

To the children of Ishmael

Speaking bluntly to Ishmael, don't allow a woman to once again get in the way of your receipt of the promise of God as Eve did with Adam. Your status as a seeming outcast was the result of two women. The one was impatient to have *ownership* of a child.

> *Now Sarai Abram's wife bare him no children: and she had an handmaid, an Egyptian, whose name was Hagar. And Sarai said unto Abram, Behold now, the LORD hath restrained me from bearing: I pray thee, go in unto my maid; it may be that I may obtain children by her. And Abram hearkened to the voice of Sarai.*

> *And Sarai Abram's wife took Hagar her maid the Egyptian, after Abram had dwelt ten years in the land of Canaan, and gave her to her husband Abram to be his wife. And he went in unto Hagar, and she conceived: and when she saw that she had conceived, her mistress was despised in her eyes.*

And Sarai said unto Abram, My wrong be upon thee: I have given my maid into thy bosom; and when she saw that she had conceived, I was despised in her eyes: the LORD judge between me and thee.

But Abram said unto Sarai, Behold, thy maid is in thy hand; do to her as it pleaseth thee.

And when Sarai dealt hardly with her, she fled from her face.
(Genesis 16:1-5)

But that was not the end of the story. It continues.

And the angel of the LORD found her by a fountain of water in the wilderness, by the fountain in the way to Shur. And he said, Hagar, Sarai's maid, whence camest thou? and whither wilt thou go?

And she said, I flee from the face of my mistress Sarai.

And the angel of the LORD said unto her, Return to thy mistress, and submit thyself under her hands. And the angel of the LORD said unto her, I will multiply thy seed exceedingly, that it shall not be numbered for multitude.

And the angel of the LORD said unto her, Behold, thou art with child, and shalt bear a son, and shalt call his name Ishmael; because the LORD hath heard thy affliction. And he will be a wild man; his hand will be against every man, and every man's hand against him; and he shall dwell in the presence of all his brethren.

And she called the name of the LORD that spake unto her, Thou God seest me: for she said, Have I also here looked after him that seeth me? Wherefore the well was called Beerlahairoi; behold, it is between Kadesh and Bered.

And Hagar bare Abram a son: and Abram called his son's name, which Hagar bare, Ishmael.
(Genesis 16:7-15)

Later Abraham's wife Sarah did have a child, who was named, Isaac. Even though there had been tension between the parents at the beginning, in the end the brothers came together to honor their father.

> *And these are the days of the years of Abraham's life which he lived, an hundred threescore and fifteen years. Then Abraham gave up the ghost, and died in a good old age, an old man, and full of years; and was gathered to his people.*
>
> *And his sons Isaac and Ishmael buried him in the cave of Machpelah, in the field of Ephron the son of Zohar the Hittite, which is before Mamre; The field which Abraham purchased of the sons of Heth: there was Abraham buried, and Sarah his wife.*
> (Genesis 25:7-10)

As the angel of the LORD proclaimed to Hagar, Ishmael became the father of a great number. God blessed him as the angel said and he was able to end his days among his brethren.

> *Now these are the generations of Ishmael, Abraham's son, whom Hagar the Egyptian, Sarah's handmaid, bare unto Abraham: And these are the names of the sons of Ishmael, by their names, according to their generations: the firstborn of Ishmael, Nebajoth; and Kedar, and Adbeel, and Mibsam, And Mishma, and Dumah, and Massa, Hadar, and Tema, Jetur, Naphish, and Kedemah: These are the sons of Ishmael, and these are their names, by their towns, and by their castles; twelve princes according to their nations.*
>
> *And these are the years of the life of Ishmael, an hundred and thirty and seven years: and he gave up the ghost and died; and was gathered unto his people. And they dwelt from Havilah unto Shur, that is before Egypt, as thou goest toward Assyria: and he died in the presence of all his brethren.*
> (Genesis 25:12-18)

Ishmael was a great man who built great nations. He did not devote his life to destroying others. This is an example that the children of Ishmael should call to mind when they think of the children of Isaac. To do otherwise is to dishonor your father Ishmael.

There are some today who would disrupt the legacy of Ishmael. They would sever Ishmael from the promise of God, by sowing in Ishmael seeds of discord. This is not done in accordance with the God of Ishmael. The angel of the LORD of Ishmael delivered to Hagar, his mother, a command for reconciliation. As a blessing God delivered to Ishmael a great prize.

There are some in Ishmael today who will disrupt the stream of blessing by moving in an opposite direction from the message given by the angel of the LORD. This should never be done, even if a very, very powerful man tells you to do so.

> *If there arise among you a prophet, or a dreamer of dreams, and giveth thee a sign or a wonder, And the sign or the wonder come to pass, whereof he spake unto thee, saying, Let us go after other gods, which thou hast not known, and let us serve them; Thou shalt not hearken unto the words of that prophet, or that dreamer of dreams: for the LORD your God proveth you, to know whether ye love the LORD your God with all your heart and with all your soul.*
> (Deuteronomy 13:1-3)

God willed that Ishmael live among his brethren. He did not say, some of his brethren only. Ishmael's brethren are all those of the line of Abraham. This proclamation from God must be honored in full: to not do so is to dishonor God.

To the children of Jacob (who is, the son of Isaac)

It was no accident that you were not allowed to totally remove the inhabitants of the land. In this directive God already knew of your unwillingness to fully accomplish the acquisition of the land. And in this, through this seeming shortfall by Israel, God set the stage for you being the instrument of salvation to the entire world.

God is pleased with the world that contains more than just the seed of Jacob. If not, He would have solved this "problem" without the requirement for any human intervention. He had already done so with the flood. And He had shown His ability to do so in Egypt.

Consider the wisdom of the LORD in allowing nations to exist around you.

> *Now these are the nations which the LORD left, to prove Israel by them, even as many of Israel as had not known all the wars of Canaan; Only that the generations of the children of Israel might know, to teach them war, at the least such as before knew nothing thereof; Namely, five lords of the Philistines, and all the Canaanites, and the Sidonians, and the Hivites that dwelt in mount Lebanon, from mount Baalhermon unto the entering in of Hamath. And they were to prove Israel by them, to know whether they would hearken unto the commandments of the LORD, which he commanded their fathers by the hand of Moses*
>
> (Judges 3:1-4)

God is gracious to all, beyond measure. Consider the number of times that you strayed from His will. Consider the number of times that He delivered you. Consider also that He has made an everlasting promise to you. This promise started with Abraham and was perfected in the time of Moses. You are to be a peculiar treasure to Him.

> *And Moses went up unto God, and the LORD called unto him out of the mountain, saying, Thus shalt thou say to the house of Jacob, and tell the children of Israel; Ye have seen what I did unto the Egyptians, and how I bare you on eagles' wings, and brought you unto myself. Now therefore, if ye will obey my voice indeed, and keep my covenant, then ye shall be a peculiar treasure unto me above all people: for all the earth is mine: And ye shall be unto me a kingdom of priests, and an holy nation. These are the words which thou shalt speak unto the children of Israel*
>
> (Exodus 19:3-6)

Not, however, the only people that He has.

> *Among the gods there is none like unto thee, O Lord; neither are there any works like unto thy works. All nations whom thou hast made shall come and worship before thee, O Lord; and shall glorify thy name. For*

thou art great, and doest wondrous things: thou art God alone.

(Psalm 86:8-10)

Petition the LORD once more to show you His redemption. His promise is that He will.

Behold, I will send my messenger, and he shall prepare the way before me: and the Lord, whom ye seek, shall suddenly come to his temple, even the messenger of the covenant, whom ye delight in: behold, he shall come, saith the LORD of hosts.

But who may abide the day of his coming? and who shall stand when he appeareth? for he is like a refiner's fire, and like fullers' soap: And he shall sit as a refiner and purifier of silver: and he shall purify the sons of Levi, and purge them as gold and silver, that they may offer unto the LORD an offering in righteousness. Then shall the offering of Judah and Jerusalem be pleasant unto the LORD, as in the days of old, and as in former years.

And I will come near to you to judgment; and I will be a swift witness against the sorcerers, and against the adulterers, and against false swearers, and against those that oppress the hireling in his wages, the widow, and the fatherless, and that turn aside the stranger from his right, and fear not me, saith the LORD of hosts. For I am the LORD, I change not; therefore ye sons of Jacob are not consumed.

Even from the days of your fathers ye are gone away from mine ordinances, and have not kept them. Return unto me, and I will return unto you, saith the LORD of hosts.

But ye said, Wherein shall we return? Will a man rob God? Yet ye have robbed me.

But ye say, Wherein have we robbed thee?

In tithes and offerings. Ye are cursed with a curse: for ye have robbed me, even this whole nation. Bring ye all the tithes into the storehouse, that there may be meat in mine house, and prove me now herewith, saith the LORD of hosts, if I will not open you the windows of heaven, and pour you out a blessing, that there shall not be room enough to receive it.

And I will rebuke the devourer for your sakes, and he shall not destroy the fruits of your ground; neither shall your vine cast her fruit before the time in the field, saith the LORD of hosts. And all nations shall call you blessed: for ye shall be a delightsome land, saith the LORD of hosts.
(Malachi 3:1-12)

To the children Adam through Noah

Though this is addressed to the children of Abraham, there is a relationship of every man to one another that needs to be addressed. To the world at large that doesn't consider itself to be the children of Abraham we say, be VERY careful how you interact with the children of Abraham. Don't be so quick to try to force your solution on those who are under the promise of Almighty God. Honor God: He will provide the solution.

You must give place to God even though the answer given to the children of Abraham by the God of Abraham, Isaac and Jacob may have a direct impact on you. Trust God to modify and mollify any impact that may come your way. And above all, stand ready to participate in the solution; as God directs your nation to do.

Petition to all the children of Abraham

I pray to God that you can learn to live in the unity of diversity. Reconcile under the tent of Abraham. Be that seed which is as the stars of heaven. As each human has physical boundaries, so must nations. And when humans intersect over a matter of space, they must not kill one another to resolve the issue: that is, not when they are living according to the God of Abraham.

The God we serve is the same God who moved Abram from his comfortable space to establish him as Abraham in a divinely selected space. This was the first example of political expedience; Abram needed his own space. Be like-minded and look to God for the means to negotiate the space that is given to you by Him. Remember the lesson of

Lot and what God moved Abraham to do against those who would hold captive his selected people.

God is the final arbiter of any and all matters that relate to Abraham and the promise. No man or nation or ethnicity or world can overrule Him. His will is done.

Oh children of Abraham,
No matter how formed,
Please don't let your witness
Be maliciously deformed

By those who would pit
You one against another;
Man against man,
Brother against brother.

Their aim is not
To show you the Way;
They only want
To cause your decay.

Great nations were promised,
By God, Whom you serve;
He gives to all peoples
What they each deserve.

One branches of Abraham,
Who he named Ishmael;
One other named Jacob,
Better known as Israel.

Both having their place,
Each to serve in their land
By the will of God,
According to His command.

Not called by Him
To war and fight,
But called to righteousness
To make evil take flight.

The strife is not with
Men of a few hours,
But with rulers of darkness,
And principalities and powers.

Truly we honor God
By receiving from above
The precious gift
Of His divine love,

To share one with another
Across every community;
To spread His love;
To live in unity.

Chapter 10a

Try the Spirits

1 John 4:1-6

Beloved, believe not every spirit, but try the spirits whether they are of God: because many false prophets are gone out into the world. Hereby know ye the Spirit of God: Every spirit that confesseth that Jesus Christ is come in the flesh is of God: And every spirit that confesseth not that Jesus Christ is come in the flesh is not of God: and this is that spirit of antichrist, whereof ye have heard that it should come; and even now already is it in the world.

Ye are of God, little children, and have overcome them: because greater is he that is in you, than he that is in the world. They are of the world: therefore speak they of the world, and the world heareth them. We are of God: he that knoweth God heareth us; he that is not of God heareth not us. Hereby know we the spirit of truth, and the spirit of error.

+=+

The prophets of God do not disagree with the prophets of God on the same word from God, unless one of them is wrong.

The prophets of God do not propose practices that are different from one another for the same mission of God, unless one of them is wrong.

The prophets of God do not present descriptions of God that have contradictory views of the nature of God unless something is wrong.

The wrong is either the prophet or the behavior of the people. Whenever the people are wrong, God will change His aspect from Loving Father, Faithful Shepherd to Jealous and Rod of Reproof.

> *For thou shalt worship no other god: for the LORD,*
> *whose name is Jealous, is a jealous God:*
>> (Exodus 34:14)

How do we know which prophet is right in a difference between prophets?

Begin with the fact that God does not change.

> *For I am the LORD, I change not; therefore ye sons of*
> *Jacob are not consumed.*
>> (Malachi 3:6)

Next, when God says it; that settles it.

> *God forbid: yea, let God be true, but every man a liar; as*
> *it is written, That thou mightest be justified in thy*
> *sayings, and mightest overcome when thou art judged.*
>> (Romans 3:4)

Being human, we can draw from our experience as either employees or employers. Let us view the evaluation of a prophet's word much like the selection of the proper candidate for a work assignment. For indeed, if we listen to the words of the prophet, we have accepted one of the highest of *work* assignments on the earth. This assignment is none other than service to God Almighty.

Therefore, take a good look at the life of the prophet to clearly understand God's manifestation in their life. If no manifestation is obvious, then no message should be followed. Where a manifestation is present; search for a God-certified record of blessing and establishment of the work and words of the prophet.

The easiest of all prophets to refer to as fully certified by God Almighty is Abraham. We all know of many who call God the God of Abraham. Right along side of Abraham is the man Moses. Consider the word of the LORD concerning this man and the honor given to him by God, and by man.

> *And Miriam and Aaron spake against Moses because of*
> *the Ethiopian woman whom he had married: for he had*
> *married an Ethiopian woman. And they said, Hath the*
> *LORD indeed spoken only by Moses? hath he not spoken*
> *also by us? And the LORD heard it.*

(Now the man Moses was very meek, above all the men which were upon the face of the earth.)

And the LORD spake suddenly unto Moses, and unto Aaron, and unto Miriam, Come out ye three unto the tabernacle of the congregation. And they three came out. And the LORD came down in the pillar of the cloud, and stood in the door of the tabernacle, and called Aaron and Miriam: and they both came forth.

And he said, Hear now my words: If there be a prophet among you, I the LORD will make myself known unto him in a vision, and will speak unto him in a dream. My servant Moses is not so, who is faithful in all mine house. With him will I speak mouth to mouth, even apparently, and not in dark speeches; and the similitude of the LORD shall he behold: wherefore then were ye not afraid to speak against my servant Moses?

And the anger of the LORD was kindled against them; and he departed. And the cloud departed from off the tabernacle; and, behold, Miriam became leprous, white as snow: and Aaron looked upon Miriam, and, behold, she was leprous.

And Aaron said unto Moses, Alas, my lord, I beseech thee, lay not the sin upon us, wherein we have done foolishly, and wherein we have sinned. Let her not be as one dead, of whom the flesh is half consumed when he cometh out of his mother's womb.

And Moses cried unto the LORD, saying, Heal her now, O God, I beseech thee.

And the LORD said unto Moses, If her father had but spit in her face, should she not be ashamed seven days? let her be shut out from the camp seven days, and after that let her be received in again.
(Numbers 12:1-14)

Finally, we must evaluate the message we are currently being given against the ones we know to be from God, by His word in Scripture. If the message, in any part, does not conform to what we find there, then it must be rejected in all parts. This, however, is where the difficulty lies. This is a very difficult thing for us to do if we don't fully search the Scriptures.

> *Of these things put them in remembrance, charging them before the Lord that they strive not about words to no profit, but to the subverting of the hearers. Study to show thyself approved unto God, a workman that needeth not to be ashamed, rightly dividing the word of truth. But shun profane and vain babblings: for they will increase unto more ungodliness.*
> (2 Timothy 2:14-16)

It is not enough just to hear an interpretation of the word, we must also study it.

> *And the brethren immediately sent away Paul and Silas by night unto Berea: who coming thither went into the synagogue of the Jews. These were more noble than those in Thessalonica, in that they received the word with all readiness of mind, and searched the scriptures daily, whether those things were so. Therefore many of them believed; also of honourable women which were Greeks, and of men, not a few.*
> (Acts 17:10-12)

Above all, we must constantly activate in our lives God's gift of understanding.

> *And ye shall know that I am in the midst of Israel, and that I am the LORD your God, and none else: and my people shall never be ashamed. And it shall come to pass afterward, that I will pour out my spirit upon all flesh; and your sons and your daughters shall prophesy, your old men shall dream dreams, your young men shall see visions: And also upon the servants and upon the handmaids in those days will I pour out my spirit.*
> (Joel 2:27-29)

These things must be done because we have an adversary. This adversary will challenge us and mislead us. The adversary is called Satan. Satan, as well as any who behaves according to his spirit, has the ability to present messages that are almost on the mark; but the result of the message is wrong, and the whole message is worthless. We have many examples of this, but let's look at only the first one. This is an example of an adversarial statement by the serpent, against the rule of God.

> *Now the serpent was more subtle than any beast of the field which the LORD God had made. And he said unto the woman, Yea, hath God said, Ye shall not eat of every tree of the garden?*

> *And the woman said unto the serpent, We may eat of the fruit of the trees of the garden: But of the fruit of the tree which is in the midst of the garden, God hath said, Ye shall not eat of it, neither shall ye touch it, lest ye die.*

> *And the serpent said unto the woman, Ye shall not surely die: For God doth know that in the day ye eat thereof, then your eyes shall be opened, and ye shall be as gods, knowing good and evil.*
> (Genesis 3:2-5)

Satan's message was almost correct. They did obtain knowledge of good and evil and they did become like gods. This was confirmed by God.

> *And the LORD God said, Behold, the man is become as one of us, to know good and evil: and now, lest he put forth his hand, and take also of the tree of life, and eat, and live for ever: Therefore the LORD God sent him forth from the garden of Eden, to till the ground from whence he was taken.*
> (Genesis 3:22-23)

Where Satan deceived was that they **did** surely die. The following passages of Scripture show just how this happened and just how it continually happens in the hearts of men and women; to this day.

> *And the LORD said unto Cain, Why art thou wroth? and why is thy countenance fallen? If thou doest well, shalt thou not be accepted? and if thou doest not well, sin lieth at the door. And unto thee shall be his desire, and thou shalt rule over him.*
> (Genesis 4:6-7)

Even from the days of your fathers ye are gone away from mine ordinances, and have not kept them. Return unto me, and I will return unto you, saith the LORD of hosts. But ye said, Wherein shall we return?
(Malachi 3:7)

For the wages of sin is death; but the gift of God is eternal life through Jesus Christ our Lord.
(Romans 6:23)

And you hath he quickened, who were dead in trespasses and sins: Wherein in time past ye walked according to the course of this world, according to the prince of the power of the air, the spirit that now worketh in the children of disobedience: Among whom also we all had our conversation in times past in the lusts of our flesh, fulfilling the desires of the flesh and of the mind; and were by nature the children of wrath, even as others.

But God, who is rich in mercy, for his great love wherewith he loved us, Even when we were dead in sins, hath quickened us together with Christ, (by grace ye are saved;) And hath raised us up together, and made us sit together in heavenly places in Christ Jesus: That in the ages to come he might show the exceeding riches of his grace in his kindness toward us through Christ Jesus. For by grace are ye saved through faith; and that not of yourselves: it is the gift of God: Not of works, lest any man should boast.
(Ephesians 2:1-9)

God says to each of us *Return unto me, and I will return unto you.* Praise God that even if we do follow an erroneous message, even from one who carries the title of prophet, He has a way for us to return to Him. The way we return to God, when we have followed a false prophet is the same way we do so whenever we sin. We return to a right status with God by each of us turning away from evil. We do this by way of individual prayer and supplication. It is not done by collective finger pointing.

Judge not, that ye be not judged. For with what judgment ye judge, ye shall be judged: and with what measure ye mete, it shall be measured to you again.

And why beholdest thou the mote that is in thy brother's eye, but considerest not the beam that is in thine own eye? Or how wilt thou say to thy brother, Let me pull out the mote out of thine eye; and, behold, a beam is in thine own eye? Thou hypocrite, first cast out the beam out of thine own eye; and then shalt thou see clearly to cast out the mote out of thy brother's eye.
(Matthew 7:1-5)

Once we have received cleansing from the Lord, we will then be able to hear the mission God has for us to perform in order to participate in transforming the nation. Sometimes the message will be simply to have patience and depend on God.

Come, behold the works of the LORD, what desolations he hath made in the earth. He maketh wars to cease unto the end of the earth; he breaketh the bow, and cutteth the spear in sunder; he burneth the chariot in the fire. Be still, and know that I am God: I will be exalted among the heathen, I will be exalted in the earth.
(Psalm 46:8-10)

Our prayer for the nation must be for the purification of our national character before God. And if God does draft us into service, we must be diligent and longsuffering. If we've strived with the nation and still see no results, we must return to God for refreshing and renewal of the word He has given us. It is not enough for *us* to say that we have done all that is humanly possible to reform our land. God is not human. His provisions for the nations are not human: they are divine.

If you only go to the highest level of humanity, as you see it, you will have missed the mark. Even the prince of this earth, Satan, knows how to reach the highest known human level. Nations of God, once having reached that level, must seek God's presence and power in their nation. Such nations will petition the LORD for a renewal to propel them well beyond even the highest known human level. Such nations will request the blanket of the Holy Ghost from God to jumpstart their efforts to rise to the next level, and the next level, and the next level, and the ---.

In this way, the nation that would be a nation of the LORD will frustrate the prince of this world, and his princes of nations who follow him. The evil one will have to pursue understanding in order to start his attack again. The prince of this world, and the princes of nations who follow him, will cease persecuting the nation of God while they try to catch up. Indeed they will have to learn anew how to effect such persecution. They will have to revise their definition of persecution for a nation of God that is seeking after God.

Understand this, however. The prince of the earth, Satan, and those princes of nations who follow him, will learn. They will surely learn if we once again rest on the "where we ares", the "What we have becomes" and the "what we have dones". The drive toward Perfection in God for a nation, or for a person, is eternal. God is eternal.

> *Before the mountains were brought forth, or ever thou hadst formed the earth and the world, even from everlasting to everlasting, thou art God.*
> (Psalm 90:2)

Furthermore, we must continue on the eternal path to Perfection, forever refreshing our petitions to God for a *flapping* of the blanket of the Holy Ghost that covers us. The *flapping* of the blanket will shake off the dust of complacency and disrupt the peace of *having arrived* in our nation. We will thus be constantly moving forward in our nation. God will then establish us and no enemy from without will be allowed to enter. In like manner, no enemy from within will be able to remain. The enemies within will be expelled by the power of God, with no need for intervention by the hand of man. God will prepare the way.

> *Behold, I send an Angel before thee, to keep thee in the way, and to bring thee into the place which I have prepared. Beware of him, and obey his voice, provoke him not; for he will not pardon your transgressions: for my name is in him.*
>
> *But if thou shalt indeed obey his voice, and do all that I speak; then I will be an enemy unto thine enemies, and an adversary unto thine adversaries. For mine Angel shall go before thee, and bring thee in unto the Amorites, and the Hittites, and the Perizzites, and the Canaanites, the Hivites, and the Jebusites: and I will cut them off.*

Thou shalt not bow down to their gods, nor serve them,
nor do after their works: but thou shalt utterly overthrow
them, and quite break down their images.
(Exodus 23:20-24)

In this time, the only holy war that will be mentioned will be the Holy Fight of God. It will be only a fight, for the time will be short and the victory is sure. God will send forth a battalion of His own army; not one of the seed of man. One of these battalions went before the children of Israel into the land.

And it came to pass, when Joshua was by Jericho, that
he lifted up his eyes and looked, and, behold, there stood
a man over against him with his sword drawn in his
hand: and Joshua went unto him, and said unto him, Art
thou for us, or for our adversaries?

And he said, Nay; but as captain of the host of the LORD
am I now come. And Joshua fell on his face to the earth,
and did worship, and said unto him, What saith my lord
unto his servant? And the captain of the LORD'S host
said unto Joshua, Loose thy shoe from off thy foot; for the
place whereon thou standest is holy. And Joshua did so.
(Joshua 5:13-15)

And one of these battalions went forth to dismiss Satan from Heaven. This was done to make way for the Saviour of mankind, by removing the accuser of mankind from his spot before God in Heaven.

And there was war in heaven: Michael and his angels
fought against the dragon; and the dragon fought and
his angels, And prevailed not; neither was their place
found any more in heaven. And the great dragon was
cast out, that old serpent, called the Devil, and Satan,
which deceiveth the whole world: he was cast out into
the earth, and his angels were cast out with him.

And I heard a loud voice saying in heaven, Now is come
salvation, and strength, and the kingdom of our God,
and the power of his Christ: for the accuser of our
brethren is cast down, which accused them before our
God day and night.
(Revelation 12:7-10)

The patriarch Job was subjected to his accusation.

And the LORD said unto Satan, Whence comest thou?

Then Satan answered the LORD, and said, From going to and fro in the earth, and from walking up and down in it.

And the LORD said unto Satan, Hast thou considered my servant Job, that there is none like him in the earth, a perfect and an upright man, one that feareth God, and escheweth evil?

Then Satan answered the LORD, and said, Doth Job fear God for nought? Hast not thou made an hedge about him, and about his house, and about all that he hath on every side? thou hast blessed the work of his hands, and his substance is increased in the land. But put forth thine hand now, and touch all that he hath, and he will curse thee to thy face.

And the LORD said unto Satan, Behold, all that he hath is in thy power; only upon himself put not forth thine hand. So Satan went forth from the presence of the LORD.
(Job 1:7-12)

But praise God; that Job, even after much suffering, still knows that the Saviour would preserve him from this evil one.

For I know that my redeemer liveth, and that he shall stand at the latter day upon the earth: And though after my skin worms destroy this body, yet in my flesh shall I see God: Whom I shall see for myself, and mine eyes shall behold, and not another; though my reins be consumed within me.
(Job 19:25-27)

The final battle, however, is not so easy for the forces of evil. The forces of evil at the final battle have no means of retreat. They are not able to regroup and fight another day; not even another second. The battle is over in an instant and this done by only one. Hear the word given by the Lord.

And I saw heaven opened, and behold a white horse; and he that sat upon him was called Faithful and True, and in righteousness he doth judge and make war. His eyes were as a flame of fire, and on his head were many crowns; and he had a name written, that no man knew, but he himself. And he was clothed with a vesture dipped in blood: and his name is called The Word of God.

And the armies which were in heaven followed him upon white horses, clothed in fine linen, white and clean. And out of his mouth goeth a sharp sword, that with it he should smite the nations: and he shall rule them with a rod of iron: and he treadeth the winepress of the fierceness and wrath of Almighty God. And he hath on his vesture and on his thigh a name written, KING OF KINGS, AND LORD OF LORDS.

And I saw an angel standing in the sun; and he cried with a loud voice, saying to all the fowls that fly in the midst of heaven, Come and gather yourselves together unto the supper of the great God; That ye may eat the flesh of kings, and the flesh of captains, and the flesh of mighty men, and the flesh of horses, and of them that sit on them, and the flesh of all men, both free and bond, both small and great.

And I saw the beast, and the kings of the earth, and their armies, gathered together to make war against him that sat on the horse, and against his army. And the beast was taken, and with him the false prophet that wrought miracles before him, with which he deceived them that had received the mark of the beast, and them that worshipped his image. These both were cast alive into a lake of fire burning with brimstone. And the remnant were slain with the sword of him that sat upon the horse, which sword proceeded out of his mouth: and all the fowls were filled with their flesh.

(Revelation 19:11-21)

And I saw an angel come down from heaven, having the key of the bottomless pit and a great chain in his hand. And he laid hold on the dragon, that old serpent, which

is the Devil, and Satan, and bound him a thousand years,
And cast him into the bottomless pit, and shut him up,
and set a seal upon him, that he should deceive the
nations no more, till the thousand years should be
fulfilled: and after that he must be loosed a little season.
(Revelation 20:1-3)

And when the thousand years are expired, Satan shall be
loosed out of his prison, And shall go out to deceive the
nations which are in the four quarters of the earth, Gog
and Magog, to gather them together to battle: the number
of whom is as the sand of the sea. And they went up on the
breadth of the earth, and compassed the camp of the
saints about, and the beloved city: and fire came down
from God out of heaven, and devoured them. And the
devil that deceived them was cast into the lake of fire and
brimstone, where the beast and the false prophet are, and
shall be tormented day and night for ever and ever.
(Revelation 20:7-10)

All these battles and many more are the direct work of God.

"Why", you ask, "would God not use his instrument, known as man? Particularly, why not use this instrument before the time of the end? Particularly why not when it pertains only to man to man, nation to nation, disagreements?

For this reason: Man is still touched by the prince of this earth and the princes of nations that follow him. As such man will seek glory for himself in war. Furthermore, other men who are either conquered by man or view the conquest from afar will give glory to man. God is Jealous. All glory must be given to Him.

"Why," you ask, "is God Jealous? Isn't man worthy of glory when he is executing the will of God?"

God is not Jealous for His sake. God is Jealous for our sake. God's will is that mankind exists in communion with the Best. And the Best is God. As happened to king Saul, so it is with all mankind. He was puffed up by his authority; and in this he reflected the state of all mankind.

And Samuel came to Saul: and Saul said unto him,
Blessed be thou of the LORD: I have performed the
commandment of the LORD.

And Samuel said, What meaneth then this bleating of the sheep in mine ears, and the lowing of the oxen which I hear?

And Saul said, They have brought them from the Amalekites: for the people spared the best of the sheep and of the oxen, to sacrifice unto the LORD thy God; and the rest we have utterly destroyed.

Then Samuel said unto Saul, Stay, and I will tell thee what the LORD hath said to me this night.

And he said unto him, Say on.

And Samuel said, When thou wast little in thine own sight, wast thou not made the head of the tribes of Israel, and the LORD anointed thee king over Israel? And the LORD sent thee on a journey, and said, Go and utterly destroy the sinners the Amalekites, and fight against them until they be consumed. Wherefore then didst thou not obey the voice of the LORD, but didst fly upon the spoil, and didst evil in the sight of the LORD?

And Saul said unto Samuel, Yea, I have obeyed the voice of the LORD, and have gone the way which the LORD sent me, and have brought Agag the king of Amalek, and have utterly destroyed the Amalekites. But the people took of the spoil, sheep and oxen, the chief of the things which should have been utterly destroyed, to sacrifice unto the LORD thy God in Gilgal.

And Samuel said, Hath the LORD as great delight in burnt offerings and sacrifices, as in obeying the voice of the LORD? Behold, to obey is better than sacrifice, and to hearken than the fat of rams. For rebellion is as the sin of witchcraft, and stubbornness is as iniquity and idolatry. Because thou hast rejected the word of the LORD, he hath also rejected thee from being king.

(1 Samuel 15:13-23)

We must understand that we were made not to receive glory from one another but to receive all things from God. Furthermore, we were created to give all glory to God. He is the only One who knows how to rightly store glory. We are not so equipped. This is the design of all mankind.

> *It is not good to eat much honey: so for men to search their own glory is not glory.*
>   (Proverbs 25:27)

When the battle is won by the LORD, all mankind will know that they have witnessed a peculiar event. Those who know Him will praise Him. Those who don't yet know Him will, in time, come to know Him.

> *The Lord is not slack concerning his promise, as some men count slackness; but is longsuffering to us-ward, not willing that any should perish, but that all should come to repentance.*
>   (2 Peter 3:9)

Furthermore, the LORD has stated that all will serve Him.

> *Look unto me, and be ye saved, all the ends of the earth: for I am God, and there is none else. I have sworn by myself, the word is gone out of my mouth in righteousness, and shall not return, That unto me every knee shall bow, every tongue shall swear. Surely, shall one say, in the LORD have I righteousness and strength: even to him shall men come; and all that are incensed against him shall be ashamed.*
>   (Isaiah 45:22-24)

When God fights the battle, what is there left for us to do? Pray!!!!!!!

> *After this manner therefore pray ye: Our Father which art in heaven, Hallowed be thy name. Thy kingdom come, Thy will be done in earth, as it is in heaven. Give us this day our daily bread. And forgive us our debts, as we forgive our debtors. And lead us not into temptation, but deliver us from evil: For thine is the kingdom, and the power, and the glory, for ever. Amen.*
>   (Matthew 6:9-13)

The Word from the Bible

Daniel 9:24-27

Seventy weeks are determined upon thy people and upon thy holy city, to finish the transgression, and to make an end of sins, and to make reconciliation for iniquity, and to bring in everlasting righteousness, and to seal up the vision and prophecy, and to anoint the most Holy.

Know therefore and understand, that from the going forth of the commandment to restore and to build Jerusalem unto the Messiah the Prince shall be seven weeks, and threescore and two weeks: the street shall be built again, and the wall, even in troublous times.

And after threescore and two weeks shall Messiah be cut off, but not for himself: and the people of the prince that shall come shall destroy the city and the sanctuary; and the end thereof shall be with a flood, and unto the end of the war desolations are determined. And he shall confirm the covenant with many for one week: and in the midst of the week he shall cause the sacrifice and the oblation to cease, and for the overspreading of abominations he shall make it desolate, even until the consummation, and that determined shall be poured upon the desolate.

Psalm 110:1-7

A Psalm of David.

The LORD said unto my Lord, Sit thou at my right hand, until I make thine enemies thy footstool. The LORD shall send the rod of thy strength out of Zion: rule thou in the midst of thine enemies. Thy people shall be willing in the day of thy power, in the beauties of holiness from the womb of the morning: thou hast the dew of thy youth.

The LORD hath sworn, and will not repent, Thou art a priest for ever after the order of Melchizedek. The Lord at thy right hand shall strike through kings in the day of his wrath. He shall judge among the heathen, he shall fill the places with the dead bodies;

he shall wound the heads over many countries. He shall drink of the brook in the way: therefore shall he lift up the head.

Isaiah 10:33-11:8

Behold, the Lord, the LORD of hosts, shall lop the bough with terror: and the high ones of stature shall be hewn down, and the haughty shall be humbled. And he shall cut down the thickets of the forest with iron, and Lebanon shall fall by a mighty one.

And there shall come forth a rod out of the stem of Jesse, and a Branch shall grow out of his roots: And the spirit of the LORD shall rest upon him, the spirit of wisdom and understanding, the spirit of counsel and might, the spirit of knowledge and of the fear of the LORD; And shall make him of quick understanding in the fear of the LORD: and he shall not judge after the sight of his eyes, neither reprove after the hearing of his ears: But with righteousness shall he judge the poor, and reprove with equity for the meek of the earth: and he shall smite the earth with the rod of his mouth, and with the breath of his lips shall he slay the wicked. And righteousness shall be the girdle of his loins, and faithfulness the girdle of his reins.

The wolf also shall dwell with the lamb, and the leopard shall lie down with the kid; and the calf and the young lion and the fatling together; and a little child shall lead them. And the cow and the bear shall feed; their young ones shall lie down together: and the lion shall eat straw like the ox. And the sucking child shall play on the hole of the asp, and the weaned child shall put his hand on the cockatrice' den.

Chapter Eleven

Why live in peace?
The Messiah!

There is no man, presently on this earth, who has the wisdom to rule all nations. There is a man who is groomed by God to do just that. He is the one who was in the world, but in whom the prince of this world had no part. God alone has a part in him. This is the Messiah, who was described by the prophet Isaiah.

> *The people that walked in darkness have seen a great light: they that dwell in the land of the shadow of death, upon them hath the light shined. Thou hast multiplied the nation, and not increased the joy: they joy before thee according to the joy in harvest, and as men rejoice when they divide the spoil. For thou hast broken the yoke of his burden, and the staff of his shoulder, the rod of his oppressor, as in the day of Midian. For every battle of the warrior is with confused noise, and garments rolled in blood; but this shall be with burning and fuel of fire.*
>
> *For unto us a child is born, unto us a son is given: and the government shall be upon his shoulder: and his name shall be called Wonderful, Counsellor, The mighty God, The everlasting Father, The Prince of Peace. Of the increase of his government and peace there shall be no end, upon the throne of David, and upon his kingdom, to order it, and to establish it with judgment and with justice from henceforth even for ever. The zeal of the LORD of hosts will perform this.*
> (Isaiah 9:2-7)

Imagine if you will, how great a sacrifice God made in creating this universe. As we say on earth, "He had to take a serious cut in pay to take on this mission". Before mankind was created, God held dominion over all in Heaven, who willingly served Him. However, instead of resting with that, He expanded existence to include beings that would, at their best, give Him grudging obedience. And this giving of obedience is dependent on Him giving to them first.

> *And we have known and believed the love that God hath to us. God is love; and he that dwelleth in love dwelleth in God, and God in him. Herein is our love made perfect, that we may have boldness in the day of judgment: because as he is, so are we in this world. There is no fear in love; but perfect love casteth out fear: because fear hath torment. He that feareth is not made perfect in love.*
>
> *We love him, because he first loved us. If a man say, I love God, and hateth his brother, he is a liar: for he that loveth not his brother whom he hath seen, how can he love God whom he hath not seen? And this commandment have we from him, That he who loveth God love his brother also.*
>   (1 John 4:16-21)

"Well, since God has at least a portion of our devotion, what else does He expect? Can't He just let us take care of one another, and relate to Him when we get around to it? Why does He have to send this Messiah person?"

God sent the Messiah because we depend on this crude thing, known as human government, to provide order. Just think about the mess the world is in under these governments. It should be no wonder that God will not trust His *precious china* of mankind to the crude *bull* of any of the governments of this earth. It should also be no surprise that He would prepare one who would have the knowledge, wisdom and authority to do so. This is a preparation that only He can engineer. This is the one who only He can train. This is the Messiah.

This is not a soul that was brought into existence at a certain time in the history of mankind. This is the soul that is from before the foundations of the world.

> *In the beginning was the Word, and the Word was with God, and the Word was God. The same was in the beginning with God. All things were made by him; and without him was not any thing made that was made. In*

him was life; and the life was the light of men. And the light shineth in darkness; and the darkness comprehended it not.

There was a man sent from God, whose name was John. The same came for a witness, to bear witness of the Light, that all men through him might believe. He was not that Light, but was sent to bear witness of that Light. That was the true Light, which lighteth every man that cometh into the world.

He was in the world, and the world was made by him, and the world knew him not. He came unto his own, and his own received him not. But as many as received him, to them gave he power to become the sons of God, even to them that believe on his name: Which were born, not of blood, nor of the will of the flesh, nor of the will of man, but of God.
(John 1:1-13)

The Messiah is also the Son of man. The Son -- trained in all matters of man and of God. He is called Son because he is the one who is, first, under the direct instruction of God the Father. The Son has also been filled with all knowledge of the ways of God toward man. By the will of God he has become equal to God in the knowledge of man's ways. This, of course, includes both the proper and improper ways that man has displayed, or even thought about, in relating to God.

Let this mind be in you, which was also in Christ Jesus: Who, being in the form of God, thought it not robbery to be equal with God: But made himself of no reputation, and took upon him the form of a servant, and was made in the likeness of men: And being found in fashion as a man, he humbled himself, and became obedient unto death, even the death of the cross. Wherefore God also hath highly exalted him, and given him a name which is above every name: That at the name of Jesus every knee should bow, of things in heaven, and things in earth, and things under the earth; And that every tongue should confess that Jesus Christ is Lord, to the glory of God the Father.
(Philippians 2:5-11)

He is the first soul of mankind born from the very essence of God. As such he is an ideal teacher for mankind. He will also serve as the ideal ruler of mankind. He is the Son of God who is totally responsible for man.

> *Giving thanks unto the Father, which hath made us meet to be partakers of the inheritance of the saints in light: Who hath delivered us from the power of darkness, and hath translated us into the kingdom of his dear Son: In whom we have redemption through his blood, even the forgiveness of sins: Who is the image of the invisible God, the firstborn of every creature: For by him were all things created, that are in heaven, and that are in earth, visible and invisible, whether they be thrones, or dominions, or principalities, or powers: all things were created by him, and for him: And he is before all things, and by him all things consist. And he is the head of the body, the church: who is the beginning, the firstborn from the dead; that in all things he might have the preeminence.*
>
> *For it pleased the Father that in him should all fulness dwell; And, having made peace through the blood of his cross, by him to reconcile all things unto himself; by him, I say, whether they be things in earth, or things in heaven.*
>
> (Colossians 1:12-20)

Why call him, "The Son"? Because of all other sons which were created by God, only the Son of God was born of the very substance of God, the Holy Ghost. Our process of birth is an image of the birth of the only begotten Son of God. It is in this way that we can understand why he is called the Son of God and not just a son of God.

> *And as Moses lifted up the serpent in the wilderness, even so must the Son of man be lifted up: That whosoever believeth in him should not perish, but have eternal life. For God so loved the world, that he gave his only begotten Son, that whosoever believeth in him should not perish, but have everlasting life. For God sent not his*

Son into the world to condemn the world; but that the
world through him might be saved.
(John 3:14-17)

From before the foundation of the world, God delivered a select one. The Son of God was delivered to prepare for a time to come, in the history of man. He was there when God created all that we know of as this universe. It was to him that God referred in performing the task of making man. God, by witness of His word, shared the glory of the creation with His Son.

> *And God said, Let us make man in our image, after our*
> *likeness: and let them have dominion over the fish of the*
> *sea, and over the fowl of the air, and over the cattle, and*
> *over all the earth, and over every creeping thing that*
> *creepeth upon the earth. So God created man in his own*
> *image, in the image of God created he him; male and*
> *female created he them. And God blessed them, and God*
> *said unto them, Be fruitful, and multiply, and replenish*
> *the earth, and subdue it: and have dominion over the fish*
> *of the sea, and over the fowl of the air, and over every*
> *living thing that moveth upon the earth.*
> (Genesis 1:26-28)

To negotiate man to man with divine authority: this is the Messiah. Through the Messiah we have the full presence of God with us. He has been trained by God in all things pertaining to this realm and by his own witness he has total authority over this creation.

> *And Jesus came and spake unto them, saying, All power*
> *is given unto me in heaven and in earth. Go ye therefore,*
> *and teach all nations, baptizing them in the name of the*
> *Father, and of the Son, and of the Holy Ghost: Teaching*
> *them to observe all things whatsoever I have*
> *commanded you: and, lo, I am with you alway, even unto*
> *the end of the world. Amen.*
> (Matthew 28:18-20)

To clearly understand the majesty of the Messiah, we must step beyond the human focus. We must try, as best we can, to see God as He is. God is the Creator. As such, He must Create. This world of ours may be just one point on the map of Creation. God may have planned, and already accomplished, the creation of other universes. To say that this is well within His power, is a severe understatement.

However, God is not remiss in taking care of His handiwork. It would seem--I speak as a human, here--negligent of Him not to establish a perfect control point for this universe. It just seems righteous for Him to create a perfect control point that will fit this universe. It seems necessary that this being be of a substance like unto God's: Spirit. It seems, for the sake of man, a necessity that he also be of the same substance as man. The children of Israel give us an example of what we would have experienced under the direct rule of God.

> *And it came to pass on the third day in the morning, that there were thunders and lightnings, and a thick cloud upon the mount, and the voice of the trumpet exceeding loud; so that all the people that was in the camp trembled. And Moses brought forth the people out of the camp to meet with God; and they stood at the nether part of the mount. And mount Sinai was altogether on a smoke, because the LORD descended upon it in fire: and the smoke thereof ascended as the smoke of a furnace, and the whole mount quaked greatly. And when the voice of the trumpet sounded long, and waxed louder and louder, Moses spake, and God answered him by a voice.*
> (Exodus 19:16-19)

> *And all the people saw the thunderings, and the lightnings, and the noise of the trumpet, and the mountain smoking: and when the people saw it, they removed, and stood afar off. And they said unto Moses, Speak thou with us, and we will hear: but let not God speak with us, lest we die.*

> *And Moses said unto the people, Fear not: for God is come to prove you, and that his fear may be before your faces, that ye sin not.*

> *And the people stood afar off, and Moses drew near unto the thick darkness where God was.*
> (Exodus 20:18-21)

Mankind has to have an intermediary. Moses was this intermediary to the children of Israel. Moses was almost perfect in his mediation between man and God. However, we are searching for the *perfect* intermediary; who can negotiate between God and man for the *entire* human race. This race of beings is one that has many nations and many temperament and many views of what authority is worthy of their devotion and capable of swaying them to obedience. The intermediary who will govern all these nations can only be one who comes from God. It is God who created all nations and it is God who owns all nations. Therefore, it is only from the realm of God that a governor for the world can come. The Son of man is that governor. He has been given a promise to be heir to the kingdom of man.

> *I will declare the decree: the LORD hath said unto me,*
> *Thou art my Son; this day have I begotten thee. Ask of*
> *me, and I shall give thee the heathen for thine*
> *inheritance, and the uttermost parts of the earth for thy*
> *possession.*
> (Psalm 2:7-8)

God the Father has reserved for Himself the nation of Israel, according to Moses and the prophets. This is the nation that has the continual duty to illustrate the Father among the nations of man. It is an eternal covenant which will never be broken. Even though there have been times when the children of Israel moved far away from the will of God, still God is constant in His promise.

> *For I am the LORD, I change not; therefore ye sons of*
> *Jacob are not consumed.*
> (Malachi 3:6)

There is, however, a huge mass of humanity outside the nation of Israel. The message of the kingdom of God is not limited to one nation. The bearer of the message cannot be the only hearer of the message. Furthermore, Israel has illustrated throughout history that it resists perfection. God requires perfection. The good news of the kingdom of God is the message of perfection. The Messiah will deliver to all mankind, including Israel, the right and the only way to perfection in the kingdom of God the Father.

The Messiah will always remember that he is the Son: by doing so he will always honor the Father. He comes as a servant, not as an earthly king. He comes to glorify the Father and not to glorify himself.

His mission is to turn the hearts of mankind back to the Father. He does not come to give mankind another focal point for worship, but only an example of the purest of worship. The Father is center in all that he does. This is the lesson that we must learn from the life that the Son lived here and that he now lives in our hearts.

> *My sheep hear my voice, and I know them, and they follow me: And I give unto them eternal life; and they shall never perish, neither shall any man pluck them out of my hand. My Father, which gave them me, is greater than all; and no man is able to pluck them out of my Father's hand.*
> (John 10:27-29)

> *Peace I leave with you, my peace I give unto you: not as the world giveth, give I unto you. Let not your heart be troubled, neither let it be afraid. Ye have heard how I said unto you, I go away, and come again unto you. If ye loved me, ye would rejoice, because I said, I go unto the Father: for my Father is greater than I.*
> (John 14:27-28)

> *And Jesus answered him, The first of all the commandments is, Hear, O Israel; The Lord our God is one Lord: And thou shalt love the Lord thy God with all thy heart, and with all thy soul, and with all thy mind, and with all thy strength: this is the first commandment. And the second is like, namely this, Thou shalt love thy neighbour as thyself. There is none other commandment greater than these.*
> (Mark 12:29-31)

The Son of God will care for and take the full burden of mankind. Not only will the government be upon his shoulders, but he also bears the responsibility for redeeming the souls of all mankind. This he will do by living the greatest example of all. Having come to be with us and performed many signs and wonders he shows his commitment to the physical well-being of mankind. By establishing the mindset of love he will have solidified the mental well-being of mankind. He will give all that he has, including his life, to show the full extent of his commitment to the total welfare of mankind.

All aspects of man are served by the Son of man. Nothing is left to chance. Nothing is left vacant for the demons of this world to enter a clean house. This he has done for the Father's inheritance as well as for his own.

Behold, my servant shall deal prudently, he shall be exalted and extolled, and be very high. As many were astonied at thee; his visage was so marred more than any man, and his form more than the sons of men: So shall he sprinkle many nations; the kings shall shut their mouths at him: for that which had not been told them shall they see; and that which they had not heard shall they consider.

Who hath believed our report? and to whom is the arm of the LORD revealed? For he shall grow up before him as a tender plant, and as a root out of a dry ground: he hath no form nor comeliness; and when we shall see him, there is no beauty that we should desire him. He is despised and rejected of men; a man of sorrows, and acquainted with grief: and we hid as it were our faces from him; he was despised, and we esteemed him not. Surely he hath borne our griefs, and carried our sorrows: yet we did esteem him stricken, smitten of God, and afflicted. But he was wounded for our transgressions, he was bruised for our iniquities: the chastisement of our peace was upon him; and with his stripes we are healed. All we like sheep have gone astray; we have turned every one to his own way; and the LORD hath laid on him the iniquity of us all.

He was oppressed, and he was afflicted, yet he opened not his mouth: he is brought as a lamb to the slaughter, and as a sheep before her shearers is dumb, so he openeth not his mouth. He was taken from prison and from judgment: and who shall declare his generation? for he was cut off out of the land of the living: for the transgression of my people was he stricken. And he made his grave with the wicked, and with the rich in his death; because he had done no violence, neither was any deceit in his mouth.

Yet it pleased the LORD to bruise him; he hath put him to grief: when thou shalt make his soul an offering for sin, he shall see his seed, he shall prolong his days, and the pleasure of the LORD shall prosper in his hand. He shall see of the travail of his soul, and shall be satisfied: by his knowledge shall my righteous servant justify many; for he shall bear their iniquities. Therefore will I divide him a portion with the great, and he shall divide the spoil with the strong; because he hath poured out his soul unto death: and he was numbered with the transgressors; and he bare the sin of many, and made intercession for the transgressors.
(Isaiah 52:13-53:12)

Since he is the Heir, the Messiah will not just give his life, he will also pick it up again. He will return to the Father to wait for the time of completion of the preparation of mankind for joining with God in eternity. He will not return according to some formula or by the will of man, but only by the will of the Father. It is the Father's timing that determines when mankind is ready for the Son to return to take fully evident control of his inheritance. It is the Father who determines when the Son may start the *final phase* of the governance of mankind.

This is the *final phase* that moves from whenever in time the Father decides it will start, and goes on into eternity. There is, however, a mission that has to be accomplished before the Father will move this world from temporality to eternity. The Son has stated that this time, called the time of the end, will not come until every nation has had an opportunity to know how to recognize him. (It is called the end only because it is the end of this temporal world. It is the beginning in that it ushers in an eternity of righteous rule.) Then will be the judgment of this world, as is described by Jesus.

When the Son of man shall come in his glory, and all the holy angels with him, then shall he sit upon the throne of his glory: And before him shall be gathered all nations: and he shall separate them one from another, as a shepherd divideth his sheep from the goats: And he shall set the sheep on his right hand, but the goats on the left.

Then shall the King say unto them on his right hand, Come, ye blessed of my Father, inherit the kingdom prepared for you from the foundation of the world: For I was an hungred, and ye gave me meat: I was thirsty, and ye gave me drink: I was a stranger, and ye took me in: Naked, and ye clothed me: I was sick, and ye visited me: I was in prison, and ye came unto me.

Then shall the righteous answer him, saying, Lord, when saw we thee an hungred, and fed thee? or thirsty, and gave thee drink? When saw we thee a stranger, and took thee in? or naked, and clothed thee? Or when saw we thee sick, or in prison, and came unto thee?

And the King shall answer and say unto them, Verily I say unto you, Inasmuch as ye have done it unto one of the least of these my brethren, ye have done it unto me.

Then shall he say also unto them on the left hand, Depart from me, ye cursed, into everlasting fire, prepared for the devil and his angels: For I was an hungred, and ye gave me no meat: I was thirsty, and ye gave me no drink: I was a stranger, and ye took me not in: naked, and ye clothed me not: sick, and in prison, and ye visited me not.

Then shall they also answer him, saying, Lord, when saw we thee an hungred, or athirst, or a stranger, or naked, or sick, or in prison, and did not minister unto thee?

Then shall he answer them, saying, Verily I say unto you, Inasmuch as ye did it not to one of the least of these, ye did it not to me.

And these shall go away into everlasting punishment: but the righteous into life eternal.
(Matthew 25:31-46)

Our first mission is to prepare our own nations for his coming. We can best do this by the witness of our example. By sharing the witness of the Son, through the witness of our lives, we are working to prepare the world for the day of his return. A message to the young man Timothy, given by the apostle Paul, is relevant to all who truly want to know God.

These things command and teach. Let no man despise thy youth; but be thou an example of the believers, in word, in conversation, in charity, in spirit, in faith, in purity. Till I come, give attendance to reading, to exhortation, to doctrine. Neglect not the gift that is in thee, which was given thee by prophecy, with the laying on of the hands of the presbytery. Meditate upon these things; give thyself wholly to them; that thy profiting may appear to all. Take heed unto thyself, and unto the doctrine; continue in them: for in doing this thou shalt both save thyself, and them that hear thee.
(1 Timothy 4:11-16)

All of us can do this by living a life that is an example of the love of God. This can be done whether young or old.

There are some who have been selected, called the elect, to carry the message of God to the world. This ministry is not a calling for everyone, but only for those who are chosen and equipped according to the will of God to do so. There is no need for anyone to feel that they are not *pulling their weight* if they don't travel the world preaching the Gospel. God chooses whom He will for this type of service.

Go ye therefore, and teach all nations, baptizing them in the name of the Father, and of the Son, and of the Holy Ghost: Teaching them to observe all things whatsoever I have commanded you: and, lo, I am with you alway, even unto the end of the world. Amen.
(Matthew 28:19-20)

There are many areas of service which honor God. Whenever you pray for the will of God on earth, as directed by the Lord, in what is called the Lord's Prayer, you are serving God. There is no service too small for God. Consider the following event as recorded in the Bible.

And Jesus sat over against the treasury, and beheld how the people cast money into the treasury: and many that were rich cast in much. And there came a certain poor widow, and she threw in two mites, which make a farthing. And he called unto him his disciples, and saith unto them, Verily I say unto you, That this poor widow hath cast more in, than all they which have cast

into the treasury: For all they did cast in of their abundance; but she of her want did cast in all that she had, even all her living.
(Mark 12:41-44)

The Messiah will make us a community. We need not strive to force another to serve God. God doesn't want our offerings in a grudging fashion; He wants them willingly. The work is not ours to complete; but only ours to do in righteous service to God.

For while one saith, I am of Paul; and another, I am of Apollos; are ye not carnal? Who then is Paul, and who is Apollos, but ministers by whom ye believed, even as the Lord gave to every man?

I have planted, Apollos watered; but God gave the increase. So then neither is he that planteth any thing, neither he that watereth; but God that giveth the increase. Now he that planteth and he that watereth are one: and every man shall receive his own reward according to his own labour. For we are labourers together with God: ye are God's husbandry, ye are God's building.

According to the grace of God which is given unto me, as a wise masterbuilder, I have laid the foundation, and another buildeth thereon. But let every man take heed how he buildeth thereupon. For other foundation can no man lay than that is laid, which is Jesus Christ.
(1 Corinthians 3:4-11)

The Messiah is the Son of God, the Christ, and the Heir to the kingdom of God here on earth. He will establish himself using the power given to him in heaven and earth. With this knowledge we can rest from our strivings with one another about politics and procedures and principalities and powers. Our duty is to deliver, through the example of our lives, the message of the good news of the kingdom of God with man; which is the Gospel.

We share the Gospel like unto the way Moses delivered the message of God, the Law, to the children of Abraham. Moses did not force the Law upon them, or present it under his own power; but under the power of God. It is in like manner that we must serve God; in love, with humility and according to our faith.

But sanctify the Lord God in your hearts: and be ready always to give an answer to every man that asketh you a reason of the hope that is in you with meekness and fear: Having a good conscience; that, whereas they speak evil of you, as of evildoers, they may be ashamed that falsely accuse your good conversation in Christ. For it is better, if the will of God be so, that ye suffer for well doing, than for evil doing.

(1 Peter 3:15-17)

The Messiah will return to us,
Flowing through Heaven's door;
In a pageant most splendid
That none on earth can ignore.

Accompanied by the angels
From Heaven, where God doth reign;
To establish peace and truth
Among all nations, once again.

The ones who have fought
To destroy his message true
Will be dispersed in his brilliance
Like the early morning dew.

Nations who thought they
Were surely in the right
Will discover their feeble logic
By his great power put to flight.

The nations of the earth,
Including all that are now,
Will in his presence
Most surely have to bow.

So what of your nation,
You think has such worth?
Is it preparing for the arrival
Of peace on all the earth?

Don't strive for ownership
Of some other's land;
It will flow through your fist
Like grains of sand.

Know ye not that God
Set the bounds of your land
When He created the nations
By His strong Right Hand?

You are bought with a price
Paid to the Father above,
By Jesus Christ, His Son,
In a marvel of great love.

Praise God for the gift
Of redemption through His Son;
May the world receive this truth,
To come together as one.

Chapter 11a

Government

I'm going to take you through a Scriptural journey on the place of governments in the kingdom of God. This journey will be somewhat sketchy and will depend heavily on the text of the Bible. I will only give a brief sentence before each section to prompt thought. Well let's be off on our journey.

From the beginning God held supreme authority over governments: He set them up and He tore them down.

Deuteronomy 32:1-9

Give ear, O ye heavens, and I will speak; and hear, O earth, the words of my mouth. My doctrine shall drop as the rain, my speech shall distil as the dew, as the small rain upon the tender herb, and as the showers upon the grass: Because I will publish the name of the LORD: ascribe ye greatness unto our God. He is the Rock, his work is perfect: for all his ways are judgment: a God of truth and without iniquity, just and right is he.

They have corrupted themselves, their spot is not the spot of his children: they are a perverse and crooked generation. Do ye thus requite the LORD, O foolish people and unwise? is not he thy father that hath bought thee? hath he not made thee, and established thee? Remember the days of old, consider the years of many generations: ask thy father, and he will show thee; thy elders, and they will tell thee.

When the Most High divided to the nations their inheritance, when he separated the sons of Adam, he set the bounds of the people according to the number of the children of Israel. For the LORD'S portion is his people; Jacob is the lot of his inheritance.

Jeremiah 1:1-10

The words of Jeremiah the son of Hilkiah, of the priests that were in Anathoth in the land of Benjamin: To whom the word of the LORD came in the days of Josiah the son of Amon king of Judah, in the thirteenth year of his reign. It came also in the days of Jehoiakim the son of Josiah king of Judah, unto the end of the eleventh year of Zedekiah the son of Josiah king of Judah, unto the carrying away of Jerusalem captive in the fifth month.

Then the word of the LORD came unto me, saying, Before I formed thee in the belly I knew thee; and before thou camest forth out of the womb I sanctified thee, and I ordained thee a prophet unto the nations.

Then said I, Ah, Lord GOD! behold, I cannot speak: for I am a child.

But the LORD said unto me, Say not, I am a child: for thou shalt go to all that I shall send thee, and whatsoever I command thee thou shalt speak. Be not afraid of their faces: for I am with thee to deliver thee, saith the LORD.

Then the LORD put forth his hand, and touched my mouth. And the LORD said unto me, Behold, I have put my words in thy mouth. See, I have this day set thee over the nations and over the kingdoms, to root out, and to pull down, and to destroy, and to throw down, to build, and to plant.

Job 12:9-23

Who knoweth not in all these that the hand of the LORD hath wrought this? In whose hand is the soul of every living thing, and the breath of all mankind. Doth not the ear try words? and the mouth taste his meat? With the ancient is wisdom; and in length of days understanding. With him is wisdom and strength, he hath counsel and understanding.

Behold, he breaketh down, and it cannot be built again: he shutteth up a man, and there can be no opening. Behold, he withholdeth the waters, and they dry up: also he sendeth them out, and they overturn the earth. With him is strength and wisdom: the deceived and the deceiver are his.

He leadeth counsellors away spoiled, and maketh the judges fools. He looseth the bond of kings, and girdeth their loins with a girdle. He leadeth princes away spoiled, and overthroweth the mighty. He removeth away the speech of the trusty, and taketh away the understanding of the aged. He poureth contempt upon princes, and weakeneth the strength of the mighty. He discovereth deep things out of darkness, and bringeth out to light the shadow of death. He increaseth the nations, and destroyeth them: he enlargeth the nations, and straiteneth them again.

As the nations were maturing God gave them some leeway to experiment in their growth toward Him.

Acts 17:24-31

God that made the world and all things therein, seeing that he is Lord of heaven and earth, dwelleth not in temples made with hands; Neither is worshipped with men's hands, as though he needed any thing, seeing he giveth to all life, and breath, and all things; And hath made of one blood all nations of men for to dwell on all the face of the earth, and hath determined the times before appointed, and the bounds of their habitation; That they should seek the Lord, if haply they might feel after him, and find him, though he be not far from every one of us: For in him we live, and move, and have our being; as certain also of your own poets have said, For we are also his offspring.

Forasmuch then as we are the offspring of God, we ought not to think that the Godhead is like unto gold, or silver, or stone, graven by art and man's device. And the times of this ignorance God winked at; but now commandeth all men every where to repent: Because he hath appointed a day, in the which he will judge the world in righteousness by that man whom he hath ordained; whereof he hath given assurance unto all men, in that he hath raised him from the dead.

Then Satan was kicked out of Heaven. The accusatory actions he performed before God were then brought to an end. The condemnation of the children of the earth before God by Satan was nullified as a result of the sacrifice made in love by the Son of God, Jesus the Messiah.

John 12:27-32

Now is my soul troubled; and what shall I say? Father, save me from this hour: but for this cause came I unto this hour. Father, glorify thy name.

Then came there a voice from heaven, saying, I have both glorified it, and will glorify it again.

The people therefore, that stood by, and heard it, said that it thundered: others said, An angel spake to him.

Jesus answered and said, This voice came not because of me, but for your sakes. Now is the judgment of this world: now shall the prince of this world be cast out. And I, if I be lifted up from the earth, will draw all men unto me.

Revelation 12:7-12

And there was war in heaven: Michael and his angels fought against the dragon; and the dragon fought and his angels, And prevailed not; neither was their place found any more in heaven. And the great dragon was cast out, that old serpent, called the Devil, and Satan, which deceiveth the whole world: he was cast out into the earth, and his angels were cast out with him.

And I heard a loud voice saying in heaven, Now is come salvation, and strength, and the kingdom of our God, and the power of his Christ: for the accuser of our brethren is cast down, which accused them before our God day and night.

And they overcame him by the blood of the Lamb, and by the word of their testimony; and they loved not their lives unto the death. Therefore rejoice, ye heavens, and ye that dwell in them. Woe to the inhabiters of the earth and of the sea! for the devil is come down unto you, having great wrath, because he knoweth that he hath but a short time.

John 12:31

Now is the judgment of this world: now shall the prince of this world be cast out.

Luke 10:18

And he said unto them, I beheld Satan as lightning fall from heaven.

However, Satan is not powerless on this earth. In fact, Satan is supreme on this earth. Satan is the prince of this earth. This is even acknowledged by the Son of God, the Messiah.

Luke 4:1-8

And Jesus being full of the Holy Ghost returned from Jordan, and was led by the Spirit into the wilderness, Being forty days tempted of the devil. And in those days he did eat nothing: and when they were ended, he afterward hungered.

And the devil said unto him, If thou be the Son of God, command this stone that it be made bread.

And Jesus answered him, saying, It is written, That man shall not live by bread alone, but by every word of God.

And the devil, taking him up into an high mountain, shewed unto him all the kingdoms of the world in a moment of time. And the devil said unto him, All this power will I give thee, and the glory of them: for that is delivered unto me; and to whomsoever I will I give it. If thou therefore wilt worship me, all shall be thine.

And Jesus answered and said unto him, Get thee behind me, Satan: for it is written, Thou shalt worship the Lord thy God, and him only shalt thou serve.

John 14:30

Hereafter I will not talk much with you: for the prince of this world cometh, and hath nothing in me.

The security blanket provided by God, in obviously controlling the affairs of government, is gone. A new blanket of peace in love is now extended. However, it must be taken up and used by mankind. God no longer **demands** man's obedience; he requests it through Jesus Christ. Jesus asks us to give our obedience to the Father; freely in love.

John 14:27-30

Peace I leave with you, my peace I give unto you: not as the world giveth, give I unto you. Let not your heart be troubled, neither let it be afraid.

Ye have heard how I said unto you, I go away, and come again unto you. If ye loved me, ye would rejoice, because I said, I go unto the Father: for my Father is greater than I.

And now I have told you before it come to pass, that, when it is come to pass, ye might believe. Hereafter I will not talk much with you: for the prince of this world cometh, and hath nothing in me.

John 14:15-26

If ye love me, keep my commandments.

And I will pray the Father, and he shall give you another Comforter, that he may abide with you for ever; Even the Spirit of truth; whom the world cannot receive, because it seeth him not, neither knoweth him: but ye know him; for he dwelleth with you, and shall be in you.

I will not leave you comfortless: I will come to you.

Yet a little while, and the world seeth me no more; but ye see me: because I live, ye shall live also. At that day ye shall know that I am in my Father, and ye in me, and I in you.

He that hath my commandments, and keepeth them, he it is that loveth me: and he that loveth me shall be loved of my Father, and I will love him, and will manifest myself to him.

Judas saith unto him, not Iscariot, Lord, how is it that thou wilt manifest thyself unto us, and not unto the world?

Jesus answered and said unto him, If a man love me, he will keep my words: and my Father will love him, and we will come unto him, and make our abode with him. He that loveth me not keepeth not my sayings: and the word which ye hear is not mine, but the Father's which sent me. These things have I spoken unto you, being yet present with you. But the Comforter, which is the Holy Ghost, whom the Father will send in my name, he shall teach you all things, and bring all things to your remembrance, whatsoever I have said unto you.

The stakes are high, for mankind in not looking to God and yielding to His way. The adversary, Satan, is not resting. With a full knowledge of his final dismissal from the presence of mankind, as he was dismissed from the presence of God, the adversary is very busy today. Though he was not able to convince the Lord Jesus to accept his offer of governmental rule, he did succeed in establishing a stronghold for himself on this earth. This stronghold, however, will be the first to go in the cleansing that God brings to mankind.

Revelation 18:1-24

And after these things I saw another angel come down from heaven, having great power; and the earth was lightened with his glory. And he cried mightily with a strong voice, saying, Babylon the great is fallen, is fallen, and is become the habitation of devils, and the hold of every foul spirit, and a cage of every unclean and hateful bird. For all nations have drunk of the wine of the wrath of her fornication, and the kings of the earth have committed fornication with her, and the merchants of the earth are waxed rich through the abundance of her delicacies.

And I heard another voice from heaven, saying, Come out of her, my people, that ye be not partakers of her sins, and that ye receive not of her plagues. For her sins have reached unto heaven, and God hath remembered her iniquities. Reward her even as she rewarded you, and double unto her double according to her works: in the cup which she hath filled fill to her double. How much she hath glorified herself, and lived deliciously, so much torment and sorrow give her: for she saith in her heart, I sit a queen, and am no widow, and shall see no sorrow. Therefore shall her plagues come in one day, death, and mourning, and famine; and she shall be utterly burned with fire: for strong is the Lord God who judgeth her.

And the kings of the earth, who have committed fornication and lived deliciously with her, shall bewail her, and lament for her, when they shall see the smoke of her burning, Standing afar off for the fear of her torment, saying, Alas, alas that great city Babylon, that mighty city! for in one hour is thy judgment come.

And the merchants of the earth shall weep and mourn over her; for no man buyeth their merchandise any more: The merchandise of gold, and silver, and precious stones, and of pearls, and fine linen, and purple, and silk, and scarlet, and all thyine wood, and all manner vessels of ivory, and all manner vessels of most precious wood, and of brass, and iron, and marble, And cinnamon, and odours, and ointments, and frankincense, and wine, and oil, and fine flour, and wheat, and beasts, and sheep, and horses, and chariots, and slaves, and souls of men. And the fruits that thy soul lusted after are departed from thee, and all things which were dainty and goodly are departed from thee, and thou shalt find them no more at all. The merchants of these things, which were made rich by her, shall stand afar off for the fear of her torment, weeping and wailing, And saying, Alas, alas, that great city, that was clothed in fine linen, and purple, and scarlet, and decked with gold, and precious stones, and pearls!

For in one hour so great riches is come to nought. And every shipmaster, and all the company in ships, and sailors, and as many as trade by sea, stood afar off, And cried when they saw the smoke of her burning, saying, What city is like unto this great city! And they cast dust on their heads, and cried, weeping and wailing, saying, Alas, alas, that great city, wherein were made rich all that had ships in the sea by reason of her costliness! for in one hour is she made desolate.

Rejoice over her, thou heaven, and ye holy apostles and prophets; for God hath avenged you on her.

And a mighty angel took up a stone like a great millstone, and cast it into the sea, saying, Thus with violence shall that great city Babylon be thrown down, and shall be found no more at all. And the voice of harpers, and musicians, and of pipers, and trumpeters, shall be heard no more at all in thee; and no craftsman, of whatsoever craft he be, shall be found any more in thee; and the sound of a millstone shall be heard no more at all in thee; And the light of a candle shall shine no more at all in thee; and the voice of the bridegroom and of the bride shall be heard no more at all in thee: for thy merchants were the great men of the earth; for by thy sorceries were all nations deceived.

And in her was found the blood of prophets, and of saints, and of all that were slain upon the earth.

As God has always done, so it will be; He will defeat the workings of the devil in the earth. He will re-establish His order among mankind and among mankind's governments.

Psalm 110:1-7

A Psalm of David.

The LORD said unto my Lord, Sit thou at my right hand, until I make thine enemies thy footstool.

The LORD shall send the rod of thy strength out of Zion: rule thou in the midst of thine enemies. Thy people shall be willing in the day of thy power, in the beauties of holiness from the womb of the morning: thou hast the dew of thy youth. The LORD hath sworn, and will not repent, Thou art a priest for ever after the order of Melchizedek.

The Lord at thy right hand shall strike through kings in the day of his wrath. He shall judge among the heathen, he shall fill the places with the dead bodies; he shall wound the heads over many countries. He shall drink of the brook in the way: therefore shall he lift up the head.

Revelation 19:11-21

And I saw heaven opened, and behold a white horse; and he that sat upon him was called

Faithful and True, and in righteousness he doth judge and make war. His eyes were as a flame of fire, and on his head were many crowns; and he had a name written, that no man knew, but he himself. And he was clothed with a vesture dipped in blood: and his name is called The Word of God. And the armies which were in heaven followed him upon white horses, clothed in fine linen, white and clean. And out of his mouth goeth a sharp sword, that with it he should smite the nations: and he shall rule them with a rod of iron: and he treadeth the winepress of the fierceness and wrath of Almighty God. And he hath on his vesture and on his thigh a name written, KING OF KINGS, AND LORD OF LORDS.

And I saw an angel standing in the sun; and he cried with a loud voice, saying to all the fowls that fly in the midst of heaven, Come and gather yourselves together unto the supper of the great God; That ye may eat the flesh of kings, and the flesh of captains, and the flesh of mighty men, and the flesh of horses, and of them that sit on them, and the flesh of all men, both free and bond, both small and great.

And I saw the beast, and the kings of the earth, and their armies, gathered together to make war against him that sat on the horse, and against his army. And the beast was taken, and with him the false prophet that wrought miracles before him, with which he deceived them that had received the mark of the beast, and them that worshipped his image. These both were cast alive into a lake of fire burning with brimstone.

And the remnant were slain with the sword of him that sat upon the horse, which sword proceeded out of his mouth: and all the fowls were filled with their flesh.

Revelation 20:1-3

And I saw an angel come down from heaven, having the key of the bottomless pit and a great chain in his hand. And he laid hold on the dragon, that old serpent, which is the Devil, and Satan, and bound him a thousand years, And cast him into the bottomless pit, and shut him up, and set a seal upon him, that he should deceive the nations no more, till the thousand years should be fulfilled: and after that he must be loosed a little season.

The dream of all mankind, the true one-world government, will come through the Messiah, the Son of God. It is only through the Son of God that the Father has determined that it will come.

Revelation 20:7-15

And when the thousand years are expired, Satan shall be loosed out of his prison, And shall go out to deceive the nations which are in the four quarters of the earth, Gog and Magog, to gather them together to battle: the number of whom is as the sand of the sea. And they went up on the breadth of the earth, and compassed the camp of the saints about, and the beloved city: and fire came down from God out of heaven, and devoured them.

And the devil that deceived them was cast into the lake of fire and brimstone, where the beast and the false prophet are, and shall be tormented day and night for ever and ever.

And I saw a great white throne, and him that sat on it, from whose face the earth and the heaven fled away; and there was found no place for them.

And I saw the dead, small and great, stand before God; and the books were opened: and another book was opened, which is the book of life: and the dead were judged out of those things which were written in the books, according to their works. And the sea gave up the dead which were in it; and death and hell delivered up the dead which were in them: and they were judged every man according to their works.

And death and hell were cast into the lake of fire. This is the second death. And whosoever was not found written in the book of life was cast into the lake of fire.

Revelation 21:1

And I saw a new heaven and a new earth: for the first heaven and the first earth were passed away; and there was no more sea. And I John saw the holy city, new Jerusalem, coming down from God out of heaven, prepared as a bride adorned for her husband.

And I heard a great voice out of heaven saying, Behold, the tabernacle of God is with men, and he will dwell with them, and they shall be his people, and God himself shall be with them, and be their God. And God shall wipe away all tears from their eyes; and there shall be no more death, neither sorrow, nor crying, neither shall there be any more pain: for the former things are passed away.

In light of these words of God, given to the messengers of God; ask God for direction as to what you must do in your governments on this earth. There is no answer to be found other than the answer that is found in God.

Ho, every one that thirsteth, come ye to the waters, and he that hath no money; come ye, buy, and eat; yea, come, buy wine and milk without money and without price. Wherefore do ye spend money for that which is not bread? and your labour for that which satisfieth not? hearken diligently unto me, and eat ye that which is good, and let your soul delight itself in fatness.

Incline your ear, and come unto me: hear, and your soul shall live; and I will make an everlasting covenant with you, even the sure mercies of David. Behold, I have given him for a witness to the people, a leader and commander to the people. Behold, thou shalt call a nation that thou knowest not, and nations that knew not thee shall run unto thee because of the LORD thy God, and for the Holy One of Israel; for he hath glorified thee.

Seek ye the LORD while he may be found, call ye upon him while he is near: Let the wicked forsake his way, and the unrighteous man his thoughts: and let him return unto the LORD, and he will have mercy upon him; and to our God, for he will abundantly pardon

For my thoughts are not your thoughts, neither are your ways my ways, saith the LORD. For as the heavens are higher than the earth, so are my ways higher than your ways, and my thoughts than your thoughts. For as the rain cometh down, and the snow from heaven, and returneth not thither, but watereth the earth, and maketh it bring forth and bud, that it may give seed to the sower, and bread to the eater: So shall my word be that goeth forth out of my mouth: it shall not return unto me void, but it shall accomplish that which I please, and it shall prosper in the thing whereto I sent it.

For ye shall go out with joy, and be led forth with peace: the mountains and the hills shall break forth before you into singing, and all the trees of the field shall clap their hands. Instead of the thorn shall come up the fir tree, and instead of the brier shall come up the myrtle tree: and it shall be to the LORD for a name, for an everlasting sign that shall not be cut off.

(Isaiah 55)

The Word from the Bible

Genesis 17:1-6

And when Abram was ninety years old and nine, the LORD appeared to Abram, and said unto him, I am the Almighty God; walk before me, and be thou perfect. And I will make my covenant between me and thee, and will multiply thee exceedingly.

And Abram fell on his face: and God talked with him, saying, As for me, behold, my covenant is with thee, and thou shalt be a father of many nations. Neither shall thy name any more be called Abram, but thy name shall be Abraham; for a father of many nations have I made thee. And I will make thee exceeding fruitful, and I will make nations of thee, and kings shall come out of thee.

Genesis 17:7-8

And I will establish my covenant between me and thee and thy seed after thee in their generations for an everlasting covenant, to be a God unto thee, and to thy seed after thee. And I will give unto thee, and to thy seed after thee, the land wherein thou art a stranger, all the land of Canaan, for an everlasting possession; and I will be their God.

Genesis 18:16-19

And the men rose up from thence, and looked toward Sodom: and Abraham went with them to bring them on the way. And the LORD said, Shall I hide from Abraham that thing which I do; Seeing that Abraham shall surely become a great and mighty nation, and all the nations of the earth shall be blessed in him? For I know him, that he will command his children and his household after him, and they shall keep the way of the LORD, to do justice and judgment; that the LORD may bring upon Abraham that which he hath spoken of him.

Deuteronomy 18:15-22

The LORD thy God will raise up unto thee a Prophet from the midst of thee, of thy brethren, like unto me; unto him ye shall hearken; According to all that thou desiredst of the LORD thy God in Horeb in the day of the assembly, saying, Let me not hear again the voice of the LORD my God, neither let me see this great fire any more, that I die not.

And the LORD said unto me, They have well spoken that which they have spoken. I will raise them up a Prophet from among their brethren, like unto thee, and will put my words in his mouth; and he shall speak unto them all that I shall command him. And it shall come to pass, that whosoever will not hearken unto my words which he shall speak in my name, I will require it of him. But the prophet, which shall presume to speak a word in my name, which I have not commanded him to speak, or that shall speak in the name of other gods, even that prophet shall die.

And if thou say in thine heart, How shall we know the word which the LORD hath not spoken? When a prophet speaketh in the name of the LORD, if the thing follow not, nor come to pass, that is the thing which the LORD hath not spoken, but the prophet hath spoken it presumptuously: thou shalt not be afraid of him.

Psalm 110:1-7

A Psalm of David.

The LORD said unto my Lord, Sit thou at my right hand, until I make thine enemies thy footstool.

The LORD shall send the rod of thy strength out of Zion: rule thou in the midst of thine enemies. Thy people shall be willing in the day of thy power, in the beauties of holiness from the womb of the morning: thou hast the dew of thy youth. The LORD hath sworn, and will not repent, Thou art a priest for ever after the order of Melchizedek.

The Lord at thy right hand shall strike through kings in the day of his wrath. He shall judge among the heathen, he shall fill the places with the dead bodies; he shall wound the heads over many countries. He shall drink of the brook in the way: therefore shall he lift up the head.

Isaiah 11:1-5

And there shall come forth a rod out of the stem of Jesse, and a Branch shall grow out of his roots: And the spirit of the LORD shall rest upon him, the spirit of wisdom and understanding, the spirit of counsel and might, the spirit of knowledge and of the fear of the LORD; And shall make him of quick understanding in the fear of the LORD: and he shall not judge after the sight of his eyes, neither reprove after the hearing of his ears: But with righteousness shall he judge the poor, and reprove with equity for the meek of the earth: and he shall smite the earth with the rod of his mouth, and with the breath of his lips shall he slay the wicked. And righteousness shall be the girdle of his loins, and faithfulness the girdle of his reins.

Psalm 90:4

For a thousand years in thy sight are but as yesterday when it is past, and as a watch in the night.

In My Conclusion

Let us recap where we've been.

All mankind belongs to God. This includes every nation on the earth. It also includes all humans who have passed from this earth through the gate of death. Furthermore, it includes all those who will enter this earth by way of the unfolding of birth. All mankind belongs to God.

God establishes all processes: whether these processes are what we call worship or whether they be what we call science. Furthermore, God controls all procedures: among these are principalities and powers. He raises them up and He quiets them down

> *Then Job arose, and rent his mantle, and shaved his head, and fell down upon the ground, and worshipped, And said, Naked came I out of my mother's womb, and naked shall I return thither: the LORD gave, and the LORD hath taken away; blessed be the name of the LORD. In all this Job sinned not, nor charged God foolishly.*
> (Job 1:20-22)

> *O thou king, the most high God gave Nebuchadnezzar thy father a kingdom, and majesty, and glory, and honour: And for the majesty that he gave him, all people, nations, and languages, trembled and feared before him: whom he would he slew; and whom he would he kept alive; and whom he would he set up; and whom he would he put down. But when his heart was lifted up, and his mind hardened in pride, he was deposed from his kingly throne, and they took his glory from him: And he was driven from the sons of men; and his heart was made like the beasts, and his dwelling was with the wild asses: they fed him with grass like oxen, and his body was wet with the dew of heaven; till he knew that the most high God ruled in the kingdom of men, and that he appointeth over it whomsoever he will.*
> (Daniel 5:18-21)

Our view of God involves placing Him in a frame of majesty. Outside this frame are events that occur in all reality. These events are said to be for the glory of God when they are done in righteousness. Alternatively, we say that they are subject to the judgment of God if they are not done in righteousness.

> *Whether therefore ye eat, or drink, or whatsoever ye do,*
> *do all to the glory of God.*
>   (1 Corinthians 10:31)

The matter of His glory goes beyond a heavenly gift of obeisance to the Father above. One need only go two steps further to see this. At the first step we must ask ourselves a question: "What is the glory of an earthly father?"

The answer is, "the prosperity of his children and of all who are in his dominion."

The next step is to ask the following: "What is the glory of our heavenly Father?"

The answer is, "It is the same."

Too often, we think of God as capriciously sitting back, looking for entertainment from human activity: we call it praise. This is not the God of the universes. This would be more in line with selfish humanity.

The God of the universes, Creates. Furthermore, He moves that which He creates to a state known as Perfection. This is another of the processes He has established. Those who have built companies, organizations, groups, friendships, and, yes, even families know the joy of creation. Furthermore, those who have worked with their creations, to move them toward perfection, know the joy of progression. This joy is not just for the creator but also for the creation.

Progression is not instant gratification. Instant gratification is more for the recipient than for anyone else. Progression and escalation of responsibility, however, are best for the creation. Progression is required for increasing responsibility: a child of two months would not make a good king, alone. God has given us many physical examples of His majesty being displayed through progression. He also has given us a history of human progression, which is directed according to His majesty: this is contained in the Bible.

We, being human, can lose sight of the majesty of God. We do so when we allow the works done by Him for our ancestors to drift solely into the past. The lessons are archived and deemed of little, if any, use for *now*. In order to prevent this archival, the LORD directs His people to honor the observances set up by Him for them. Furthermore, they are to do so throughout their generations.

> *Then Moses called for all the elders of Israel, and said unto them, Draw out and take you a lamb according to your families, and kill the passover. And ye shall take a bunch of hyssop, and dip it in the blood that is in the bason, and strike the lintel and the two side posts with the blood that is in the bason; and none of you shall go out at the door of his house until the morning. For the LORD will pass through to smite the Egyptians; and when he seeth the blood upon the lintel, and on the two side posts, the LORD will pass over the door, and will not suffer the destroyer to come in unto your houses to smite you.*
>
> *And ye shall observe this thing for an ordinance to thee and to thy sons for ever. And it shall come to pass, when ye be come to the land which the LORD will give you, according as he hath promised, that ye shall keep this service. And it shall come to pass, when your children shall say unto you, What mean ye by this service? That ye shall say, It is the sacrifice of the LORD's passover, who passed over the houses of the children of Israel in Egypt, when he smote the Egyptians, and delivered our houses. And the people bowed the head and worshipped.*
> (Exodus 12:21-27)

The nation of Israel received this commandment, but still they drifted away from the observances. This does not mean that every nation must observe these celebrations and commemorations set up for Israel. These are specific to the nation of Israel; refreshing God's presence with that nation in its history. Each nation on this earth has its own unique presence in God. Therefore, all nations must serve God, the Creator, and honor His Messiah.

Our honor of God does not, however, include any of the man-made services. These are those which were created by a human or an organization to either replace or exceed the service given by God. Such things are an affront to God. Only God knows the type, form and level of service that each nation, and each person, must deliver to Him.

Consider how precise He was with Noah in describing the ark. Consider also, the precision of the temple blueprint given by God to Moses.

On the other hand, once a service has been ruled by God as being obsolete, it must be abandoned. Our thoughts must be on the present. We cannot change the past. We cannot force the future: God has set the entire course of mankind for all generations. The services are a part of His method for accomplishing this flow.

> *But seek ye first the kingdom of God, and his righteousness; and all these things shall be added unto you. Take therefore no thought for the morrow: for the morrow shall take thought for the things of itself. Sufficient unto the day is the evil thereof.*
> (Matthew 6:33-34)

Again, let's look at the nation of Israel. The sacrifices were once the way for them to move toward righteousness, anew. This is a precise form of worship. It was replaced by the better way of obedience to God and righteous living before God.

> *And Samuel said, Hath the LORD as great delight in burnt offerings and sacrifices, as in obeying the voice of the LORD? Behold, to obey is better than sacrifice, and to hearken than the fat of rams.*
> (1 Samuel 15:22)

> *For I desired mercy, and not sacrifice; and the knowledge of God more than burnt offerings.*
> (Hosea 6:6)

For the world, including the nation of Israel when they accept it fully, God sent the best and final way to righteousness. Let's follow the logic through the Bible.

The law and the prophets were until John

> *And he said unto them, Ye are they which justify yourselves before men; but God knoweth your hearts: for that which is highly esteemed among men is abomination in the sight of God. The law and the prophets were until John: since that time the kingdom of God is preached, and every man presseth into it.*
> (Luke 16:15-16)

he shall save his people from their sins

Now the birth of Jesus Christ was on this wise: When as his mother Mary was espoused to Joseph, before they came together, she was found with child of the Holy Ghost. Then Joseph her husband, being a just man, and not willing to make her a publick example, was minded to put her away privily.

But while he thought on these things, behold, the angel of the LORD appeared unto him in a dream, saying, Joseph, thou son of David, fear not to take unto thee Mary thy wife: for that which is conceived in her is of the Holy Ghost. And she shall bring forth a son, and thou shalt call his name JESUS: for he shall save his people from their sins.

Now all this was done, that it might be fulfilled which was spoken of the Lord by the prophet, saying, Behold, a virgin shall be with child, and shall bring forth a son, and they shall call his name Emmanuel, which being interpreted is, God with us.
(Matthew 1:18-23)

Christ is the end of the law for righteousness

Brethren, my heart's desire and prayer to God for Israel is, that they might be saved. For I bear them record that they have a zeal of God, but not according to knowledge. For they being ignorant of God's righteousness, and going about to establish their own righteousness, have not submitted themselves unto the righteousness of God. For Christ is the end of the law for righteousness to every one that believeth.
(Romans 10:1-4)

Believe on the Lord Jesus Christ

And at midnight Paul and Silas prayed, and sang praises unto God: and the prisoners heard them. And suddenly there was a great earthquake, so that the foundations of the prison were shaken: and immediately all the doors were opened, and every one's bands were loosed. And the keeper of the prison awaking out of his sleep, and seeing the prison doors open, he drew out his sword, and would have killed himself, supposing that the prisoners had been fled.

But Paul cried with a loud voice, saying, Do thyself no harm: for we are all here.

Then he called for a light, and sprang in, and came trembling, and fell down before Paul and Silas, And brought them out, and said, Sirs, what must I do to be saved?

And they said, Believe on the Lord Jesus Christ, and thou shalt be saved, and thy house. And they spake unto him the word of the Lord, and to all that were in his house.
(Acts 16:25-32)

Confess with thy mouth the Lord Jesus

But what saith it? The word is nigh thee, even in thy mouth, and in thy heart: that is, the word of faith, which we preach; That if thou shalt confess with thy mouth the Lord Jesus, and shalt believe in thine heart that God hath raised him from the dead, thou shalt be saved. For with the heart man believeth unto righteousness; and with the mouth confession is made unto salvation. For the scripture saith, Whosoever believeth on him shall not be ashamed.
(Romans 10:8-11)

Wherefore hear the word of the LORD, ye scornful men, that rule this people which is in Jerusalem. Because ye have said, We have made a covenant with death, and with hell are we at agreement; when the overflowing scourge shall pass through, it shall not come unto us: for we have made lies our refuge, and under falsehood have we hid ourselves: Therefore thus saith the Lord GOD, Behold, I lay in Zion for a foundation a stone, a tried stone, a precious corner stone, a sure foundation: he that believeth shall not make haste.

Judgment also will I lay to the line, and righteousness to the plummet: and the hail shall sweep away the refuge of lies, and the waters shall overflow the hiding place. And your covenant with death shall be disannulled, and your agreement with hell shall not stand; when the overflowing scourge shall pass through, then ye shall be trodden down by it. From the time that it goeth forth it shall take you: for morning by morning shall it pass over, by day and by night: and it shall be a vexation only to understand the report. For the bed is shorter than that a man can stretch himself on it: and the covering narrower than that he can wrap himself in it.
(Isaiah 28:14-20)

And I, if I be lifted up from the earth, will draw all men unto me.

And Jesus answered them, saying, The hour is come, that the Son of man should be glorified. Verily, verily, I say unto you, Except a corn of wheat fall into the ground and die, it abideth alone: but if it die, it bringeth forth much fruit. He that loveth his life shall lose it; and he that hateth his life in this world shall keep it unto life eternal. If any man serve me, let him follow me; and where I am, there shall also my servant be: if any man serve me, him will my Father honour.

Now is my soul troubled; and what shall I say? Father, save me from this hour: but for this cause came I unto this hour. Father, glorify thy name.

Then came there a voice from heaven, saying, I have both glorified it, and will glorify it again.

The people therefore, that stood by, and heard it, said that it thundered: others said, An angel spake to him.

Jesus answered and said, This voice came not because of me, but for your sakes. Now is the judgment of this world: now shall the prince of this world be cast out. And I, if I be lifted up from the earth, will draw all men unto me.

This he said, signifying what death he should die.

(John 12:23-33)

Our mission is to honor God by living the kind of life that He has selected for us. This is our service to God: this is our worship of Him. We can do this in a peaceful forward flow or we can perform like a child throwing a tantrum. The first is the route of peace; the latter is the anguish of strife. We honor God by the former; we dishonor God to our own hurt by the latter. Either way, the Father's way is the final way; all others will be removed.

> *Assemble yourselves and come; draw near together, ye that are escaped of the nations: they have no knowledge that set up the wood of their graven image, and pray unto a god that cannot save. Tell ye, and bring them near; yea, let them take counsel together: who hath declared this from ancient time? who hath told it from that time? have not I the LORD? and there is no God else beside me; a just God and a Saviour; there is none beside me. Look unto me, and be ye saved, all the ends of the earth: for I am God, and there is none else. I have sworn by myself, the word is gone out of my mouth in righteousness, and shall not return, That unto me every knee shall bow, every tongue shall swear. Surely, shall one say, in the LORD have I righteousness and strength: even to him shall men come; and all that are incensed against him shall be ashamed. In the LORD shall all the seed of Israel be justified, and shall glory.*
> (Isaiah 45:20-25)

> *And at that time shall Michael stand up, the great prince which standeth for the children of thy people: and there shall be a time of trouble, such as never was since there was a nation even to that same time: and at that time thy people shall be delivered, every one that shall be found written in the book. And many of them that sleep in the dust of the earth shall awake, some to everlasting life, and some to shame and everlasting contempt. And they that be wise shall shine as the brightness of the firmament; and they that turn many to righteousness as the stars for ever and ever.*
> (Daniel 12:1-3)

And the angel said unto me, Wherefore didst thou marvel? I will tell thee the mystery of the woman, and of the beast that carrieth her, which hath the seven heads and ten horns. The beast that thou sawest was, and is not; and shall ascend out of the bottomless pit, and go into perdition: and they that dwell on the earth shall wonder, whose names were not written in the book of life from the foundation of the world, when they behold the beast that was, and is not, and yet is.
(Revelation 17:7-8)

And I saw a great white throne, and him that sat on it, from whose face the earth and the heaven fled away; and there was found no place for them. And I saw the dead, small and great, stand before God; and the books were opened: and another book was opened, which is the book of life: and the dead were judged out of those things which were written in the books, according to their works. And the sea gave up the dead which were in it; and death and hell delivered up the dead which were in them: and they were judged every man according to their works.

And death and hell were cast into the lake of fire. This is the second death. And whosoever was not found written in the book of life was cast into the lake of fire.
(Revelation 20:11-15)

Nations are the vessels which God created to promote the development of mankind toward the best it can be. These are the rulers of thousands; like those Moses established. Within these nations are princes as there were princes over the twelve families of Israel.

And it came to pass on the morrow, that Moses sat to judge the people: and the people stood by Moses from the morning unto the evening. And when Moses' father in law saw all that he did to the people, he said, What is this thing that thou doest to the people? why sittest thou thyself alone, and all the people stand by thee from morning unto even?

And Moses said unto his father in law, Because the people come unto me to enquire of God: When they have a matter, they come unto me; and I judge between one and another, and I do make them know the statutes of God, and his laws.

And Moses' father in law said unto him, The thing that thou doest is not good. Thou wilt surely wear away, both thou, and this people that is with thee: for this thing is too heavy for thee; thou art not able to perform it thyself alone.

Hearken now unto my voice, I will give thee counsel, and God shall be with thee: Be thou for the people to God-ward, that thou mayest bring the causes unto God: And thou shalt teach them ordinances and laws, and shalt shew them the way wherein they must walk, and the work that they must do. Moreover thou shalt provide out of all the people able men, such as fear God, men of truth, hating covetousness; and place such over them, to be rulers of thousands, and rulers of hundreds, rulers of fifties, and rulers of tens: And let them judge the people at all seasons: and it shall be, that every great matter they shall bring unto thee, but every small matter they shall judge: so shall it be easier for thyself, and they shall bear the burden with thee.

If thou shalt do this thing, and God command thee so, then thou shalt be able to endure, and all this people shall also go to their place in peace.

So Moses hearkened to the voice of his father in law, and did all that he had said. And Moses chose able men out of all Israel, and made them heads over the people, rulers of thousands, rulers of hundreds, rulers of fifties, and rulers of tens. And they judged the people at all seasons: the hard causes they brought unto Moses, but every small matter they judged themselves.
(Exodus 18:13-26)

But what is it that we are called to do as nations? What are we called to do as the children of Abraham?

We are called to serve and to grow within our nations. We will find it sufficient unto us to govern within our given responsibilities. For some this will be the family, for others it will be our friends. Some will be selected to rule powers and then move forward to govern principalities. Still others will be shackled by God with the responsibility to rule a nation. None will be allowed to rule the world. This is for the Messiah.

The various nations, having been established by God, are ruled by Him and for Him. Let us, therefore, serve God in truth within our nations. When we have done this, we will find the message of God, in us, expanding to the world. It will do this by the witness of our lives as we travel the world. It will not be done by the force of our armies sent into the world. God will keep us contained in this regard. He who hath an ear let him hear.

My Christian brothers are probably waiting for my closing with what is called the *invitation*. As many understand it to be given, this will not be done here. In the search for the presence of God and for His Messiah, I say to my readers, seek your answer from God. I am only His very low level servant. He must be approached either directly or through the witness of His Son or through the indwelling of the Holy Ghost, which was sent at the request of His Son. To all who find this odd, I leave you with the following insight.

> *And I, brethren, could not speak unto you as unto spiritual, but as unto carnal, even as unto babes in Christ. I have fed you with milk, and not with meat: for hitherto ye were not able to bear it, neither yet now are ye able. For ye are yet carnal: for whereas there is among you envying, and strife, and divisions, are ye not carnal, and walk as men? For while one saith, I am of Paul; and another, I am of Apollos; are ye not carnal?*
>
> *Who then is Paul, and who is Apollos, but ministers by whom ye believed, even as the Lord gave to every man? I have planted, Apollos watered; but God gave the increase. So then neither is he that planteth any thing, neither he that watereth; but God that giveth the increase.*
>
> *Now he that planteth and he that watereth are one: and every man shall receive his own reward according to his*

own labour. For we are labourers together with God: ye are God's husbandry, ye are God's building. According to the grace of God which is given unto me, as a wise masterbuilder, I have laid the foundation, and another buildeth thereon. But let every man take heed how he buildeth thereupon. For other foundation can no man lay than that is laid, which is Jesus Christ.

Now if any man build upon this foundation gold, silver, precious stones, wood, hay, stubble; Every man's work shall be made manifest: for the day shall declare it, because it shall be revealed by fire; and the fire shall try every man's work of what sort it is. If any man's work abide which he hath built thereupon, he shall receive a reward. If any man's work shall be burned, he shall suffer loss: but he himself shall be saved; yet so as by fire.
(1 Corinthians 3:1-15)

Abraham;
A most special son,
Who by his faith
From God hath won

A place of honor
Among all who live,
According to the promise
To him the LORD did give.

He received the promise
Of a brand new land,
Which God would provide
By His mighty hand.

No need for Abraham
To select the place,
Or to say which
Of mankind's race

Would live or die
To give him the jewel
Over which his seed
Will surely rule.

His faith was enough
To move the Most High
To secure his possession
By and by.

The only thing needed
Was that he love the Lord,
And teach all his children
To stay on board

With the promise of God,
Most Faithful and True;
By walking before Him,
To receive what was due

To Abraham and his family,
Because of faith most clear,
Serving the LORD God
In a love deep and dear.

As promised by God to Abraham,
He is more than just one nation.
Let us glorify Him now, by our
Reconciliation.

Dis'ing the Children

In Luke 6:6-11, we have the following event recorded.

> *And it came to pass also on another sabbath, that he entered into the synagogue and taught: and there was a man whose right hand was withered. And the scribes and Pharisees watched him, whether he would heal on the sabbath day; that they might find an accusation against him. But he knew their thoughts, and said to the man which had the withered hand, Rise up, and stand forth in the midst. And he arose and stood forth.*

> *Then said Jesus unto them, I will ask you one thing; Is it lawful on the sabbath days to do good, or to do evil? to save life, or to destroy it? And looking round about upon them all, he said unto the man, Stretch forth thy hand. And he did so: and his hand was restored whole as the other.*

> *And they were filled with madness; and communed one with another what they might do to Jesus.*

Some things will never cease to amaze me. There are still to this day, and probably will always be, those who call themselves religious, but who don't think that God should perform wonders with anyone but them; and only according to their rules. They are unwilling to allow that God has done a work through Jesus Christ that is for the sake of the entire world. They even use Scripture to support this opinion. Chief among these Scriptures is the one that says

> *But now the righteousness of God without the law is manifested, being witnessed by the law and the prophets; Even the righteousness of God which is by faith of Jesus Christ unto all and upon all them that believe: for there is no difference: For all have sinned, and come short of the glory of God; Being justified freely by his grace through the redemption that is in Christ Jesus: Whom God hath set forth to be a propitiation through faith in his blood, to declare his righteousness for the remission of sins that are past, through the forbearance of God; To declare, I say, at this time his righteousness: that*

he might be just, and the justifier of him which believeth
in Jesus.
(Romans 3:21-26)

This is such an obvious thing that it really should not need comment. Of course, all have sinned. This is easily understood, for we are imperfect and God is perfect. In the light of perfection, we who are shackled to imperfection will, at least once in our lives, sin. However, as a statement by itself it does not indict man to an eternity of suffering. This is precisely the reason that the Messiah came to the earth: because all have sinned. This is the reason that the Messiah had to be born of God: because Jesus had to bypass the *curiosity toward unrighteousness* that comes from being born of man alone. This is the reason the Holy Ghost has to indwell man: because without it man has no way of consistently knowing what are the things of God; and what he doesn't know he can only do by accident, at best, and not at all, at worst.

There is, however, a step from this statement and others like it in the Scriptures, which can cause some serious damage to all humanity. It is when we suddenly make the jump from individual sin to original sin: this is when we develop a really serious problem. It is especially damaging when we assign to every child born on this earth a place that is distant from God because they have this *original sin.*

For the sake of this study, let us consider the term parent in its broadest sense. In this sense it can mean pastor, teacher, counselor or anyone else who has the responsibility of bringing a human from a child-like pattern of thought to one closer to adulthood in some area of life. As parents we are admonished to be very diligent about our responsibility to develop our charges.

Train up a child in the way he should go: and when he is
old, he will not depart from it.
(Proverbs 22:6)

Sometimes I think that this directive frightens many people; especially those who are parents. When this is taken as written, we know that it is not the responsibility of the child to be born behaving: it is the responsibility of the parent to teach them how to do so. This is where the fright comes in.

We know from Proverbs 22:6 that God will hold us responsible for the training of the child; and not the child for the lack of training from the parent. Oh, of course, there comes a time when the child will become a physical adult and is called upon to rise above any failure of their parents. This, however, is done through the grace of God in that person's life. God can send another parent to raise the child, if the one originally designated by God does not do so. However, we are without excuse when we do not, as the originally selected parent, do that for which we were selected.

The parent-child relationship is an extremely serious one.

> *Thou shalt not bow down thyself to them, nor serve them: for I the LORD thy God am a jealous God, visiting the iniquity of the fathers upon the children unto the third and fourth generation of them that hate me;*
> (Exodus 20:5)

We may think of this as a matter of bookkeeping. That is to say, we think that God keeps a record of the sins of the father, and then applies them to the son. It is much more automatic than that. The sins of the father will set the pattern for the son; which the son will follow. It is not God that causes the sins of the father to be visited upon the son; it is the father who sets the pattern for such visitation. This, however, is overcome when the father turns to God for forgiveness.

> *And shewing mercy unto thousands of them that love me, and keep my commandments.*
> (Exodus 20:6)

The matter of the sins of the father being a condemnation from God to the sons was very potent in the nation of Israel. It was believed, during the time of the revelation of Jesus of Nazareth, that such passed on sins would not just cause mental and emotional damage, but also physical damage.

> *And as Jesus passed by, he saw a man which was blind from his birth. And his disciples asked him, saying, Master, who did sin, this man, or his parents, that he was born blind?*
>
> *Jesus answered, Neither hath this man sinned, nor his parents: but that the works of God should be made manifest in him.*
> (John 9:1-3)

The concept of passing on sins from the fathers is one of the most serious of burdens acquired by the children. However, the matter of the false imputation to children of original sin is much more egregious. Some men are so focused on this concept that they indict the smallest of God's human creations as damnable from the start. They totally ignore the message that was presented by Jesus Christ.

> *Take heed that ye despise not one of these little ones; for*
> *I say unto you, That in heaven their angels do always*
> *behold the face of my Father which is in heaven.*
> (Matthew 18:10)

Let us say, for the sake of discussion, that original sin exists. If it does it must be somewhat impotent to affect the standing of the child with God. If original sin was so potent that it even caused children to be cut off from God, then how in the world can we accept the kingdom of God that is filled with something that is by its nature abhorrent to God? Such abhorrent creations cannot stand the sight of God. Such abhorrent creations would not have angels that behold the face of God. No such state of original sin exists in the children of this earth.

> *Then were there brought unto him little children, that*
> *he should put his hands on them, and pray: and the*
> *disciples rebuked them. But Jesus said, Suffer little*
> *children, and forbid them not, to come unto me: for of*
> *such is the kingdom of heaven. And he laid his hands on*
> *them, and departed thence.*
> (Matthew 19:13-15)

We have already read the message of Scripture that says that children can lead a life where they adhere to the tenants of God. (*Train up a child in the way he should go*). Jesus, however, goes even further. He states that the image of the child is the very one we must have to become a part of the Kingdom of Heaven.

> *At the same time came the disciples unto Jesus, saying,*
> *Who is the greatest in the kingdom of heaven?*
>
> *And Jesus called a little child unto him, and set him in*
> *the midst of them, And said, Verily I say unto you, Except*
> *ye be converted, and become as little children, ye shall*
> *not enter into the kingdom of heaven. Whosoever*
> *therefore shall humble himself as this little child, the*

same is greatest in the kingdom of heaven. And whoso shall receive one such little child in my name receiveth me. But whoso shall offend one of these little ones which believe in me, it were better for him that a millstone were hanged about his neck, and that he were drowned in the depth of the sea.

(Matthew 18:1-6)

God Himself also gave a message about the children in the nation of Israel. This is not isolated to the nation of Israel. It applies to all children, especially the newborn, infants and most toddlers.

And the LORD heard the voice of your words, and was wroth, and sware, saying, Surely there shall not one of these men of this evil generation see that good land, which I sware to give unto your fathers, Save Caleb the son of Jephunneh; he shall see it, and to him will I give the land that he hath trodden upon, and to his children, because he hath wholly followed the LORD.

Also the LORD was angry with me for your sakes, saying, Thou also shalt not go in thither. But Joshua the son of Nun, which standeth before thee, he shall go in thither: encourage him: for he shall cause Israel to inherit it.

Moreover your little ones, which ye said should be a prey, and your children, which in that day had no knowledge between good and evil, they shall go in thither, and unto them will I give it, and they shall possess it.

(Deuteronomy 1:34-39)

This excuse--to give some impression that mankind must accept the sorry state of being automatically evil--is itself evil. Using this excuse, we can then say as parents that we have an insurmountable handicap in raising our children. That only when they come to God will we be able to control them. This excuse, which shifts the blame for the sorry state of mankind from the parents to the children, must stop. Sin is a willful act, not an incidental occurrence. The LORD stressed this when he provided for cities of refuge in the nation of Israel.

And the LORD spake unto Moses, saying, Speak unto the children of Israel, and say unto them, When ye be come over Jordan into the land of Canaan; Then ye shall appoint you cities to be cities of refuge for you; that the slayer may flee thither, which killeth any person at unawares. And they shall be unto you cities for refuge from the avenger; that the manslayer die not, until he stand before the congregation in judgment. And of these cities which ye shall give six cities shall ye have for refuge. Ye shall give three cities on this side Jordan, and three cities shall ye give in the land of Canaan, which shall be cities of refuge. These six cities shall be a refuge, both for the children of Israel, and for the stranger, and for the sojourner among them: that every one that killeth any person unawares may flee thither.
(Numbers 35:9-15)

By attempting to accomplish this shift, man continues to show a hatred of God's way. And this hatred is freely expressed, even among those who profess to love Him. There is much discussion about the Scripture which indicates that through one man sin came into the world. This does not mean that all infants must instantaneously be born as sinners. No, sin is an *acquired taste*. Yes, it is one that is readily accessed by mankind and easily achieved, but it is not the requirement for mankind.

Let's wake up and get back to biblical principles of man being able to excel in God. And even more so, let's get back to the position where we are willing to take responsibility for the requirements of God for the children in this world. Let's not blame them for the failings of the adults, but let's seek God's forgiveness for our shortfall, and His guidance in our up building.

In this way we honor God, we equip the children and we send redemption into the world. Remember, John the Baptist was filled with the Holy Ghost from his birth. Does this mean that there was a fraction of a second before the entry of the Holy Ghost when he had original sin? I think, not!!!

There was in the days of Herod, the king of Judaea, a certain priest named Zacharias, of the course of Abia: and his wife was of the daughters of Aaron, and her name was Elisabeth. And they were both righteous before God, walking in all the commandments and ordinances of the Lord blameless. And they had no child, because that Elisabeth was barren, and they both were now well stricken in years.

And it came to pass, that while he executed the priest's office before God in the order of his course, According to the custom of the priest's office, his lot was to burn incense when he went into the temple of the Lord. And the whole multitude of the people were praying without at the time of incense. And there appeared unto him an angel of the Lord standing on the right side of the altar of incense. And when Zacharias saw him, he was troubled, and fear fell upon him.

But the angel said unto him, Fear not, Zacharias: for thy prayer is heard; and thy wife Elisabeth shall bear thee a son, and thou shalt call his name John. And thou shalt have joy and gladness; and many shall rejoice at his birth. For he shall be great in the sight of the Lord, and shall drink neither wine nor strong drink; and he shall be filled with the Holy Ghost, even from his mother's womb. And many of the children of Israel shall he turn to the Lord their God. And he shall go before him in the spirit and power of Elias, to turn the hearts of the fathers to the children, and the disobedient to the wisdom of the just; to make ready a people prepared for the Lord.

(Luke 1:5-17)

Terms, Terms, Terms

There seem to be three categories of terms that are used in presentation of the message of the Creator. We will describe some of those terms, and their uses. We will focus on some uses that need to be evaluated and corrected.

First among these categories are those that were used by Moses in describing the Law to the children of Israel. These are examples of terms of judgment.

There is also the mysterious use of terms which was done by the prophets. In this use the Creator often wrapped the message in a mystery. These include the terms that are only for the ones to whom He gives understanding.

Then there are terms that are related neither to judgment nor to prophecy, but to everyday righteous living.

All these terms will lead us to a relationship with God. Within these categories we will explore three ways that terms help us develop this relationship. There are terms that give an understanding of the presence of God. There are also terms that guide those who are in service to God. And then there are terms that reveal positive and Godly methods for us to use in establishing our relationships man to man in God.

The Presence of God

This is important for all peoples: those who are of the children of Abraham and those who are not. The terms that we will concentrate on here, to highlight this relationship, relate to the nature of the Creator as He reveals Himself through actions. The first of these involve the nature of the Creator.

There are many different names for the Creator that are used by different nations. Among these names, in their English equivalents, are the following: Him, God, Allah, YHWH, Yahweh, Jehovah, LORD, and El. There are a host of others based on the particular language that is being spoken. We will refer to the Creator as Him, and sometimes God.

Some other terms are used to describe attributes of Him and of the heavenly community. Among these that are mentioned in the Scriptures are Father, Jealous, Godhead, and some others, that use the *El* prefix.

They became a part of man's vocabulary when man started to call on God's name.

> *And to Seth, to him also there was born a son; and*
> *he called his name Enos: then began men to call upon*
> *the name of the LORD.*
> (Genesis 11:28)

There are others that have crept into our communications, through the mind of man, such as trinity. These latter types of terms are not listed in the Scriptures and so they will not be used as valid identifiers for God. It really is not significant that someone feels that they can be derived from passages of the Scripture. If they can be derived from passages of Scripture then we must use these passages rather than a man-made shortcut.

Too often shortcuts don't have any clear definition, and serve only to confuse and alienate the uninitiated. We will, therefore, not use them or accept them as useful for educating mankind about Him. They do not move the heart of mankind closer to Him. We want to, in all things, reflect Jesus of Nazareth in his inclusive nature; to the lowest common denominator.

> *Come unto me, all ye that labour and are heavy laden,*
> *and I will give you rest. Take my yoke upon you, and*
> *learn of me; for I am meek and lowly in heart: and ye*
> *shall find rest unto your souls. For my yoke is easy, and*
> *my burden is light.*
> (Matthew 11:28-30)

With this in mind, if the meaning is not clear, then the burden is not light. We must not slip into difficulties by trying to use shortcuts in public prayer or preaching. Maybe that should be our goal; to stay with the Scriptural terms because we can use them in prayer to God, and edification of one another. We should remember that we have a responsibility to the *least* of our brethren.

> *And before him shall be gathered all nations: and*
> *he shall separate them one from another, as a shepherd*
> *divideth his sheep from the goats: And he shall set the*
> *sheep on his right hand, but the goats on the left. Then*
> *shall the King say unto them on his right hand, Come, ye*
> *blessed of my Father, inherit the kingdom prepared for*

you from the foundation of the world: For I was an hungred, and ye gave me meat: I was thirsty, and ye gave me drink: I was a stranger, and ye took me in: Naked, and ye clothed me: I was sick, and ye visited me: I was in prison, and ye came unto me.

Then shall the righteous answer him, saying, Lord, when saw we thee an hungred, and fed thee? or thirsty, and gave thee drink? When saw we thee a stranger, and took thee in? or naked, and clothed thee? Or when saw we thee sick, or in prison, and came unto thee?

And the King shall answer and say unto them, Verily I say unto you, Inasmuch as ye have done it unto one of the least of these my brethren, ye have done it unto me.
(Matthew 25:32-40)

Let us, therefore, return to the Scriptural terms that are used to glorify God.

This matter of glorifying God brings to light another issue among mankind. There is some tension among mankind about the proper name to be given to Him. In some factions it reaches the point where it is a mortal sin to use the *wrong* name. However, though it is said to be a mortal sin, it is left up to men to carry out the sentence. This does not honor the power of Him.

One would think that if there was only one proper way to refer to Him, that this would be a matter that would be settled without the need for human intervention. This seems so because unlike the sin of adultery, this is something which can occur where there are no witnesses. If I go into my closet and say the *wrong* name, who will know but me? If it is not up to Him to deliver judgment for this type of behavior, then the sin has to be revised. If it is up to mankind to mete out judgment then the sin is only a sin where there is discovery. This does not account for the omnipresence of Him. Also, it just doesn't seem reasonable for someone to go around and ask every member of their community to say the name of Him. What happens if a person can't speak? They can still say the *wrong* name in their mind.

In the Christian faith, of which I am a part, the only admonition that was given by Him to the people was not to use the name in vain.

Thou shalt not take the name of the LORD thy God in vain; for the LORD will not hold him guiltless that taketh his name in vain.
(Exodus 20:7)

This seems to allow for any calling to Him, as long as it is not done in an irreverent fashion.

Therefore shall ye keep my commandments, and do them: I am the LORD. Neither shall ye profane my holy name; but I will be hallowed among the children of Israel: I am the LORD which hallow you, That brought you out of the land of Egypt, to be your God: I am the LORD.
(Leviticus 22:31-33)

I have a very strong concern for those who are on the other side of either advantage or maturity. These are the ones referred to as the handicapped and the child. When we establish these man-made rules about what should and should not be done relative to the things of God, we introduce opportunities for trouble. This refers to those titles and rules that apply to Him as well as rules formulated on behalf of those who are revered as ambassadors of Him; such as Muhammad.

Sometimes we establish rules that are not given by the words we received directly from Him. When we do so we will leave those on the other side of advantage and maturity exposed to inadvertent errors. Is this a case where ignorance is an excuse for the law? Scripture says, yes!

And the LORD heard the voice of your words, and was wroth, and sware, saying, Surely there shall not one of these men of this evil generation see that good land, which I sware to give unto your fathers, Save Caleb the son of Jephunneh; he shall see it, and to him will I give the land that he hath trodden upon, and to his children, because he hath wholly followed the LORD.

Also the LORD was angry with me for your sakes, saying, Thou also shalt not go in thither. But Joshua the son of Nun, which standeth before thee, he shall go in thither: encourage him: for he shall cause Israel to inherit it.

Moreover your little ones, which ye said should be a prey, and your children, which in that day had no

knowledge between good and evil, they shall go in thither, and unto them will I give it, and they shall possess it.
(Deuteronomy 1:34-39)

Don't place stumbling blocks in the path of others. Don't do anything that would limit the entry of others into the presence of Him. You will be held accountable to Him for any action that quenches the spirit of another toward entering the presence of Him. You will be held accountable for anything that attempts to limit the working of the Spirit in others, or in the world.

See that none render evil for evil unto any man; but ever follow that which is good, both among yourselves, and to all men.

Rejoice evermore.

Pray without ceasing.

In every thing give thanks: for this is the will of God in Christ Jesus concerning you.

Quench not the Spirit.

Despise not prophesyings.

Prove all things; hold fast that which is good.

Abstain from all appearance of evil.
(1 Thessalonians 5:15-22)

In Service to Him

The next types of terms are those referring to the nature of mankind as men and women in their type of service to Him. Such terms as prophet, priest, apostle, disciple, elect, followers, saved and condemned, are a few. These things can be seriously confused when being presented by even the most well-meaning of the servants of Him. An example from the teaching of Christianity, that sometimes occurs, is the merging of follower, saved, disciple, elect and apostle under one set of rules of conduct.

Often when Christian leaders are reading the Scriptures they see statements by Jesus Christ that are directed to particular groups of people. They then try to generalize them into application to all of the people of Christ. Let me give you passages which describe specific groups that are referred to in Scripture.

Follower: *Jesus answered them and said, Verily, verily, I say unto you, Ye seek me, not because ye saw the miracles, but because ye did eat of the loaves, and were filled. Labour not for the meat which perisheth, but for that meat which endureth unto everlasting life, which the Son of man shall give unto you: for him hath God the Father sealed.* (John 6:26-27)

Saved: *And the keeper of the prison awaking out of his sleep, and seeing the prison doors open, he drew out his sword, and would have killed himself, supposing that the prisoners had been fled.*

But Paul cried with a loud voice, saying, Do thyself no harm: for we are all here.

Then he called for a light, and sprang in, and came trembling, and fell down before Paul and Silas, And brought them out, and said, Sirs, what must I do to be saved?

And they said, Believe on the Lord Jesus Christ, and thou shalt be saved, and thy house. (Acts 16:27-31)

And he said to them all, If any man will come after me, let him deny himself, and take up his cross daily, and follow me. For whosoever will save his life shall lose it: but whosoever will lose his life for my sake, the same shall save it. For what is a man advantaged, if he gain the whole world, and lose himself, or be cast away? (Luke 9:23-25)

Disciple: *When Jesus knew in himself that his disciples murmured at it, he said unto them, Doth this offend you? What and if ye shall see the Son of man ascend up where he was before? It is the spirit that quickeneth; the flesh profiteth nothing:*

the words that I speak unto you, they are spirit, and they are life. But there are some of you that believe not. For Jesus knew from the beginning who they were that believed not, and who should betray him. And he said, Therefore said I unto you, that no man can come unto me, except it were given unto him of my Father.

From that time many of his disciples went back, and walked no more with him.
     (John 6:61)

For I am come to set a man at variance against his father, and the daughter against her mother, and the daughter in law against her mother in law. And a man's foes shall be they of his own household. He that loveth father or mother more than me is not worthy of me: and he that loveth son or daughter more than me is not worthy of me.
     (Matthew 10:35-37)

And there went great multitudes with him: and he turned, and said unto them, If any man come to me, and hate not his father, and mother, and wife, and children, and brethren, and sisters, yea, and his own life also, he cannot be my disciple. And whosoever doth not bear his cross, and come after me, cannot be my disciple. For which of you, intending to build a tower, sitteth not down first, and counteth the cost, whether he have sufficient to finish it? Lest haply, after he hath laid the foundation, and is not able to finish it, all that behold it begin to mock him, Saying, This man began to build, and was not able to finish. Or what king, going to make war against another king, sitteth not down first, and consulteth whether he be able with ten thousand to meet him that cometh against him with twenty thousand? Or else, while the other is yet a great way off, he sendeth an ambassage, and desireth

conditions of peace. So likewise, whosoever
he be of you that forsaketh not all that he hath,
he cannot be my disciple.
(Luke 14:25-33)

Christian: *Then departed Barnabas to Tarsus, for to seek*
Saul: And when he had found him, he brought
him unto Antioch. And it came to pass, that
a whole year they assembled themselves with the
church, and taught much people. And the
disciples were called Christians first in Antioch.
(Acts 11:25-26)

Elect: *And when the king came in to see the guests,*
he saw there a man which had not on a wedding
garment: And he saith unto him, Friend, how
camest thou in hither not having a wedding
garment? And he was speechless. Then said the
king to the servants, Bind him hand and foot, and
take him away, and cast him into outer darkness,
there shall be weeping and gnashing of teeth.
For many are called, but few are chosen.
(Matthew 22:11-14)

Now ye are the body of Christ, and members in
particular.   And God hath set some in the
church, first apostles, secondarily prophets,
thirdly teachers, after that miracles, then gifts of
healings, helps, governments, diversities of
tongues. Are all apostles? are all prophets? are
all teachers? are all workers of miracles? Have
all the gifts of healing? do all speak with
tongues? do all interpret?
(1 Corinthians 12:27-30)

Neglect not the gift that is in thee, which was
given thee by prophecy, with the laying on of the
hands of the presbytery. Meditate upon these
things; give thyself wholly to them; that thy
profiting may appear to all. Take heed unto
thyself, and unto the doctrine; continue in them:

> *for in doing this thou shalt both save thyself, and
> them that hear thee.*
> (1 Timothy 4:14-16)

Apostle: *Afterward he appeared unto the eleven as they
sat at meat, and upbraided them with their
unbelief and hardness of heart, because they
believed not them which had seen him after
he was risen. And he said unto them, Go ye into
all the world, and preach the gospel to every
creature. He that believeth and is baptized shall
be saved; but he that believeth not shall be
damned. And these signs shall follow them that
believe; In my name shall they cast out devils;
they shall speak with new tongues; They shall
take up serpents; and if they drink any deadly
thing, it shall not hurt them; they shall lay hands
on the sick, and they shall recover.*
(Mark 16:14-18)

There are levels of responsibility for the things of Him: as with all
things in life, we have to start somewhere. Furthermore, we are not all
called to rise to the highest level of human understanding or service to
Him. Some of us will serve more by example than by being in the
limelight. Such, for example, is the virtuous woman.

> *Who can find a virtuous woman? for her price is far
> above rubies. The heart of her husband doth safely trust
> in her, so that he shall have no need of spoil. She will do
> him good and not evil all the days of her life.*
>
> *She seeketh wool, and flax, and worketh willingly with her
> hands. She is like the merchants' ships; she bringeth her
> food from afar. She riseth also while it is yet night, and
> giveth meat to her household, and a portion to her maidens.*
>
> *She considereth a field, and buyeth it: with the fruit of
> her hands she planteth a vineyard. She girdeth her loins
> with strength, and strengtheneth her arms.
> She perceiveth that her merchandise is good: her candle
> goeth not out by night. She layeth her hands to the
> spindle, and her hands hold the distaff.*

She stretcheth out her hand to the poor; yea, she reacheth forth her hands to the needy.

She is not afraid of the snow for her household: for all her household are clothed with scarlet. She maketh herself coverings of tapestry; her clothing is silk and purple. Her husband is known in the gates, when he sitteth among the elders of the land.

She maketh fine linen, and selleth it; and delivereth girdles unto the merchant.

Strength and honour are her clothing; and she shall rejoice in time to come. She openeth her mouth with wisdom; and in her tongue is the law of kindness. She looketh well to the ways of her household, and eateth not the bread of idleness. Her children arise up, and call her blessed; her husband also, and he praiseth her.

Many daughters have done virtuously, but thou excellest them all. Favour is deceitful, and beauty is vain: but a woman that feareth the LORD, she shall be praised. Give her of the fruit of her hands; and let her own works praise her in the gates.
(Proverbs 31:10-31)

Of such also is the widow with her mite. Though she was praised by Jesus in the light, the person is unknown.

And he looked up, and saw the rich men casting their gifts into the treasury. And he saw also a certain poor widow casting in thither two mites. And he said, Of a truth I say unto you, that this poor widow hath cast in more than they all: For all these have of their abundance cast in unto the offerings of God: but she of her penury hath cast in all the living that she had.
(Luke 21:1-4)

We are called into service each according to the will of Him. We are called to participate in the development of the entire sphere of heaven and earth.

Let me interject a real simple thought: we are not all called to, nor will we all be President of the United States. This is a power level that is ordained by Him, and the person to fill this position is selected by Him. Those who know Him know that the outcome of the elections of kings, princes, presidents and any other ruler has been determined before there was even a mankind to experience the outcome. But this is a matter for another time.

man to man in Him

There is a third type of term. These are the terms that refer to the ways in which men and women relate to one another within Him. This category shows forth the major amount of power of Him that is expressed in the earth. Without a mastery of this category of existence it is very, very difficult, if not impossible to please Him. Some of the terms in this category include love, forbearance, peace, charity, husband, head, submission, and wife. All these types of terms have been summed up for Christians in two marvelous passages in the New Testament.

The Bible sets forth how man is to relate to man, in general: by the mouth of two or three witnesses.

> *But when the Pharisees had heard that he had put the Sadducees to silence, they were gathered together. Then one of them, which was a lawyer, asked him a question, tempting him, and saying, Master, which is the great commandment in the law?*
>
> *Jesus said unto him,*
>
> *Thou shalt love the Lord thy God with all thy heart, and with all thy soul, and with all thy mind. This is the first and great commandment.*
>
> *And the second is like unto it, Thou shalt love thy neighbour as thyself.*
>
> *On these two commandments hang all the law and the prophets.*
> (Matthew 22:34-40)
>
> *For, brethren, ye have been called unto liberty; only use not liberty for an occasion to the flesh, but by love serve*

one another. For all the law is fulfilled in one word, even in this; Thou shalt love thy neighbour as thyself.
(Galatians 5:13-14)

If ye fulfil the royal law according to the scripture, Thou shalt love thy neighbour as thyself, ye do well: But if ye have respect to persons, ye commit sin, and are convinced of the law as transgressors. For whosoever shall keep the whole law, and yet offend in one point, he is guilty of all.
(James 2:8-10)

And one of the scribes came, and having heard them reasoning together, and perceiving that he had answered them well, asked him, Which is the first commandment of all?

And Jesus answered him,

The first of all the commandments is, Hear, O Israel; The Lord our God is one Lord: And thou shalt love the Lord thy God with all thy heart, and with all thy soul, and with all thy mind, and with all thy strength: this is the first commandment.

And the second is like, namely this, Thou shalt love thy neighbour as thyself.

There is none other commandment greater than these.

And the scribe said unto him, Well, Master, thou hast said the truth: for there is one God; and there is none other but he: And to love him with all the heart, and with all the understanding, and with all the soul, and with all the strength, and to love his neighbour as himself, is more than all whole burnt offerings and sacrifices.

And when Jesus saw that he answered discreetly, he said unto him, Thou art not far from the kingdom of God. And no man after that durst ask him any question.
(Mark 12:28-34)

There is specific Scripture telling us how families must be structured.

Likewise, ye wives, be in subjection to your own husbands; that, if any obey not the word, they also may without the word be won by the conversation of the wives; While they behold your chaste conversation coupled with fear. Whose adorning let it not be that outward adorning of plaiting the hair, and of wearing of gold, or of putting on of apparel; But let it be the hidden man of the heart, in that which is not corruptible, even the ornament of a meek and quiet spirit, which is in the sight of God of great price. For after this manner in the old time the holy women also, who trusted in God, adorned themselves, being in subjection unto their own husbands: Even as Sara obeyed Abraham, calling him lord: whose daughters ye are, as long as ye do well, and are not afraid with any amazement.

Likewise, ye husbands, dwell with them according to knowledge, giving honour unto the wife, as unto the weaker vessel, and as being heirs together of the grace of life; that your prayers be not hindered.
     (1 Peter 3:1-7)

If these two are done within the family, and then within the community, we will find that we will have a very easy time spreading the love of Him into the entire world. This is the directive that was given to the apostles by Jesus Christ.

The former treatise have I made, O Theophilus, of all that Jesus began both to do and teach, Until the day in which he was taken up, after that he through the Holy Ghost had given commandments unto the apostles whom he had chosen: To whom also he showed himself alive after his passion by many infallible proofs, being seen of them forty days, and speaking of the things pertaining to the kingdom of God: And, being assembled together with them, commanded them that they should not depart from Jerusalem, but wait for the promise of the Father, which, saith he, ye have heard of me. For John truly baptized with water; but ye shall be baptized with the Holy Ghost not many days hence.

When they therefore were come together, they asked of him, saying, Lord, wilt thou at this time restore again the kingdom to Israel?

And he said unto them, It is not for you to know the times or the seasons, which the Father hath put in his own power. But ye shall receive power, after that the Holy Ghost is come upon you: and ye shall be witnesses unto me both in Jerusalem, and in all Judaea, and in Samaria, and unto the uttermost part of the earth.

(Acts 1:1-8)

Jesus knew that they would first have to understand the needs of their own people. Then they would have to incorporate the things of Him into practice in their community. From this point they could go out into the broader nation, and then finally into the entire world. Understand this, however, the preaching that was to be done was the good news, also called, the Gospel. It was not the commanded edicts or the things to avoid *biblical capital punishment*. This is a free-will request to turn to Him. It was not a, "do it or we kill you," methodology.

And when he had called unto him his twelve disciples, he gave them power against unclean spirits, to cast them out, and to heal all manner of sickness and all manner of disease. Now the names of the twelve apostles are these; The first, Simon, who is called Peter, and Andrew his brother; James the son of Zebedee, and John his brother; Philip, and Bartholomew; Thomas, and Matthew the publican; James the son of Alphaeus, and Lebbaeus, whose surname was Thaddaeus; Simon the Canaanite, and Judas Iscariot, who also betrayed him.

These twelve Jesus sent forth, and commanded them, saying, Go not into the way of the Gentiles, and into any city of the Samaritans enter ye not: But go rather to the lost sheep of the house of Israel. And as ye go, preach, saying, The kingdom of heaven is at hand. Heal the sick, cleanse the lepers, raise the dead, cast out devils: freely ye have received, freely give. Provide neither gold, nor silver, nor brass in your purses, Nor scrip for your journey, neither two coats, neither shoes, nor yet staves: for the workman is worthy of his meat. And into

> *whatsoever city or town ye shall enter, enquire who in it is worthy; and there abide till ye go thence. And when ye come into an house, salute it. And if the house be worthy, let your peace come upon it: but if it be not worthy, let your peace return to you.*
> (Matthew 10:1-13)

In other words, you go tell them what is the will of Him. If they receive it, then you have accomplished your mission and blessings will come from Him to the community. If they do not hear it, leave them to Him. In fact, you are then directed to leave **with attitude**.

> *And whosoever shall not receive you, nor hear your words, when ye depart out of that house or city, shake off the dust of your feet. Verily I say unto you, It shall be more tolerable for the land of Sodom and Gomorrha in the day of judgment, than for that city.*
> (Matthew 10:14-15)

This seems more in keeping with the awesome power of Him. If someone doesn't want to listen to a human; then let Him do it.

> *He that despised Moses' law died without mercy under two or three witnesses: Of how much sorer punishment, suppose ye, shall he be thought worthy, who hath trodden under foot the Son of God, and hath counted the blood of the covenant, wherewith he was sanctified, an unholy thing, and hath done despite unto the Spirit of grace? For we know him that hath said, Vengeance belongeth unto me, I will recompense, saith the Lord. And again, The Lord shall judge his people.*
>
> *It is a fearful thing to fall into the hands of the living God.*
> (Hebrews 10:28-31)

Now don't start jumping up and down, thinking that surely when they fall into the Hands of Him, they will be, as they say, toast. Before you do that you might want to read the following portion of the book of Jonah, from the Bible.

And Jonah began to enter into the city a day's journey, and he cried, and said, Yet forty days, and Nineveh shall be overthrown.

So the people of Nineveh believed God, and proclaimed a fast, and put on sackcloth, from the greatest of them even to the least of them. For word came unto the king of Nineveh, and he arose from his throne, and he laid his robe from him, and covered him with sackcloth, and sat in ashes. And he caused it to be proclaimed and published through Nineveh by the decree of the king and his nobles, saying, Let neither man nor beast, herd nor flock, taste any thing: let them not feed, nor drink water: But let man and beast be covered with sackcloth, and cry mightily unto God: yea, let them turn every one from his evil way, and from the violence that is in their hands. Who can tell if God will turn and repent, and turn away from his fierce anger, that we perish not?

And God saw their works, that they turned from their evil way; and God repented of the evil, that he had said that he would do unto them; and he did it not.

But it displeased Jonah exceedingly, and he was very angry. And he prayed unto the LORD, and said, I pray thee, O LORD, was not this my saying, when I was yet in my country? Therefore I fled before unto Tarshish: for I knew that thou art a gracious God, and merciful, slow to anger, and of great kindness, and repentest thee of the evil. Therefore now, O LORD, take, I beseech thee, my life from me; for it is better for me to die than to live.

Then said the LORD, Doest thou well to be angry?

So Jonah went out of the city, and sat on the east side of the city, and there made him a booth, and sat under it in the shadow, till he might see what would become of the city.

And the LORD God prepared a gourd, and made it to come up over Jonah, that it might be a shadow over his head, to deliver him from his grief. So Jonah was exceeding glad of the gourd. But God prepared a worm when the morning rose the next day, and it smote the gourd that it withered. And it came to pass, when the sun did arise, that God prepared a vehement east wind; and the sun beat upon the head of Jonah, that he fainted, and wished in himself to die, and said, It is better for me to die than to live.

And God said to Jonah, Doest thou well to be angry for the gourd? And he said, I do well to be angry, even unto death. Then said the LORD, Thou hast had pity on the gourd, for the which thou hast not laboured, neither madest it grow; which came up in a night, and perished in a night: And should not I spare Nineveh, that great city, wherein are more than sixscore thousand persons that cannot discern between their right hand and their left hand; and also much cattle?
(Jonah 3:4-4:11)

The passage from Jonah shows us the power of God, to manifest His power in ways that man just didn't think possible; or in this case, that the man Jonah didn't want to happen. Jonah was intent on seeing the fiery vengeance of Him. Jonah was extremely disappointed when that didn't happen. I hope both Jonah and you can accept the explanation given by the LORD, as one other method available to Him to bring all mankind to God. Please accept it.

Body Systems

(for the building of the organism of mankind
in the kingdom of God on earth)

This thought was started toward the beginning of the book and it is only fair that it be completed before you leave the book.

You might think of this writing as food for thought, as you ponder the body of the kingdom of God. These are thoughts about the components and about their functions.

In all existence, the One that is of most importance is, of course, God. Therefore, we start with God.

Respiratory System

> ***Respiratory System*** - the system of organs in the body responsible for the intake of oxygen and the expiration of carbon dioxide.

God is the creator of man and it is He who gives us life. He forms the body and carries us through the birth process. Then He starts our external existence by triggering the newly independent functioning of the system which we have selected to remind you of Him, the respiratory system.

God　　　*And the LORD God formed man of the dust of the ground, and breathed into his nostrils the breath of life; and man became a living soul.*
(Genesis 2:7)

All of us, who are humans, know that none of the other systems are of much use if we don't have a strong respiratory system. If we can't acquire breath we will not live. When a situation arises where there are multiple injuries leading to a cessation of breathing, the first order of business is to stabilize the breathing. And we humans have many spiritual injuries that cause us to strain to receive the breath of God's presence. These injuries require attention from God and His kingdom.

The selection of this system also highlights the fact that God does not just activate life and leave. God is continually there sustaining our life. Furthermore, from this point of view, everyone who is alive contains a piece of God, in the breath of life. This is the piece that is housed in the soul (those who have passed on, through death, retain this piece, because the soul is eternal). This piece is one that must be honored and nurtured. Quite a serious responsibility, isn't it?

Endocrine System

Endocrine System - It's a little-known system made up of a whole collection of glands and it does very BIG things. It regulates, coordinates and controls an extraordinary number of your body's functions. How? While your nervous system uses electricity to orchestrate all sorts of things in your body, your endocrine system does even more through the wonder of chemicals.

The Holy Ghost is placed here in the order, not because it is "greater than" the Son. There is no mention in Scripture of the importance level of the Holy Ghost. However, it is related to the Son by gifting to the believers in him.

These things have I spoken unto you, being yet present with you. But the Comforter, which is the Holy Ghost, whom the Father will send in my name, he shall teach you all things, and bring all things to your remembrance, whatsoever I have said unto you.
(John 14:25-26)

The Holy Ghost is sent by the Father, as requested by the Son.

And I will pray the Father, and he shall give you another Comforter, that he may abide with you for ever; Even the Spirit of truth; whom the world cannot receive, because it seeth him not, neither knoweth him: but ye know him; for he dwelleth with you, and shall be in you.
(John 14:16-17)

Thus, it seems reasonable to have the Holy Ghost in a position where it joins the Father and the Son in textual proximity. If the Holy Ghost had been placed below the discussion of the Son, it might be more difficult for you to see their relationship within the kingdom of God, as described here; and this is something of which one should never lose sight. For this reason, the Holy Ghost is set in the intersection of the Father and the Son.

To describe why the endocrine system seems to fit the functioning of the Holy Ghost, I will revise the definition of the system given above as follows:

The Holy Ghost - it is a little-known Spirit made up of a whole collection of activities and utterances and it does very BIG things. It regulates, coordinates and controls an extraordinary number of mankind's spiritual communion with God. How? While your nervous system uses electricity to orchestrate all sorts of things in the body of the church, the Holy Ghost does even more through the wonder of its indwelling presence.

Holy Ghost   *When they therefore were come together, they asked of him, saying, Lord, wilt thou at this time restore again the kingdom to Israel? And he said unto them, It is not for you to know the times or the seasons, which the Father hath put in his own power. But ye shall receive power, after that the Holy Ghost is come upon you: and ye shall be witnesses unto me both in Jerusalem, and in all Judaea, and in Samaria, and unto the uttermost part of the earth.*
    (Acts 1:6-8)

Likewise the Spirit also helpeth our infirmities: for we know not what we should pray for as we ought: but the Spirit itself maketh intercession for us with groanings which cannot be uttered. And he that searcheth the hearts knoweth what is the mind of the Spirit, because he maketh intercession for the saints according to the will of God.
    (Romans 8:26-27)

Circulatory System (also called the Cardiovascular System)

> **Circulatory**, also known as, Cardiovascular: includes a transport system (blood) and a pump (the heart) that keeps the transport system moving.

> **Lymphatic System** - The lymphatic system is a specialized component of the circulatory system. Its two most important functions are maintenance of fluid balance in the internal environment and immunity.

Once breathing is stabilized, then blood loss is taken care of. Does this remind you of the order of reverence described by Christ?

> *Ye have heard how I said unto you, I go away, and come again unto you. If ye loved me, ye would rejoice, because I said, I go unto the Father: for my Father is greater than I.*
> (John 14:28)

He also constantly directs our attention to God for sustenance, and away from him. This is especially true in his closing words recorded in the Bible.

> *And he said unto me, These sayings are faithful and true: and the Lord God of the holy prophets sent his angel to show unto his servants the things which must shortly be done. Behold, I come quickly: blessed is he that keepeth the sayings of the prophecy of this book.*

> *And I John saw these things, and heard them. And when I had heard and seen, I fell down to worship before the feet of the angel which showed me these things.*

> *Then saith he unto me, See thou do it not: for I am thy fellowservant, and of thy brethren the prophets, and of them which keep the sayings of this book: worship God.*
> (Revelation 22:6-9)

The Bible describes the Son and his working in accomplishing the proper flow of the blood of his sacrifice in the body of the church.

Son of God   *The next day John seeth Jesus coming unto him, and saith, Behold the Lamb of*

God, which taketh away the sin of the world. This is he of whom I said, After me cometh a man which is preferred before me: for he was before me. And I knew him not: but that he should be made manifest to Israel, therefore am I come baptizing with water.

And John bare record, saying, I saw the Spirit descending from heaven like a dove, and it abode upon him. And I knew him not: but he that sent me to baptize with water, the same said unto me, Upon whom thou shalt see the Spirit descending, and remaining on him, the same is he which baptizeth with the Holy Ghost. And I saw, and bare record that this is the Son of God.
     (John 1:29-34)

And almost all things are by the law purged with blood; and without shedding of blood is no remission. It was therefore necessary that the patterns of things in the heavens should be purified with these; but the heavenly things themselves with better sacrifices than these. For Christ is not entered into the holy places made with hands, which are the figures of the true; but into heaven itself, now to appear in the presence of God for us: Nor yet that he should offer himself often, as the high priest entereth into the holy place every year with blood of others; For then must he often have suffered since the foundation of the world: but now once in the end of the world hath he appeared to put away sin by the sacrifice of himself. And as it is appointed unto men once to die, but after this the

judgment: So Christ was once offered to bear the sins of many; and unto them that look for him shall he appear the second time without sin unto salvation.
(Hebrews 9:22-28)

Blessed be the God and Father of our Lord Jesus Christ, who hath blessed us with all spiritual blessings in heavenly places in Christ: According as he hath chosen us in him before the foundation of the world, that we should be holy and without blame before him in love: Having predestinated us unto the adoption of children by Jesus Christ to himself, according to the good pleasure of his will, To the praise of the glory of his grace, wherein he hath made us accepted in the beloved. In whom we have redemption through his blood, the forgiveness of sins, according to the riches of his grace; Wherein he hath abounded toward us in all wisdom and prudence; Having made known unto us the mystery of his will, according to his good pleasure which he hath purposed in himself:
(Ephesians 1:3-9)

We use the following relationship to visualize the working of the Son as the blood of the body of mankind in God.

1. The plasma and other lymphatic fluids may be likened to the milk of the Word

2. The white blood cells may be likened to the sword of the Word

3. The red blood cells may be likened to the meat of the Word

We can also look at some historical evidences of the impact of the Son by the Word in his representation as the blood of the Circulatory System.

1. Blood on the doorposts and lentils - Word in the dwelling so that when the angels of God arrived they could see the Word of God there and act according to the will of God.

    And the LORD spake unto Moses and Aaron in the land of Egypt saying, This month shall be unto you the beginning of months: it shall be the first month of the year to you. Speak ye unto all the congregation of Israel, saying, In the tenth day of this month they shall take to them every man a lamb, according to the house of their fathers, a lamb for an house: And if the household be too little for the lamb, let him and his neighbour next unto his house take it according to the number of the souls; every man according to his eating shall make your count for the lamb. Your lamb shall be without blemish, a male of the first year: ye shall take it out from the sheep, or from the goats: And ye shall keep it up until the fourteenth day of the same month: and the whole assembly of the congregation of Israel shall kill it in the evening. And they shall take of the blood, and strike it on the two side posts and on the upper door post of the houses, wherein they shall eat it. And they shall eat the flesh in that night, roast with fire, and unleavened bread; and with bitter herbs they shall eat it. Eat not of it raw, nor sodden at all with water, but roast with fire; his head with his legs, and with the purtenance thereof. And ye shall let nothing of it remain until the morning; and that which remaineth of it until the morning ye shall burn with fire.

    And thus shall ye eat it; with your loins girded, your shoes on your feet, and your staff in your hand; and ye shall eat it in haste: it is the LORD's passover. For I will pass through the land of Egypt this night, and will smite all the firstborn in the land of Egypt, both man and

beast; and against all the gods of Egypt I will execute judgment: I am the LORD. And the blood shall be to you for a token upon the houses where ye are: and when I see the blood, I will pass over you, and the plague shall not be upon you to destroy you, when I smite the land of Egypt. And this day shall be unto you for a memorial; and ye shall keep it a feast to the LORD throughout your generations; ye shall keep it a feast by an ordinance for ever.
(Exodus 12:1-14)

2. Blood sacrifices of animals - a constant pointer to the need for the Word of God. This was a temporary solution which affected a restart of the flow of the Word of God by the shedding of blood of the animal sacrifice. The children of Israel showed by their behavior during the deliverance from Egypt that, like most children, the reminder, was only a temporary one. This is especially true when it depends on the action of the child to produce the reminder. The Law of Moses as the reminder, was often bypassed by the children when it was convenient for them to do so.

Another solution was needed: and another solution was given.

And Samuel said, Hath the LORD as great delight in burnt offerings and sacrifices, as in obeying the voice of the LORD? Behold, to obey is better than sacrifice, and to hearken than the fat of rams. For rebellion is as the sin of witchcraft, and stubbornness is as iniquity and idolatry. Because thou hast rejected the word of the LORD, he hath also rejected thee from being king.
(1 Samuel 15:22-23)

3. The best solution: blood sacrifice of Christ (*without shedding of blood is no remission* (Hebrews 9:22)) - a permanent answer done not by man but by the will of God, using a sacrifice created by God from a heavenly resident; not an earth-bound animal. This heavenly resident resided in flesh as the Lord Jesus Christ.

The shedding of the blood of this sacrifice started the flow of the Word not just on earth, but also in Heaven. This shedding of blood called for a heavenly reminder not from Laws written on tablets but from the Word written on the hearts of mankind.

> *Behold, the days come, saith the LORD, that I will make a new covenant with the house of Israel, and with the house of Judah: Not according to the covenant that I made with their fathers in the day that I took them by the hand to bring them out of the land of Egypt; which my covenant they brake, although I was an husband unto them, saith the LORD: But this shall be the covenant that I will make with the house of Israel; After those days, saith the LORD, I will put my law in their inward parts, and write it in their hearts; and will be their God, and they shall be my people. And they shall teach no more every man his neighbour, and every man his brother, saying, Know the LORD: for they shall all know me, from the least of them unto the greatest of them, saith the LORD: for I will forgive their iniquity, and I will remember their sin no more.*
>   (Jeremiah 31:31-34)

The stirring of this Word is done by the indwelling of the Holy Ghost; which is an eternal reminder, not one that comes and goes at the whim of human emotion, pride or convenience. The Holy Ghost stays and challenges human emotions and pride. It also highlights the damage that is done by mankind's search for convenience. It does this with the Word of comfort that leads to fullness in God. The Holy Ghost does this by defending against attack from Satan, or any other force that would attempt to overthrow the presence of God in man.

> *And ye shall know that I am in the midst of Israel, and that I am the LORD your God, and none else: and my people shall never be ashamed. And it shall come to pass afterward, that I will pour*

out my spirit upon all flesh; and your sons and your daughters shall prophesy, your old men shall dream dreams, your young men shall see visions: And also upon the servants and upon the handmaids in those days will I pour out my spirit.

And I will show wonders in the heavens and in the earth, blood, and fire, and pillars of smoke. The sun shall be turned into darkness, and the moon into blood, before the great and the terrible day of the LORD come.

And it shall come to pass, that whosoever shall call on the name of the LORD shall be delivered: for in mount Zion and in Jerusalem shall be deliverance, as the LORD hath said, and in the remnant whom the LORD shall call.
    (Joel 2:27-32)

Thus, the blood sacrifices of Christ now carries the breath of God from the Circulatory System as the Word of God through the Respiratory System of mankind's conformance to the principles of God with the indwelling of the Endocrine System of the Holy Ghost to regulate and energize mankind in properly handling the breath of God through the Word of God.

Listed below are some thoughts about the functioning of the manifestation of the kingdom of God with man which is likened unto the lymphatic system.

Maintenance of balance in the internal environment

These things have I spoken unto you, being yet present with you. But the Comforter, which is the Holy Ghost, whom the Father will send in my name, he shall teach you all things, and bring all things to your remembrance, whatsoever I have said unto you.
    (John 14:25-26)

Then the eleven disciples went away into Galilee, into a mountain where Jesus had appointed them. And when they saw him, they worshipped him: but some doubted.

And Jesus came and spake unto them, saying, All power is given unto me in heaven and in earth. Go ye therefore, and teach all nations, baptizing them in the name of the Father, and of the Son, and of the Holy Ghost: Teaching them to observe all things whatsoever I have commanded you: and, lo, I am with you alway, even unto the end of the world. Amen.

(Matthew 28:16-20)

Immunity

Jesus said unto her, I am the resurrection, and the life: he that believeth in me, though he were dead, yet shall he live: And whosoever liveth and believeth in me shall never die. Believest thou this?

She saith unto him, Yea, Lord: I believe that thou art the Christ, the Son of God, which should come into the world.

(John 11:25-27)

But this is that which was spoken by the prophet Joel; And it shall come to pass in the last days, saith God, I will pour out of my Spirit upon all flesh: and your sons and your daughters shall prophesy, and your young men shall see visions, and your old men shall dream dreams: And on my servants and on my handmaidens I will pour out in those days of my Spirit; and they shall prophesy: And I will show wonders in heaven above, and signs in the earth beneath; blood, and fire, and vapour of smoke: The sun shall be turned into darkness, and the moon into blood, before that great and notable day of the Lord come: And it shall come to pass, that whosoever shall call on the name of the Lord shall be saved.

Ye men of Israel, hear these words; Jesus of Nazareth, a man approved of God among you by miracles and wonders and signs, which God did by him in the midst of you, as ye yourselves also know: Him, being delivered by the determinate counsel and foreknowledge of God, ye have taken, and by wicked hands have crucified and slain: Whom God hath raised up, having loosed the pains of death: because it was not possible that he should be holden of it.

For David speaketh concerning him, I foresaw the Lord always before my face, for he is on my right hand, that I should not be moved: Therefore did my heart rejoice, and my tongue was glad; moreover also my flesh shall rest in hope: Because thou wilt not leave my soul in hell, neither wilt thou suffer thine Holy One to see corruption. Thou hast made known to me the ways of life; thou shalt make me full of joy with thy countenance.

Men and brethren, let me freely speak unto you of the patriarch David, that he is both dead and buried, and his sepulchre is with us unto this day. Therefore being a prophet, and knowing that God had sworn with an oath to him, that of the fruit of his loins, according to the flesh, he would raise up Christ to sit on his throne; He seeing this before spake of the resurrection of Christ, that his soul was not left in hell, neither his flesh did see corruption. This Jesus hath God raised up, whereof we all are witnesses.

Therefore being by the right hand of God exalted, and having received of the Father the promise of the Holy Ghost, he hath shed forth this, which ye now see and hear. For David is not ascended into the heavens: but he saith himself, The Lord said unto my Lord, Sit thou on my right hand, Until I make thy foes thy footstool. Therefore let all the house of Israel know assuredly, that God hath made that same Jesus, whom ye have crucified, both Lord and Christ.

(Acts 2:16-36)

Excretory System

> **Excretory** System - the agents operating in the body
> that have a role in removing spiritual contaminants.

When we think about angels, for many of us, we may have to broaden our minds. Angels do not just come to mankind in the form of physical beings. Angels include any of the operatives that have specific duties from God; many of which they are given to perform on behalf of mankind. It is with this in mind that we have chosen the excretory system to give an image of their working in the realm of mankind.

In the normal functioning of the body there are substances that come about which are not necessary for life. Indeed, in high concentrations, these substances can be toxic to the body. They must be removed; either all at once or by little and little.

In the body of mankind, metabolic wastes can be by-products of our mental struggles to accomplish the will of God. We will have to discard many things such as malice, envy and strife. These are transported out of the body by the angels of God; angels replace malicious emotions by delivering others such as peace, joy, submission, longsuffering, etc. In the olden times, the angels appeared in physical form to perform the cleanup of the waste products of the spiritual journey of the nation of Israel. These were characteristically seen in strife, such as wars. They were, however, seen in other types of strife such as arguments. God gave clear reasons why the angels were required in the nation of Israel.

> *I will send my fear before thee, and will destroy all the people to whom thou shalt come, and I will make all thine enemies turn their backs unto thee. And I will send hornets before thee, which shall drive out the Hivite, the Canaanite, and the Hittite, from before thee. I will not drive them out from before thee in one year; lest the land become desolate, and the beast of the field multiply against thee. By little and little I will drive them out from before thee, until thou be increased, and inherit the land. And I will set thy bounds from the Red sea even unto the sea of the Philistines, and from the desert unto the river: for I will deliver the inhabitants of the land into your hand; and thou shalt drive them out before thee.*

(Exodus 23:27-31)

Behold, I send an Angel before thee, to keep thee in the way, and to bring thee into the place which I have prepared. Beware of him, and obey his voice, provoke him not; for he will not pardon your transgressions: for my name is in him. But if thou shalt indeed obey his voice, and do all that I speak; then I will be an enemy unto thine enemies, and an adversary unto thine adversaries. For mine Angel shall go before thee, and bring thee in unto the Amorites, and the Hittites, and the Perizzites, and the Canaanites, the Hivites, and the Jebusites: and I will cut them off. Thou shalt not bow down to their gods, nor serve them, nor do after their works: but thou shalt utterly overthrow them, and quite break down their images.
      (Exodus 23:20-24)

Thou shalt make no covenant with them, nor with their gods. They shall not dwell in thy land, lest they make thee sin against me: for if thou serve their gods, it will surely be a snare unto thee.
      (Exodus 23:32-33)

Angel - <u>Removing toxic malice</u>

And Sarai said unto Abram, My wrong be upon thee: I have given my maid into thy bosom; and when she saw that she had conceived, I was despised in her eyes: the LORD judge between me and thee.

But Abram said unto Sarai, Behold, thy maid is in thy hand; do to her as it pleaseth thee.

And when Sarai dealt hardly with her, she fled from her face.

And the angel of the LORD found her by a fountain of water in the wilderness, by the fountain in the way to Shur. And he said, Hagar, Sarai's maid, whence camest thou? and whither wilt thou go?

And she said, I flee from the face of my mistress Sarai.

And the angel of the LORD said unto her, Return to thy mistress, and submit thyself under her hands.
      (Genesis 16:5-9)

Angel - <u>Buffering toxic self-sufficiency</u>

And the children of Israel encamped in Gilgal, and kept the passover on the fourteenth day of the month at even in the plains of Jericho. And they did eat of the old corn of the land on the morrow after the passover, unleavened cakes, and parched corn in the selfsame day. And the manna ceased on the morrow after they had eaten of the old corn of the land; neither had the children of Israel manna any more; but they did eat of the fruit of the land of Canaan that year.

And it came to pass, when Joshua was by Jericho, that he lifted up his eyes and looked, and, behold, there stood a man over against him with his sword drawn in his hand: and Joshua went unto him, and said unto him, Art thou for us, or for our adversaries?

And he said, Nay; but as captain of the host of the LORD am I now come.

And Joshua fell on his face to the earth, and did worship, and said unto him, What saith my lord unto his servant?

And the captain of the LORD'S host said unto Joshua, Loose thy shoe from off thy foot; for the place whereon thou standest is holy.

And Joshua did so.
(Joshua 5:10-15)

Angel - <u>Removing destructive feeling of defeat</u>

And, behold, an hand touched me, which set me upon my knees and upon the palms of my hands. And he said unto me, O Daniel, a man greatly beloved, understand the words that I speak unto thee, and stand upright: for unto thee am I now sent.

And when he had spoken this word unto me, I stood trembling.

Then said he unto me, Fear not, Daniel: for from the first day that thou didst set thine heart to understand, and to chasten thyself before thy God, thy words were heard, and I am come for thy words. But the prince of the kingdom of Persia withstood me one and twenty days: but, lo, Michael, one of the chief princes, came to help me; and I remained there with the kings of Persia. Now I am come to make thee understand what shall befall thy people in the latter days: for yet the vision is for many days.

And when he had spoken such words unto me, I set my face toward the ground, and I became dumb. And, behold, one like the similitude of the sons of men touched my lips: then I opened my mouth, and spake, and said unto him that stood before me, O my lord, by the vision my sorrows are turned upon me, and I have retained no strength. For how can the servant of this my lord talk with this my lord? for as for me, straightway there remained no strength in me, neither is there breath left in me.

Then there came again and touched me one like the appearance of a man, and he strengthened me, And said, O man greatly beloved, fear not: peace be unto thee, be strong, yea, be strong.

And when he had spoken unto me, I was strengthened, and said, Let my lord speak; for thou hast strengthened me.

Then said he, Knowest thou wherefore I come unto thee? and now will I return to fight with the prince of Persia: and when I am gone forth, lo, the prince of Grecia shall come. But I will show thee that which is noted in the scripture of truth: and there is none that holdeth with me in these things, but Michael your prince.
(Daniel 10:10-21)

Furthermore, there are angel visitations in the New Testament times; extending into this era.

Then was Jesus led up of the spirit into the wilderness to be tempted of the devil. And when he had fasted forty days and forty nights, he was afterward an hungred.

And when the tempter came to him, he said, If thou be the Son of God, command that these stones be made bread.

But he answered and said, It is written, Man shall not live by bread alone, but by every word that proceedeth out of the mouth of God.

Then the devil taketh him up into the holy city, and setteth him on a pinnacle of the temple, And saith unto him, If thou be the Son of God, cast thyself down: for it is written, He shall give his angels charge concerning thee: and in their hands they shall bear thee up, lest at any time thou dash thy foot against a stone.

Jesus said unto him, It is written again, Thou shalt not tempt the Lord thy God.

Again, the devil taketh him up into an exceeding high mountain, and sheweth him all the kingdoms of the world, and the glory of them; And saith unto him, All these things will I give thee, if thou wilt fall down and worship me.

Then saith Jesus unto him, Get thee hence, Satan: for it is written, Thou shalt worship the Lord thy God, and him only shalt thou serve.

Then the devil leaveth him, and, behold, angels came and ministered unto him.
(Matthew 4:1-11)

And he came out, and went, as he was wont, to the mount of Olives; and his disciples also followed him. And when he was at the place, he said unto them, Pray that ye enter not into temptation. And he was withdrawn from them about a stone's cast, and kneeled down, and prayed, Saying, Father, if thou be willing, remove this cup from me: nevertheless not my will, but thine, be done. And there appeared an angel unto him from heaven, strengthening him.
(Luke 22:39-43)

I Jesus have sent mine angel to testify unto you these things in the churches. I am the root and the offspring of David, and the bright and morning star.   And   the Spirit and the bride say, Come. And let him that heareth say, Come. And let him that is athirst come. And whosoever will, let him take the water of life freely.

For I testify unto every man that heareth the words of the prophecy of this book, If any man shall add unto these things, God shall add unto him the plagues that are written in this book: And if any man shall take away from the words of the book of this prophecy, God shall take away his part out of the book of life, and out of the holy city, and from the things which are written in this book.

He which testifieth these things saith, Surely I come quickly. Amen. Even so, come, Lord Jesus.
          (Revelation 22:16-20)

Nervous System

> **Nervous** System - Uses electricity to orchestrate
> all sorts of things in your body.

The prophets are not shy about challenging people in formerly unheard of ways. They are well known for pushing nations, through their explosive statements, to admonish the nations to strive for excellence in God. They are definitely vocal when a nation is straying from the ways of the LORD. They have provided the shock needed to put many righteous things back into focus and motion. Such is the power of the electricity of prophecy; such is the driving force behind the nervous system of mankind.

Prophets   *So Ahab sent unto all the children of Israel, and gathered the prophets together unto mount Carmel. And Elijah came unto all the people, and said, How long halt ye between two opinions? if the LORD be God, follow him: but if Baal, then follow him. And the people answered him not a word. Then said Elijah unto the people, I, even I only, remain a prophet of the LORD; but Baal's prophets are four hundred and fifty men. Let them therefore give us two bullocks; and let them choose one bullock for themselves, and cut it in pieces, and lay it on wood, and put no fire under: and I will dress the other bullock, and lay it on wood, and put no fire under: And call ye on the name of your gods, and I will call on the name of the LORD: and the God that answereth by fire, let him be God.*

And all the people answered and said, It is well spoken.

And Elijah said unto the prophets of Baal, Choose you one bullock for yourselves, and dress it first; for ye are many; and call on the name of your gods, but put no fire under. And they took the bullock which was given them, and they dressed it, and called on the name of Baal from morning even until noon, saying, O Baal, hear us. But there was no voice, nor any that answered. And they leaped upon the altar which was made.

And it came to pass at noon, that Elijah mocked them, and said, Cry aloud: for he is a god; either he is talking, or he is pursuing, or he is in a journey, or peradventure he sleepeth, and must be awaked.

And they cried aloud, and cut themselves after their manner with knives and lancets, till the blood gushed out upon them. And it came to pass, when midday was past, and they prophesied until the time of the offering of the evening sacrifice, that there was neither voice, nor any to answer, nor any that regarded.

And Elijah said unto all the people, Come near unto me. And all the people came near unto him. And he repaired the altar of the LORD that was broken down. And Elijah took twelve stones, according to the number of the tribes of the sons of Jacob, unto whom the word of the LORD came, saying, Israel shall be thy name: And with the stones he built an altar in the name of the LORD: and he made a trench about the altar, as great as would contain two measures of seed. And he put the wood in order, and cut the bullock in pieces, and laid him on the wood, and said, Fill four barrels with water, and pour it on the burnt sacrifice, and on the wood. And he said, Do it the second time. And they did it the second time. And he said, Do it the third time. And they did it the third time. And the water ran round about the altar; and he filled the trench also with water.

And it came to pass at the time of the offering of the evening sacrifice, that Elijah the prophet came near, and said, LORD God of Abraham, Isaac, and of Israel, let it be known this day that thou art God in Israel, and that I am thy servant, and that I have done all these things at thy word. Hear me, O LORD, hear me, that this people may know that thou art the LORD God, and that thou hast turned their heart back again.

Then the fire of the LORD fell, and consumed the burnt sacrifice, and the wood, and the stones, and the dust, and licked up the water that was in the trench.

And when all the people saw it, they fell on their faces: and they said, The LORD, he is the God; the LORD, he is the God.

And Elijah said unto them, Take the prophets of Baal; let not one of them escape. And they took them: and Elijah brought them down to the brook Kishon, and slew them there.
(1 Kings 18:20-40)

Then the king sent unto him a captain of fifty with his fifty. And he went up to him: and, behold, he sat on the top of an hill. And he spake unto him, Thou man of God, the king hath said, Come down.

And Elijah answered and said to the captain of fifty, If I be a man of God, then let fire come down from heaven, and consume thee and thy fifty. And there came down fire from heaven, and consumed him and his fifty.

Again also he sent unto him another captain of fifty with his fifty. And he answered and said unto him, O man of God, thus hath the king said, Come down quickly.

And Elijah answered and said unto them, If I be a man of God, let fire come down from heaven, and consume thee and thy fifty. And the fire of God came down from heaven, and consumed him and his fifty.

And he sent again a captain of the third fifty with his fifty. And the third captain of fifty went up, and came and fell on his knees before Elijah, and besought him, and said unto him, O man of God, I pray thee, let my life, and the life of these fifty thy servants, be precious in thy sight. Behold, there came fire down from heaven, and burnt up the two captains of the former fifties with their fifties: therefore let my life now be precious in thy sight.

And the angel of the LORD said unto Elijah, Go down with him: be not afraid of him. And he arose, and went down with him unto the king.

(2 Kings 1:9-15)

And it came to pass, afore Isaiah was gone out into the middle court, that the word of the LORD came to him, saying, Turn again, and tell Hezekiah the captain of my people, Thus saith the LORD, the God of David thy father, I have heard thy prayer, I have seen thy tears: behold, I will heal thee: on the third day thou shalt go up unto the house of the LORD. And I will add unto thy days fifteen years; and I will deliver thee and this city out of the hand of the king of Assyria; and I will defend this city for mine own sake, and for my servant David's sake.

And Isaiah said, Take a lump of figs.

And they took and laid it on the boil, and he recovered.

And Hezekiah said unto Isaiah, What shall be the sign that the LORD will heal me, and that I shall go up into the house of the LORD the third day?

And Isaiah said, This sign shalt thou have of the LORD, that the LORD will do the thing that he hath spoken: shall the shadow go forward ten degrees, or go back ten degrees?

And Hezekiah answered, It is a light thing for the shadow to go down ten degrees: nay, but let the shadow return backward ten degrees.

And Isaiah the prophet cried unto the LORD: and he brought the shadow ten degrees backward, by which it had gone down in the dial of Ahaz.
(2 Kings 20:4-11)

The hand of the LORD was upon me, and carried me out in the spirit of the LORD, and set me down in the midst of the valley which was full of bones, And caused me to pass by them round about: and, behold, there were very many in the open valley; and, lo, they were very dry. And he said unto me, Son of man, can these bones live?

And I answered, O Lord GOD, thou knowest.

Again he said unto me, Prophesy upon these bones, and say unto them, O ye dry bones, hear the word of the LORD. Thus saith the Lord GOD unto these bones; Behold, I will cause breath to enter into you, and ye shall live: And I will lay sinews upon you, and will bring up flesh upon you, and cover you with skin, and put breath in you, and ye shall live; and ye shall know that I am the LORD.

So I prophesied as I was commanded: and as I prophesied, there was a noise, and behold a shaking, and the bones came together, bone to his bone. And when I beheld, lo, the sinews and the flesh came up upon them, and the skin covered them above: but there was no breath in them.

Then said he unto me, Prophesy unto the wind, prophesy, son of man, and say to the wind, Thus saith the Lord GOD; Come from the four winds, O breath, and breathe upon these slain, that they may live.

So I prophesied as he commanded me, and the breath came into them, and they lived, and stood up upon their feet, an exceeding great army.

Then he said unto me, Son of man, these bones are the whole house of Israel: behold, they say, Our bones are dried, and our hope is lost: we are cut off for our parts. Therefore prophesy and say

unto them, Thus saith the Lord GOD;
Behold, O my people, I will open your
graves, and cause you to come up out of
your graves, and bring you into the land
of Israel. And ye shall know that I am the
LORD, when I have opened your graves,
O my people, and brought you up out of
your graves, And shall put my spirit in
you, and ye shall live, and I shall place
you in your own land: then shall ye know
that I the LORD have spoken it, and
performed it, saith the LORD.
(Ezekiel 37:1-14)

Muscular System

Israel   *See Chapter 1a*

Skeletal System

Ishmael   *See Chapter 2a*

Digestive System

> **Digestive** System - Helps humans turn the food they eat into energy.

The Gentile (sometimes called the heathen) nations were vigorous in breaking down the nation of Israel. In doing this they caused to be extracted from it the nutritious remnant. This extraction process continued until the time of Christ, at which time the process of digestion of the food of God placed in the nation of Israel was continued after the crucifixion of Christ.

Gentiles - the extract of God's chosen

> *And the children of Israel went away, and did as the LORD had commanded Moses and Aaron, so did they.*

> *And it came to pass, that at midnight the LORD smote all the firstborn in the land of Egypt, from the firstborn of Pharaoh that sat on his throne unto the firstborn of the captive that was in the dungeon; and all the firstborn of cattle. And Pharaoh rose up in the night, he, and all his servants, and all the Egyptians; and there was a great cry in Egypt; for there was not a house where there was not one dead. And he called for Moses and Aaron by night, and said, Rise up, and get you forth from among my people, both ye and the children of Israel; and go, serve the LORD, as ye have said. Also take your flocks and your herds, as ye have said, and be gone; and bless me also.*

> *And the Egyptians were urgent upon the people, that they might send them out of the land in haste; for they said, We be all dead men.*

> *And the people took their dough before it was leavened, their kneadingtroughs being bound up in their clothes upon their shoulders. And the children of Israel did according to the word of Moses; and they borrowed of the Egyptians*

jewels of silver, and jewels of gold, and raiment: And the LORD gave the people favour in the sight of the Egyptians, so that they lent unto them such things as they required. And they spoiled the Egyptians.

And the children of Israel journeyed from Rameses to Succoth, about six hundred thousand on foot that were men, beside children. And a mixed multitude went up also with them; and flocks, and herds, even very much cattle. And they baked unleavened cakes of the dough which they brought forth out of Egypt, for it was not leavened; because they were thrust out of Egypt, and could not tarry, neither had they prepared for themselves any victual.

Now the sojourning of the children of Israel, who dwelt in Egypt, was four hundred and thirty years. And it came to pass at the end of the four hundred and thirty years, even the selfsame day it came to pass, that all the hosts of the LORD went out from the land of Egypt. It is a night to be much observed unto the LORD for bringing them out from the land of Egypt: this is that night of the LORD to be observed of all the children of Israel in their generations.

(Exodus 12:28-42)

Gentiles - <u>the extract of boldness in God</u>

Wherefore at that time certain Chaldeans came near, and accused the Jews. They spake and said to the king Nebuchadnezzar, O king, live for ever. Thou, O king, hast made a decree, that every man that shall hear the sound of the cornet, flute, harp, sackbut, psaltery, and dulcimer, and all kinds of music, shall fall down and worship the golden image: And whoso falleth not down and worshippeth, that he should be cast into the midst of a burning fiery furnace. There are certain Jews whom thou hast set over the affairs of the province of Babylon, Shadrach, Meshach, and Abednego; these men, O king, have not regarded thee: they serve not thy gods, nor worship the golden image which thou hast set up.

Then Nebuchadnezzar in his rage and fury commanded to bring Shadrach, Meshach, and Abednego. Then they brought these men before the king. Nebuchadnezzar spake and said unto them, Is it true, O Shadrach, Meshach, and Abednego, do not ye serve my gods, nor worship the golden image which I have set up? Now if ye be ready that at what time ye hear the sound of the cornet, flute, harp, sackbut, psaltery, and dulcimer, and all kinds of music, ye fall down and worship the image which I have made; well: but if ye worship not, ye shall be cast the same hour into the midst of a burning fiery furnace; and who is that God that shall deliver you out of my hands?

Shadrach, Meshach, and Abednego, answered and said to the king, O Nebuchadnezzar, we are not careful to answer thee in this matter. If it be so, our God whom we serve is able to deliver us from the burning fiery furnace, and he will deliver us out of thine hand, O king. But if not, be it known unto thee, O king, that we will not serve thy gods, nor worship the golden image which thou hast set up.

Then was Nebuchadnezzar full of fury, and the form of his visage was changed against Shadrach, Meshach, and Abednego: therefore he spake, and commanded that they should heat the furnace one seven times more than it was wont to be heated. And he commanded the most mighty men that were in his army to bind Shadrach, Meshach, and Abednego, and to cast them into the burning fiery furnace.

Then these men were bound in their coats, their hosen, and their hats, and their other garments, and were cast into the midst of the burning fiery furnace. Therefore because the king's commandment was urgent, and the furnace exceeding hot, the flame of the fire slew those men that took up Shadrach, Meshach, and Abednego. And these three men, Shadrach, Meshach, and Abednego, fell down bound into the midst of the burning fiery furnace.

Then Nebuchadnezzar the king was astonied, and rose up in haste, and spake, and said unto his counsellors, Did not we cast three men bound into the midst of the fire?

They answered and said unto the king, True, O king.

He answered and said, Lo, I see four men loose, walking in the midst of the fire, and they have no hurt; and the form of the fourth is like the Son of God.

Then Nebuchadnezzar came near to the mouth of the burning fiery furnace, and spake, and said, Shadrach, Meshach, and Abednego, ye servants of the most high God, come forth, and come hither. Then Shadrach, Meshach, and Abednego, came forth of the midst of the fire. And the princes, governors, and captains, and the king's counsellors, being gathered together, saw these men, upon whose bodies the fire had no power, nor was an hair of their head singed, neither were their coats changed, nor the smell of fire had passed on them.

Then Nebuchadnezzar spake, and said, Blessed be the God of Shadrach, Meshach, and Abednego, who hath sent his angel, and delivered his servants that trusted in him, and have changed the king's word, and yielded their bodies, that they might not serve nor worship any god, except their own God. Therefore I make a decree, That every people, nation, and language, which speak any thing amiss against the God of Shadrach, Meshach, and Abednego, shall be cut in pieces, and their houses shall be made a dunghill: because there is no other God that can deliver after this sort.

(Daniel 3:8-29)

Gentiles - <u>the extract of perseverance under fire</u>

All the presidents of the kingdom, the governors, and the princes, the counsellors, and the captains, have consulted together to establish a royal statute, and to make a firm decree, that whosoever shall ask a petition of any God or man for thirty days, save of thee, O king, he shall be cast into the den of lions. Now, O king, establish the decree, and sign the writing, that it be not changed, according to the law of the Medes and Persians, which altereth not. Wherefore king Darius signed the writing and the decree.

Now when Daniel knew that the writing was signed, he went into his house; and his windows being open in his chamber toward Jerusalem, he kneeled upon his knees three times a day, and prayed, and gave thanks before his God, as he did aforetime. Then these men assembled, and found Daniel praying and making supplication before his God.

Then they came near, and spake before the king concerning the king's decree; Hast thou not signed a decree, that every man that shall ask a petition of any God or man within thirty days, save of thee, O king, shall be cast into the den of lions?

The king answered and said, The thing is true, according to the law of the Medes and Persians, which altereth not.

Then answered they and said before the king, That Daniel, which is of the children of the captivity of Judah, regardeth not thee, O king, nor the decree that thou hast signed, but maketh his petition three times a day.

Then the king, when he heard these words, was sore displeased with himself, and set his heart on Daniel to deliver him: and he laboured till the going down of the sun to deliver him.

Then these men assembled unto the king, and said unto the king, Know, O king, that the law of the Medes and Persians is, That no decree nor statute which the king establisheth may be changed.

Then the king commanded, and they brought Daniel, and cast him into the den of lions. Now the king spake and said unto Daniel, Thy God whom thou servest continually, he will deliver thee.

And a stone was brought, and laid upon the mouth of the den; and the king sealed it with his own signet, and with the signet of his lords; that the purpose might not be changed concerning Daniel. Then the king went to his palace, and passed the night fasting: neither were instruments of music brought before him: and his sleep went from him.

Then the king arose very early in the morning, and went in haste unto the den of lions. And when he came to the den, he cried with a lamentable voice unto Daniel: and the king spake and said to Daniel, O Daniel, servant of the living God, is thy God, whom thou servest continually, able to deliver thee from the lions?

Then said Daniel unto the king, O king, live for ever. My God hath sent his angel, and hath shut the lions' mouths, that they have not hurt me: forasmuch as before him innocency was found in me; and also before thee, O king, have I done no hurt.

Then was the king exceeding glad for him, and commanded that they should take Daniel up out of the den. So Daniel was taken up out of the den, and no manner of hurt was found upon him, because he believed in his God. And the king commanded, and they brought those men which had accused Daniel, and they cast them into the den of lions, them, their children, and their wives; and the lions had the mastery of them, and brake all their bones in pieces or ever they came at the bottom of the den.

Then king Darius wrote unto all people, nations, and languages, that dwell in all the earth; Peace be multiplied unto you. I make a decree, That in every dominion of my kingdom men tremble and fear before the God of Daniel: for he is the living God, and stedfast for ever, and his kingdom that which shall not be destroyed, and his dominion shall be even unto the end.
(Daniel 6:7-26)

Gentiles - the extract of peace in despair

Now in the first year of Cyrus king of Persia, that the word of the LORD by the mouth of Jeremiah might be fulfilled, the LORD stirred up the spirit of Cyrus king of Persia, that he made a proclamation throughout all his kingdom, and put it also in writing, saying, Thus saith Cyrus king of Persia, The LORD God of heaven hath given me all the kingdoms of the earth; and he hath charged me to build him an house at Jerusalem, which is in Judah. Who is there among you of all his people? his God be with him, and let him go up to Jerusalem, which is in Judah, and build the house of the LORD God of Israel, (he is the God,) which is in Jerusalem. And whosoever remaineth in any place where he sojourneth, let the men of his place help him with silver, and with gold, and with goods, and with beasts, beside the freewill offering for the house of God that is in Jerusalem.

Then rose up the chief of the fathers of Judah and Benjamin, and the priests, and the Levites, with all them whose spirit God had raised, to go up to build the house of the LORD which is in Jerusalem. And all they that were about them strengthened their hands with vessels of silver, with gold, with goods, and with beasts, and with precious things, beside all that was willingly offered. Also Cyrus the king brought forth the vessels of the house of the LORD, which Nebuchadnezzar had brought forth out of Jerusalem, and had put them in the house of his gods; Even those did Cyrus king of Persia bring forth by the hand of Mithredath the treasurer, and numbered them unto Sheshbazzar, the prince of Judah.

(Ezra 1:1-8)

Gentiles - <u>the extract of leaning on God</u>

And it came to pass in the month Nisan, in the twentieth year of Artaxerxes the king, that wine was before him: and I took up the wine, and gave it unto the king. Now I had not been beforetime sad in his presence. Wherefore the king said unto me, Why is thy countenance sad, seeing thou art not sick? this is nothing else but sorrow of heart.

Then I was very sore afraid, And said unto the king, Let the king live for ever: why should not my countenance be sad, when the city, the place of my fathers' sepulchres, lieth waste, and the gates thereof are consumed with fire?

Then the king said unto me, For what dost thou make request?

So I prayed to the God of heaven. And I said unto the king, If it please the king, and if thy servant have found favour in thy sight, that thou wouldest send me unto Judah, unto the city of my fathers' sepulchres, that I may build it.

And the king said unto me, (the queen also sitting by him,) For how long shall thy journey be? and when wilt thou return?

So it pleased the king to send me; and I set him a time. Moreover I said unto the king, If it please the king, let letters be given me to the governors beyond the river, that they may convey me over till I come into Judah; And a letter unto Asaph the keeper of the king's forest, that he may give me timber to make beams for the gates of the palace which appertained to the house, and for the wall of the city, and for the house that I shall enter into.

And the king granted me, according to the good hand of my God upon me.
     (Nehemiah 2:1-8)

Gentiles - the extract of perceiving the mind of God

They provoked him to jealousy with strange gods, with abominations provoked they him to anger. They sacrificed unto devils, not to God; to gods whom they knew not, to new gods that came newly up, whom your fathers feared not. Of the Rock that begat thee thou art unmindful, and hast forgotten God that formed thee. And when the LORD saw it, he abhorred them, because of the provoking of his sons, and of his daughters. And he said, I will hide my face from them, I will see what their end shall be: for they are a very froward generation, children in whom is no faith. They have moved me to jealousy with that which is not God; they have provoked me to anger with their vanities: and I will move them to jealousy with those which are not a people; I will provoke them to anger with a foolish nation.

(Deuteronomy 32:16-21)

Gentiles - the extract of pure worship

And when ye shall see Jerusalem compassed with armies, then know that the desolation thereof is nigh. Then let them which are in Judaea flee to the mountains; and let them which are in the midst of it depart out; and let not them that are in the countries enter thereinto. For these be the days of vengeance, that all things which are written may be fulfilled. But woe unto them that are with child, and to them that give suck, in those days! for there shall be great distress in the land, and wrath upon this people. And they shall fall by the edge of the sword, and shall be led away captive into all nations: and Jerusalem shall be trodden down of the Gentiles, until the times of the Gentiles be fulfilled.

(Luke 21:20-24)

Reproductive System

Reproductive System - Hopefully, this needs no further explanation than the following.

Apostles *Then Peter said unto them, Repent, and be baptized every one of you in the name of Jesus Christ for the remission of sins, and ye shall receive the gift of the Holy Ghost. For the promise is unto you, and to your children, and to all that are afar off, even as many as the Lord our God shall call. And with many other words did he testify and exhort, saying, Save yourselves from this untoward generation.*

Then they that gladly received his word were baptized: and the same day there were added unto them about three thousand souls. And they continued stedfastly in the apostles' doctrine and fellowship, and in breaking of bread, and in prayers. And fear came upon every soul: and many wonders and signs were done by the apostles.

And all that believed were together, and had all things common; And sold their possessions and goods, and parted them to all men, as every man had need. And they, continuing daily with one accord in the temple, and breaking bread from house to house, did eat their meat with gladness and singleness of heart, Praising God, and having favour with all the people. And the Lord added to the church daily such as should be saved.
(Acts 2:38-47)

And by the hands of the apostles were many signs and wonders wrought among the people; (and they were all with one accord in Solomon's porch. And of the rest durst no man join himself to them: but the people magnified them. And believers were the more added to the Lord,

*multitudes both of men and women.) Insomuch
that they brought forth the sick into the streets,
and laid them on beds and couches, that at the
least the shadow of Peter passing by might
overshadow some of them. There came also
a multitude out of the cities round about unto
Jerusalem, bringing sick folks, and them which
were vexed with unclean spirits: and they were
healed everyone.*

(Acts 5:12-26)

*Now they which were scattered abroad upon the
persecution that arose about Stephen travelled
as far as Phenice, and Cyprus, and Antioch,
preaching the word to none but unto the Jews
only. And some of them were men of Cyprus and
Cyrene, which, when they were come to Antioch,
spake unto the Grecians, preaching the Lord
Jesus. And the hand of the Lord was with them:
and a great number believed, and turned unto
the Lord.*

*Then tidings of these things came unto the ears of
the church which was in Jerusalem: and they
sent forth Barnabas, that he should go as far as
Antioch. Who, when he came, and had seen the
grace of God, was glad, and exhorted them all,
that with purpose of heart they would cleave unto
the Lord. For he was a good man, and full of the
Holy Ghost and of faith: and much people was
added unto the Lord.*

(Acts 11:19-24)

Appendix A

Bible references to *'Son of man'* from the Old Testament (emphasizing, 'Son')

(not including The book of the prophet Ezekiel)

Daniel 7:13-14

I saw in the night visions, and, behold, one like the Son of man came with the clouds of heaven, and came to the Ancient of days, and they brought him near before him. And there was given him dominion, and glory, and a kingdom, that all people, nations, and languages, should serve him: his dominion is an everlasting dominion, which shall not pass away, and his kingdom that which shall not be destroyed.

+=+
+=+

Like-kind
Bible references to *'Son of God'*
from the Old Testament

Daniel 3:21-25

Then these men were bound in their coats, their hosen, and their hats, and their other garments, and were cast into the midst of the burning fiery furnace. Therefore because the king's commandment was urgent, and the furnace exceeding hot, the flame of the fire slew those men that took up Shadrach, Meshach, and Abednego. And these three men, Shadrach, Meshach, and Abednego, fell down bound into the midst of the burning fiery furnace.

Then Nebuchadnezzar the king was astonied, and rose up in haste, and spake, and said unto his counsellors, Did not we cast three men bound into the midst of the fire?

They answered and said unto the king, True, O king.

He answered and said, Lo, I see four men loose, walking in the midst of the fire, and they have no hurt; and the form of the fourth is like the Son of God.

Appendix B

Bible references to *'son of man'*
from the Old Testament
(not including The book of the prophet Ezekiel)

Numbers 23:19

God is not a man, that he should lie; neither the son of man, that he should repent: hath he said, and shall he not do it? or hath he spoken, and shall he not make it good?

Job 25:5-6

Behold even to the moon, and it shineth not; yea, the stars are not pure in his sight. How much less man, that is a worm? and the son of man, which is a worm?

Psalm 8:4-5

What is man, that thou art mindful of him? and the son of man, that thou visitest him? For thou hast made him a little lower than the angels, and hast crowned him with glory and honour.

Psalm 80:14-19

Return, we beseech thee, O God of hosts: look down from heaven, and behold, and visit this vine; And the vineyard which thy right hand hath planted, and the branch that thou madest strong for thyself. It is burned with fire, it is cut down: they perish at the rebuke of thy countenance. Let thy hand be upon the man of thy right hand, upon the son of man whom thou madest strong for thyself. So will not we go back from thee: quicken us, and we will call upon thy name. Turn us again, O LORD God of hosts, cause thy face to shine; and we shall be saved.

Psalm 144:3

LORD, what is man, that thou takest knowledge of him! or the son of man, that thou makest account of him!

Psalm 146:3

Put not your trust in princes, nor in the son of man, in whom there is no help.

Isaiah 51:11-13

Therefore the redeemed of the LORD shall return, and come with singing unto Zion; and everlasting joy shall be upon their head: they shall obtain gladness and joy; and sorrow and mourning shall flee away. I, even I, am he that comforteth you: who art thou, that thou shouldest be afraid of a man that shall die, and of the son of man which shall be made as grass; And forgettest the LORD thy maker, that hath stretched forth the heavens, and laid the foundations of the earth; and hast feared continually every day because of the fury of the oppressor, as if he were ready to destroy? and where is the fury of the oppressor?

Isaiah 56:1-2

Thus saith the LORD, Keep ye judgment, and do justice: for my salvation is near to come, and my righteousness to be revealed. Blessed is the man that doeth this, and the son of man that layeth hold on it; that keepeth the sabbath from polluting it, and keepeth his hand from doing any evil.

Jeremiah 49:16-18

Thy terribleness hath deceived thee, and the pride of thine heart, O thou that dwellest in the clefts of the rock, that holdest the height of the hill: though thou shouldest make thy nest as high as the eagle, I will bring thee down from thence, saith the LORD. Also Edom shall be a desolation: every one that goeth by it shall be astonished, and shall hiss at all the plagues thereof. As in the overthrow of Sodom and Gomorrah and the neighbour cities thereof, saith the LORD, no man shall abide there, neither shall a son of man dwell in it.

Jeremiah 49:33

And Hazor shall be a dwelling for dragons, and a desolation for ever: there shall no man abide there, nor any son of man dwell in it.

Jeremiah 50:40

As God overthrew Sodom and Gomorrah and the neighbour cities thereof, saith the LORD; so shall no man abide there, neither shall any son of man dwell therein.

Jeremiah 51:42-43

The sea is come up upon Babylon: she is covered with the multitude of the waves thereof. Her cities are a desolation, a dry land, and a wilderness, a land wherein no man dwelleth, neither doth any son of man pass thereby.

Appendix C

Bible references to 'Son of man' from the New Testament

Matthew 8:18-20

Now when Jesus saw great multitudes about him, he gave commandment to depart unto the other side. And a certain scribe came, and said unto him, Master, I will follow thee whithersoever thou goest.

And Jesus saith unto him, The foxes have holes, and the birds of the air have nests; but the Son of man hath not where to lay his head.

Matthew 9:1-6

And he entered into a ship, and passed over, and came into his own city. And, behold, they brought to him a man sick of the palsy, lying on a bed: and Jesus seeing their faith said unto the sick of the palsy; Son, be of good cheer; thy sins be forgiven thee.

And, behold, certain of the scribes said within themselves, This man blasphemeth.

And Jesus knowing their thoughts said, Wherefore think ye evil in your hearts? For whether is easier, to say, Thy sins be forgiven thee; or to say, Arise, and walk? But that ye may know that the Son of man hath power on earth to forgive sins, (then saith he to the sick of the palsy,) Arise, take up thy bed, and go unto thine house.

Mark 2:5-12

When Jesus saw their faith, he said unto the sick of the palsy, Son, thy sins be forgiven thee.

But there was certain of the scribes sitting there, and reasoning in their hearts, Why doth this man thus speak blasphemies? who can forgive sins but God only?

And immediately when Jesus perceived in his spirit that they so reasoned within themselves, he said unto them, Why reason ye these things in your hearts? Whether is it easier to say to the sick of the palsy, Thy sins be forgiven thee; or to say, Arise, and take up thy bed, and walk? But that ye may know that the Son of man hath power on earth to forgive sins, (he saith to the sick of the palsy,) I say unto thee, Arise, and take up thy bed, and go thy way into thine house. And immediately he arose, took up the bed, and went forth before them all; insomuch that they were all amazed, and glorified God, saying, We never saw it on this fashion.

Luke 5:20-26

And when he saw their faith, he said unto him, Man, thy sins are forgiven thee.

And the scribes and the Pharisees began to reason, saying, Who is this which speaketh blasphemies? Who can forgive sins, but God alone?

But when Jesus perceived their thoughts, he answering said unto them, What reason ye in your hearts? Whether is easier, to say, Thy sins be forgiven thee; or to say, Rise up and walk? But that ye may know that the Son of man hath power upon earth to forgive sins, (he said unto the sick of the palsy,) I say unto thee, Arise, and take up thy couch, and go into thine house.

And immediately he rose up before them, and took up that whereon he lay, and departed to his own house, glorifying God. And they were all amazed, and they glorified God, and were filled with fear, saying, We have seen strange things to day.

Matthew 10:16-24

Behold, I send you forth as sheep in the midst of wolves: be ye therefore wise as serpents, and harmless as doves. But beware of men: for they will deliver you up to the councils, and they will scourge you in their synagogues; And ye shall be brought before governors and kings for my sake, for a testimony against them and the Gentiles. But when they deliver you up, take no thought how or what ye shall speak: for it shall be given you in that same hour what ye shall speak. For it is not ye that speak, but the Spirit of your Father which speaketh in you.

And the brother shall deliver up the brother to death, and the father the child: and the children shall rise up against their parents, and cause them to be put to death. And ye shall be hated of all men for my name's sake: but he that endureth to the end shall be saved.

But when they persecute you in this city, flee ye into another: for verily I say unto you, Ye shall not have gone over the cities of Israel, till the Son of man be come.

The disciple is not above his master, nor the servant above his lord.

Matthew 11:16-19

But whereunto shall I liken this generation? It is like unto children sitting in the markets, and calling unto their fellows, And saying, We have piped unto you, and ye have not danced; we have mourned unto you, and ye have not lamented. For John came neither eating nor drinking, and they say, He hath a devil. The Son of man came eating and drinking, and they say, Behold a man gluttonous, and a winebibber, a friend of publicans and sinners. But wisdom is justified of her children

Luke 7:31-35

And the Lord said, Whereunto then shall I liken the men of this generation? and to what are they like? They are like unto children sitting in the marketplace, and calling one to another, and saying, We have piped unto you, and ye have not danced; we have mourned to you, and ye have not wept. For John the Baptist came neither eating bread nor drinking wine; and ye say, He hath a devil. The Son of man is come eating and drinking; and ye say, Behold a gluttonous man, and a winebibber, a friend of publicans and sinners! But wisdom is justified of all her children.

~~~~~~

Matthew 12:3-8

But he said unto them, Have ye not read what David did, when he was an hungred, and they that were with him; How he entered into the house of God, and did eat the shewbread, which was not lawful for him to eat, neither for them which were with him, but only for the priests? Or have ye not read in the law, how that on the sabbath days the priests in the temple profane the sabbath, and are blameless? But I say unto you, That in this place is one greater than the temple.

But if ye had known what this meaneth, I will have mercy, and not sacrifice, ye would not have condemned the guiltless. For the Son of man is Lord even of the sabbath day.

Mark 2:23-28

And it came to pass, that he went through the corn fields on the sabbath day; and his disciples began, as they went, to pluck the ears of corn. And the Pharisees said unto him, Behold, why do they on the sabbath day that which is not lawful?

And he said unto them, Have ye never read what David did, when he had need, and was an hungred, he, and they that were with him? How he went into the house of God in the days of Abiathar the high priest, and did eat the shewbread, which is not lawful to eat but for the priests, and gave also to them which were with him? And he said unto them, The sabbath was made for man, and not man for the sabbath: Therefore the Son of man is Lord also of the sabbath.

Luke 6:1-5

And it came to pass on the second sabbath after the first, that he went through the corn fields; and his disciples plucked the ears of corn, and did eat, rubbing them in their hands. And certain of the Pharisees said unto them, Why do ye that which is not lawful to do on the sabbath days?

And Jesus answering them said, Have ye not read so much as this, what David did, when himself was an hungred, and they which were with him; How he went into the house of God, and did take and eat the shewbread, and gave also to them that were with him; which it is not lawful to eat but for the priests alone? And he said unto them, That the Son of man is Lord also of the sabbath

Matthew 12:31-32

Wherefore I say unto you, All manner of sin and blasphemy shall be forgiven unto men: but the blasphemy against the Holy Ghost shall not be forgiven unto men. And whosoever speaketh a word against the Son of man, it shall be forgiven him: but whosoever speaketh against the Holy Ghost, it shall not be forgiven him, neither in this world, neither in the world to come.

Matthew 12:38-40

Then certain of the scribes and of the Pharisees answered, saying, Master, we would see a sign from thee.

But he answered and said unto them, An evil and adulterous generation seeketh after a sign; and there shall no sign be given to it, but the sign of the prophet Jonas: For as Jonas was three days and three nights in the whale's belly; so shall the Son of man be three days and three nights in the heart of the earth.

Matthew 13:36-43

Then Jesus sent the multitude away, and went into the house: and his disciples came unto him, saying, Declare unto us the parable of the tares of the field.

He answered and said unto them, He that soweth the good seed is the Son of man; The field is the world; the good seed are the children of the kingdom; but the tares are the children of the wicked one; The enemy that sowed them is the devil; the harvest is the end of the world; and the reapers are the angels. As therefore the tares are gathered and burned in the fire; so shall it be in the end of this world. The Son of man shall send forth his angels, and they shall gather out of his kingdom all things that offend, and them which do iniquity; And shall cast them into a furnace of fire: there shall be wailing and gnashing of teeth. Then shall the righteous shine forth as the sun in the kingdom of their Father. Who hath ears to hear, let him hear.

Matthew 16:13-16

When Jesus came into the coasts of Caesarea Philippi, he asked his disciples, saying, Whom do men say that I the Son of man am?

And they said, Some say that thou art John the Baptist: some, Elias; and others, Jeremias, or one of the prophets.

He saith unto them, But whom say ye that I am?

And Simon Peter answered and said, Thou art the Christ, the Son of the living God.

Luke 9:18-26

And it came to pass, as he was alone praying, his disciples were with him: and he asked them, saying, Whom say the people that I am?

They answering said, John the Baptist; but some say, Elias; and others say, that one of the old prophets is risen again.

He said unto them, But whom say ye that I am?

Peter answering said, The Christ of God.

And he straitly charged them, and commanded them to tell no man that thing; Saying, The Son of man must suffer many things, and be rejected of the elders and chief priests and scribes, and be slain, and be raised the third day. And he said to them all, If any man will come after me, let him deny himself, and take up his cross daily, and follow me. For whosoever will save his life shall lose it: but whosoever will lose his life for my sake, the same shall save it. For what is a man advantaged, if he gain the whole world, and lose himself, or be cast away? For whosoever shall be ashamed of me and of my words, of him shall the Son of man be ashamed, when he shall come in his own glory, and in his Father's, and of the holy angels.

Matthew 16:24-28

Then said Jesus unto his disciples, If any man will come after me, let him deny himself, and take up his cross, and follow me. For whosoever will save his life shall lose it: and whosoever will lose his life for my sake shall find it. For what is a man profited, if he shall gain the whole world, and lose his own soul? or what shall a man give in exchange for his soul?

For the Son of man shall come in the glory of his Father with his angels; and then he shall reward every man according to his works. Verily I say unto you, There be some standing here, which shall not taste of death, till they see the Son of man coming in his kingdom.

Matthew 17:1-13

And after six days Jesus taketh Peter, James, and John his brother, and bringeth them up into an high mountain apart, And was transfigured before them: and his face did shine as the sun, and his raiment was white as the light. And, behold, there appeared unto them Moses and Elias talking with him.

Then answered Peter, and said unto Jesus, Lord, it is good for us to be here: if thou wilt, let us make here three tabernacles; one for thee, and one for Moses, and one for Elias.

While he yet spake, behold, a bright cloud overshadowed them: and behold a voice out of the cloud, which said, This is my beloved Son, in whom I am well pleased; hear ye him.

And when the disciples heard it, they fell on their face, and were sore afraid. And Jesus came and touched them, and said, Arise, and be not afraid. And when they had lifted up their eyes, they saw no man, save Jesus only.

And as they came down from the mountain, Jesus charged them, saying, Tell the vision to no man, until the Son of man be risen again from the dead.

And his disciples asked him, saying, Why then say the scribes that Elias must first come?

And Jesus answered and said unto them, Elias truly shall first come, and restore all things. But I say unto you, That Elias is come already, and they knew him not, but have done unto him whatsoever they listed. Likewise shall also the Son of man suffer of them.

Then the disciples understood that he spake unto them of John the Baptist.

Mark 9:2-13

And after six days Jesus taketh with him Peter, and James, and John, and leadeth them up into an high mountain apart by themselves: and he was transfigured before them. And his raiment became shining, exceeding white as snow; so as no fuller on earth can white them. And there appeared unto them Elias with Moses: and they were talking with Jesus.

And Peter answered and said to Jesus, Master, it is good for us to be here: and let us make three tabernacles; one for thee, and one for Moses, and one for Elias. For he wist not what to say; for they were sore afraid.

And there was a cloud that overshadowed them: and a voice came out of the cloud, saying, This is my beloved Son: hear him.

And suddenly, when they had looked round about, they saw no man any more, save Jesus only with themselves. And as they came down from the mountain, he charged them that they should tell no man what things they had seen, till the Son of man were risen from the dead. And they kept that saying with themselves, questioning one with another what the rising from the dead should mean.

And they asked him, saying, Why say the scribes that Elias must first come?

And he answered and told them, Elias verily cometh first, and restoreth all things; and how it is written of the Son of man, that he must suffer many things, and be set at nought. But I say unto you, That Elias is indeed come, and they have done unto him whatsoever they listed, as it is written of him.

Matthew 17:22-23

And while they abode in Galilee, Jesus said unto them, The Son of man shall be betrayed into the hands of men: And they shall kill him, and the third day he shall be raised again.

And they were exceeding sorry.

Matthew 18:10-13

Take heed that ye despise not one of these little ones; for I say unto you, That in heaven their angels do always behold the face of my Father which is in heaven. For the Son of man is come to save that which was lost.

How think ye? if a man have an hundred sheep, and one of them be gone astray, doth he not leave the ninety and nine, and goeth into the mountains, and seeketh that which is gone astray? And if so be that he find it, verily I say unto you, he rejoiceth more of that sheep, than of the ninety and nine which went not astray.

Matthew 19:27-30

Then answered Peter and said unto him, Behold, we have forsaken all, and followed thee; what shall we have therefore?

And Jesus said unto them, Verily I say unto you, That ye which have followed me, in the regeneration when the Son of man shall sit in the throne of his glory, ye also shall sit upon twelve thrones, judging the twelve tribes of Israel. And every one that hath forsaken houses, or brethren, or sisters, or father, or mother, or wife, or children, or lands, for my name's sake, shall receive an hundredfold, and shall inherit everlasting life. But many that are first shall be last; and the last shall be first

Matthew 20:17-19

And Jesus going up to Jerusalem took the twelve disciples apart in the way, and said unto them, Behold, we go up to Jerusalem; and the Son of man shall be betrayed unto the chief priests and unto the scribes, and they shall condemn him to death, And shall deliver him to the Gentiles to mock, and to scourge, and to crucify him: and the third day he shall rise again.

Matthew 20:25-28

But Jesus called them unto him, and said, Ye know that the princes of the Gentiles exercise dominion over them, and they that are great exercise authority upon them. But it shall not be so among you: but whosoever will be great among you, let him be your minister; And whosoever will be chief among you, let him be your servant: Even as the Son of man came not to be ministered unto, but to minister, and to give his life a ransom for many.

Matthew 24:26-30

Wherefore if they shall say unto you, Behold, he is in the desert; go not forth: behold, he is in the secret chambers; believe it not. For as the lightning cometh out of the east, and shineth even unto the west; so shall also the coming of the Son of man be. For wheresoever the carcase is, there will the eagles be gathered together.

Immediately after the tribulation of those days shall the sun be darkened, and the moon shall not give her light, and the stars shall fall from heaven, and the powers of the heavens shall be shaken: And then shall appear the sign of the Son of man in heaven: and then shall all the tribes of the earth mourn, and they shall see the Son of man coming in the clouds of heaven with power and great glory.

Matthew 24:37-44

But as the days of Noe were, so shall also the coming of the Son of man be. For as in the days that were before the flood they were eating and drinking, marrying and giving in marriage, until the day that Noe entered into the ark, And knew not until the flood came, and took them all away; so shall also the coming of the Son of man be. Then shall two be in the field; the one shall be taken, and the other left. Two women shall be grinding at the mill; the one shall be taken, and the other left. Watch therefore: for ye know not what hour your Lord doth come.

But know this, that if the goodman of the house had known in what watch the thief would come, he would have watched, and would not have suffered his house to be broken up. Therefore be ye also ready: for in such an hour as ye think not the Son of man cometh.

Matthew 25:1-13

Then shall the kingdom of heaven be likened unto ten virgins, which took their lamps, and went forth to meet the bridegroom. And five of them were wise, and five were foolish. They that were foolish took their lamps, and took no oil with them: But the wise took oil in their vessels with their lamps. While the bridegroom tarried, they all slumbered and slept.

And at midnight there was a cry made, Behold, the bridegroom cometh; go ye out to meet him. Then all those virgins arose, and trimmed their lamps.

And the foolish said unto the wise, Give us of your oil; for our lamps are gone out.

But the wise answered, saying, Not so; lest there be not enough for us and you: but go ye rather to them that sell, and buy for yourselves.

And while they went to buy, the bridegroom came; and they that were ready went in with him to the marriage: and the door was shut.

Afterward came also the other virgins, saying, Lord, Lord, open to us. But he answered and said, Verily I say unto you, I know you not.

25:13   Watch therefore, for ye know neither the day nor the hour wherein the Son of man cometh.

Matthew 25:31-46

When the Son of man shall come in his glory, and all the holy angels with him, then shall he sit upon the throne of his glory: And before him shall be gathered all nations: and he shall separate them one from another, as a shepherd divideth his sheep from the goats: And he shall set the sheep on his right hand, but the goats on the left.

Then shall the King say unto them on his right hand, Come, ye blessed of my Father, inherit the kingdom prepared for you from the foundation of the world: For I was an hungred, and ye gave me meat: I was thirsty, and ye gave me drink: I was a stranger, and ye took me in: Naked, and ye clothed me: I was sick, and ye visited me: I was in prison, and ye came unto me.

Then shall the righteous answer him, saying, Lord, when saw we thee an hungred, and fed thee? or thirsty, and gave thee drink? When saw we thee a stranger, and took thee in? or naked, and clothed thee? Or when saw we thee sick, or in prison, and came unto thee?

And the King shall answer and say unto them, Verily I say unto you, Inasmuch as ye have done it unto one of the least of these my brethren, ye have done it unto me.

Then shall he say also unto them on the left hand, Depart from me, ye cursed, into everlasting fire, prepared for the devil and his angels: For I was an hungred, and ye gave me no meat:

I was thirsty, and ye gave me no drink: I was a stranger, and ye took me not in: naked, and ye clothed me not: sick, and in prison, and ye visited me not.

Then shall they also answer him, saying, Lord, when saw we thee an hungred, or athirst, or a stranger, or naked, or sick, or in prison, and did not minister unto thee?

Then shall he answer them, saying, Verily I say unto you, Inasmuch as ye did it not to one of the least of these, ye did it not to me.

And these shall go away into everlasting punishment: but the righteous into life eternal.

Matthew 26:1-2

And it came to pass, when Jesus had finished all these sayings, he said unto his disciples, Ye know that after two days is the feast of the passover, and the Son of man is betrayed to be crucified.

Matthew 26:23-24

And he answered and said, He that dippeth his hand with me in the dish, the same shall betray me. The Son of man goeth as it is written of him: but woe unto that man by whom the Son of man is betrayed! it had been good for that man if he had not been born.

Matthew 26:44-46

And he left them, and went away again, and prayed the third time, saying the same words. Then cometh he to his disciples, and saith unto them, Sleep on now, and take your rest: behold, the hour is at hand, and the Son of man is betrayed into the hands of sinners. Rise, let us be going: behold, he is at hand that doth betray me.

Matthew 26:62-64

And the high priest arose, and said unto him, Answerest thou nothing? what is it which these witness against thee? But Jesus held his peace, And the high priest answered and said unto him, I adjure thee by the living God, that thou tell us whether thou be the Christ, the Son of God.

Jesus saith unto him, Thou hast said: nevertheless I say unto you, Hereafter shall ye see the Son of man sitting on the right hand of power, and coming in the clouds of heaven.

Mark 8:31-38

And he began to teach them, that the Son of man must suffer many things, and be rejected of the elders, and of the chief priests, and scribes, and be killed, and after three days rise again. And he spake that saying openly.

And Peter took him, and began to rebuke him.

But when he had turned about and looked on his disciples, he rebuked Peter, saying, Get thee behind me, Satan: for thou savourest not the things that be of God, but the things that be of men.

And when he had called the people unto him with his disciples also, he said unto them, Whosoever will come after me, let him deny himself, and take up his cross, and follow me. For whosoever will save his life shall lose it; but whosoever shall lose his life for my sake and the gospel's, the same shall save it. For what shall it profit a man, if he shall gain the whole world, and lose his own soul? Or what shall a man give in exchange for his soul? Whosoever therefore shall be ashamed of me and of my words in this adulterous and sinful generation; of him also shall the Son of man be ashamed, when he cometh in the glory of his Father with the holy angels.

Mark 9:31

For he taught his disciples, and said unto them, The Son of man is delivered into the hands of men, and they shall kill him; and after that he is killed, he shall rise the third day.

Mark 10:32-34

And they were in the way going up to Jerusalem; and Jesus went before them: and they were amazed; and as they followed, they were afraid. And he took again the twelve, and began to tell them what things should happen unto him, Saying, Behold, we go up to Jerusalem; and the Son of man shall be delivered unto the chief priests, and unto the scribes; and they shall condemn him to death, and shall deliver him to the Gentiles: And they shall mock him, and shall scourge him, and shall spit upon him, and shall kill him: and the third day he shall rise again.

Mark 10:41-45

And when the ten heard it, they began to be much displeased with James and John. But Jesus called them to him, and saith unto them, Ye know that they which are accounted to rule over the Gentiles exercise lordship over them; and their great ones exercise authority upon them. But so shall it not be among you: but whosoever will be great among you, shall be your minister: And whosoever of you will be the chiefest, shall be servant of all. For even the Son of man came not to be ministered unto, but to minister, and to give his life a ransom for many.

Mark 13:21-34

And then if any man shall say to you, Lo, here is Christ; or, lo, he is there; believe him not: For false Christs and false prophets shall rise, and shall shew signs and wonders, to seduce, if it were possible, even the elect. But take ye heed: behold, I have foretold you all things.

But in those days, after that tribulation, the sun shall be darkened, and the moon shall not give her light, And the stars of heaven shall fall, and the powers that are in heaven shall be shaken. And then shall they see the Son of man coming in the clouds with great power and glory. And then shall he send his angels, and shall gather together his elect from the four winds, from the uttermost part of the earth to the uttermost part of heaven. Now learn a parable of the fig tree; When her branch is yet tender, and putteth forth leaves, ye know that summer is near: So ye in like manner, when ye shall see these things come to pass, know that it is nigh, even at the doors. Verily I say unto you, that this generation shall not pass, till all these things be done. Heaven and earth shall pass away: but my words shall not pass away.

But of that day and that hour knoweth no man, no, not the angels which are in heaven, neither the Son, but the Father. Take ye heed, watch and pray: for ye know not when the time is.

For the Son of Man is as a man taking a far journey, who left his house, and gave authority to his servants, and to every man his work, and commanded the porter to watch.

Mark 14:21

The Son of man indeed goeth, as it is written of him: but woe to that man by whom the Son of man is betrayed! good were it for that man if he had never been born.

Mark 14:39-42

And again he went away, and prayed, and spake the same words. And when he returned, he found them asleep again, (for their eyes were heavy,) neither wist they what to answer him. And he cometh the third time, and saith unto them, Sleep on now, and take your rest: it is enough, the hour is come; behold, the Son of man is betrayed into the hands of sinners. Rise up, let us go; lo, he that betrayeth me is at hand.

Mark 14:60-62

And the high priest stood up in the midst, and asked Jesus, saying, Answerest thou nothing? what is it which these witness against thee? But he held his peace, and answered nothing. Again the high priest asked him, and said unto him, Art thou the Christ, the Son of the Blessed?

And Jesus said, I am: and ye shall see the Son of man sitting on the right hand of power, and coming in the clouds of heaven.

Luke 9:42-45

And as he was yet a coming, the devil threw him down, and tare him. And Jesus rebuked the unclean spirit, and healed the child, and delivered him again to his father.

And they were all amazed at the mighty power of God. But while they wondered every one at all things which Jesus did, he said unto his disciples, Let these sayings sink down into your ears: for the Son of man shall be delivered into the hands of men.

But they understood not this saying, and it was hid from them, that they perceived it not: and they feared to ask him of that saying.

Luke 9:51-58

And it came to pass, when the time was come that he should be received up, he stedfastly set his face to go to Jerusalem, And sent messengers before his face: and they went, and entered into a village of the Samaritans, to make ready for him. And they did not receive him, because his face was as though he would go to Jerusalem.

And when his disciples James and John saw this, they said, Lord, wilt thou that we command fire to come down from heaven, and consume them, even as Elias did?

But he turned, and rebuked them, and said, Ye know not what manner of spirit ye are of. For the Son of man is not come to destroy men's lives, but to save them.

And they went to another village.

And it came to pass, that, as they went in the way, a certain man said unto him, Lord, I will follow thee whithersoever thou goest.

And Jesus said unto him, Foxes have holes, and birds of the air have nests; but the Son of man hath not where to lay his head.

Luke 11:29-30

And when the people were gathered thick together, he began to say, This is an evil generation: they seek a sign; and there shall no sign be given it, but the sign of Jonas the prophet. For as Jonas was a sign unto the Ninevites, so shall also the Son of man be to this generation.

Luke 12:8-10

Also I say unto you, Whosoever shall confess me before men, him shall the Son of man also confess before the angels of God: But he that denieth me before men shall be denied before the angels of God. And whosoever shall speak a word against the Son of man, it shall be forgiven him: but unto him that blasphemeth against the Holy Ghost it shall not be forgiven.

Luke 12:37-40

Blessed are those servants, whom the lord when he cometh shall find watching: verily I say unto you, that he shall gird himself, and make them to sit down to meat, and will come forth and serve them. And if he shall come in the second watch, or come in the third watch, and find them so, blessed are those servants.

And this know, that if the goodman of the house had known what hour the thief would come, he would have watched, and not have suffered his house to be broken through. Be ye therefore ready also: for the Son of man cometh at an hour when ye think not.

Luke 17:22-30

And he said unto the disciples, The days will come, when ye shall desire to see one of the days of the Son of man, and ye shall not see it. And they shall say to you, See here; or, see there: go not after them, nor follow them. For as the lightning, that lighteneth out of the one part under heaven, shineth unto the other part under heaven; so shall also the Son of man be in his day. But first must he suffer many things, and be rejected of this generation.

And as it was in the days of Noe, so shall it be also in the days of the Son of man. They did eat, they drank, they married wives, they were given in marriage, until the day that Noe entered into the ark, and the flood came, and destroyed them all.

Likewise also as it was in the days of Lot; they did eat, they drank, they bought, they sold, they planted, they builded; But the same day that Lot went out of Sodom it rained fire and brimstone from heaven, and destroyed them all. Even thus shall it be in the day when the Son of man is revealed.

Luke 18:1-8

And he spake a parable unto them to this end, that men ought always to pray, and not to faint; Saying, There was in a city a judge, which feared not God, neither regarded man: And there was a widow in that city; and she came unto him, saying, Avenge me of mine adversary. And he would not for a while: but afterward he said within himself, Though I fear not God, nor regard man; Yet because this widow troubleth me, I will avenge her, lest by her continual coming she weary me.

And the Lord said, Hear what the unjust judge saith. And shall not God avenge his own elect, which cry day and night unto him, though he bear long with them? I tell you that he will avenge them speedily. Nevertheless when the Son of man cometh, shall he find faith on the earth?

Luke 18:31-33

Then he took unto him the twelve, and said unto them, Behold, we go up to Jerusalem, and all things that are written by the prophets concerning the Son of man shall be accomplished. For he shall be delivered unto the Gentiles, and shall be mocked, and spitefully entreated, and spitted on: And they shall scourge him, and put him to death: and the third day he shall rise again.

Luke 19:1-10

And Jesus entered and passed through Jericho. And, behold, there was a man named Zacchaeus, which was the chief among the publicans, and he was rich. And he sought to see Jesus who he was; and could not for the press, because he was little of stature. And he ran before, and climbed up into a sycomore tree to see him: for he was to pass that way.

And when Jesus came to the place, he looked up, and saw him, and said unto him, Zacchaeus, make haste, and come down; for to day I must abide at thy house.

And he made haste, and came down, and received him joyfully.

And when they saw it, they all murmured, saying, That he was gone to be guest with a man that is a sinner. And Zacchaeus stood, and said unto the Lord; Behold, Lord, the half of my goods I give to the poor; and if I have taken any thing from any man by false accusation, I restore him fourfold.

And Jesus said unto him, This day is salvation come to this house, forsomuch as he also is a son of Abraham. For the Son of man is come to seek and to save that which was lost.

Luke 21:20-27

And when ye shall see Jerusalem compassed with armies, then know that the desolation thereof is nigh. Then let them which are in Judaea flee to the mountains; and let them which are in the midst of it depart out; and let not them that are in the countries enter thereinto. For these be the days of vengeance, that all things which are written may be fulfilled. But woe unto them that are with child, and to them that give suck, in those days! for there shall be great distress in the land, and wrath upon this people. And they shall fall by the edge of the sword, and shall be led away captive into all nations: and Jerusalem shall be trodden down of the Gentiles, until the times of the Gentiles be fulfilled.

And there shall be signs in the sun, and in the moon, and in the stars; and upon the earth distress of nations, with perplexity; the sea and the waves roaring; Men's hearts failing them for fear, and for looking after those things which are coming on the earth: for the powers of heaven shall be shaken. And then shall they see the Son of man coming in a cloud with power and great glory.

Luke 21:36

Watch ye therefore, and pray always, that ye may be accounted worthy to escape all these things that shall come to pass, and to stand before the Son of man.

Luke 22:21-22

But, behold, the hand of him that betrayeth me is with me on the table. And truly the Son of man goeth, as it was determined: but woe unto that man by whom he is betrayed!

Luke 22:47-48

And while he yet spake, behold a multitude, and he that was called Judas, one of the twelve, went before them, and drew near unto Jesus to kiss him.

But Jesus said unto him, Judas, betrayest thou the Son of man with a kiss?

Luke 22:66-69

And as soon as it was day, the elders of the people and the chief priests and the scribes came together, and led him into their council, saying, Art thou the Christ? tell us.

And he said unto them, If I tell you, ye will not believe: And if I also ask you, ye will not answer me, nor let me go. Hereafter shall the Son of man sit on the right hand of the power of God.

Luke 24:1-7

Now upon the first day of the week, very early in the morning, they came unto the sepulchre, bringing the spices which they had prepared, and certain others with them. And they found the stone rolled away from the sepulchre. And they entered in, and found not the body of the Lord Jesus.

And it came to pass, as they were much perplexed thereabout, behold, two men stood by them in shining garments: And as they were afraid, and bowed down their faces to the earth, they said unto them, Why seek ye the living among the dead? He is not here, but is risen: remember how he spake unto you when he was yet in Galilee, Saying, The Son of man must be delivered into the hands of sinful men, and be crucified, and the third day rise again.

John 1:49-51

Nathanael answered and saith unto him, Rabbi, thou art the Son of God; thou art the King of Israel.

Jesus answered and said unto him, Because I said unto thee, I saw thee under the fig tree, believest thou? thou shalt see greater things than these. And he saith unto him, Verily, verily, I say unto you, Hereafter ye shall see heaven open, and the angels of God ascending and descending upon the Son of man.

John 3:11-15

Verily, verily, I say unto thee, We speak that we do know, and testify that we have seen; and ye receive not our witness. If I have told you earthly things, and ye believe not, how shall ye believe, if I tell you of heavenly things? And no man hath ascended up to heaven, but he that came down from heaven, even the Son of man which is in heaven. And as Moses lifted up the serpent in the wilderness, even so must the Son of man be lifted up: That whosoever believeth in him should not perish, but have eternal life.

John 5:25-27

Verily, verily, I say unto you, The hour is coming, and now is, when the dead shall hear the voice of the Son of God: and they that hear shall live. For as the Father hath life in himself; so hath he given to the Son to have life in himself; And hath given him authority to execute judgment also, because he is the Son of man.

John 6:26-27

Jesus answered them and said, Verily, verily, I say unto you, Ye seek me, not because ye saw the miracles, but because ye did eat of the loaves, and were filled. Labour not for the meat which perisheth, but for that meat which endureth unto everlasting life, which the Son of man shall give unto you: for him hath God the Father sealed.

John 6:53-62

Then Jesus said unto them, Verily, verily, I say unto you, Except ye eat the flesh of the Son of man, and drink his blood, ye have no life in you. Whoso eateth my flesh, and drinketh my blood, hath eternal life; and I will raise him up at the last day. For my flesh is meat indeed, and my blood is drink indeed. He that eateth my flesh, and drinketh my blood, dwelleth in me, and I in him. As the living Father hath sent me, and I live by the Father: so he that eateth me, even he shall live by me. This is that bread which came down from heaven: not as your fathers did eat manna, and are dead: he that eateth of this bread shall live for ever.

These things said he in the synagogue, as he taught in Capernaum. Many therefore of his disciples, when they had heard this, said, This is an hard saying; who can hear it?

When Jesus knew in himself that his disciples murmured at it, he said unto them, Doth this offend you? What and if ye shall see the Son of man ascend up where he was before?

John 8:25-29

Then said they unto him, Who art thou?

And Jesus saith unto them, Even the same that I said unto you from the beginning. I have many things to say and to judge of you: but he that sent me is true; and I speak to the world those things which I have heard of him.

They understood not that he spake to them of the Father.

Then said Jesus unto them, When ye have lifted up the Son of man, then shall ye know that I am he, and that I do nothing of myself; but as my Father hath taught me, I speak these things. And he that sent me is with me: the Father hath not left me alone; for I do always those things that please him.

John 12:23

And Jesus answered them, saying, The hour is come, that the Son of man should be glorified.

John 12:34

The people answered him, We have heard out of the law that Christ abideth for ever: and how sayest thou, The Son of man must be lifted up? who is this Son of man?

John 13:31-32

Therefore, when he was gone out, Jesus said, Now is the Son of man glorified, and God is glorified in him. If God be glorified in him, God shall also glorify him in himself, and shall straightway glorify him.

Acts 7:54-56

When they heard these things, they were cut to the heart, and they gnashed on him with their teeth.

But he, being full of the Holy Ghost, looked up stedfastly into heaven, and saw the glory of God, and Jesus standing on the right hand of God, And said, Behold, I see the heavens opened, and the Son of man standing on the right hand of God.

Revelation 1:9-18

I John, who also am your brother, and companion in tribulation, and in the kingdom and patience of Jesus Christ, was in the isle that is called Patmos, for the word of God, and for the testimony of Jesus Christ. I was in the Spirit on the Lord's day, and heard behind me a great voice, as of a trumpet, Saying, I am Alpha and Omega, the first and the last: and, What thou seest, write in a book, and send it unto the seven churches which are in Asia; unto Ephesus, and unto Smyrna, and unto Pergamos, and unto Thyatira, and unto Sardis, and unto Philadelphia, and unto Laodicea.

And I turned to see the voice that spake with me. And being turned, I saw seven golden candlesticks; And in the midst of the seven candlesticks one like unto the Son of man, clothed with a garment down to the foot, and girt about the paps with a golden girdle. His head and his hairs were white like wool, as white as snow; and his eyes were as a flame of fire; And his feet like unto fine brass, as if they burned in a furnace; and his voice as the sound of many waters. And he had in his right hand seven stars: and out of his mouth went a sharp twoedged sword: and his countenance was as the sun shineth in his strength. And when I saw him, I fell at his feet as dead.

And he laid his right hand upon me, saying unto me, Fear not; I am the first and the last: I am he that liveth, and was dead; and, behold, I am alive for evermore, Amen; and have the keys of hell and of death.

Revelation 14:13-14

And I heard a voice from heaven saying unto me, Write, Blessed are the dead which die in the Lord from henceforth: Yea, saith the Spirit, that they may rest from their labours; and their works do follow them. And I looked, and behold a white cloud, and upon the cloud one sat like unto the Son of man, having on his head a golden crown, and in his hand a sharp sickle.

Appendix D

Bible references to 'son of man' from the New Testament

Hebrews 2:1-8

Therefore we ought to give the more earnest heed to the things which we have heard, lest at any time we should let them slip. For if the word spoken by angels was stedfast, and every transgression and disobedience received a just recompense of reward; How shall we escape, if we neglect so great salvation; which at the first began to be spoken by the Lord, and was confirmed unto us by them that heard him; God also bearing them witness, both with signs and wonders, and with divers miracles, and gifts of the Holy Ghost, according to his own will?

For unto the angels hath he not put in subjection the world to come, whereof we speak. But one in a certain place testified, saying, What is man, that thou art mindful of him? or the son of man, that thou visitest him? Thou madest him a little lower than the angels; thou crownedst him with glory and honour, and didst set him over the works of thy hands: Thou hast put all things in subjection under his feet.

For in that he put all in subjection under him, he left nothing that is not put under him. But now we see not yet all things put under him.

Appendix E

**Bible references to '*son of man*'
and '*Son of man*'
in a generic sense
from the Old Testament
in The book of the prophet Ezekiel**

**Pertaining to the beginning of the
reconciliation
of the tribes of the house of Israel
to the LORD God**

Ezekiel 2:1-8

And he said unto me, Son of man, stand upon thy feet, and I will speak unto thee.

And the spirit entered into me when he spake unto me, and set me upon my feet, that I heard him that spake unto me.

And he said unto me, Son of man, I send thee to the children of Israel, to a rebellious nation that hath rebelled against me: they and their fathers have transgressed against me, even unto this very day. For they are impudent children and stiffhearted. I do send thee unto them; and thou shalt say unto them, Thus saith the Lord GOD. And they, whether they will hear, or whether they will forbear, (for they are a rebellious house,) yet shall know that there hath been a prophet among them.

And thou, son of man, be not afraid of them, neither be afraid of their words, though briers and thorns be with thee, and thou dost dwell among scorpions: be not afraid of their words, nor be dismayed at their looks, though they be a rebellious house. And thou shalt speak my words unto them, whether they will hear, or whether they will forbear: for they are most rebellious.

But thou, son of man, hear what I say unto thee; Be not thou rebellious like that rebellious house: open thy mouth, and eat that I give thee.

Ezekiel 3:1-11

Moreover he said unto me, Son of man, eat that thou findest; eat this roll, and go speak unto the house of Israel.

So I opened my mouth, and he caused me to eat that roll.

And he said unto me, Son of man, cause thy belly to eat, and fill thy bowels with this roll that I give thee.

Then did I eat it; and it was in my mouth as honey for sweetness.

And he said unto me, Son of man, go, get thee unto the house of Israel, and speak with my words unto them. For thou art not sent to a people of a strange speech and of an hard language, but to the house of Israel; Not to many people of a strange speech and of an hard language, whose words thou canst not understand. Surely, had I sent thee to them, they would have hearkened unto thee. But the house of Israel will not hearken unto thee; for they will not hearken unto me: for all the house of Israel are impudent and hardhearted. Behold, I have made thy face strong against their faces, and thy forehead strong against their foreheads. As an adamant harder than flint have I made thy forehead: fear them not, neither be dismayed at their looks, though they be a rebellious house.

Moreover he said unto me, Son of man, all my words that I shall speak unto thee receive in thine heart, and hear with thine ears. And go, get thee to them of the captivity, unto the children of thy people, and speak unto them, and tell them, Thus saith the Lord GOD; whether they will hear, or whether they will forbear.

Ezekiel 3:16-17

And it came to pass at the end of seven days, that the word of the LORD came unto me, saying, Son of man, I have made thee a watchman unto the house of Israel: therefore hear the word at my mouth, and give them warning from me.

Ezekiel 3:24-27

Then the spirit entered into me, and set me upon my feet, and spake with me, and said unto me, Go, shut thyself within thine house. But thou, O son of man, behold, they shall put bands upon thee, and shall bind thee with them, and thou shalt not go out among them: And I will make thy tongue cleave to the roof of thy mouth, that thou shalt be dumb, and shalt not be to them a reprover: for they are a rebellious house. But when I speak with thee, I will open thy mouth, and thou shalt say unto them, Thus saith the Lord GOD; He that heareth, let him hear; and he that forbeareth, let him forbear: for they are a rebellious house.

Ezekiel 4:1-2

Thou also, son of man, take thee a tile, and lay it before thee, and portray upon it the city, even Jerusalem: And lay siege against it, and build a fort against it, and cast a mount against it; set the camp also against it, and set battering rams against it round about.

Ezekiel 4:16-17

Moreover he said unto me, Son of man, behold, I will break the staff of bread in Jerusalem: and they shall eat bread by weight, and with care; and they shall drink water by measure, and with astonishment: That they may want bread and water, and be astonied one with another, and consume away for their iniquity.

Ezekiel 5:1-4

And thou, son of man, take thee a sharp knife, take thee a barber's razor, and cause it to pass upon thine head and upon thy beard: then take thee balances to weigh, and divide the hair. Thou shalt burn with fire a third part in the midst of the city, when the days of the siege are fulfilled: and thou shalt take a third part, and smite about it with a knife: and a third part thou shalt scatter in the wind; and I will draw out a sword after them. Thou shalt also take thereof a few in number, and bind them in thy skirts. Then take of them again, and cast them into the midst of the fire, and burn them in the fire; for thereof shall a fire come forth into all the house of Israel.

Ezekiel 6:1-2

And the word of the LORD came unto me, saying, Son of man, set thy face toward the mountains of Israel, and prophesy against them,

Ezekiel 7:1-2

Moreover the word of the LORD came unto me, saying, Also, thou son of man, thus saith the Lord GOD unto the land of Israel; An end, the end is come upon the four corners of the land.

Ezekiel 8:4-12

And, behold, the glory of the God of Israel was there, according to the vision that I saw in the plain. Then said he unto me, Son of man, lift up thine eyes now the way toward the north.

So I lifted up mine eyes the way toward the north, and behold northward at the gate of the altar this image of jealousy in the entry.

He said furthermore unto me, Son of man, seest thou what they do? even the great abominations that the house of Israel committeth here, that I should go far off from my sanctuary? but turn thee yet again, and thou shalt see greater abominations.

And he brought me to the door of the court; and when I looked, behold a hole in the wall.

Then said he unto me, Son of man, dig now in the wall: and when I had digged in the wall, behold a door.

And he said unto me, Go in, and behold the wicked abominations that they do here.

So I went in and saw; and behold every form of creeping things, and abominable beasts, and all the idols of the house of Israel, portrayed upon the wall round about. And there stood before them seventy men of the ancients of the house of Israel, and in the midst of them stood Jaazaniah the son of Shaphan, with every man his censer in his hand; and a thick cloud of incense went up.

Then said he unto me, Son of man, hast thou seen what the ancients of the house of Israel do in the dark, every man in the chambers of his imagery? for they say, The LORD seeth us not; the LORD hath forsaken the earth.

Ezekiel 11:1-4

Moreover the spirit lifted me up, and brought me unto the east gate of the LORD'S house, which looketh eastward: and behold at the door of the gate five and twenty men; among whom I saw Jaazaniah the son of Azur, and Pelatiah the son of Benaiah, princes of the people. Then said he unto me, Son of man, these are the men that devise mischief, and give wicked counsel in this city: Which say, It is not near; let us build houses: this city is the caldron, and we be the flesh. Therefore prophesy against them, prophesy, O son of man.

Ezekiel 11:14-17

Again the word of the LORD came unto me, saying, Son of man, thy brethren, even thy brethren, the men of thy kindred, and all the house of Israel wholly, are they unto whom the inhabitants of Jerusalem have said, Get you far from the LORD: unto us is this land given in possession. Therefore say, Thus saith the Lord GOD; Although I have cast them far off among the heathen, and although I have scattered them among the countries, yet will I be to them as a little sanctuary in the countries where they shall come. Therefore say, Thus saith the Lord GOD; I will even gather you from the people, and assemble you out of the countries where ye have been scattered, and I will give you the land of Israel.

Ezekiel 12:1-3

The word of the LORD also came unto me, saying, Son of man, thou dwellest in the midst of a rebellious house, which have eyes to see, and see not; they have ears to hear, and hear not: for they are a rebellious house. Therefore, thou son of man, prepare thee stuff for removing, and remove by day in their sight; and thou shalt remove from thy place to another place in their sight: it may be they will consider, though they be a rebellious house.

Ezekiel 12:8-11

And in the morning came the word of the LORD unto me, saying, Son of man, hath not the house of Israel, the rebellious house, said unto thee, What doest thou? Say thou unto them, Thus saith the Lord GOD; This burden concerneth the prince in Jerusalem, and all the house of Israel that are among them. Say, I am your sign: like as I have done, so shall it be done unto them: they shall remove and go into captivity.

Ezekiel 12:17-28

Moreover the word of the LORD came to me, saying, Son of man, eat thy bread with quaking, and drink thy water with trembling and with carefulness; And say unto the people of the land, Thus saith the Lord GOD of the inhabitants of Jerusalem, and of the land of Israel; They shall eat their bread with carefulness, and drink their water with astonishment, that her land may be desolate from all that is therein, because of the violence of all them that dwell therein. And the cities that are inhabited shall be laid waste, and the land shall be desolate; and ye shall know that I am the LORD.

And the word of the LORD came unto me, saying, Son of man, what is that proverb that ye have in the land of Israel, saying, The days are prolonged, and every vision faileth? Tell them therefore, Thus saith the Lord GOD; I will make this proverb to cease, and they shall no more use it as a proverb in Israel; but say unto them, The days are at hand, and the effect of every vision. For there shall be no more any vain vision nor flattering divination within the house of Israel. For I am the LORD: I will speak, and the word that I shall speak shall come to pass; it shall be no more prolonged: for in your days, O rebellious house, will I say the word, and will perform it, saith the Lord GOD.

Again the word of the LORD came to me, saying, Son of man, behold, they of the house of Israel say, The vision that he seeth is for many days to come, and he prophesieth of the times that are far off. Therefore say unto them, Thus saith the Lord GOD; There shall none of my words be prolonged any more, but the word which I have spoken shall be done, saith the Lord GOD.

Ezekiel 13:1-3

And the word of the LORD came unto me, saying, Son of man, prophesy against the prophets of Israel that prophesy, and say thou unto them that prophesy out of their own hearts, Hear ye the word of the LORD; Thus saith the Lord GOD; Woe unto the foolish prophets, that follow their own spirit, and have seen nothing!

Ezekiel 13:17-18

Likewise, thou son of man, set thy face against the daughters of thy people, which prophesy out of their own heart; and prophesy thou against them, And say, Thus saith the Lord GOD; Woe to the women that sew pillows to all armholes, and make kerchiefs upon the head of every stature to hunt souls! Will ye hunt the souls of my people, and will ye save the souls alive that come unto you?

Ezekiel 14:2-5

And the word of the LORD came unto me, saying, Son of man, these men have set up their idols in their heart, and put the stumblingblock of their iniquity before their face: should I be inquired of at all by them?

Therefore speak unto them, and say unto them, Thus saith the Lord GOD; Every man of the house of Israel that setteth up his idols in his heart, and putteth the stumblingblock of his iniquity before his face, and cometh to the prophet; I the LORD will answer him that cometh according to the multitude of his idols; That I may take the house of Israel in their own heart, because they are all estranged from me through their idols.

Ezekiel 14:12-14

The word of the LORD came again to me, saying, Son of man, when the land sinneth against me by trespassing grievously, then will I stretch out mine hand upon it, and will break the staff of the bread thereof, and will send famine upon it, and will cut off man and beast from it: Though these three men, Noah, Daniel, and Job, were in it, they should deliver but their own souls by their righteousness, saith the Lord GOD.

Ezekiel 15:1-3

And the word of the LORD came unto me, saying, Son of man, What is the vine tree more than any tree, or than a branch which is among the trees of the forest? Shall wood be taken thereof to do any work? or will men take a pin of it to hang any vessel thereon?

Ezekiel 16:1-3

Again the word of the LORD came unto me, saying, Son of man, cause Jerusalem to know her abominations, And say, Thus saith the Lord GOD unto Jerusalem; Thy birth and thy nativity is of the land of Canaan; thy father was an Amorite, and thy mother an Hittite.

Ezekiel 17:1-4

And the word of the LORD came unto me, saying, Son of man, put forth a riddle, and speak a parable unto the house of Israel; And say, Thus saith the Lord GOD; A great eagle with great wings, longwinged, full of feathers, which had divers colours, came unto Lebanon, and took the highest branch of the cedar: He cropped off the top of his young twigs, and carried it into a land of traffic; he set it in a city of merchants.

Ezekiel 20:1-7

And it came to pass in the seventh year, in the fifth month, the tenth day of the month, that certain of the elders of Israel came to inquire of the LORD, and sat before me. Then came the word of the LORD unto me, saying, Son of man, speak unto the elders of Israel, and say unto them, Thus saith the Lord GOD; Are ye come to inquire of me? As I live, saith the Lord GOD, I will not be inquired of by you.

Wilt thou judge them, son of man, wilt thou judge them? cause them to know the abominations of their fathers: And say unto them, Thus saith the Lord GOD; In the day when I chose Israel, and lifted up mine hand unto the seed of the house of Jacob, and made myself known unto them in the land of Egypt, when I lifted up mine hand unto them, saying, I am the LORD your God; In the day that I lifted up mine hand unto them, to bring them forth of the land of Egypt into a land that I had espied for them, flowing with milk and honey, which is the glory of all lands: Then said I unto them, Cast ye away every man the abominations of his eyes, and defile not yourselves with the idols of Egypt: I am the LORD your God.

Ezekiel 20:27-29

Therefore, son of man, speak unto the house of Israel, and say unto them, Thus saith the Lord GOD; Yet in this your fathers have blasphemed me, in that they have committed a trespass against me. For when I had brought them into the land, for the which I lifted up mine hand to give it to them, then they saw every high hill, and all the thick trees, and they offered there their sacrifices, and there they presented the provocation of their offering: there also they made their sweet savour, and poured out there their drink offerings. Then I said unto them, What is the high place whereunto ye go? And the name thereof is called Bamah unto this day.

Ezekiel 20:45-49

Moreover the word of the LORD came unto me, saying, Son of man, set thy face toward the south, and drop thy word toward the south, and prophesy against the forest of the south field; And say to the forest of the south, Hear the word of the LORD; Thus saith the Lord GOD; Behold, I will kindle a fire in thee, and it shall devour every green tree in thee, and every dry tree: the flaming flame shall not be quenched, and all faces from the south to the north shall be burned therein. And all flesh shall see that I the LORD have kindled it: it shall not be quenched.

Then said I, Ah Lord GOD! they say of me, Doth he not speak parables?

Ezekiel 21:1-20

And the word of the LORD came unto me, saying, Son of man, set thy face toward Jerusalem, and drop thy word toward the holy places, and prophesy against the land of Israel, And say to the land of Israel, Thus saith the LORD; Behold, I am against thee, and will draw forth my sword out of his sheath, and will cut off from thee the righteous and the wicked. Seeing then that I will cut off from thee the righteous and the wicked, therefore shall my sword go forth out of his sheath against all flesh from the south to the north: That all flesh may know that I the LORD have drawn forth my sword out of his sheath: it shall not return any more. Sigh therefore, thou son of man, with the breaking of thy loins; and with bitterness sigh before their eyes. And it shall be, when they say unto thee, Wherefore sighest thou? that thou shalt answer, For the tidings; because it cometh: and every heart shall melt, and all hands shall be feeble, and every spirit shall faint, and all knees shall be weak as water: behold, it cometh, and shall be brought to pass, saith the Lord GOD.

Again the word of the LORD came unto me, saying, Son of man, prophesy, and say, Thus saith the LORD; Say, A sword, a sword is sharpened, and also furbished: It is sharpened to make a sore slaughter; it is furbished that it may glitter: should we then make mirth? it contemneth the rod of my son, as every tree. And he hath given it to be furbished, that it may be handled: this sword is sharpened, and it is furbished, to give it into the hand of the slayer. Cry and howl, son of man: for it shall be upon my people, it shall be upon all the princes of Israel: terrors by reason of the sword shall be upon my people: smite therefore upon thy thigh. Because it is a trial, and what if the sword contemn even the rod? it shall be no more, saith the Lord GOD. Thou therefore, son of man, prophesy, and smite thine hands together, and let the sword be doubled the third time, the sword of the slain: it is the sword of the great men that are slain, which entereth into their privy chambers. I have set the point of the sword against all their gates, that their heart may faint, and their ruins be multiplied: ah! it is made bright, it is wrapped up for the slaughter. Go thee one way or other, either on the right hand, or on the left, whithersoever thy face is set. I will also smite mine hands together, and I will cause my fury to rest: I the LORD have said it.

The word of the LORD came unto me again, saying, Also, thou son of man, appoint thee two ways, that the sword of the king of Babylon may come: both twain shall come forth out of one land: and choose thou a place, choose it at the head of the way to the city. Appoint a way, that the sword may come to Rabbath of the Ammonites, and to Judah in Jerusalem the defenced.

Ezekiel 21:26-30

Thus saith the Lord GOD; Remove the diadem, and take off the crown: this shall not be the same: exalt him that is low, and abase him that is high. I will overturn, overturn, overturn, it: and it shall be no more, until he come whose right it is; and I will give it him.

And thou, son of man, prophesy and say, Thus saith the Lord GOD concerning the Ammonites, and concerning their reproach; even say thou, The sword, the sword is drawn: for the slaughter it is furbished, to consume because of the glittering: Whiles they see vanity unto thee, whiles they divine a lie unto thee, to bring thee upon the necks of them that are slain, of the wicked, whose day is come, when their iniquity shall have an end. Shall I cause it to return into his sheath? I will judge thee in the place where thou wast created, in the land of thy nativity

Ezekiel 22:1-4

Moreover the word of the LORD came unto me, saying, Now, thou son of man, wilt thou judge, wilt thou judge the bloody city? yea, thou shalt show her all her abominations.

Then say thou, Thus saith the Lord GOD, The city sheddeth blood in the midst of it, that her time may come, and maketh idols against herself to defile herself. Thou art become guilty in thy blood that thou hast shed; and hast defiled thyself in thine idols which thou hast made; and thou hast caused thy days to draw near, and art come even unto thy years: therefore have I made thee a reproach unto the heathen, and a mocking to all countries.

Ezekiel 22:17-25

And the word of the LORD came unto me, saying, Son of man, the house of Israel is to me become dross: all they are brass, and tin, and iron, and lead, in the midst of the furnace; they are even the dross of silver. Therefore thus saith the Lord GOD; Because ye are all become dross, behold, therefore I will gather you into the midst of Jerusalem. As they gather silver, and brass, and iron, and lead, and tin, into the midst of the furnace, to blow the fire upon it, to melt it; so will I gather you in mine anger and in my fury, and I will leave you there, and melt you.Yea, I will gather you, and blow upon you in the fire of my wrath, and ye shall be melted in the midst thereof. As silver is melted in the midst of the furnace, so shall ye be melted in the midst thereof; and ye shall know that I the LORD have poured out my fury upon you.

And the word of the LORD came unto me, saying, Son of man, say unto her, Thou art the land that is not cleansed, nor rained upon in the day of indignation. There is a conspiracy of her prophets in the midst thereof, like a roaring lion ravening the prey; they have devoured souls; they have taken the treasure and precious things; they have made her many widows in the midst thereof.

Ezekiel 23:1-3

The word of the LORD came again unto me, saying, Son of man, there were two women, the daughters of one mother: And they committed whoredoms in Egypt; they committed whoredoms in their youth: there were their breasts pressed, and there they bruised the teats of their virginity.

Ezekiel 23:35-37

Therefore thus saith the Lord GOD; Because thou hast forgotten me, and cast me behind thy back, therefore bear thou also thy lewdness and thy whoredoms. The LORD said moreover unto me; Son of man, wilt thou judge Aholah and Aholibah? yea, declare unto them their abominations; That they have committed adultery, and blood is in their hands, and with their idols have they committed adultery, and have also caused their sons, whom they bare unto me, to pass for them through the fire, to devour them.

Ezekiel 24:1-5

Again in the ninth year, in the tenth month, in the tenth day of the month, the word of the LORD came unto me, saying, Son of man, write thee the name of the day, even of this same day: the king of Babylon set himself against Jerusalem this same day. And utter a parable unto the rebellious house, and say unto them, Thus saith the Lord GOD; Set on a pot, set it on, and also pour water into it: Gather the pieces thereof into it, even every good piece, the thigh, and the shoulder; fill it with the choice bones. Take the choice of the flock, and burn also the bones under it, and make it boil well, and let them seethe the bones of it therein.

Ezekiel 24:15-27

Also the word of the LORD came unto me, saying, Son of man, behold, I take away from thee the desire of thine eyes with a stroke: yet neither shalt thou mourn nor weep, neither shall thy tears run down. Forbear to cry, make no mourning for the dead, bind the tire of thine head upon thee, and put on thy shoes upon thy feet, and cover not thy lips, and eat not the bread of men.

So I spake unto the people in the morning: and at even my wife died; and I did in the morning as I was commanded.

And the people said unto me, Wilt thou not tell us what these things are to us, that thou doest so?

Then I answered them, The word of the LORD came unto me, saying, Speak unto the house of Israel, Thus saith the Lord GOD; Behold, I will profane my sanctuary, the excellency of your strength, the desire of your eyes, and that which your soul pitieth; and your sons and your daughters whom ye have left shall fall by the sword. And ye shall do as I have done: ye shall not cover your lips, nor eat the bread of men. And your tires shall be upon your heads, and your shoes upon your feet: ye shall not mourn nor weep; but ye shall pine away for your iniquities, and mourn one toward another. Thus Ezekiel is unto you a sign: according to all that he hath done shall ye do: and when this cometh, ye shall know that I am the Lord GOD.

Also, thou son of man, shall it not be in the day when I take from them their strength, the joy of their glory, the desire of their eyes, and that whereupon they set their minds, their sons and their daughters, That he that escapeth in that day shall come unto thee, to cause thee to hear it with thine ears? In that day shall thy mouth be opened to him which is escaped, and thou shalt speak, and be no more dumb: and thou shalt be a sign unto them; and they shall know that I am the LORD.

Ezekiel 25:1-4

The word of the LORD came again unto me, saying, Son of man, set thy face against the Ammonites, and prophesy against them; And say unto the Ammonites, Hear the word of the Lord GOD; Thus saith the Lord GOD; Because thou saidst, Aha, against my sanctuary, when it was profaned; and against the land of Israel, when it was desolate; and against the house of Judah, when they went into captivity; Behold, therefore I will deliver thee to the men of the east for a possession, and they shall set their palaces in thee, and make their dwellings in thee: they shall eat thy fruit, and they shall drink thy milk.

Ezekiel 26:1-3

And it came to pass in the eleventh year, in the first day of the month, that the word of the LORD came unto me, saying, Son of man, because that Tyrus hath said against Jerusalem, Aha, she is broken that was the gates of the people: she is turned unto me: I shall be replenished, now she is laid waste: Therefore thus saith the Lord GOD; Behold, I am against thee, O Tyrus, and will cause many nations to come up against thee, as the sea causeth his waves to come up.

Ezekiel 27:1-3

The word of the LORD came again unto me, saying, Now, thou son of man, take up a lamentation for Tyrus; And say unto Tyrus, O thou that art situate at the entry of the sea, which art a merchant of the people for many isles, Thus saith the Lord GOD; O Tyrus, thou hast said, I am of perfect beauty.

Ezekiel 28:1-7

The word of the LORD came again unto me, saying, Son of man, say unto the prince of Tyrus, Thus saith the Lord GOD; Because thine heart is lifted up, and thou hast said, I am a God, I sit in the seat of God, in the midst of the seas; yet thou art a man, and not God, though thou set thine heart as the heart of God: Behold, thou art wiser than Daniel; there is no secret that they can hide from thee: With thy wisdom and with thine understanding thou hast gotten thee riches, and hast gotten gold and silver into thy treasures: By thy great wisdom and by thy traffic hast thou increased thy riches, and thine heart is lifted up because of thy riches: Therefore thus saith the Lord GOD; Because thou hast set thine heart as the heart of God; Behold, therefore I will bring strangers upon thee, the terrible of the nations: and they shall draw their swords against the beauty of thy wisdom, and they shall defile thy brightness.

Ezekiel 28:11-15

Moreover the word of the LORD came unto me, saying, Son of man, take up a lamentation upon the king of Tyrus, and say unto him, Thus saith the Lord GOD; Thou sealest up the sum, full of wisdom, and perfect in beauty. Thou hast been in Eden the garden of God; every precious stone was thy covering, the sardius, topaz, and the diamond, the beryl, the onyx, and the jasper, the sapphire, the emerald, and the carbuncle, and gold: the workmanship of thy tabrets and of thy pipes was prepared in thee in the day that thou wast created. Thou art the anointed cherub that covereth; and I have set thee so: thou wast upon the holy mountain of God; thou hast walked up and down in the midst of the stones of fire. Thou wast perfect in thy ways from the day that thou wast created, till iniquity was found in thee.

Ezekiel 28:20-22

Again the word of the LORD came unto me, saying, Son of man, set thy face against Zidon, and prophesy against it, And say, Thus saith the Lord GOD; Behold, I am against thee, O Zidon; and I will be glorified in the midst of thee: and they shall know that I am the LORD, when I shall have executed judgments in her, and shall be sanctified in her

Ezekiel 29:1-3

In the tenth year, in the tenth month, in the twelfth day of the month, the word of the LORD came unto me, saying, Son of man, set thy face against Pharaoh king of Egypt, and prophesy against him, and against all Egypt: Speak, and say, Thus saith the Lord GOD; Behold, I am against thee, Pharaoh king of Egypt, the great dragon that lieth in the midst of his rivers, which hath said, My river is mine own, and I have made it for myself.

Ezekiel 29:17-19

And it came to pass in the seven and twentieth year, in the first month, in the first day of the month, the word of the LORD came unto me, saying, Son of man, Nebuchadrezzar king of Babylon caused his army to serve a great service against Tyrus: every head was made bald, and every shoulder was peeled: yet had he no wages, nor his army, for Tyrus, for the service that he had served against it: Therefore thus saith the Lord GOD; Behold, I will give the land of Egypt unto Nebuchadrezzar king of Babylon; and he shall take her multitude, and take her spoil, and take her prey; and it shall be the wages for his army.

Ezekiel 30:1-4

The word of the LORD came again unto me, saying, Son of man, prophesy and say, Thus saith the Lord GOD; Howl ye, Woe worth the day! For the day is near, even the day of the LORD is near, a cloudy day; it shall be the time of the heathen. And the sword shall come upon Egypt, and great pain shall be in Ethiopia, when the slain shall fall in Egypt, and they shall take away her multitude, and her foundations shall be broken down.

Ezekiel 30:20-22

And it came to pass in the eleventh year, in the first month, in the seventh day of the month, that the word of the LORD came unto me, saying, Son of man, I have broken the arm of Pharaoh king of Egypt; and, lo, it shall not be bound up to be healed, to put a roller to bind it, to make it strong to hold the sword. Therefore thus saith the Lord GOD; Behold, I am against Pharaoh king of Egypt, and will break his arms, the strong, and that which was broken; and I will cause the sword to fall out of his hand.

Ezekiel 31:1-2

And it came to pass in the eleventh year, in the third month, in the first day of the month, that the word of the LORD came unto me, saying, Son of man, speak unto Pharaoh king of Egypt, and to his multitude; Whom art thou like in thy greatness?

Ezekiel 32:1-3

And it came to pass in the twelfth year, in the twelfth month, in the first day of the month, that the word of the LORD came unto me, saying, Son of man, take up a lamentation for Pharaoh king of Egypt, and say unto him, Thou art like a young lion of the nations, and thou art as a whale in the seas: and thou camest forth with thy rivers, and troubledst the waters with thy feet, and fouledst their rivers. Thus saith the Lord GOD; I will therefore spread out my net over thee with a company of many people; and they shall bring thee up in my net.

Ezekiel 32:17-19

It came to pass also in the twelfth year, in the fifteenth day of the month, that the word of the LORD came unto me, saying, Son of man, wail for the multitude of Egypt, and cast them down, even her, and the daughters of the famous nations, unto the nether parts of the earth, with them that go down into the pit. Whom dost thou pass in beauty? go down, and be thou laid with the uncircumcised.

Ezekiel 33:1-12

Again the word of the LORD came unto me, saying, Son of man, speak to the children of thy people, and say unto them, When I bring the sword upon a land, if the people of the land take a man of their coasts, and set him for their watchman: If when he seeth the sword come upon the land, he blow the trumpet, and warn the people; Then whosoever heareth the sound of the trumpet, and taketh not warning; if the sword come, and take him away, his blood shall be upon his own head. He heard the sound of the trumpet, and took not warning; his blood shall be upon him. But he that taketh warning shall deliver his soul.

But if the watchman see the sword come, and blow not the trumpet, and the people be not warned; if the sword come, and take any person from among them, he is taken away in his iniquity; but his blood will I require at the watchman's hand. So thou, O son of man, I have set thee a watchman unto the house of Israel; therefore thou shalt hear the word at my mouth, and warn them from me. When I say unto the wicked, O wicked man, thou shalt surely die; if thou dost not speak to warn the wicked from his way, that wicked man shall die in his iniquity; but his blood will I require at thine hand. Nevertheless, if thou warn the wicked of his way to turn from it; if he do not turn from his way, he shall die in his iniquity; but thou hast delivered thy soul.

Therefore, O thou son of man, speak unto the house of Israel; Thus ye speak, saying, If our transgressions and our sins be upon us, and we pine away in them, how should we then live? Say unto them, As I live, saith the Lord GOD, I have no pleasure in the death of the wicked; but that the wicked turn from his way and live: turn ye, turn ye from your evil ways; for why will ye die, O house of Israel? Therefore, thou son of man, say unto the children of thy people, The righteousness of the righteous shall not deliver him in the day of his transgression: as for the wickedness of the wicked, he shall not fall thereby in the day that he turneth from his wickedness; neither shall the righteous be able to live for his righteousness in the day that he sinneth.

Ezekiel 33:23-30

Then the word of the LORD came unto me, saying, Son of man, they that inhabit those wastes of the land of Israel speak, saying, Abraham was one, and he inherited the land: but we are many; the land is given us for inheritance. Wherefore say unto them, Thus saith the Lord GOD; Ye eat with the blood, and lift up your eyes toward your idols, and shed blood: and shall ye possess the land? Ye stand upon your sword, ye work abomination, and ye defile every one his neighbour's wife: and shall ye possess the land?

Say thou thus unto them, Thus saith the Lord GOD; As I live, surely they that are in the wastes shall fall by the sword, and him that is in the open field will I give to the beasts to be devoured, and they that be in the forts and in the caves shall die of the pestilence. For I will lay the land most desolate, and the pomp of her strength shall cease; and the mountains of Israel shall be desolate, that none shall pass through. Then shall they know that I am the LORD, when I have laid the land most desolate because of all their abominations which they have committed.

Also, thou son of man, the children of thy people still are talking against thee by the walls and in the doors of the houses, and speak one to another, every one to his brother, saying, Come, I pray you, and hear what is the word that cometh forth from the LORD.

Ezekiel 34:1-3

And the word of the LORD came unto me, saying, Son of man, prophesy against the shepherds of Israel, prophesy, and say unto them, Thus saith the Lord GOD unto the shepherds; Woe be to the shepherds of Israel that do feed themselves! should not the shepherds feed the flocks? Ye eat the fat, and ye clothe you with the wool, ye kill them that are fed: but ye feed not the flock.

Ezekiel 35:1-3

Moreover the word of the LORD came unto me, saying, Son of man, set thy face against mount Seir, and prophesy against it, And say unto it, Thus saith the Lord GOD; Behold, O mount Seir, I am against thee, and I will stretch out mine hand against thee, and I will make thee most desolate.

Ezekiel 36:1-5

Also, thou son of man, prophesy unto the mountains of Israel, and say, Ye mountains of Israel, hear the word of the LORD: Thus saith the Lord GOD; Because the enemy hath said against you, Aha, even the ancient high places are ours in possession: Therefore prophesy and say, Thus saith the Lord GOD; Because they have made you desolate, and swallowed you up on every side, that ye might be a possession unto the residue of the heathen, and ye are taken up in the lips of talkers, and are an infamy of the people: Therefore, ye mountains of Israel, hear the word of the Lord GOD; Thus saith the Lord GOD to the mountains, and to the hills, to the rivers, and to the valleys, to the desolate wastes, and to the cities that are forsaken, which became a prey and derision to the residue of the heathen that are round about; Therefore thus saith the Lord GOD; Surely in the fire of my jealousy have I spoken against the residue of the heathen, and against all Idumea, which have appointed my land into their possession with the joy of all their heart, with despiteful minds, to cast it out for a prey.

Ezekiel 36:16-17

Moreover the word of the LORD came unto me, saying, Son of man, when the house of Israel dwelt in their own land, they defiled it by their own way and by their doings: their way was before me as the uncleanness of a removed woman.

Ezekiel 37:1-11

The hand of the LORD was upon me, and carried me out in the spirit of the LORD, and set me down in the midst of the valley which was full of bones, And caused me to pass by them round about: and, behold, there were very many in the open valley; and, lo, they were very dry.

And he said unto me, Son of man, can these bones live?

And I answered, O Lord GOD, thou knowest.

Again he said unto me, Prophesy upon these bones, and say unto them, O ye dry bones, hear the word of the LORD. Thus saith the Lord GOD unto these bones; Behold, I will cause breath to enter into you, and ye shall live: And I will lay sinews upon you, and will bring up flesh upon you, and cover you with skin, and put breath in you, and ye shall live; and ye shall know that I am the LORD.

So I prophesied as I was commanded: and as I prophesied, there was a noise, and behold a shaking, and the bones came together, bone to his bone. And when I beheld, lo, the sinews and the flesh came up upon them, and the skin covered them above: but there was no breath in them.

Then said he unto me, Prophesy unto the wind, prophesy, son of man, and say to the wind, Thus saith the Lord GOD; Come from the four winds, O breath, and breathe upon these slain, that they may live.

So I prophesied as he commanded me, and the breath came into them, and they lived, and stood up upon their feet, an exceeding great army.

Then he said unto me, Son of man, these bones are the whole house of Israel: behold, they say, Our bones are dried, and our hope is lost: we are cut off for our parts.

Ezekiel 37:15-17

The word of the LORD came again unto me, saying, Moreover, thou son of man, take thee one stick, and write upon it, For Judah, and for the children of Israel his companions: then take another stick, and write upon it, For Joseph, the stick of Ephraim, and for all the house of Israel his companions: And join them one to another into one stick; and they shall become one in thine hand.

Ezekiel 38:1-6

And the word of the LORD came unto me, saying, Son of man, set thy face against Gog, the land of Magog, the chief prince of Meshech and Tubal, and prophesy against him, And say, Thus saith the Lord GOD; Behold, I am against thee, O Gog, the chief prince of Meshech and Tubal: And I will turn thee back, and put hooks into thy jaws, and I will bring thee forth, and all thine army, horses and horsemen, all of them clothed with all sorts of armour, even a great company with bucklers and shields, all of them handling swords: Persia, Ethiopia, and Libya with them; all of them with shield and helmet: Gomer, and all his bands; the house of Togarmah of the north quarters, and all his bands: and many people with thee.

Ezekiel 38:14-16

Therefore, son of man, prophesy and say unto Gog, Thus saith the Lord GOD; In that day when my people of Israel dwelleth safely, shalt thou not know it? And thou shalt come from thy place out of the north parts, thou, and many people with thee, all of them riding upon horses, a great company, and a mighty army: And thou shalt come up against my people of Israel, as a cloud to cover the land; it shall be in the latter days, and I will bring thee against my land, that the heathen may know me, when I shall be sanctified in thee, O Gog, before their eyes.

Ezekiel 39:1-3

Therefore, thou son of man, prophesy against Gog, and say, Thus saith the Lord GOD; Behold, I am against thee, O Gog, the chief prince of Meshech and Tubal: And I will turn thee back, and leave but the sixth part of thee, and will cause thee to come up from the north parts, and will bring thee upon the mountains of Israel: And I will smite thy bow out of thy left hand, and will cause thine arrows to fall out of thy right hand.

Ezekiel 39:17

And, thou son of man, thus saith the Lord GOD; Speak unto every feathered fowl, and to every beast of the field, Assemble yourselves, and come; gather yourselves on every side to my sacrifice that I do sacrifice for you, even a great sacrifice upon the mountains of Israel, that ye may eat flesh, and drink blood.

Ezekiel 40:1-5

In the five and twentieth year of our captivity, in the beginning of the year, in the tenth day of the month, in the fourteenth year after that the city was smitten, in the selfsame day the hand of the LORD was upon me, and brought me thither. In the visions of God brought he me into the land of Israel, and set me upon a very high mountain, by which was as the frame of a city on the south. And he brought me thither, and, behold, there was a man, whose appearance was like the appearance of brass, with a line of flax in his hand, and a measuring reed; and he stood in the gate. And the man said unto me, Son of man, behold with thine eyes, and hear with thine ears, and set thine heart upon all that I shall show thee; for to the intent that I might show them unto thee art thou brought hither: declare all that thou seest to the house of Israel. And behold a wall on the outside of the house round about, and in the man's hand a measuring reed of six cubits long by the cubit and an hand breadth: so he measured the breadth of the building, one reed; and the height, one reed.

Ezekiel 43:1-11

Afterward he brought me to the gate, even the gate that looketh toward the east: And, behold, the glory of the God of Israel came from the way of the east: and his voice was like a noise of many waters: and the earth shined with his glory. And it was according to the appearance of the vision which I saw, even according to the vision that I saw when I came to destroy the city: and the visions were like the vision that I saw by the river Chebar; and I fell upon my face.

And the glory of the LORD came into the house by the way of the gate whose prospect is toward the east. So the spirit took me up, and brought me into the inner court; and, behold, the glory of the LORD filled the house. And I heard him speaking unto me out of the house; and the man stood by me. And he said unto me, Son of man, the place of my throne, and the place of the soles of my feet, where I will dwell in the midst of the children of Israel for ever, and my holy name, shall the house of Israel no more defile, neither they, nor their kings, by their whoredom, nor by the carcases of their kings in their high places. In their setting of their threshold by my thresholds, and their post by my posts, and the wall between me and them, they have even defiled my holy name by their abominations that they have committed: wherefore I have consumed them in mine anger. Now let them put away their whoredom, and the carcases of their kings, far from me, and I will dwell in the midst of them for ever.

Thou son of man, show the house to the house of Israel, that they may be ashamed of their iniquities: and let them measure the pattern. And if they be ashamed of all that they have done, show them the form of the house, and the fashion thereof, and the goings out thereof, and the comings in thereof, and all the forms thereof, and all the ordinances thereof, and all the forms thereof, and all the laws thereof: and write it in their sight, that they may keep the whole form thereof, and all the ordinances thereof, and do them.

Ezekiel 43:18-21

And he said unto me, Son of man, thus saith the Lord GOD; These are the ordinances of the altar in the day when they shall make it, to offer burnt offerings thereon, and to sprinkle blood thereon. And thou shalt give to the priests the Levites that be of the seed of Zadok, which approach unto me, to minister unto me, saith the Lord GOD, a young bullock for a sin offering. And thou shalt take of the blood thereof, and put it on the four horns of it, and on the four corners of the settle, and upon the border round about: thus shalt thou cleanse and purge it. Thou shalt take the bullock also of the sin offering, and he shall burn it in the appointed place of the house, without the sanctuary.

Ezekiel 44:1-5

Then he brought me back the way of the gate of the outward sanctuary which looketh toward the east; and it was shut. Then said the LORD unto me; This gate shall be shut, it shall not be opened, and no man shall enter in by it; because the LORD, the God of Israel, hath entered in by it, therefore it shall be shut. It is for the prince; the prince, he shall sit in it to eat bread before the LORD; he shall enter by the way of the porch of that gate, and shall go out by the way of the same.

Then brought he me the way of the north gate before the house: and I looked, and, behold, the glory of the LORD filled the house of the LORD: and I fell upon my face. And the LORD said unto me, Son of man, mark well, and behold with thine eyes, and hear with thine ears all that I say unto thee concerning all the ordinances of the house of the LORD, and all the laws thereof; and mark well the entering in of the house, with every going forth of the sanctuary.

Ezekiel 47:1-6

Afterward he brought me again unto the door of the house; and, behold, waters issued out from under the threshold of the house eastward: for the forefront of the house stood toward the east, and the waters came down from under from the right side of the house, at the south side of the altar. Then brought he me out of the way of the gate northward, and led me about the way without unto the utter gate by the way that looketh eastward; and, behold, there ran out waters on the right side. And when the man that had the line in his hand went forth eastward, he measured a thousand cubits, and he brought me through the waters; the waters were to the ankles. Again he measured a thousand, and brought me through the waters; the waters were to the knees. Again he measured a thousand, and brought me through; the waters were to the loins. Afterward he measured a thousand; and it was a river that I could not pass over: for the waters were risen, waters to swim in, a river that could not be passed over. And he said unto me, Son of man, hast thou seen this? Then he brought me, and caused me to return to the brink of the river.